BECOMING LITERATE

THE CONSTRUCTION
OF INNER CONTROL

MARIE M. CLAY

BECOMING LITERATE

THE CONSTRUCTION OF INNER CONTROL

HEINEMANN

Published by Heinemann Education, a Division of Octopus
Publishing Group (NZ) Ltd, 39 Rawene Road, Birkenhead,
Auckland. Associated companies, branches and representatives
throughout the world.

In the United States: Heinemann Educational Books, Inc. 361
Hanover St, Portsmouth. N.H. 03801-3959

ISBN 0 86863-279-1 (NZ)

© 1991, Marie M. Clay
First published 1991
Reprinted 1991 (twice)

Library of Congress Cataloging-in-Publication Data

Clay, Marie M.
  Becoming literate: the construction of inner control / Marie M.
  Clay.
       p.   cm.
  Includes bibliographical references (p.) and index.
  ISBN 0-435-08574-3
  1. Reading (Primary) 2. Reading (Preschool) 3. Language arts
  (Primary)   I. Title.
  LB1525.C57   1991
  372.4—dc20   90-24897
                                                         CIP

Produced and printed by SRM Production Services Sdn Bhd,
Malaysia

The pronouns she and he have often been used in this text to
refer to the teacher and the child respectively. Despite a possible
charge of sexist bias it makes for clearer, easier reading if such
references are consistent.

Contents

Children are Active Constructors of Their Own Learning
Changes in Ways of Learning
Where is that Zone of Proximal Development?
Teaching as Interaction
When the Programme Goes to the Child
When the Child Has to Meet the Programme's Demands
Entry to School — Many Transitions

Text Characteristics Influence the Child's Expectations
Three Challenging Ideas
Three Major Text Types
Teaching with Transition or Story Book Texts
A Gradient of Difficulty in Texts
In Summary

**PART FOUR: THE DEEP STRUCTURE OF SUCCESS:
                READING STRATEGIES   231**

Introduction

I planned to write a new book about learning to read. My own understanding of literacy acquisition had changed as a result of close observation of children engaged in reading work, and frequent opportunities to watch superb teaching, and the ideas and research reports of many authorities. However, when I came to the task of writing I realized that the ideas I wrote about in my first book on reading were still the fundamental core of the theory I work with. Where I had previously said 'I do not know what occurs here' new ideas had taken shape. The task began to look more like a need to fine-tune my explanations in the light of recent research, new critiques, and emerging emphases provided by numbers of authorities in the professional literature.

A theory emerges which hypothesizes that out of early reading and writing experiences the young learner creates a network of competencies which power subsequent independent literacy learning. It is a theory of generic learning, that is, learning which generates further learning. The generic competencies are constructed by the learner as he works on many kinds of information coming from the printed page in reading or going to the printed page in writing.

In one sense, then, this book is a revision of my earlier work, but my view of literacy acquisition has been enriched by many debates. I have not attempted to compile the ideas of these debates nor provide a general overview. I am often charged with ignoring the views of authorities whose work I value highly. My position is that when a colleague has written something we should all take note of I should not demean it by giving it superficial reference. I like to have my students read original sources. An interesting literature on emerging literacy is part of the dialogue of the early part of this book but is not reviewed here. This is not a book about my favourite authorities: they speak for themselves.

I have tried to present an integrated and somewhat innovative explanation of changes that occur over time in a young child's control over literacy learning, limiting my discussion to the period from the formal introduction of instruction in school until the relative independence of the third year of schooling. I acknowledge that social contexts have a controlling influence on children's opportunities to learn but this book turns the spotlight on how children use those opportunities to construct an inner control over literacy tasks. In the end it is the children who learn to actively integrate their experiences and the parent or teacher is powerless to do more than contribute to this active construction completed by the learner.

Two criticisms of my previous work have been that I neglect the central role of meaning and I do not seem to understand that a reader brings a meaning to a text. In fact I regard meaning as the 'given' in all reading — the source of anticipation, the guide to being on track, and the outcome and reward of the effort. Meanings provide the purpose of reading and writing. But different readers bring different meanings to texts, just as one theorist interpreting another's theory brings a different meaning to it.

The third criticism is not so easy to answer briefly. The criticism is that I want children to read correctly and write correctly. Since I am not very interested in items of knowledge — letters, sounds and words — this argument is hard to sustain. What I am interested in is a gradual increase in effective processing strategies, so I ask teachers to think about what the child does when meaningfulness does not match with word-form and to observe the problem-solving that the child does. I encourage teachers to interact or teach at these points but why? To develop the child's strategies for working independently with text, to increase the child's processing power, not to get the response correct.

This book presents a cognitive view of literacy processes in developmental perspective. In this case 'developmental' does not mean unfolding all by itself without contextual support from the environment. It means an approach which looks at active learners *changing over time* within their contexts. Looking closely at the reading and writing work that children do out in the real world leads us to assumptions about what it is that they are learning 'in their heads.' So, in addition to describing the changes in literacy behaviours that we might observe in young learners my account leads from the observation of reading behaviours towards a model of how the constructive, problem-solving activities inside children's heads allow competent readers to increase their reading power every time they read.

The text asks many questions about two groups of children, those learning with ease and those who could be at risk of having difficulty. I assume that what the successful child learns to do is what the less successful child needs to learn. There is now extensive evidence from a 'prevention of failure' strategy used in three countries that less successful children can become successful readers in an intervention which uses many of the ideas in this book. This gives me some confidence that I am writing about patterns of literacy acquisition (in English) which are generally possible to achieve and explanations which have enough generality to be taken seriously.

As I think that theorists should check whether their formulations do in fact occur in real life, many of my examples are the ones I have available to me from my own research and that of my colleagues. For that reason the examples are grounded in New Zealand practice. However, this is not a book written to help only New Zealand children with the transition into formal education, nor is it directed to those who work mostly with children who are struggling with literacy tasks. From my background in developmental psychology I judge the matters I am addressing to apply to children learning about literacy in any country or language, or in any programme of instruction.

Teachers who learn to be observers of successful and unsuccessful learners have data on which to test their assumptions. I think that effective teachers must continually test their assumptions about children and learning against such observations. I believe that teachers must question their own assumptions, and what authorities are telling them to do. They should ask, 'Do my children actually do what authorities say they do as they read texts?' This is a book that could help teachers to develop ways of asking questions of their own practice and self-correcting their own thinking about learning to read. It is an account of what any teacher needs to pay attention to as he or she works with young children and observes them closely.

For that reason I cannot become prescriptive about teaching methodologies. Effective teaching is an interaction and a major part of that interaction is outside the teacher's control. However, in order to judge what to teach, and which way to set about the task, a teacher needs to have an overview of changes to watch for along the way. I have been building myself a clearer map of what those changes are.

I do not write about teaching methodology because I think the underlying structure of literacy behaviours might be achieved in several different ways. Successful readers and writers do emerge from many different types of programmes. I have attempted to construct a model of literacy behaviours which respects the complexity, studies the cross-referencing of knowledge, expects different skills to be interactive, and assumes that control of this orchestration is something the child has learned. I find the big debates divisive, for people feel obliged to take up opposing positions on matters like phonological awareness, the reader's use of context, and the nature of getting meaning from texts.

Like any good drama my explanations gradually unfold, teasing out the various concepts or sets of behaviours. In this way the book calls for more and more understanding from the reader as the discussion leads towards the last chapter and the overarching concept of a self-extending system of strategies. (In this book a strategy cannot be seen — it is some activity 'in the head,' a move directed by the child during reading work to problem-solve a section of text and it belongs to an orchestrated set of strategies needed in literacy activities.)

In writing this book I have assumed that some teachers will want to think about the learning children already have when they enter school, others will want to fine tune their understanding of the 'engagement period' as children begin to use literacy knowledge to access texts. As the children move further into literacy the teacher needs to understand more complex concepts of what underlies the surface behaviours she or he can observe. Some teachers will want to think more critically and theoretically about two teasing questions:

How do readers become independent?
How do good readers get better as a result of reading?

Thus the organization of the text is developmental in two senses: it traces the range of child responses from preschool through entry, to reading and writing without much teacher help, and it allows teachers to move as far into the explanations as they feel is useful for them. Perhaps it is a book to stay with over a period of years — an inservice tool rather than a preservice preparation.

The first chapters describe the emerging literacy of preschool children who are approaching the time they will enter formal instruction in school. Then the transition into school and the translation of existing competencies into two new systems of behaviour for reading and writing are discussed. The middle section traces in some detail what children are learning and where some children are getting confused. By the time children are beginning to move through a gradient of increasing difficulty in their early reading books, which may be little story books, an observant teacher can watch the formation of several important reading strategies — how children use meaning to control what they are doing, how they draw upon and use the language competencies they have, how they manage to detect errors themselves, and what they do to correct these. All this attempts to capture and describe patterns of change over time in reading and writing processes, the changes that occur as children accumulate experience with literacy activities.

In the last section of the book the discussion turns to a problem recently brought into sharp focus by Stanovich (1986) whose review of a large amount of research showed that the good readers get better while the poor readers fall further behind as they accumulate years of schooling. In the past we have explained failure to learn to read in terms of a lack of certain competencies in poor readers, blaming the learner or his background. However, what now needs to be explained is what it is about reading and writing that helps the good reader to become better as a result of his own efforts. Something about the ways in which they read creates a forward thrust, and perhaps this is something that poor readers have not managed to learn. The forward thrust is currently explained by phonological skills, and rapidly expanding vocabulary brought about by quantity of reading. To formulate the question in a different way we could ask 'What is the generating power controlled by the independent reader that gives him or her such easy access to quantities of reading, and what processes does that reader need to control to get a rapid expansion of vocabulary?' It seems to me that controlling letter-sound relationships and learning more and more words do not suffice as explanations of this forward thrust in reading power. So the book ends with my attempt to draw together some of the characteristics of what I call a self-extending system.

PART ONE

A Framework of Issues

1   A Framework of Issues

Reading people have many different theories, many preferred programmes and many rationales for doing what they do. If such differences were critical we would be producing mostly problem readers and only a few successful readers. Fortunately that is not the case. Despite the diversity of approaches to instruction most children learn to read and they learn in very different programmes.

What is Reading?

I define reading as a message-getting, problem-solving activity which increases in power and flexibility the more it is practised. My definition states that within the directional constraints of the printer's code, language and visual perception responses are purposefully directed by the reader in some integrated way to the problem of extracting meaning from cues in a text, in sequence, so that the reader brings a maximum of understanding to the author's message.

As we progress along the lines of a text it is not unlike the process of finding footholds when climbing up a cliff-face, yet the achievement is in the single completed task.

We ask questions all the time as we read and our theories of what might occur work so well that we are scarcely aware that they exist. We only become aware of our questioning when our answers fail to match the information before us. Asking questions is a means of eliminating alternatives. We can encourage children to ask themselves questions and develop their strategies for improving predictions. All this applies to reading and writing. We must read by asking and answering questions if we are to understand what we are reading. Palincsar and Brown (1984, 1986) have provided an excellent example of this view of reading in a large body of careful research on reciprocal teaching.

Observing Some Aspects of Reading

To help adults to understand something of the way we react when we are reading efficiently researchers have from time to time produced strange reading tasks. Here are some such tasks.

Take a piece of paper and number 1–12 and 1–26. Read the first paragraph below and write down against each number

- *what you look at*
- *where you search*
- *what you look for.*

Do not write the words that are missing.

- *The second time through, write down the missing words.*
- *Then read the second paragraph in the same way. First, observe your own behaviour, then try to get to the author's words.*

Paragraph 1   An extract on TV for children.

But school's out, and for
the next three hours it's
switch and mix according
to your age group. For how
_____ you talk of children's
_____ as an entity
_____ you mean pro-
_____ for children aged
_____ nine and twelve, for early
_____ and late adoles
_____ to say nothing of
_____ -from-work dads and
_____ grannies, each
_____ with a viewing pre-
_____ that may be an
_____ to the others.

Paragraph 2   A comment on cartoons.

Yet, as one who has, I
hope, survived unscathed
a youthful addiction to
comic _____ and _____ still
_____ secret _____ of _____ Flint-
stones, _____ like _____ think _____
children _____ every _____ as
capable _____ the _____ of _____ at
distinguishing _____
reality _____ harmless
_____ believe. And they _____ less
influenced _____ what _____
see _____ television _____ by
_____ example _____ the _____
of _____ elders _____
developing values.

Missing words

1 can; programmes; when; -grammes; six; teenagers; -cents; home; weary; group; -ference; anathema.

2 papers; is; a; fan; the; I; to; that; are; bit; as; rest; us; between; and; make; are; by; they; on; than; the; of; attitudes; their; in.

Another way to observe the reading process is to have volunteers read unseen texts aloud to a group of observers who do not have a copy of the text. Choose texts carefully and you can break down the fluent reading skills of the best readers to reveal some of the processes they use. Some challenging texts would be:

- an upside down book
- a poor copy of a text blurred in some way
- difficult handwriting
- a highly specialized scientific text
- a text written in the initial teaching alphabet (i.t.a.)
- a text typed with very wide spacing of letters and words
- a text typed with no spacing of words.

Have the observers write down what they notice about the reading behaviours of the reader. Talk about what the readers were trying to do and why it was necessary for them to behave the way they did.

Few adults have occasion to think of the ways in which they identify words while reading or how they produce them in writing. Their perception of words is automatic; a mature reader responds to most printed words accurately and quickly, for that is one aspect of what reading is. It is certainly not decoding nonsense words like 'tham', 'blep' or 'drimplet.' Decoding nonsense words cannot be used as the ultimate test for the final explanation of reading. We must be interested in both the means used by mature readers to identify unfamiliar words when they meet them and also what they do when they read faultlessly and speedily.

In efficient rapid word perception the reader relies mostly on the sentence and its meaning and some selected features of the forms of words. Awareness of the sentence context (and often the general context of the text as a whole) and a glance at the word enables the reader to respond instantly. This type of word perception occurs in most of the reading done by experienced mature readers. For example, you had no difficulty in perceiving the words in this and the preceding paragraph. You did not stop to study the form of the separate words. Nor did you analyse words consciously noting root words, prefixes and suffixes, or 'reading' phoneme by phoneme. It is highly unlikely that you consulted a dictionary for the pronunciation or for the meaning of any word. This was not necessary because every word was familiar. You have used each one yourself many times — except for 'tham', 'blep' and 'drimplet' which might have irritated you a little. However, second time around you probably dealt with those words more fluently. In what sense did you 'read' them?

Observe your own behaviour as you read the next three selections.

● When he first came there she had resented him; after that she had gone on to ignore him. It had been clear enough at first that she did not like his being there. The companionship and the interest that he had there was with Stenning in their work and in the farm. She had a habit whenever they were in the house together of always interrupting Johnson when he spoke. She always helped him last at meal-times, so that it should be plain that he was their servant and not one of them.

● The making and breaking of chemical bonds is the job of a particular and very varied group of substances found in every living cell and in many body fluids such as saliva and gastric juices — the enzymes. These compounds speed up the forming or decomposing of polymers and other complex substances by making or breaking the chemical bonds between the various parts of these giant molecules. Any one enzyme can usually act on only one particular bond, say, for example, the bond between two glucose molecules in a starch chain. Thus every different chemical reaction needs its own enzyme.

● From the brain the *circumoesophageal commissures* pass around the gut to the suboesophageal ganglion lying ventrally in the head. Nerves arising from here innervate the mouth parts. From the suboesophageal ganglion paired connectives pass back to the pro-thoracic ganglion in the floor of the *prothorax*. Then follow the next two thoracic ganglia. The ganglia supplying the first two abdominal segments have probably fused with the meta-thoracic ganglion.

When we are reading about learning to read we can always check what authorities are claiming against what we are able to observe in our own behaviour as readers. It is helpful to use this resource as one way of checking whether some claim about literacy learning makes sense to you.

This Complex Learning Begins Before School

If we think about the four or five or six year old children who enter school we realize that although they have learned a great deal about their worlds, and about language, they have much more to learn in everything they do. They are not experts and a particular challenge for schools is to work out how to help those with limited knowledge and skills to be effective in learning to read and write.

However, recent research has shown that many children have begun literacy learning before they enter school. We have rich descriptions of what preschoolers have been learning from their environments about books and writing (Strickland and Morrow, 1989). What used to be regarded as due to individual differences in intelligence turns out to have a great deal to do with opportunities to learn about books and writing. Teachers used to think they had to wait for children to gain more mental age before they were 'ready for reading': now we are faced with giving them more make-up opportunities with print and stories as soon as possible to enhance their potential for literacy learning.

Teaching practices today have to take into account

- what children can already do with print when they come to school and
- any need for enriched opportunities for booksharing and exploring with a pencil; for these are things that are learned through interactions with people and with print. They do not merely 'mature'.

By the End of Early Childhood

It is common to refer to the period of early childhood as birth to eight years, and so we could ask what is the status of literacy learning by the end of this period? There will be no one answer because different countries begin formal instruction at different times, varying between four and seven years.

Many authorities divide literacy learning into two phases—the acquisition of literacy skills and the application of the skills to other learning. Searching for practical criteria of a changeover from acquisition to application we might consider Stanovich's analysis of research supporting the Matthew effect (1986). He found that the (mainly American) research literature pointed to about eight years of age as a time when readers can be divided into (a) those who get better every time they read, learning more and more about coping with the task, and (b) those who have already begun to fall further and further behind their achieving classmates.

What would be reasonable goals for literacy acquisition by about eight years of age? (A list will suffice because the ideas will be treated more fully in later sections of this book.) Later education could build upon a firm foundation if the achievements of early childhood education was a child who was:

- tuned to the meanings of texts
- eager to talk and read and write
- able to compose and write simple texts
- able to read narrative and non-narrative texts.

Through engaging with many reading and writing opportunities the child would have learned how to call up and use a range of strategies (hidden from our view) for understanding texts such as:

- using feedback, monitoring and self-correction strategies in both reading and writing
- having direct and rapid access to words in a reading vocabulary

- having direct and rapid access to a writing vocabulary
- using ways of getting to new words in reading from words already known
- using ways of getting to new words in writing from words already known
- using many cognitive processes to learn more about reading and writing
- using equivalent processes in each language if one is a bilingual child learning to be biliterate.

Although this list might seem like a tall order, competent readers at these ages achieve all these things easily while average readers are well on the way and there are ways in which school entrants with the lowest achievements can be helped to develop most of these strategies (Clay, 1985). The last section of this book discusses how such achievements could make up a system of responses which extends itself, a self-improving system, which would allow the good reader to get better from reading.

One would not deny that we continue to expand and amplify our literacy skills throughout life, and in fact there is reason to believe that what happens to reading competencies between eight and twelve years is a vast unplotted landscape of change. The emphasis in this book is on the relationship of this later learning to the foundation laid by the child in the first two to three years of literacy learning.

Longitudinal Research on Change Over Time

I had many questions about how instruction affected children's learning when I began to record in detail what children did as they read books. From a background in Developmental Psychology I began field research designed to prepare accounts of progressions in reading and writing achievements that occurred in Auckland classrooms in the 1960s.

The programme of research included two longitudinal studies. Data for the first of these was gathered in 1963 and 1964. A record was taken *every week* of what children were saying and doing in reading and writing from the time they entered school at 5:0* (that is on their fifth birthday) through until their sixth birthdays (Clay, 1967, 1982) and a group of co-operative mothers kept diary records of what literacy activities the children were producing at home. I recorded in minute detail the observable aspects of reading and writing 'behaviours.' Behaviour is a key word here. The records described what the children did and what they said, and I made no prior assumptions as to how or why they did these things. Following this intensive documentation of how literacy responding changed during the first year of schooling in New Zealand in the 1960s, further observations were made at 7:0 and 8:0 to capture progress in subsequent years.

---

* The convention used for recording age and months in this book is a colon, i.e. 6:11 is six years and eleven months.

The progress that I described (Clay, 1967, 1982) did not match closely with that described by Biemiller (1970), and I do not find that surprising because the children we studied were probably being taught in quite different ways. More important, I suspect, was the fact that he used a probe test approach at different ages and the averaged findings look like a stage-wise description of progress. If you follow children over time at weekly intervals you get results which are very difficult to fit into the 'accepted' description of stages in American reports (Biemiller, 1970; Chall, 1983; Ehri and Wilce, 1985). Failure to explore the longitudinal approach using frequent observations seems to have produced a description of reading acquisition in terms of global averages which do not help us to teach individuals. They also mask the effects that different types of instruction might have on individual progress.

Data for a second longitudinal research study were gathered in Auckland in 1967 (Clay, 1970, 1976, 1982). The children were selected from four very different backgrounds of language experience. One group was bilingual in Samoan and English. Another was a group of Maori children who were monolingual in English. The third was an average group of children whose parents spoke English as their mother tongue. The fourth group also had parents who spoke English and came from homes where one parent had professional training. This was not selection on socio-economic grounds; what was needed was a group for whom one could assume that the dialect of English used in their homes would represent a wide range of usage since this group would represent some kind of optimum performance for age in oral language. Four age groups were followed, starting at 5:0, 5:6, 6:0 and 6:6, at fortnightly intervals over six months.

Those studies demonstrated on both majority and minority groups that while most children began a slow accumulation of achievements towards effective literacy behaviours others, in their first year of schooling, began to establish less productive ways of responding. The problem was not immaturity or unwillingness to learn but seemed to result from dedicated efforts by children to respond to the school's demands. Slowly their achievements fell further behind those of their successful classmates. (See Ferreiro and Teberosky, 1982 for a similar description for children in Argentina.) Obviously the important question was 'Could the trajectory of progress be altered?'

Another way to phrase my question in the light of more recent knowledge would be to ask 'Can we see the trajectories of progress for good and poor readers (Stanovich, 1986) beginning to draw away from each other in the first year of school?' Wording the question in that way it becomes obvious why I had to study both groups together.

The Prevention of Reading Failure

The important question behind these research studies was the prevention of reading failure and the assumption was that to prevent failure we needed to know the pattern of progress made by successful children. The reader will find three emphases in this book which flow from those early research projects.

- Firstly, there is an emphasis on the early detection of children who are beginning to drop behind compared with their age-mates whatever the method of classroom instruction.

- Secondly, there is comment on *behaviour* which is readily observed rather than on aspects of important learning which are hidden from sight such as hidden cognitive processes, comprehension and understanding. This is because it is evidence that is before the teacher and to which she responds, knowingly or not, and it is evidence against which teachers can check their assumptions.

- Thirdly, the children I observed in my studies entered a formal instruction programme at 5:0. Early reading and writing behaviours will look somewhat different if beginning readers are older children or when new entrants come from a wider age group. However, my work in several different countries has convinced me that successful readers are acquiring the same processing strategies, even though instructional emphases can bring about apparent differences.

It used to be unusual for remedial reading instruction to begin before 8:0 in many countries although there may have been a shift to earlier interventions in recent years. If we can detect the process of learning to read 'going wrong' within a year of school entry then it would be folly to wait several years before providing children with extra help. An earlier offer of effective help to the child might reduce the magnitude of the reading problems in later schooling.

Of Theories About Reading

No reader is likely to render all texts accurately without some problem-solving and therefore every reader has to be able to operate a system of checks and balances to achieve either understanding of a text or error-free reading (either or both of which might be legitimate goals for a reader).

Such a system of checks and balances is possible because the messages in language have high redundancy. Language is organized in several ways. We can focus on the sound system, or on the ways in which we put words together in phrases or utterances, or on the meaningfulness of the language. In reading we have the letters with some systematic links to the sounds of language, the structures of sentences, and the meanings of messages. At each of these 'levels' there are rules which govern the occurrence of language features and we can make predictions because some things are more likely to occur than others (Smith 1978). Certain letters occur in certain positions more than others and combinations of letters are predictable. Some words occur much more often than others, again in predictable sequences, and as for meanings our real world knowledge tells us what is likely to occur and that some things will never go together. If you think about several layers of knowledge within the same text, and several ways of judging whether things are likely to occur together or not we have a rich source of data for telling when things are going well in our reading and when a miscue may have occurred. Usually we have more than one option for checking whether we could be correct.

Reading acquisition involves learning to use all these redundant sources of information in texts to problem-solve the meanings. It is a complex activity. It is a multifaceted learning task in which the relationship of one facet to another changes in importance at different stages of the acquisition process.

In the last 25 years there has been an intensive search for theories that will explain how children learn to read but rather than lead us to clear explanations and predictions our present theories compete for support.

Theories of reading cluster around two main views. One group of theories sees reading as an exact process of seeing and saying words. I have two problems with this:

- The demand for precision does not seem to match the inexactitude of the young learner in many of his interactions with his world.

- This view assumes that the reader uses the visual details of print to get access to his memory. He attends to a word, links what he sees with similar detail that he remembers from past experiences, recognizes the word, and in some kind of cognitive operation gets meaning from the text. However, while I think I sometimes do this when I read I am also rather sure that there are many times when I use as little visual information as I can get away with.

A competing group of theories sees reading as a questioning or problem-solving process in which we search for meaning, sampling only enough visual information to be satisfied that we have grasped the message of the text so far. Critics of this theory say, 'If a person reads a passage up to a point and then makes an estimate of the next word, he will be wrong far more often than he will be correct,' and so a theory of hypothesis-testing will be a weak theory. Yet hypothesis-testing is a strategy that is used in human perception and cognition (Bruner, 1957) and in the way that we coordinate movement (Bruner, 1974). Such feedback and feedforward processes which control all responses also operate in reading and writing.

It is difficult to see how one could avoid forming hypotheses in an activity like reading which is both perceptual and cognitive. This was tested in my recent encounter with two lines of print.

It was a matter of prest-
ige that we try.........

It was also illustrated by a story told to me by a remedial teacher in England. An older failing reader was being encouraged to tell her which words in the first paragraph of a simple story he knew. The task was merely to point along the line saying 'Yes' or 'No' to each word. Completing the task he came to the last two words and said, 'I can read *bear* but I can't read *polar!*' Did this child only allow himself a direct perception theory of reading and did he believe that he was not reading the word 'polar'? If so did his theory limit his ability to extend his own reading skill?

The problem-solving theory is probably a satisfactory description of the responding of mature readers for the mature reader has the control to expertly sample information from the text if he should choose to do so. When we are thinking about child learners beginning to interact with print it is helpful to consider how the child is learning to use such information-sampling processes.

Recent experimental research on the cognitive processes involved in reading acquisition has focussed on two particular debates, one general and the other specific. The general debate is about the ways in which cognitive abilities contribute to reading acquisition, and this has included discussion about the converse effect, the ways in which reading may contribute to the formation or enhancement of cognitive processes.

The specific debate provides one illustration of the general issue. The reader's awareness of how sounds are represented in print has emerged as a prominent area of study. The topic has many names, variously termed phonological awareness or phonological segmentation, phonemics and phonetics. These terms sometimes refer to regularities in letter-sound correspondences, or to the ways in which sounds are represented in clusters of letters (spelling patterns) or to some more abstract associations which we form from our pronunciation of language and which have been called systematic phonemes. Authorities differ as to whether phonological awareness develops in oral language *before* literacy, or *in interaction with* reading, or *after* introduction to reading; whether it is a cause or outcome of reading progress; whether it involves the ear in segmenting speech, the eye in segmenting print, or the brain in learning about the inter-relationships between the two. The issue is important but it is by no means clear from many research papers whether phonological processes (which are cognitive processes) precede and contribute to reading acquisition, or whether they could be cognitive outcomes of being a reader.

To complicate the debate, two further hypotheses about the 'sounds of reading' are worthy of serious consideration.

- Firstly, gaining skill in reading and in phonological awareness may work interactively throughout the acquisition of both.

- Secondly, children may develop this awareness of sounds in reading in another learning activity such as playing with *rhyme* or exploring *beginning writing* because an essential component of recording one's speech in print is to work out how what is heard can be recorded by letters.

Theories Usually Ignore the Effects of Instruction

Sometimes teachers ask me to talk about research which is leading teaching. They seem to assume that theorists pose questions, find answers, and then recommend things to do in classrooms. This is not the case. Researchers rarely ask the questions which teachers want answered (and there are good reasons why this will be so, see Clay, 1990) and educators rarely work to implement the implications of particular research findings. Researchers tend to prepare a more general 'curriculum' of recent advances in understanding. We may well do better if practice and theory were considered together in ongoing research to inform each other.

Reading is made up of various component behaviours and because of this the starting point of programmes of instruction can vary from one to another. Two authorities have suggested that differences between theorists might be better understood if we thought of the sequence or order in instructional programmes as the central issue (Carroll, 1976; Donaldson, 1978). Perhaps the debates are really about the order in which component behaviours are learned. Is an 'order of acquisition' the key issue for becoming an effective or less effective reader?

We seem to believe that sequences of instruction make a difference and continually look for better methods and better materials. One school selects a diagnostic-prescriptive instruction programme, knowing that a neighbouring school has adopted an individualized reading programme: each must believe that one approach is better than the another. There may be various ways and orders in which one can learn all the processes needed by an effective reader, and the guidelines of a programme will state the order in which skills are emphasized in that programme. This illustrates how adults preselect what children have an opportunity to learn: they or the programme they use decree that this must be learned before that can be introduced. Children's learning is constrained by our schemes and our scheming, by our allegiences and our theories. We construct the learning situations for the children and then we try to build general theories about how they learn when they have been in very different instruction.

In the construction of efficient reading strategies does it matter which starting points we choose? Probably the answer is a qualified '*Yes.*' Flexible children may approach the task by any of the paths plotted by publishers or curriculum designers, and for such children one may not be better than another. I am not convinced that children are infinitely flexible and I suspect that the more formalized the teaching sequence and the more committed the teachers are to it, the larger could be the group of children who cannot keep in step with that particular programme. Unfortunately when teachers say of a child 'He cannot make progress in reading and writing' or 'He is not ready for reading and writing' too often that is only true if he has to learn by that teacher's programme. There is probably another route by which he could learn and in that case the instruction would start, not where the teacher is, but where the child is.

One reason to value the current advocacy for 'whole language' approaches to literacy instruction is because they do not try to control which sources of information in a text the child shall learn first. They do not prevent the child's exposure to any aspect of the task. However, the problem that the 'whole language' teacher then has is knowing what cues in texts (or sources of information) individual children are attending to and whether children are moving forward. It becomes more difficult to notice the children who are losing their way in the complexities of whole language approaches unless special efforts are made.

Do our programme decisions or those of some publishers of reading programmes, ever make literacy learning more difficult for children? Once particular theoretical assumptions have been made about reading acquisition and a curriculum has been built around those assumptions, then unusual individuals who need a different kind of instruction from that highlighted in the programme will have their learning placed in jeopardy. In this way instructional programmes are responsible for producing reading failure.

Every programme involves risks to individuals. All teaching is not perfect and in the real world of education we are always faced with less than a perfect delivery system. Therefore any programme from direct phonic instruction to enriched and individualized whole language curricula has its risk areas. This is another way in which instructional programmes are responsible for producing reading failure.

It follows from the last two paragraphs that we should expect every programme to provide itself with safeguards against its risk areas.

It is easy to conclude that our usual sequences of instruction are the necessary sequences, but are they? If children succeed in a programme that is a demonstration of a satisfactory sequence; it does not prove that it is a necessary sequence. Theorists and researchers have proceeded in the last decade with too little attention to the role of instruction, and the distinction between usual sequences and necessary sequences for learning.

The Need to Look More Closely and Think More Clearly

In this book I hope the reader will find ideas which will guide their observations of children who are not following the majority path, children who will succeed if we can only tune into the way they are seeing and doing things at some particular point in their progress towards literacy. By thinking more clearly about reading acquisition the teacher may be able to aid the child who cannot 'get his ducklings all in a row' to become effective.

Three concepts that developed to increase our understanding of children's progress in learning to read have now become insurmountable barriers, blocking the development of early intervention programmes. These are the belief that 'intelligence will out' and the concepts of reading age and reading readiness.

Intelligence will out

There is an unbounded optimism among teachers and parents that children who are late starters will indeed catch up. Given time, something will happen. A temporary backwardness will eventually be relieved by suitable teaching and children may even grow out of it themselves! In particular, there is a belief that the intelligent child who fails to learn to read will catch up to his intelligent classmates once he has made a start. Do we have any evidence that this is the case? Is there documented evidence of accelerated progress in late starters? Isolated examples may support this hope but correlations from a long-term study of 100 school entrants showed that two or three years after a child had entered school, where he stood in relation to his age-mates at the end of the first year at school (i.e. his rank order in relation to his classmates) was roughly where one could expect to find him at 7:0 or 8:0. This is what one would expect if learning to read depended on the cumulative acquisition of a complex set of learned behaviours and was not the product of sudden insights.

The concept of reading age

A child's level of performance on a reading test has traditionally been expressed as a reading age. Classroom teachers tend to teach according to a particular, prescribed or preferred method, and to evaluate progress according to the easy-to-administer standardized test. The main criterion for a test's selection by teachers is that it is prescribed by some authority or it does not take much time. When the test isolates a failing child there is no ready means of translating the test score into the classroom practices of the teacher. There is not enough information in the test score and it is not information of the kind needed for instruction. The reading age unit as such does not describe the skills a child has, or the skills he has yet to be taught. It tells the teacher nothing about the teaching required. A reading age tells nothing about the child's reading skills; one has to interpret it.

A more serious criticism of a reading age concept for the early identification of reading difficulty is that it tends to force us to delay for several years. Because tests involve test error, small differences in scores cannot be considered significant. They may have occurred by chance. If we have to rely on reading tests to select readers who are falling behind their classmates then only a sizeable difference between reading age and chronological age can ever be reliable. It is commonly recommended that a difference of two years indicates that special tuition is necessary.

By such a criterion reading difficulty might be detected at 7:0 if the child began school at 5:0 but in fact children are likely to be 8:0 with three or more years of failure behind them before special help is considered in the form of complementary or compensatory teaching. And yet, in all probability classroom teachers have always classified these children as 'my lowest reading group' from about the time they entered school! That is the anomaly.

The concept of reading readiness

School entry is not the beginning of development or of education in its broadest sense, but it is the beginning of society's formal attempts to instruct all children, in groups, in skills that are considered important. It is supposed to coincide with a state of reading readiness in the average child, although studies of preschool children who have taught themselves to read have been reported. Despite lip service paid to a developmental concept of reading readiness there remains the cultural anomaly which allows New Zealand and British children to face formal instruction and learn to read at 5:0, American children at 6:0 and Swedish or Russian children at 7:0.

The term 'reading readiness' has many definitions but usually it implies that children become ready for formal reading at different times as a result of different rates of maturing, and that there is a stage at which the child is not yet a reader (Stallman, A. C. and Pearson, P. D., 1990). However, recent accounts of preschool children's interest in literacy have used the term 'emerging literacy' to describe how children go through a long and gradual process of 'becoming literate' (Teale and Sulzby, 1986). This position implies that when children enter school they will be at different points in the emerging literacy process.

One consequence of the readiness concept is that the education system, the schools and the teacher expect all children to get to where the programme starts before they are ready for formal instruction and some will be identified as 'not ready.' If the concept of emerging literacy is accepted, then the school's programme must go to wherever each child is and take his learning on from that point. (See Chapter 3.)

There have been extensive critiques of these three problematic concepts — that intelligence will become apparent no matter how limited a child's opportunities to learn are; that reading ages are a helpful way to summarize literacy learning; and that children become ready to be taught to read at some single moment of time. However, if teachers are to go to wherever each child is and take his learning on from that point then they need to be astute observers of children's interactions with literacy tasks during the preschool and early years of school.

Transitions and Transformations: An Alternate View

In the first part of this book I have tried to present an alternate view of how children with different profiles of achievement engage with school programmes, each in his or her own way. There is a period of transition extending from a few days for some but to several months for others during which time the child gradually changes from a nonreader to a beginning reader.

I see this as a time of transitions and translations. At this time the school entrant's programme couples his past learning with new learning so that he can use it in new contexts. Many of the child's old ways of responding undergo change so that they can be applied to the new tasks. For example, the preschooler who has learnt to look at picture books will scan the objects and colours back and forth in irregular patterns extracting meaning from the pictures. We do not see a picture as a whole but rather our eyes focus and move, focus and move again moving around the picture. In the early stages of learning to read the new entrant to school must confine this free-ranging, scanning behaviour to particular directional patterns suitable for moving across lines of print.

In oral language the child's ways of talking undergo transformations when the child develops new expectations about the links between oral and written language—a new theory of the task. This transformation cannot occur with three-dimensional blocks and shapes, nor with two-dimensional picture materials. These materials will certainly have value for the development of visual perception in the child whose preschool life has been barren of similar experiences. However, the appropriate transformations at the early reading stage take place only in the presence of print and when the child is actively seeking to discover how oral and written language are related.

Both visual perception and language behaviour were patterned in intricate ways during the preschool years but they must now be linked to achieve progress in reading and this must call for some reorganization or transformation to take place when the child is introduced to printed language. This creates a kind of developmental discontinuity. For some children this linking has already begun in the preschool years but then it was optional: now it is obligatory.

Reading instruction places new demands on the child. He must use his old preschool ways of responding in novel situations and he must discover or invent new co-ordinations. The initiative for this active learning comes from the child engaging with his new environment and it bears little relation to the passive control of readiness suggested by the idea of maturation.

Preschool children learn to respond to the messages in children's stories which are told or read to them and in doing this they use the kind of language and thought processes that they will use in learning to read later on. They acquire control over the more formal language of books if they are read to. Yet formal reading instruction presents children with a new set of problems and places them under some pressure to get them solved. The pressure may be slight and the experience may be enjoyable but the formal demands of school create a discontinuity with the child's past experience. *For something between a year and three years all children struggle with a new and complex problem—how to draw upon several things they know, and how to direct this knowledge collectively to the task of producing reading responses, and then how to check out the messages they get.*

It follows that children may have developed good visual perception for forms and shapes and yet fail to learn to read because they think the task depends on visual memory for particular letters or forms, and do not appreciate that their power to produce language has anything to do with the task. Similarly, other children with good language may be unsuccessful in applying this knowledge to reading because they do not pay the visual cues sufficient attention.

The need to transform preschool competencies into new ways of responding creates the developmental discontinuity, makes the early reading success a product of learning, and discredits the adequacy of a maturation concept of readiness.

When entry to school is seen as a period of transition we can begin to understand the cultural anomaly. If entrants have only five years of preschool learning they will need a different programme from those who have had seven years of prior learning. Each of the school systems that admit children at five or six or seven years must have designed different types of transitional instruction. In this book the new entrant stage of being introduced to printed language will be heavily influenced by the transitional instruction for five year olds that I have observed in my research in New Zealand, and have referred to as the 'early reading stage.' The terms 'preparation for reading' or 'reading readiness training' or 'pre-reading' will be avoided.

This concept of the early reading period as a time of transition when various preschool behaviours change into new forms, suggests that there will be wide variations in the patterns of progress one might find among children during their first year at school. Do beginning instruction programmes allow for this? And do interpretations of research studies consider the possibility of different paths to a similar goal?

Short and Long Transitions

The transitions and transformations may occur on different time-schedules for different children and may occur on different materials. The instruction delivers the opportunities to learn something: individual children will take different learning from group or class activities. This flexible approach to curriculum and progress is sustained in New Zealand classrooms by the long-standing practice of children entering school on their fifth birthday. Teachers try to meet them where they are when they arrive. My research studies showed different rates of progress.

Some move fast. A few children, well-prepared by their preschool experiences, will learn the early reading skills quickly under conditions of good instruction and pass on within weeks to reading books.

Some must be average. Many children will need to extend their preschool experiences as well as learn transitional skills but the dual task can be accomplished by the average child within the first six months of school.

Some take a long time. Usually children are unable to progress during the first year at school because teachers are not able to reach and build on to their particular preschool skills. (Cultural and linguistic differences, or not having had the opportunities to learn preschool literacy skills create such situations.)

Other slow learners are children whose experiences during their first year at school have tied their *previously adequate* preschool responses into tangles of cognitive confusion, overlaid with emotional reactions to failure. Confusion was observed in children close to six years who sometimes moved from right to left or bottom to top across a page of print, or who still confused the concept of a letter with a concept of a word, or who claimed 'I can read this book without looking at it.' Children, like anyone faced with novel learning, can easily become confused even in the best of classroom programmes, but when someone is quietly watching for the tangles and working to unpick them (i.e. they are detected) then they can be overcome.

To relax and wait for 'maturation' when it is experience that is lacking would appear to be deliberately depriving the child of opportunities to learn. To fail to observe that the child's early reading progress is blocked either by inadequate prior learning or by current confusion, and not provide the required complementary activities, must be poor teaching.

While the old concept of 'reading readiness' as a question of maturation has outlived its usefulness I would want teachers of new entrants to observe them closely as they engage with classroom activities. The programme should then take each child from where she or he is into new aspects of literacy learning suited to the individual patterns of responding the teacher was able to observe. Children making slow progress after six months in such a programme could use some extra time interacting with the teacher because they may be able to do with personal assistance what they have been unable to achieve alone and so be able to establish early literacy behaviours.

After a year at school New Zealand children whose progress is in the lowest 10–20% of their age-group receive an individual one-to-one programme designed to use the strengths they already have in literacy and accelerate their transition with more finely tuned instruction. It is called Reading Recovery. Children are usually working within the average band of their class in twenty weeks (Clay, 1985). This is one example of how a school system has tried to deal with differences that show up towards the end of the transition period but which do not need to persist throughout the whole of the child's schooling.

In Summary

Reading is a process by which children can, on the run, extract a sequence of cues from printed texts and relate these, one to the other, so that they understand the message of the text. Children continue to gain in this complex processing throughout their formal education, interpreting statements of ever-increasing complexity.

What then are 'problem readers'? Presumably they have had much more difficulty than most children in coping with the day-to-day lessons in reading and therefore they seem to have accumulated processing competencies at a slower rate than average learners, slipping further and further behind. This way of approaching the problem allows us to escape from having to state how far behind children are in the earliest years of schooling. They do not have to be two years retarded to be problem readers. They are falling behind because they are not learning as effectively as their peers on this particular set of tasks under these particular classroom conditions. The new questions that should then be asked are 'Need this be so?' and 'Does closer attention, more help and a different kind of teaching interaction change this pattern?'

The concepts of reading age, reading readiness and an optimism that 'intelligence will eventually win out,' tend to operate as barriers to identifying children who need help with the transition. Better descriptions of literacy processes are needed both to improve teaching interactions and to identify where their problems lie. How children make the transition from preschool types of responding to working in a formal programme and how they transform one set of responding into the other would be interesting questions for research.

If different programmes stress different aspects of the reading process at different times, teachers need to give more sensitive attention to the sequential accumulation of reading processes by individual children. We need to recognize and work with different paths to the same outcome and we need to offer more expert teaching interactions to children who are not assuming a normal trajectory of progress.

PART TWO

Transitions and Translations

2   Literacy Before Schooling

This chapter discusses aspects of emerging literacy in the preschool years which are particularly important for what schools do to help or hinder the transition into formal schooling. How can the teacher of four or five or six year olds view the child's competencies?

Learning How to Learn Language

How a child learns to use his home language in the preschool years is impressive and many interesting accounts of these achievements from research and from biographies are available.

'Everything changes if we suppose that individuals learning to read and write already possess a notable knowledge of their mother tongue.'

(Ferreiro and Teberosky, 1982)

We have for some time understood the importance of oral language for literacy learning (see Chapter 4) but more recently our attention has been drawn to other areas of preschool learning that are relevant to becoming literate. If we could design instruction so that children could learn to read and write as a natural follow-on from what they have already learned to do well then that instruction might be particularly effective. However, if teachers are to recognize what achievements children bring to school they need to become good observers of young children, and even better listeners than they usually are.

Learning to Communicate

The young child has learned to use the adult to help him to make sense of the world. If ambiguity exists the young child negotiates with the adult to find out where the sense lies. The young child's ability to communicate is well-developed and has allowed him to construct a good control of his mother tongue by the time he enters school. In particular he has learned how to learn language.

It is important for teachers to remind themselves of this when they seem to hear differences in a particular child's speech. The child may not know as much about language as some of his peers, or he may find the rules for talking in school are different from those in his culture or ethnic group, or he may see little similarity between talking in his family and the more formal teacher-pupil talk of the classroom (Cazden, 1988), or he may even speak a different language from the teacher's. Yet in all these cases the child has already learned how to learn language.

The teacher's task is to help children to make links between what they can already do with language and the new challenges of school.

Gaining Access to Meaning

What account is taken in the first years of school of how well the child has already learned to negotiate and communicate his messages, to develop his understandings of the world and its regularities, and to test these with adults. Little children go around doing these things every day (Wells, 1986; Tizard and Hughes, 1984). The child has experience of using his interaction with people and things to make language match with what he experiences in the environment.

The child has also developed models of his own about what goes on in the world and what the steady state of that world is. He can carry out actions, or talk about carrying these out, and can make links and predictions about what will happen if... The child is actively seeking out and finding regularity in the experience he has with the world, and he is able to work out what some of the invariances are. He is able to act on this knowledge even though he cannot always describe what it is he knows.

Noting some or all of the points made above preschool teachers:

- create opportunities for learning of all kinds
- relate frequently and personally to individual children
- challenge children to talk, to think, and to learn
- ask critical questions while listening to the child's negotiations for meaning
- act as a back-up resource and support system which allows the child to extend his own interactions with the world.

Adding Value

Through the things a preschool teacher attends to she reveals to children what she values about their activities. Every time she talks with a child about his activity she places a value on it, irrespective of what she says about it. Such valuing of preschoolers' efforts and involvements are continuous, individual, personal, and powerful. Careful management of teacher attention can encourage children to change, and to take more control of their own activities and learning.

Emerging Literacy

The past decade has been rich with reports of literacy behaviours acquired by child learners before they come to school. Many facets of emerging literacy have received the attention of researchers and have been widely reported (Teale and Sulzby, 1986; Strickland and Morrow, 1989). There has been strong advocacy for acknowledging what the child is able to do (Donaldson, 1978), how the contexts of his life influence this (Harste, Burke and Woodward, 1984; Heath, 1982) and how parents and preschools can interact with the child's learning (Morrow, 1989).

One discovers that preschool children are exploring the detail of print in their environment, on signs, cereal packets and television advertisements. They are writing in primitive ways. They are developing concepts about books, newspapers and messages, and what it is to read these. A few reports of longitudinal research showed how children change over time and how more advanced concepts emerge out of earlier understandings.

Preschool children already know something about the world of print from their environment. This leads them to form primitive hypotheses about letters, words or messages in books, or in handwritten messages. Although some authorities claim that what the preschool child learns about print is not closely linked to success in learning to read (Bertelson, 1986) it is a more widely held view that learning to read and write in school will be easier for the child with rich preschool literacy experiences than it is for the child with almost no literacy experience.

Learning About Books

Favourite story books apparently teach far more than we have understood (Spencer, 1987) — story schema, the structures of plots, anticipation of events, memory for what happened from a previous reading, and the ways in which language is used to create the effects of surprise, climax, and humour. Spencer points out that:

> Being read to offers them longer stretches of written language than at any other time, and moreover, this is language put together by someone that isn't there to be seen. The reader, adult or child, lends the text a different voice, so that 'I'll huff and I'll puff and I'll blow your house down' becomes a language event of a particular kind.

Children who have been read to a great deal will already know, in some way, that the language of books is different from the language that they speak. They will be developing 'an ear' for bookish or literary forms of language.

The child who asks, 'What's that say?' in response to a television advertisement shows his awareness that language messages can be written down. The child who charges his parent with having read his favourite story incorrectly because part of the story was missed out has a basic awareness that there is a specific message to be read and that sequence is very important. When such children are given their first books in school they already understand that the captions bear some relation to the picture and to the sort of things they can say about the picture.

The most valuable preschool preparation for school learning is to love books, and to know that there is a world of interesting ideas in them (Butler and Clay, 1979). Today there are many wonderful books for preschool children and parents who love to share books with children transmit their feelings, their understanding and their language patterns to their little listeners. Some books enrich children's thinking from their plots, their ideas or their language. Books that are very simple will draw children's attention to print. *Titch* (Hutchins) is one example of a very simple book with an exciting text for a preschooler's story time.

Learning About Reading

If a child shows an interest in words and in print any parent would do well to respond to that interest for it is wisdom to enrich the child's experience. Sometimes parents wonder whether they should try to teach their pre-schoolers to read. Some parents are concerned lest they 'spoil' the unspoilt child for the teacher. Others are rather anxious to prove something to themselves about their children's abilities. Some have thought an early start in the preschool years might forestall failure in the classroom. In recent years reports have been published about children who have taught them-selves to read (Clark, 1976) so the task is not so very difficult if you are lucky enough to get the right sort of opportunities. Yet a loud warning must be sounded to over-eager parents! It is folly to kill curiosity and interest with over-instruction. Resist the temptation to tell the child what to attend to. Follow the child's line of interest and support what he or she is trying to figure out.

There are several negative things to be said about over-zealous efforts by parents. Children can certainly be taught to read letters and words, if you want to call that reading. I think that reading is better described as a sequential activity in which a message is extracted from a continuous text. So stories have more value than letter lessons. The complex process of learning to read is slow-growing from the first encounters of listening to preschool stories to the independent reading of the young school child.

In one piece of research a three year child of superior intelligence was taught to read as well as children who were five years old, in school, and of the same superior intelligence level (Begg and Clay, 1968). However, the quality of the child's learning differed from that of the five year olds in certain ways. A careful comparison of this three year old with two average school entrants showed that while his word reading and book level at 3:9 was similar to the school children at 5:6, the preschooler's performance on visual perception activities like spatial drawing, letter identification and knowing the conventions of written language was inferior to that of the older children. In the area of spatial relationships and the visual perception of differences in print his development lagged well behind the older group. A school entrant who can already read may need to develop further his control over the motor, spatial and visual perception aspects of the task despite his apparent control of the reading process. A serious limitation for the child when he was studied as a three year old seemed to be his inability to use several sources of information in print sequentially, alternatively or integratively, as the older reader does. He tended to focus on one type of information which often led him to false conclusions. The child's loss of skill when the lessons stopped for three months was almost total, although perhaps he was able to relearn these skills more quickly when he started school.

Perhaps more importantly, the reading progress and the mother-child relationship became intermingled and thrived or suffered conjointly. The programme was intensive, to fit the mother's research schedule, and she wrote 'There were times when the boy did love to learn to read and the reading appeared to be a considerable satisfaction and pleasure, but there were times when he seemed to resent reading and showed discouragement and behavioural difficulties. It seemed that he finally regarded his reading experiences as a task in which he had failed rather than a source of enjoyment and satisfaction it had been at the early stages.' A relaxed programme would have been more desirable. When an older child struggles with learning to read at school, failure is bad enough but an accepting parent at home is a refuge from that failure. If the preschool child who is taught by a parent at home is allowed to feel he is failing when his parent becomes irritated or comments negatively on his efforts, this is an earlier encounter with failure in a much more intense relationship with a much more fundamental person.

Just as too much attention to the correction of efforts to talk can be very detrimental to language development, so the child's early attempts to read can be inhibited by over-correction and an urge to 'put him right.' Parents who respond with enthusiasm to the child's attempts to discover things about print for himself are providing a rich foundation for schooling, and they do not generate tension and stress as they instruct the child. Parents and teachers can provide help, support and correct models by sharing tasks interactively with children, carrying some of the load.

It is not easy to interact effectively with children's first attempts but parents quickly learn how to contribute to constructive interactions. I witnessed the frustration of a three and a half year old recently, at the very beginning of the struggle of understanding how we put speech into writing. He wrote his name by making the letter 'M' (which his parents believed was his entire 'writing repertoire'). He must have discovered rhyme because he took pencil and paper to his mother and asked her to write 'Devon/seven!' She tried to reduce the task by saying, 'First you need the "s" for seven and then . . .' He bridled in anger and demanded 'Devon/seven!' As an observer I wondered whether he was asking for D-evon/S-even as though it were D + X and S + X which would have been an interesting analysis on his part. Both parents tried but neither responded well to his request and he went off in a huff. On the spur of the moment I do not know how I would have reacted to his interesting request, and I thought at the time how difficult it would be to probe his thinking. The incident confirmed for me a recommendation I made to parents in a book on early writing, 'Let the child lead' (Clay, 1987).

Studying What Preschoolers Understand About Print

Diary records and descriptive accounts of emerging literacy tell their own story of things we can readily observe (Baghdan, 1984; Bissex, 1980; Taylor, 1983; Taylor and Strickland, 1986).

Remarkable in its insights and detail is the study of Argentinian children by Ferreiro and Teberosky (1982). It was research using Piagetian methodology to explore early reading and writing. The authors used Piagetian theory to interpret their findings about the conceptual development of children in reading and writing. The study reported findings from a sample of children aged four to six years which can be compared with results from a study of New Zealand children from the first day they entered school until one year later when they were six years old (Clay, 1966). Similarities in the behaviours that these two studies describe are surprising and interesting since they cover children learning different languages and entering school programmes that are very different. Studies in other languages are now available (Y. Goodman, 1990). The findings have important implications for my arguments about the transition into school and the gradual development of cognitive (inner) control, so they are reviewed here in some detail.

'Reading' with the help of pictures
Texts that adults share with preschool children usually have illustrations. What attention do children pay to pictures and to text, and do they think about the relationships between these? Ferreiro and Teberosky (1982) showed that young children could learn to make several distinctions. They distinguished:

- drawing from writing
- pictures from print
- letters from numerals
- letters from punctuation
- letters from words
- print from cursive writing.

Clay (1975) identified all but the cursive distinction being made by many five year old children after entry to school in either the reading or the writing situation. In the New Zealand material imitation of cursive writing only occurred in the early stage of scribble streamers at about two to three years whereas in the Argentinian children who are taught to write in cursive script when they first enter school it was a recurrent aspect of preschool children's attempts to write.

The distinction between writing and drawing is interesting because both drawing and writing are symbolic. While drawing is obvious in its attempts to represent things in the world or in imaginary worlds, it is not immediately obvious what writing substitutes for. Written language is a particular type of substitutable object.

Picture and word   Ferreiro and Teberosky gave children a picture and word reading task and described a sequence of change in the responses that they discovered.

- At first the text and the picture are not differentiated.

- Then the children expected the text to be a label for the picture.

- At the third stage the text is expected to provide cues with which to confirm predictions based on the picture.

This was the beginning of a process of searching for confirmation in the text so that if the letters of 'bear' were not there it could not say 'bear.' When the Argentinian children were questioned about the relationship of pictures to print they expected print to contain the name of the picture.

Picture with sentence   When the authors gave the children a picture with a sentence reading task somewhat similar levels appeared.

- At first the children went from one system to the other as if together they expressed a meaning. There was little appreciation that writing was a transcription of oral language.

- If asked to read the story they would generate text from the picture and from oral language. They would construct an oral text inferring the content from the picture, imitating the style of readers, and using intonation patterns and gestures. To be able to do this they must have observed readers reading aloud and probably had been read to. The same text under different pictures would, at this stage, take on the meaning of the pictures.

- At the third level children gave some thought to the graphic properties of the text. They expected the text to name things that were pictured, but only things in pictures. To them print must represent sentences that they could associate with the picture.

- A new stage was reached when correspondence was expected between (syllabic) segments of a word that named something and selected graphic segments of the text. This depended upon the possibility of achieving breaks in enunciation.

- Finally, print represented sentences associated with the picture and some measure of correspondence was established between segmentation of the utterance and of the graphic parts of the text.

This is a sequence which Clay found in five year old children who were followed longitudinally in their first year at school and the distribution of understanding among competent and less competent children overlapped with that found in the research with Argentinian children. McKenzie (1985) reports similar behaviours among children observed in British infant classes.

In their description of these progressions Ferreiro and Teberosky stress two points.

Firstly, *the conception of print as a label for the picture is an important moment in the child's understanding of written language because the child has begun to work out what kind of representational system written language is.*

Secondly, a point directed particularly to teachers, *attention to the formal properties of print and correspondence with sound segments is the final step in a progression*, not the entry point to understanding what written language is. Many conceptual shifts about the nature of written language have to occur before the child begins to use the alphabetic principle of letter-sound relationships which is often considered to be the beginning of reading. When the child first finds some one-to-one correspondence it is between a particular segment of the graphic forms and a particular segment of the utterance.

An understanding of how print represents language cannot be taught instantly once children begin school. The Piagetian argument would be that children have their own theories about the nature of print and will shift to new hypotheses only when their current theory conflicts with new experiences and they then see the need to attend to new elements. This conflict theory of cognitive change has been challenged by Bryant (1986) who asked 'How would children know what theory to change to?' He proposed an alternative cognitive agreement theory, hypothesising that change occurs when children get two different sources of information which both support a particular change. This position has possibilities for explaining aspects of children's learning about messages in print.

Spatial orientation to reading

Orientation to the conventions of written language in Spanish (as in English) requires attention to the left-right and top-bottom directional conventions. Research in Argentina established that four year olds did not understand these conventions at all well. About half the six year old children entering school got both the directions correct. The researchers believed that children must have learned this from watching readers of texts. There are no printed signs in Spanish to signal directional behaviours and so the authors argued that text exploration on the part of the preschool children would not be sufficient on its own. The children must have witnessed acts of reading by those around them where there were some specific gestural cues such as general or specific pointing.

The other half had not adopted directional conventions but they had their own ideas about proceeding across text. They were observed to alternate direction, moving left to right and then right to left, establishing continuity in some way and avoiding leaps and jumps and return sweeps. As the conventions are arbitrary the children need models who provide them with opportunities to observe repeated demonstrations of the acts of reading, and opportunities to observe the acts of writing. In this way children can learn something about the spatial characteristics of print which are important in learning to read. In preschools it is important to have pencil and paper available in each activity corner, and for the teacher who acts as a scribe to model or demonstrate the activity.

There are further complications when we get beyond the simple directional constraints of two or three lines of print. Which page is to be read first? And how to proceed through a book? In 1963 I designed a simple book-sharing task to observe the child's use and understanding of directional relationships in print and some other concepts in this area. This Concepts About Print task (Clay, 1985) has allowed teachers to observe these directional behaviours in a systematic way. It has been used in other languages and non-Western cultures and seems to be tapping an important set of behaviours to be learned around the transition to formal reading instruction. The behaviours observed on this task are consistent with the detailed descriptions of the Argentinian children.

The other place where one can observe children's problem-solving over the spatial characteristics of text is in their attempts to write (Clay, 1975, 1987). Even seven year olds are still mastering what to do with leftover bits at the end of lines and pages.

Children need to pick up information in reading in a particular order otherwise the messages will be garbled. Children have opportunities to learn about directional constraints if adults model directional behaviours for them in book-sharing and in writing.

The concept of a word

Children explain the features of print to themselves in their own ways and develop their own rules for what text has to be read, according to the Argentinian study. Their hypotheses do not necessarily correspond with the rules of the adult world. That is also true in oral language development and the children manage to gradually sort out the problems and produce correct grammar for their mother tongue.

Researchers have pointed to the difficulty many children have on entry to school distinguishing a letter from a word. These concepts are not easily sorted out by instruction. 'Telling is not enough.' Why are the concepts and their hierarchical relationships hard to understand?

We know that children operate on some kind of language rules to form plurals and the past tense of verbs, and negatives, and we also know that many of the rules they seem to use could not have emerged from anything they have heard adults use. They must have been constructed by the children themselves. Analogously, the Argentinian children held hypotheses about print which they could not have learned from people around them.

They thought that text could not be read when there were only two letters nor if the string was only a string of repeated letters. They demanded at least three letters and some variability in the characters used. (Of course when you question children in any inquiry situation you can elicit rationales which they did not actually use but in these studies the authors were able to draw their conclusions from a wide sampling of behaviours and ages to counter this factor.)

What Ferreiro and Teberosky's children seemed to believe was that a big house needed more letters than a little house, a cow needed more letters than a fly and that three girls needed more letters than one girl. They thought that the same signs could be used in different names (that is 'hens' and 'chickens' could be written in the same way) and sometimes they did not object to quite different texts for the same name.

The nature of the letter-word-sentence hierarchy is hard to learn for the three to six year old group, although they are not lacking in hypotheses about the relationships. With relative ease children do learn to write letters, and construct their names and other words, but even in this particular case there is often an early confusion of a single initial standing for the whole name. Typically this experience with the letter-word hierarchy in writing does not generate an appropriate hypothesis about how letters relate to words.

Reading without pictures

In text, groups of letters separated by blanks do correspond to words we emit but do not correspond to the actual pauses in oral language. How do children relate utterances to texts? When Ferreiro and Teberosky gave children texts without pictures and read the text orally to them the authors concluded that written language acts as a prompt to say something in accordance with the rules of one's own internal grammar. Reading at this stage appears to be an act of oral language construction. They described the children's responses in a series of progressions like these:

- Only nouns are represented in the text so written language is a particular way of representing objects.

- A whole sentence is attributed to one written segment.

- The child attempts but has no facility to segment the utterance into parts that can be matched to parts of the text.

- Nouns appear to be broken out of the sentence but the verb is linked to the whole sentence or predicate. The child is often satisfied that print is not an exact representation of the oral text.

- Everything is written down except the articles.

- Everything is written including the articles.

They also identified a conflict between the preschool learning of their children and what they were required to do in school. The school instruction they observed failed to build upon the learning children had already acquired. Only those children who had reached advanced levels of analysis were able to adapt to the school's demands. Children with low levels of differentiation of the reading task faced confusion (referred to by Downing and Leong as 'cognitive confusion,' 1982). These children had great difficulty in reconciling the teacher's instruction or questions with their hypotheses about texts and were particularly disadvantaged by the instructional methodology or schemes of the schools. They tried to find solutions to their problems.

- They used meaning and ignored deciphering.

- They used deciphering and ignored meaning.

- They experienced conflict between meaning and deciphering and re-solved this conflict by alternating from one to the other, or they gave primacy to the meaning of the text.

- They became able to co-ordinate deciphering and meaning approaches to reading.

These strategies divorce deciphering from meaning and sometimes reject meaning at the expense of deciphering. The authors saw them as products of school instruction.

There probably are mismatches between instruction and preparedness on entry to school even when children are taught in an instructional programme more hospitable and attentive to such differences than the programme described by Ferreiro and Teberosky.

Where are the breaks in language?

Clay (1979) and Ferreiro and Teberosky (1982) describe how some of the child's difficulties in matching oral sentence construction with printed sentences are with finding the units of speech and the units in print and co-ordinating the two sets of units. One of the origins of this problem is finding units in one's speech.

- Ferreiro and Teberosky's children took a decisive step when they tried to match part of the writing to part of a name. Usually one letter corre-sponded to a spoken Spanish syllable. The children were quite skilful at adjusting what they were saying to match with what was written.

- Children must have an awareness at some level of the distinctions between the phonemes of their language because they make use of such distinctions as they listen and talk. They become more conscious of this knowledge which they already possess when they have to manipulate it for the purposes of reading and writing but this is not new knowledge for they already know the contrastive differences between the phonemes of their language.

- One can also argue that the ability to inflect words according to the (regular) rules of the language is a naturally occurring example of children's ability to segment the language they use (Berko, 1958; Clay, Gill, Glynn, McNaughton, Salmon, 1983).

- Many parents play linguistic games, use songs, nursery rhymes and poetry with children. Maclean, Bryant and Bradley (1987) asked whether these were indicators of phonological awareness in three year old children. How well do three year olds know nursery rhymes? The research found that many children could not produce a complete version, although the range was wide, from children who could do nothing to those who could accurately recite a whole rhyme. Using a longitudinal analysis these British researchers were able to ask whether early knowledge of nursery rhymes is related to the recognition of letters and written words. The answer was 'Yes.' There was a highly specific relationship between knowledge of nursery rhymes and ability to detect rhyme in 3–4 year olds and a longitudinal connection to detecting rhymes at older ages.

The team's results went further than this. Their results showed that the awareness of rhyme and alliteration, which children acquire before they go to school possibly as a result of their experience at home, has an influence on their eventual success in learning to read and to spell. Although others have suggested a link between phonological awareness and reading, the authors claim that their study is the first adequate empirical evidence that the link is causal. (This matter is discussed further in chapters 13 and 14.)

Preparing for Success in the School's Literacy Programme

Specific experiences which a child has before he goes to school may affect his progress once he gets there. What is it about new entrants' learning that may help or hinder their progress in reading?

Opportunities for learning oral language

The preschool child's language development is vital to his progress in reading. We are concerned not only with the development of his vocabulary, or his articulation of sounds, but with the range and flexibility of the patterns of sentences which he is able to control. His development in this behaviour is critically dependent on the preschool opportunities he gets to converse with an adult. The more of this experience he enjoys, the more mature his language will be on entering school. Children, like adults, like to talk about themselves, their possessions, their home, family and pets, their friends, neighbours, relatives. Children need to be engaged in conversation about the things they know about because the familiar content provides them with opportunities to experiment with ways of expressing themselves.

It is not surprising that children who have not been as active in exploring what they can do with language should have more difficulty with reading than other children. After all, reading is a language activity. If children have been slow to acquire speech, or have been offered fewer opportunities to hold conversations (for many different reasons), or have had health problems like intermittent deafness, there can be limitations in the grammar they control which might mean that they have difficulties with comprehending oral or written language. Such children may not have control of some of the most common sentence structures used in story book English and therefore are unable to anticipate what may happen next in the sentences of their reading texts.

Long before the preschool child enters school he has learned to discriminate between vocal sounds sufficiently to differentiate words one from another. Auditory discrimination activities can aim to have children perceive likenesses and differences in non-vocal sounds, and to perceive the sounds of rhymes in language games, favourite stories, poems and songs. This should prepare them to hear the words that rhyme and contrast them with words that do not rhyme, and to recognize that spoken words can begin with the same consonant sound when they begin to read. Rhymes provide activities for frequent and varied repetition and capture the ear with rhythmic movement, alliteration and voice modulation.

Some residual effects of health problems like poor auditory discrimination of sounds, words or sentence structures may not be obvious but when learning to read these children can have particular difficulty in breaking up language into its parts or in synthesizing separate sounds into whole words. For such children, important learning in the area of auditory discrimination has yet to take place.

Literacy has a visual learning side to it

Reading is also an activity which demands the analysis of complex visual stimuli. What does this mean? It means searching a picture or text with the eye and with the brain to pick up information which one can interpret. There are children whose visual analysis of complex shapes has been poorly developed by their preschool opportunities to learn. Individual differences show up in children's ability to scan and analyse pictures, geometric forms and letters merely because they have neglected to pay this kind of material significant attention during their preschool years. So they arrive at school with far less skill in analysing two-dimensional space than other children whose interests have led them to develop this skill for attending to visual detail.

Visual perception is not easy to observe, yet just as there is gradually increasing control over language in the preschool years, and over movement and body control, so there is a similar continuing increase in the ability to scan new material, organize one's perception of it, remember it, perhaps refer to it by some label, or assign meaning in some other way. The child gains this experience in play, in conversation with people who point out features of objects and pictures to the child, and in contact with books. One of the places where we can get a guide to what features of print the child is noticing is in their early attempts to produce print features in their writing. At least what they reproduce must have caught their attention (although the inverse is not necessarily true).

However, preschool visual experiences tend to differ from school experiences. In preschool days children are constantly looking upon a wide view, viewing much and seeing or remembering little detail. In formal literacy instruction seeing must go beyond just looking: it must become a systematic search for precise information and an ability to structure a mental representation of the forms that are seen. Schoolwork requires the development of new and precise discrimination and focussing skills using near-point vision.

There is one particular feature about this management of visual skills in reading to note. Until he reaches school the child has been free to scan objects, people, scenes, pictures, even books in any direction that he chooses and he has not been required to limit his pattern of search in any way. Immediately he becomes a candidate for reading he must learn that in the printed text there is only one appropriate direction in which he can proceed. It is a one-way street. If he is reading a language that is read from left to right then he must learn to go from top-left across to the right and then to return to the next top left position and go again across to the right. For the five year old school entrant of average ability that may be a challenging piece of learning. We have for too long underestimated the magnitude of this task and its particular relevance to subsequent success in learning to read. This directional behaviour, moving in a controlled way across a line of print, is related to motor behaviour or movement. This then is another area in which a child may have difficulty. If his muscular co-ordinations are not well-developed, if he has not gained good control over his hand and eye movements, he may not move across print in consistent and appropriate ways. Then his attempts to relate what he hears to what he sees may result in further difficulties.

Relating language and print

These two analytic aspects of the reading process, the language learning and the analysis of visual stimuli, have to be related to each other. There has to develop a facility for associating speech sounds with printed shapes. The child may find it difficult to link the visual and auditory stimuli or, more precisely, to match the flow of spoken language rhythms coming to his ear with the flow of attention to visual patterns across the page of his text. He may have trouble relating auditory experience to visual experience. Or more specifically, he may have trouble in relating the timing of the auditory experience to the spacing of the visual experience. Children may make a beginning on the learning before they get to school (and Ferreiro and Teberosky's children showed this) but it is in the first year of school that this becomes a challenge to the learner.

Making sense and making meaning

While attention to language and visual features have an analytic emphasis, the child's need to make sense of the world gives an overarching intactness to all this learning. Things have to make sense and seem worthy of attention, and meaningfulness brings all kinds of satisfactions. The hypotheses which Spanish children were forming about print illustrate the need to make sense of this small part of their world.

Children who are read to regularly at home and from an early age have someone in the family who enjoys sharing the stories and answering the children's questions about the meanings, the words, and the world (Durkin, 1966; Clark, 1976; Paley, 1981; White, 1956, 1984; Baghdan, 1984). The things that children learn from books about the meanings of texts and how they relate to the real world are rounded out in the discussions which children have with parents about plots and literary devices. In booksharing, children begin to become aware of the linguistic and visual features of books and texts but they do this within the wholeness of stories understood in their own way. Before they get to school they can be found retelling their favourite stories prompted by the sequence of pictures.

Self-management

The child's ability to control his own behaviour, and in particular the movement patterns of his body, is related to reading and writing progress. His ability to learn from his sensory interchanges with his environment, and to relate this sensory input of information to the output in language or movement activities, is an important foundation for the input of reading experience and the output in understanding or action.

Self-confidence

A child starting school does so with mixed feelings and some misgivings. Security, self-confidence, acceptance, and a sense of belonging are a foundation for attitudes that encourage participation in effective learning experiences. Happy, relaxed, stimulating relationships between children and between child and teacher promote growth of personality which in turn advances achievement. Some important guidelines for parents and teachers which could encourage the young child's self-acceptance are:

- Recognize the individuality of the child.
- Listen to and use the child's opinions.
- Accept his feelings.
- Accept the exuberant youngster's rough and tumble play.
- Plan work and play so that a particular child can use his particular strengths.
- Give time and thought to individual children's needs.
- Participate with the child in his selection of activities.
- Make it rewarding for the child to enter activities which seem to be his weakness.
- Consider the child's home culture and whether you are knowledgeable about it or not.

The above analysis has uncovered areas of preschool learning critical for successful literacy learning in schools. Preschool children will be well-prepared for school if they have:

- developed a good control of oral language
- taken an interest in the visual detail of their environment
- reached the level of experience which enables them to co-ordinate what they hear in language with what they see in print
- acquired enough movement flexibility, or motor co-ordination of hand and eye, to learn to control the directional movement patterns required for reading.

Problems the Child Might Take to School

These problems are included here because they can be reduced or minimized by the kinds of opportunities preschools can provide.

Sensory losses

Reading involves vision, hearing, and senses associated with movement (which we may call kinaesthetic sensation). A child with sensory losses in any of these areas will inevitably have deficits in his experience. A blind child will have to learn to read in a different way to compensate for his handicap. A deaf child will have considerable problems with learning to read because he does not develop the control of language which the average child uses in reading. The deaf child may have to learn much of his language through his eyes and may have to be taught to read early in order to develop facility in oral language. The child with cerebral palsy or some physical disability may have his experience gained from movement limited and this may affect both his control over movement (which may affect the reading process) and the development of his visual scanning behaviour.

However, while the extreme cases of sensory loss will probably be located and special provision made for them, in their preschool years other children may enter school with slight or undetected losses in each of these areas. Mild degrees of visual defect do not usually handicap the child in learning to read unless he has frequently avoided visual experiences in his preschool years. On the other hand, mild degrees of hearing loss, particularly intermittent ear trouble between two and four years, can have severe effects in limiting the richness of oral language which the child develops and also limiting the experiences he has to bring to bear on understanding the stories in books. Least obvious are the motor inco-ordinations which make it particularly difficult for the child to learn specific motor patterns such as the directional movements in reading. These children are least likely to be noticed and given extra encouragement in their preschool years.

Limited opportunities to learn some things

A second reason why children may not have the skills that are necessary for good progress in reading when they enter school is that they have not had an adequate range of experiences in their preschool years. Their homes may not have provided a wide range of interesting experiences appropriate to their making an early and easy start in learning to read and write. More specifically, the child who has not had many opportunities to converse with adults will have limited oral language skills which in turn make learning to read more difficult. More than this, the child who has not learned that books contain interesting ideas and that the language which he listens to is related in some way to the story in the book, has missed some valuable learning experience. The child who has had limited experience to run around, to climb, to use his body effectively in activities which demand gross motor skill, will not be ready for the finer adjustments that are required in the motor skills of the eye movement and hand-eye co-ordination in school activities. A child severely deprived in this way could be one who had spent most of the preschool years in hospital.

Emotional disturbance

Every child must feel that he is important, that he is wanted, and that he can accomplish things. Many children get these feelings effortlessly through the process of growing up. Some do not. Feelings of security and adequacy play an important role in achievement. The children who start school having acquired positive views of self are fortunate because they have been accepted and taught how to succeed. A positive view of self can be learned and preschool teachers can help if they create a climate where each child is respected for his uniqueness and where children are listened to, as well as spoken to.

Another reason why emotional disturbance can interfere with reading progress is that learning to read requires a great deal of personal initiative and a willingness to take risks which the insecure child is unwilling to take. It is easier for him to apply to the new learning tasks of school his old emotional reactions of withdrawing, or attacking, distorting or ignoring, and so, by applying old habits to the new situation, causing himself to fail again.

Physical difficulties or specific impairments

A group of possible causes of reading difficulty for a tiny percentage of children lie in the neurological or physical makeup of the child. In rare cases genetic or hereditary factors could be involved but we can only suspect and rarely prove this. We are always left with the task of teaching the child to read in spite of any difficulties. Various kinds of brain injury might interfere with parts of the complex act of reading—with visual perception, or with spoken language, or with the relating of visual and language behaviours, or with extracting the essential features from all this information, or with determining the meaning of the messages. Brain injury often implies in addition other symptoms which can interfere with the learning process. The child may find it difficult to attend for long periods of time, or he may attend to too much detail and be unable to tolerate the complexity of the task. A neurological condition may make him a hyperactive child who flits from task to task assimilating little with each new learning experience. It is possible that nutritional or chemical imbalance or metabolic disorders may influence the child's intellectual functioning, or sensory efficiency, and so contribute to inadequate preparation in reading. The exotic explanation of reading difficulty as due to brain damage accounts for only a very small proportion of children finding it hard to learn. Most difficulties in learning to read stem from inappropriate experiences rather than from impaired structures. Unfortunately they are equally difficult to overcome.

Another possible area of difficulty is described as a 'developmental lag,' a notion which implies that to some extent maturation in the brain and in the nervous system is going on continually and that there is a steady increase in capacity to deal with information from the environment. It is suspected that for some children this unfolding of learning potential proceeds at a slower rate than for others, although their ceiling capacity may not in the end differ. This is easy to understand when one thinks of the child's height. One child may grow very fast at an early age, then slow down, whereas another child may begin more slowly, have a growth spurt at a later age and finish the same height as the first child. Applying this concept to development of the nervous system and its ability to handle learning experience, we can see that one child could be at a disadvantage compared with another if an activity like reading were introduced at the same age for both children. However, reading difficulties caused by developmental lags are difficult to predict and prevent because there are no specific and clear signs. Although we may look at a child and say that his behaviour suggests an immaturity which could be a developmental lag, it might just as easily be due to limitations in his previous experiences that cause the very same behaviour.

Preschoolers are Different One from Another

Individual differences are an asset rather than a liability. A constellation of factors will affect the child's interactions with his first school lessons—his physical, mental, social and emotional development and the things he has had an opportunity to learn. The patterning of individual life experiences will be unique to any one child. It will be different even for siblings, so the school's 'knowledge' of other members of his family should not colour their expectations of this individual child, entering into formal learning. Ideally, preschool experiences should develop individuality, enriching children in areas of strength and interest, fostering their entry into areas for which they show less skill, helping them into the things they tend to avoid, and building up confident children who feel adequate.

It then becomes the responsibility of the school to arrange the early reading programme in ways that do not require all five year olds to fit a single shoe size. One cannot expect them to move into a narrowly conceived, preselected sequence of learning. Because the individuality of new entrants and a belief in group instruction are, initially, out of step, an important quality of a good teacher of new entrants will be an ability to use diverse responses in her pupils.

In Summary

The preschool child does a wonderful job of learning to communicate and the more he talks the more his talking improves. He learns other important general strategies like making sense of the world, in his own terms, making tasks interesting, asking questions and negotiating help. He learns about print and stories and many studies of this early attention to literacy matters have described the period as one of 'emerging literacy' (Morrow and Strickland, 1989). That term captures the 'little by little' accumulation of early knowledge upon which the child will build when he enters formal instruction.

An emphasis on individual differences in preschool children's experiences (stemming largely from their different ways of exploring their environments) signals the need for schools to plan and provide for activities in the first year of school which allow all children to widen the range of their preschool experiences, *wherever they are starting from*. Success in school will be fostered by a programme that goes to where each individual child is in his or her exploration of literacy and provides appropriate experiences for building on to that existing knowledge. Each child should be introduced to the school's programme at some level with which he or she can engage.

3 School Entry — A Transition

Kevin, I would say, is generally unconcerned about starting school — but when he does remember he seems quite happy and has spells of great excitement about it. He is rather on a high at the moment with the acquisition of a new school bag and coat for school.

The only indication of fear perhaps occurred some time ago whilst we were talking about the progression from kindy to school. Kevin asked, 'Why do we go to school — what for?' I told him about these special skills we need to learn and some time later he said — 'but what if I just can't learn?' I felt really sorry for him and since then I have illustrated through various things he does — recognising his name and other letters as the beginning of reading, and being able to draw circles and crosses as the beginning of printing, to build up his confidence in this respect.

I can see that the simple fact of being a 'schoolboy' makes Kevin feel a whole lot more grown-up, better and rather important.

A parent's diary

Rachel is extremely excited — obviously it is all-important for her to start school as this will corroborate her own feeling of having grown up. She is now becoming daily more anxious — she can't read or write yet, which she thinks she should be able to do. She said this evening that she doesn't want to go to school because of the visits to the dental clinic. She isn't impressed by our assurance that she won't have to visit the clinic on her first day at school. She is worried she hasn't got her school bag and lunch box yet. Her last remaining close friend goes to school this week and Rachel says she doesn't want to stay at playcentre on Friday, her last day there. She does seem more irritable than usual and less able to settle at home. She listens avidly to all the girls tell her of school rules — 'Can't call out.' 'Don't run.' 'Don't go anywhere without asking.' She may be oppressed by all this, but I don't think so; she seems to want to conform because school people do.

A parent's diary

The parents' diary extracts above are from Margery Renwick's 'The Transition to School: The Children's Experience' in SET 2, Wellington: New Zealand Council for Educational Research, 1987.

When a child enters school he has a private frame of reference which stems from his personal preschool experiences. His particular parents in his particular home have given him opportunities to explore some things and not others so that he knows a great deal about a limited number of personal experiences. The language he uses mirrors his parents' language; the forms, idioms and dialect he uses reflect the language of his community used by his parents when they talk with him. His feelings, pleasant or unpleasant, are the product of intense experiences he has had with significant adults in the past.

From the challenges and failures of his first five years of growth the child brings to school a store of responses for meeting new situations. Some of these responses are his strengths and the observer labels them 'mature.' Other responses are less effective, the product of unsuccessful attempts to cope in the past, and too often the observer labels these 'weaknesses.' All the child's past confidence may melt to a state of weak wonder as he tries to discover how his usual ways of doing things fit with the strange new situation in which he finds himself (Murphy, 1962). Even adults face such 'newness shock' in strange situations!

It is very common for professionals who are evaluating young children's progress to respond well to the competent child or to a child's strengths. Making comparisons they may too readily use the label 'immature' and the summing up 'he can't do anything' with less competent children. However, if they looked more closely, they would see that both those allegations are plainly wrong—there are few children who do not show maturity in some respect, and no children entering school who have not learned anything.

Life's Balance Sheet Thus Far

How different children are, even at five years! Not only are they different in gender and in styles of interacting with the physical and social environment, but they also have learned quite different things from the environments they live in. They are complex beings whose responses are bound mysteriously into patterns we can sense but are not always able to describe. They are very different one from another.

Sometimes parents and teachers search for this or that single cause that might explain a particular child's behaviour. But every little incident in a child's day occurs against a backdrop of the whole context around him at that time. The impact of that incident is determined in one sense by all his experiences in life so far. The child, however young, is not just taking in experience. He is actively approaching or withdrawing, coping or failing. He brings his personal resources to bear on his life problems learning to cope 'in the widening world of childhood' (Murphy, 1962).

We should look from time to time at the balance sheet to see whether a good life is emerging from the daily interchange of our children with the world around them.

Depending on how we handle such daily interactions our children's personality and their relationship to life will take one of several courses. No single event need have specially great impact but it is amazing how ... little experiences make up, in the long run, a good life or a pretty miserable one. And all this occurs without anything terribly important having happened, good or bad.

(Bettleheim, 1962)

So, children are complex, development is complex and educators must observe carefully life's balance sheet as it is detailed for each individual child.

Individuality and Change

A child's first five years have been peopled with attentive human beings. How does he see them? How does he draw them? (Harris, 1963.)

Primitive messages
One five old girl drew a lady with a baby. She pointed out the lady's hand, arms, body and leg (one only) and the baby, a much smaller figure, alongside.

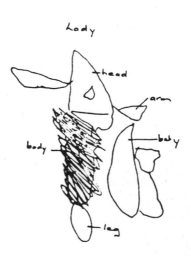

A five year old boy of superior intelligence produced an equally odd man with a body (centre line), legs (side lines), arms and fingers, toes, hair, eyes and nose. The ideas were clear in his mind. It is the transformation into a statement on paper that is difficult, not unlike the ease with which I recognize the face of a friend but the difficulty I would have painting her portrait.

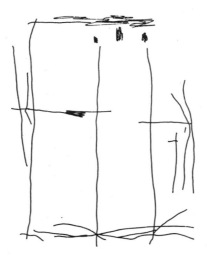

This primitive creature was produced by a five year old boy of above average ability who became an excellent reader within the year. His ability to transmit what he knew into a clear statement on paper was very limited at entry to school. One thing is fairly certain. Preschool experience had provided him with only limited opportunity to explore a two-dimensional pencil and paper world.

What a variety!

New entrants differ more, one from another, than at any other time for the next few years. This is because, in their preschool years, they have had very different kinds of experiences, whereas in school they have many shared opportunities to learn. So, at the point of entering school, children express their ideas in very individual ways.

Not haphazard

If you save several drawings made by one particular child over two or three weeks you will often find that he is working to a basic plan. His ideas are organized and he produces the same pattern or schema again and again.

It seems as if the child has learned a plan of action which produces the pattern or schema. This gives the child enough control over pencil and paper to play with variations, which often leads to new discoveries.

Even twins are individuals

Fraternal twins are like brothers and sisters. They do not have identical heredity but they have been reared in the same home and are likely to have had similar preschool experiences. At five years one might expect them to do similar kinds of things but at that age their drawings are often very different. This underlines the fact that they are individuals, making different use of similar experiences.

What does 'big' mean?

When children were asked to draw a man or a lady and to 'make it big,' this was intended to avoid the minuscule creatures that they sometimes draw in one corner of a page. Five year olds found some interesting ways to make the human figure 'big.' Even common words have different meanings for young children who tend to focus on one aspect of a problem at a time.

Rapid change

Some children's drawings change very greatly within six months, partly as a result of new experiences at school. Compare the drawings of five year olds with their own productions six months later.

Continuity

Yet underlying the changes one can often detect the persistence of a basic pattern reminding us that experience is cumulative and early experiences are the foundation upon which a child builds.

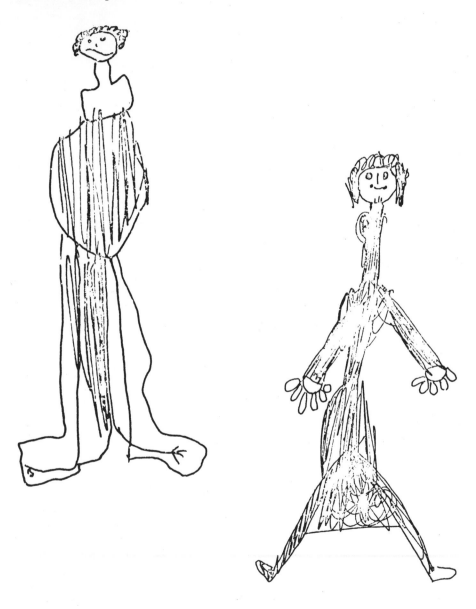

Change, Continuity and Individuality

There was no curriculum for drawing people in these children's schools, yet change was occurring. No one told them to build new responses out of what they could already do, but that seemed to be what happened. And although change was evident across all children they changed from different starting points and they changed in different ways. There is a useful analogy here for what is happening in other areas of learning. When children give their attention to particular aspects of their environments their responses to those things undergo change.

Adjustment to School Entry

There are many reasons why the child and parents alike have butterflies in their stomachs on the first days of school. From the child's point of view, starting school means leaving the safety and comfort of home for a long time every day. He is still small physically, and the school building appears as a large and unfamiliar structure for him to investigate. The child has undoubtedly heard about school from siblings or other children, and some of the butterflies must represent excitement at embarking on an adventure that is associated with growing up. While the school experience is anticipated with some knowledge, expectation, and excitement, there is still much about it that is unknown. The uncertainty about what really happens at school and the imaginative fantasies about what happens at mysterious places away from home can be sources of anxiety for the child. From the parents' perspective, the beginning of school has a strong symbolic meaning. The first day is only the beginning of a long sequence of school-related experiences which have become incorporated into the adult's self-concept. The school represents external evaluation; opportunities for success and failure; the setting for peer group formation and social evaluation; and the initiation of a set of experiences which in adulthood may lead to advancement of socio-economic status. At a more immediate level, the school represents a new source of influence on the child beyond the family. Beliefs and practices which are followed in the home will come under the scrutiny and challenge of community norms and values. The personal hopes and aspirations which parents have for their children now will be tempered by the reality of performance (Newman and Newman, 1975).

Tensions occur in many families at the time a child enters school. For the parents and the child it is a relatively sudden change. Many parents have an inner concern about some of the difficulties they think their children could encounter. For example they may fear physical attack, or criticism of the child. Some anticipate that the home will be criticised. Their concern runs like this. 'I've been spending five years doing my job. Now everyone will see whether I'm a success or not.' When the child enters school parents may feel relief and sadness at the same time. One mother asked, 'Why do I feel so near tears when I expected to feel relieved and happy that my child is growing up.' Such reactions to separation are not uncommon (Klein and Ross, 1958).

Children show signs of increased stress during the first few weeks of school and they express this in many different ways. Some show physical reactions with the loss of appetite, fatigue and stomach upsets. Others return to old problems they had given up, like bedwetting, thumbsucking, and dawdling. Irritability, fighting with brothers and sisters, talkativeness or reticence, keyed-up behaviour, a worried expression — all these behaviours have been reported by parents.

On the credit side there are often signs of growth as the children begin to feel that they can manage the new classroom situation. These changes in the children come from an increase in independent behaviours:

- acting like a big shot
- not wanting to have a baby-sitter
- playing further from home
- visiting neighbours' homes more often

or from the feeling that they are more grown-up:

- more responsibility for self-help
- increased co-operation
- imitation of older children
- more responsible with younger brothers and sisters

or from new attitudes and interests:

- more interest in other children
- new interest in music, and painting
- wanting to 'work' rather than 'play'.

Entry to school calls for a rapid transition from old adjustments to new ones for both the child and his parents. Important feelings are involved and the child is not the only one making the change. Going to school calls for adjustments by the parents who may wonder:

- about the school as an authority
- how their child will measure up
- what is happening to the child for large parts of his day
- about the teacher's handling of problem behaviours.

A satisfactory transition to school will be important for the child in two ways. He must feel able to grasp the new experiences and grow in the new environment. And, for the continuing richness of his education in future years, his parents must weather the transition so that they feel comfortable in their interaction with the school and the teachers. Time spent on these two adjustments could be valuable.

Settling in

The welcome is important. This is one teacher's account of her practices.

Reading ability often depends on whether the child settles easily into the school routine and so it is most important that he comes into a pleasant, friendly room. In fact most children are given the opportunity to visit the school before they turn five. They come on regular visits with playcentre or kindergarten groups or if they do not attend either of these they come with mother to sit for an hour or so. Most mothers with older children at school bring the little ones into the infant room several times before their fifth birthday. On entry the child finds many interesting pictures, captions, wall stories and exhibits to look at and plenty of activities in the reading, maths and science corners to occupy him. He finds that the teacher has arranged her work so that she is free to talk with him when he arrives at school each morning. This is often the only time that shy children will talk. They must be made to feel secure and as routine helps this feeling of security the sooner they become familiar with the class routine the better.

The unlucky or unusual child

When the child enters school the teacher is in a privileged position for gathering significant information about him. Parents in interviews want to explain their child and his past development to the teacher, the preschool can provide further background, general practitioners will make themselves available to teachers to comment on what they know of this unusual child so as to ease his passage into formal education. School psychologists will be prepared to give guidance to teachers in order to prevent a pattern of failure.

Children who have been unfortunate in their early childhood experiences or whose development has been unusual for other reasons, such as long hospitalizations for example, probably need quite different programmes. Their different behaviours at entry should trigger in the teacher an openness in observing their interaction with the new environment, and creative solutions for alternative activities when these are needed. To illustrate this I include a description of some children who were in one junior class of 30 children:

Grant brought problems to school from an emotionally disturbed home.

Frank came from a Samoan home, had the challenge of learning English as a second language, and had partial hearing loss in one ear.

Betty was a very active child with what seemed to be a very short attention span.

Tina had a speech impediment and her speech was very nasal and hard to understand.

David had defective eyesight that had only just been detected and corrected with glasses. His good eye was covered with sticking plaster to make the other eye work and then he had to have his left eye corrected by an operation. He also had defective hearing, and poor motor co-ordination. He was tiny and attended growth clinic. He was very aggressive and had frequent tantrums. For him life's balance sheet had many negatives on it at the time he entered school.

Len was an adopted child and there was a negative attitude to him at home. Before he arrived at school he had a reputation for being naughty and had received severe punishments. He found great difficulty handling excitement or any change in his home or school environment. He became extremely difficult in the middle term when his mother went to work and an older cousin came with an aunt to live with them. This occurred at the same time as a change of class and teacher at his school. He had a very negative attitude to himself. His motor co-ordination was very poor. He had a very short attention span and was extremely easily distracted. He was not able to listen to a whole story read to the class.

The unresponsive child

Once in a while a teacher of new entrant children finds a child who will not offer any responses. The teaching process is impotent if no interaction with the child can be established. The child who is emotionally upset by leaving home, by the crowd of other children or by the impact of newness and strangeness in his environment will sometimes over-react, and sometimes take refuge in neutrality. As the teacher wins him over to the activities of the new setting he normally begins to participate eagerly, a little at first and later wholeheartedly, almost in spite of himself.

There is another type of child who seems to be afraid to perform rather than being emotionally upset in the new environment. Perhaps he is afraid to be wrong. His reticence sometimes seems to be related to a lack of confidence in his own ability; on other occasions it seems to stem from a vague awareness that he is 'no good' at a particular activity. Someone or something in his past experience has made him feel this way. For example, after six months at school one boy put an easy story book on the observer's table and stood motionless and speechless. Both child and observer waited. The observer read the title aloud and ran her finger across the text. The child offered no response despite encouragement and several patient invitations. The observer read several pages of the book. Slowly the child moved his finger towards the print and in an approximate way traced left to right and right to left across the print as the book was read. He was not totally unresponsive; he could be coaxed to move in the reading situation, making a global, tentative response to print in a situation that was relaxed and unhurried.

Another child was quite happy to say the text, repeating what he had heard, but refused to point, to move his hand, to put a response of his body or hand into the situation. For six months one little boy maintained, 'I'll read to you but I won't write my name!' 'Won't' really meant 'can't', and his stance was a defensive one protecting himself from criticism and failure.

A child who is reluctant to point, refuses to speak, or will not look searchingly at print, is like a child out for a walk with his group, but limping with an injured leg. The reading process will be learned haltingly, until he is confident enough to respond in the troublesome area. Coaxing that is not carping, support that is not demanding, confidence in him that does not deny the reality of his sense of inadequacy, these are the fine distinctions that must determine the teacher's behaviour and attitude towards the unresponsive child.

Tuning in to Individual Differences

What kind of person is this child? What does his preschool teacher remember about him? Was he active? Slow-moving? Was he talkative or quiet? Was he usually contented or miserable? More specifically, what gave him a feeling of mastery and assurance? What did he dislike or avoid? How did he use his eyes to explore things? his language to communicate to people? his curiosity to seek new understanding? To what does this particular child give his attention? Is he reaching out for language experiences? Is he eager to explore written symbols? Is he oriented to manipulative movement in his play world? He will not attend exclusively to one mode rather than the other but will often show a preference.

When his parents enrol him for school they will want to meet the people in charge as well as his class teacher to whom they are transferring the care of their child. Can one assess how his mother is feeling about this moment of enrolment? What do you think she may have said to the child to prepare him for this experience? What does this particular parent expect for her child and for herself from the school?

A school would do well to send a parent away confident that her child's individuality will be respected, that his weaknesses will find support and that his family will not be blamed for his failures. If the parent has some responsibilities like supplying equipment or coming to school to collect the child or to participate in parent discussions, these should be explained. An invitation to come and discuss the child's settling period after four to six weeks could be extended at this time.

Children who are to move confidently into literacy must feel happy and comfortable in their new classroom and school (Renwick, 1984). Fearful children will be inarticulate, unable to listen, awed by the teacher, and withdrawing into their old competencies rather than reaching out for new ones. One way to increase children's confidence is to have child and parent visit the class and take part in activities some weeks before the child is enrolled at the school.

How do teachers weigh up individual differences?

A group of teachers of five year olds at an inservice course were asked that question.

They were convinced they got an impression of a new entrant as soon as he or she walked into the classroom. They thought they could pick the very bright and the very slow children but were less sure about children in the large middle group. They looked for confidence and willingness to settle in. When challenged they admitted there were dangers in such judgements and that preconceptions which were false could be prejudicial to the child. They agreed that perhaps teachers of new entrants would have little evidence at this time for making such judgements. They would observe the activities that the child participated in during the first days at school, activities like drawing, writing, and looking at books, talking, mixing with other children, being confident or shy in social situations, being creative or reserved about free activities.

New entrants have to learn about school and school routines, including recess and lunchtime which sometimes make children feel even more insecure than the classroom. They also have to learn to be more independent as they move through the school day. Teachers expected children to be able to sit relatively still on the mat for class activities, to participate and to be able to tune in to some of what was being done in lessons. They liked children to try new tasks even if they did not do them well. Children had to learn to be members of the groups they worked with, putting away egocentric attitudes, whereas in preschool they could have been more individual in their play.

As these were New Zealand teachers they were thinking about placing a child in a group according to his learning needs. Did the teachers notice differences in the children's control of language? One teacher explained how she called for extended statements from her children, so that they progressed from single word demands over six months to extended sentences in their conversations with her. This teacher was not thinking about polite behaviour but rather about how to encourage children to try to use well-structured and longer sentences and to feel confident about doing this. On the whole these experienced teachers found it difficult to explain to others how they fostered oral language development. They tried to be very responsive to what children were talking about, not coming in too soon, and when they paused encouraging them to say some more about the topic. They tried to focus in on the child's choice of topic and to gain a sense of what the child understood.

The discussion focussed on the need for new entrant teachers to be constantly working to draw children out, using different questioning techniques for different children. It was thought to be a good idea to greet children individually and by name, if necessary in their own language.

Children are Active Constructors of Their Own Learning

There has been great interest in recent years in children as cognitive beings, children who selectively attend to aspects of their environments seeing, searching, remembering, monitoring, correcting, validating and problem-solving — activities which build cognitive competencies. A wave of experimental challenges to Piagetian formulations (Donaldson, 1978; Bryant, 1986) has not reduced our interest in cognitive development: on the contrary there has been a heightened interest in preschool learners changing over time. Because of what we now know about oral language acquisition we have to accept that children can be active constructors of their own language competencies. Too often we adopt teaching strategies which proceed as if this were not true.

These active constructive learners are not accounted for by the empty vessel metaphor in education which suggests that the role of teachers is to pour learning into children.

Nor do they fit the growth-from-within model of the child learning through activity, through discovery and self-directed learning. Cashdan (1976) summarized this model well.

> There are two ways in which we can help a child to learn. One of them is by attempting to teach him; the other is by facilitating his attempts to teach himself. We need to give the child freedom to explore and to learn on his own ... The child is self-stimulating and self-starting provided conditions are right for him.

It now appears as though it is not enough to only give the child freedom to explore and learn on his own although this remains very important. We must not crowd out his scope for doing such learning, but we must consider some further evidence (Deardon, 1984).

There are three bodies of recent knowledge about children's learning which we must consider. These are:

1 research on child behaviours which shows that the child is affected by what immediately follows what he had done, that is what is contingent on behaviour

2 research about the importance of contexts which tells that children select what they attend to, shape their own learning environments to some extent, and evoke responses from those environments in consistent ways

3 research on parent-child and teacher-child interactions.

When we interact with children who are learning we take the context into account, and we respond to what we think are the constructions being built up in their minds. As part of the teacher's careful observation he or she attends more contingently, responds more appropriately. The teacher provides temporary scaffolds and support systems which help the child to function effectively and can lead to the child taking over independent action before long (Clay and Cazden, in press).

These new sources of information are important because it is now possible to argue how some styles of teaching may facilitate the development of independent, constructive learners and some styles of teaching may either confuse the learners or impede progress towards independence.

Changes in Ways of Learning

Important changes take place in the character of learning at the end of the preschool years.

- The older child plans, more than the younger child does.
- The older child's learning is often mediated by words whereas that of the younger child is less often mediated.
- The older child can deal with several features at a time and in some structured relationships while the younger child tends to manage one aspect at a time and depends on the properties he can perceive rather than those he knows about.
- The younger child operates on items in their contexts while the older child depends less on contextual settings and is able to bring together experiences from several settings.

By five years the child begins more actively to organize and relate his information about the world — coding, categorizing, sorting, and applying learned coding systems to new events. He depends less on the association of things that have occurred together or on responses that have produced contingent results. He tries to solve an incongruity, direct his thinking to some past event, organize his experiences in related categories, label things, recall verbally things he has observed, drawing on things that he has heard about. He has been doing all these things in some sense since he was an infant but now he does more of these things deliberately.

This has been described in relation to some research on memory. At three to four years the child cannot yet set himself a goal to memorize or to recall. Memorizing, like recalling, is accomplished unintentionally at this age. The three to four year old children mainly memorize and recall connections formed by constantly repeating the spatial and temporal contiguity of impinging objects and phenomena.

A young child does well in memorizing a connected text — nursery rhymes, stories and fairy tales. In this case, along with a number of repetitions, a number of conditions are present that favour memorizing such as:

- emotional content of the text
- clear images
- evocation of empathy

- rhythm of speech and rhythm of body movement which facilitate the construction of a verbal-motor image
- memorable play on words.

Before five years we see the appearance and gradual development of intentional memorizing and recalling. Then we can note the single intentional repetition of material that must be kept in memory and by six or seven years the child, with improved efficiency, is able to:

- analyse the material to be remembered
- group it
- establish logical connections, and
- systematize representations of the surrounding environment.

Experimental evidence suggests that the memory is more than a copying device. It uses what it already knows to reconstruct the material that it is supposed to remember.

The five to seven year age group is a particularly interesting one for cognitive development. Piaget has described this as a period of transition from perceptual learning to the thinking operations of the child who can classify and consider inverse relationships. Writers like Margaret Donaldson have emphasized that the effects of environment and instructions are greater than Piaget allowed and that this may allow for a powerful teaching environment to accelerate development in limited areas. Russian child psychologists like Vygotsky and his colleagues have described a transition from self-instructions, spoken aloud, to inner self-instructions in the five to seven year period. Experimental studies of children's learning have suggested some interesting transitions taking place at this time which speed up the process of acquiring new skills or re-applying old ones. (For example, the child can produce a whole new set of behaviour merely by applying the concept of 'opposite' to old learning.) It is a period when the child learns strategies or ways of proceeding which help him to find his own way around new learning. He learns a great deal more about how to instruct himself.

It is the aim of most reading and writing programmes to bring children through the beginning reading programme to a stage of independence in reading and writing. At that point the teacher has to do less teaching. She provides the structure, acts as a resource and schedules time and activities, but the child pursues a large amount of the activity himself, pushing the boundaries of his own knowledge as he tries more and more tasks of increasing difficulty. Having control of his current behaviours the child tries new things. As he advances he needs less outside help to confirm whether he is right or wrong or has a good quality response. The child becomes his own evaluator. Notice that, firstly, this is a gradual process. Secondly, it does not begin with the teacher merely exposing the child to an environment rich in books and writing materials. Thirdly, if the child's repertoire of entry behaviours is limited the teacher may have to engage in more shared activity with that child—not less.

The fast learner

Many well-prepared children have already had experiences in their pre-schools and homes which have fostered early reading behaviours and motivated them to begin to solve the reading puzzle (Clark, 1976). Improved liaison with kindergartens and play centres will help teachers to identify the children who are showing an early interest in reading. Discussion with parents in the first weeks of school will provide additional information.

The fast learners will soon indicate their interest in books and they will move quickly into writing words and learning early book skills. When the teacher has had sufficient opportunity to observe the child's response to books, she has two or three options for the placement of the fast-learning child. She may provide a programme designed for his individual strengths using a vast supply of story books and lots of opportunity for the child to write stories. She has to be alert to aspects of his development that lag behind his notable strengths and not neglect those weaknesses. But the trick is to use the strengths as a context within which weaknesses can be attended to. She might consider promotion to a slightly older group of children whose reading needs are close to those of this child. Or she may use the opportunities of flexible grouping in the new entrant class or the open plan classroom to group this child appropriately in reading. If this fast learner enters a school where most children have had enriched pre-school opportunities then most of his classmates will be starting school with similar advantages and this child will look like an average learner within his group.

The slow learner

Some children who have responded well to their opportunities in the preschool years nonetheless make a slow transition into school learning. There are many different reasons for this. Some school entrants will be slower than others at responding to instruction. The translation of the child's entry achievements into those needed for the particular programme may be too difficult for the child to make, left to himself. Flexible grouping helps here as it did with the fast learner; the child is moved with groups of other children whose responses to new learning are more or less keeping pace with his own. The teacher's particular focus is how to work with that child's response system to bring him more quickly into full participation with the group's work.

For the slow learner it takes longer to get adjusted to the new place and new people. He does not find many familiar tasks around him. He joins in the group activities but when the teacher asks questions he does not know what to say. Perhaps he is not keen on talking anyway. If she is hard to understand he tunes out. He does not notice many of the things that are going on around him.

If all goes well the teacher establishes a good relationship with the slow learner and he begins to respond to some of the early reading tasks. From time to time he is joined by smaller and younger children who have reached his stage of learning but they may pass on before he is ready to move to the next hard task.

The teacher's task during that first year is to get the slow child responsive to instruction, happy to try and to discover for himself, steadily accumulating the early reading behaviours and not losing his buoyancy and bounce. Most slow learners gaining confidence in this way are ready for book reading by the beginning of their second year at school. If they are not, whatever their intelligence, the school might well take out an insurance against expenditure of effort in later years and provide the child with individual tutoring (as in a Reading Recovery programme, Clay, 1985).

Where is that Zone of Proximal Development?

We may accept the child's drawing on a particular day in its present stage of primitive thought, expressing his individuality, and limited to the features that have caught his attention for the moment. How do we know whether he has anything more to give? And if he has, how do we reach towards it?

- If we present all children with the same task we are not testing the zone of proximal development of either the more competent or the least competent.

- If we present children with very simple tasks we do not have an opportunity to observe the great variety of individual differences that do exist because most children will perform successfully.

Preschool and new entrant rooms must be rich in opportunities for the child to move beyond today's statement in the direction of personal growth. The foundation of personal success is to discover one's particular competencies. The essence of successful teaching is to know where the frontier of learning is for any one pupil on a particular task. This has been referred to as the zone of proximal development (Vygotsky, 1962; Clay and Cazden, in press) within which the child can not yet learn independently but can learn with appropriate adult support.

This 'cutting edge of learning' concept can be applied to anything the child learns and has many applications to literacy learning. It is a theory which is being widely discussed in education and psychology today and at this point I want only to provide an illustration of its application in one task which was a drawing task given to new entrants.

In the figure below, four children, A,B,C,D, were asked to copy some shapes. All completed the circles well. Child A failed Item 2 but the other three succeeded, more or less. By Item 3 only children B and D could copy the master figure which was a triangle inside a circle. By Item 4 only child D succeeded in producing a divided diamond.

These examples suggest that a teacher must do more than provide the child with stimulating experiences and opportunities for growth. If she works alongside a child letting him do all that he can but supporting the activity when he reaches some limit by sharing the task she is more likely to uncover the cutting edges of his learning. He, on the other hand, will not be bored by doing ten times over something he already knows how to do, but is likely to be challenged to risk attempting the novel, knowing that help will be offered for shared completion of the task if he cannot do it alone.

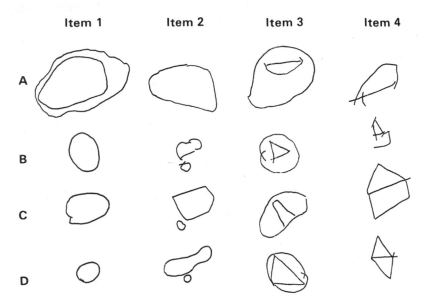

Teaching as Interaction

After careful longitudinal research on reading and early prevention pro-grammes in Sweden, Malmquist urged teachers, parents and pupils to have a little patience at the beginning of instruction.

> Growth in reading cannot be hurried without undesirable and even damaging effects on some children. Yet dalliance can mean the consolidation and habituation at best of low-order processing habits which resist reorganization at later stages of instruction; at worst the training in of erroneous concepts and handicapping procedures.
>
> It pays to seem to waste time, to start easily, by introducing a variety of reading experiences and using materials on a difficulty level far below the capacity level of many children. This make haste slowly policy permeates the teaching of reading with emphasis on interest and easily won achievement.
>
> ... when it is time to begin instruction in the various reading skills the teacher is urged to use materials systematized as to sequence so that the child is steadily challenged to raise his level of performance.

> (Malmquist, 1973)

That is an excellent guideline statement. What it omits is clear direction as to how to use the initial learning time so as to recognize 'when it is time to begin instruction.' Writings in expert-novice interaction and how learning takes place in such interactions fill this gap (Vygotsky, 1962; Bruner, 1983; McNaughton, 1987; Cazden, 1988).

When the Programme Goes to the Child

A good teacher supports an individual child in finding his personal solution to coping with the new school situation. After the child has come to terms, in his own way, with the new place and the new people, the teacher encourages him to share experiences with other members of his group in the classroom. The good teacher of new entrants needs this important quality of being able to use the unique background of each pupil so that in time he comes to share common experiences with his learning group. One should ask of any education system, 'What measures have you taken to address the individual differences of school entrants?' and 'How do these operate in the real world of classrooms?'

When the Child Has to Meet the Programme's Demands

A different approach is possible. An education system can decide upon a sequence of learning which the child must master. The teacher can programme his progress step by step, teaching and observing. With many children she will be successful because they are flexible and able to re-orient their previous learning to the teacher's demands. But for some children the first steps of the curriculum's pre-determined sequences may be an insurmountable barrier which turns them off into a side-road of failure. If a teacher thinks a child should write his name before he begins to try to read a simple book, the child with poor eye-hand co-ordination may be handicapped whereas he could have learnt to read his name and gone on from there. If naming letters is an early step in the programme, children who could have used their oral control of sentences to support their learning may become confused with the large and incomprehensible task of learning funny names for many symbols.

The inevitable inflexibility of publishers' programmes makes it almost impossible for teachers to overcome this problem. Their difficulties are increased by administrators who base evaluations on lock-step progressions and allocate good grades to high achievers rather than good learners.

Whose responsibility is it to provide the poorer performers with the opportunities to learn the prerequisites of the school programme if the children's preschool environments did not provide the opportunities to learn these? The absurd conclusion in many settings is that it is the child's responsibility to get to where the programme starts.

Schools have created policies which exclude unready children from opportunities to learn to be ready. Sometimes they are found to be unready to attend school; sometimes they are retained in a class where they did not learn in the hope that second time around something surprising will happen. Schools demand from the child performances which the school itself should be developing. It is not some ripening process which will eventually prepare the child but opportunities to learn through expert-novice interaction.

Entry to School — Many Transitions

How can the behaviours which the child does control be translated into behaviours that are:

- useful for learning beginning reading and writing, and
- common to a group of children who can be instructed together?

Common ground for group instruction will probably be achieved more rapidly by translating the child's available responses into appropriate reading responses than by insisting upon a preselected sequence of learning which the teacher has chosen. This argument favours an 'experience' emphasis to beginning reading rather than an emphasis on learning a sequence of skills. The question of what to observe in new entrant behaviour is therefore important.

When we review such a range of individual differences it is easy to see that the school must be run in such a way that it can adjust itself to the needs of such very different children. However, to take a stand fairly and squarely on the side of encouraging success and preventing failure in this new environment, the school must orient itself to such special needs at the time the child enters school so that programmes first meet the individuals at their personal learning points and bring them slowly but surely to common ground so they can learn in class and small group activities.

Although education systems will engineer this shift from individual to collective learning at different ages and in different ways, this is one of the functions of the new entrants class in New Zealand, the kindergarten in the United States, and the infants school in Britain.

4   Oral Language Support for Early Literacy

One transition we expect the five year old to make is from spoken to written communication. Adults who understand language development and who listen closely to children's spoken language will notice some of the changes that occur.

Between the ages of two and three years

The child has at first a 'private' language usually understood best by the parent or caregiver. But at this time a child usually has this caregiver with him most of the time. Caregivers are emotionally responsive to the child's big efforts and take the trouble to try to understand his private references. The efforts to understand the child's communications bring him through this stage to a three year old level of language that is quite easily understood by an outsider. The child without special attention from a caregiver, or with many changing caregivers, misses out on this shepherding—an orphanage child, a hospitalized child, a child handed over to his siblings to be minded. He needs somebody who will study his private frame of reference. When the child cannot make himself understood the communication process breaks down because when the listener does not reply the child's efforts are not rewarded. For continuing development towards mature language we have to engage in conversations with him. Our efforts should never make him reluctant to offer up his ungrammatical but expressive attempts to construct sentences. As we talk with a child he revises and refines his language, experimenting, making funny errors but gaining all the while in control over the expressiveness and the complexity of the language.

Every sentence the child constructs is an hypothesis about language. If he is understood his hypothesis is confirmed—the idea could be expressed that way. When a listener is puzzled, the hypothesis is rejected and a different sentence is formed. In this process the terms 'mother tongue' or 'home language' are well-chosen because the parents' role is so important. The child is deprived without the close, understanding, warm, readily available listener, talker, and speech model. If the child's language development seems to be lagging it is misplaced sympathy to do his talking for him. Instead, put your ear closer, concentrate more sharply, smile more rewardingly and spend more time in genuine conversation, difficult though it is. To foster children's language development, create opportunities for them to talk, and then talk with them (not at them).

Questions may be exasperating but they are sometimes used by the child in systematic search for information about language. 'What's that?' questions draw a list of nouns. 'Why?' questions usually require answers with 'because' and 'if' and therefore introduce the child to the more complex structures of the language and to qualifications in thought.

Adults Provide the Language Model

For the first five years the child's language growth is entirely dependent on what people say to him—on how much they speak to him, about what things, in what dialect or language, and in what manner, whether gentle and explaining or peremptory and imperative.

We have known for a long time that conversation in the company of an adult was the best tutorial situation in which to raise the child's language functioning to a high level. Descriptive studies of language development gave us sliding scales of proficiency from 'only' children at the highest levels of maturity, to those in small families, to those in large families, to twins and triplets, to institution children and to deaf children—an apparent correlation between the amount of mature conversation the child has with adults and the maturity of language used by the child. Adults have been shown to be effective models in this role. Other young children do not provide such satisfactory models.

What is it in the adult's behaviour that fosters increased maturity in the child's language? So far research has provided some interesting leads but no clear answers. When adults are not sure of whether they have understood a young child they may repeat some of what the child said, a kind of imitation in reverse. The adult echoes the child. But children's sentences often leave out important words or inflections and parents, in their imitations, replace the missing parts and give a completely grammatical version of what the child wanted to say. Adults do this to check their understanding of what the child said. This process has been called 'expansion.' In normal conversation the child's sentence, particularly his questions, are reformulated in some way in the answers, an immediate feedback of correct information. 'That a boy?' 'Yes, that's a boy.'

Most parents are convinced that children have something to say that is worthy of their attention. Parents who are not child-centred will spend less time expanding their child's speech. This would leave the child to struggle with the rules of English language from the haphazard flow of difficult speech around him. When adults speak with children they usually adapt or simplify their language but their conversation among themselves is more complex in construction. From this the child may find it more difficult to find the critical components of language which make his utterances meaningful to others. Children need frequent opportunities to test the rules of the language they are discovering. These opportunities arise on many occasions because children like to hold an adult's attention with a little conversation about the spontaneous activities they engage in.

A correcting or tutoring approach to language development is fraught with dangers. If a child's language gets attention only when it is in error, will he understand that all the other things he says are approved of? Or will he come to feel that his speech is defective? All children make errors in speech. It is a sign of remarkable progress when the child says 'bringed,' 'throwed' and 'writed.' He has acquired a rule for past tense verb endings that is regularly applied in English. That he has applied the rule to irregular verb endings is of little concern in a young child because the regularities are mastered before the irregularities in the language.

Parents may be disconcerted to find that a child's language which at three years is apparently error-free and highly grammatical, becomes full of errors a year later. But research has shown that this often indicates progress. At each successive stage the child masters a limited range of simple structures. When he tries to use more complicated structures to deal with his more complicated thinking, his attempts again become hypotheses which are again tested by whether he is understood or not. 'Can you say it this way?' is the test for both the linguist writing down an unwritten language and for the child who doesn't really know that he is testing out his own productions. At each successive stage the child makes errors, but only because he is trying to use more and more of the available possibilities of the English language.

Children learn the language of their caregivers and playmates. They learn the dialect or usage of a particular group. A dialect may differ from the language of education in sounds, accent or intonation, in vocabulary, in the grammatical forms and in the type and range of sentence forms used. My favourite example comes from an English county dialect where two children playing together ignored the call of a third child's mother, because one child explained, 'Her b'aint a-calling we: us don't belong-a she.' If you study this example you will find that every pronoun is used differently in this dialect from its use in standard English. The children are not making errors; they have learned to use the rules that their parents and community use in their home dialect.

In the preschool years almost all children acquire the sounds and structures of the local dialect. Some children acquire through parents and neighbourhood what has been called a 'nonstandard' dialect. It is an intimate possession, understood by loved ones. It reflects their membership of a particular speech group and identifies them with that group. It is personal and valuable and not just an incorrect version of a standard dialect.

A good teacher would not destroy this first language that children use so fluently. She would try to add to their speech a dialect for standard English to be used in some oral situations and to open the world of books to them. She would leave them their first dialect for family and friends. This poses two real problems for the teacher. She must first establish communication with the child despite the fact that she may speak a strange and unusual dialect. Beyond this she must help the child to work in the new dialect, knowing that for most of his waking life he is going to live and speak among people who use his home dialect. For every child, entry to school places heavy demands on his existing language skills as he learns to do new things that relate to educational success.

How easy it would be for the child in this situation not to speak more than is necessary in that classroom where the standard dialect is used; to choose instead the self-limiting strategy of opting out of conversation, instead of increasing his efforts to add to his range of language.

Strangely enough, the provision of stimulating preschool environments does not necessarily boost language learning. Interesting play and work activities may be of great value in themselves and still not produce much language behaviour. We need to ask 'Does the play activity bring the child into conversational exchange with a mature speaker of the language?' What opportunities are there for one-to-one conversational exchange with an adult who understands the child's frame of reference (for it seems that being understood has a great deal to do with shaping up the word and grammar skills of a child)? When we try to provide experiences that will compensate for limited language learning opportunities we must go beyond the usual bounds of spontaneous learning in a free play group situation. The child's wish to communicate about something which interests him at one particular moment should draw the attention of an adult who will talk with him, in simple, varied and grammatical language. We should arrange for language-producing activities — activities where adult and child must communicate in order to co-operate. Most of the caretaking activities of changing clothes, feeding and toileting provide excellent scope for conversations.

Compensatory programmes in language development must bear the same principles in mind. Scheduled periods of close interaction with a familiar adult are needed and activities should stimulate a flow of ideas from the child and personal responses from the helper or teacher.

Some Changes That Occur

The everyday speech which a child uses when he enters school will be unlike the language of his books. Firstly we do not speak as we write. Oral language sentences are often ungrammatical; the usage is conversational or casual. Secondly, the child's language shows immaturity and ignorance of some of the formal features of his language which he will learn later. As the child becomes familiar with the language of books that are read aloud his attempts at reading become more 'book-like.' Gradually he begins to produce sentences which replicate those of his books.

There are three major directions in which the language changes during the first six months of school for the five year old entrant.

- Firstly, there is an increasing ability in the child to understand speakers who speak differently from the 'people at home' and to make himself understood by teachers and peers who do not know his particular individual frames of reference. This is not merely a matter of the accuracy with which he uses the language, but also the flexibility with which he can adapt his language and rephrase his utterance so that his listeners understand.

- Secondly, there is continuing development and increasing precision in the use of the sound system, the vocabulary, the sentence patterns and the rules for combining words and making them agree, and a growing richness in the way he puts his meanings into words.

- Thirdly, the child begins to acquire a feeling for the kinds of language that he can expect to find in books. Some of his oral language is unlikely to be found in books, some will be found and some new features that occur in books will be very rarely or never heard in his speech.

Being in school and having to communicate provides opportunities for such development. Each of the three trends is open-ended so that at whatever level the child functions on entry to school there is always room for further differentiation, flexibility, and new applications of skill. There is always something more to be learned.

As a speaker and listener, in instruction or in play, the child learns language. He tries to construct a message that will be understood and he learns something about his effort if it is understood. He listens to a speaker and if he catches the drift he has matched the input to the correct meanings. Failing as a speaker or listener is disconcerting if not upsetting and the child is usually willing to struggle to be understood or to reach the meaning of another speaker. From such brief tussles in moments of not quite understanding the child learns more about language.

The teacher can provide opportunities for drawing the child's attention to those three lines of development, to flexibility in communication, control over linguistic features, and an awareness of book language. How can a teacher find out about the child's control of the English language?

Observing Language

Observe the child in conversation
If the child can carry on a conversation with the teacher then each is using a flexibility of language that is suitable for good communication to take place. The child who does not like to talk with the teacher or who has some difficulty in understanding what the teacher is saying may be a child at risk.

Be strong-minded about talking with a child with whom it is difficult to hold a conversation. The human reaction is not to spend much time talking to such children. The educator's reaction should be to create more opportunities for talking.

Language tests
A second approach to language observation is to use language observation tests to discover a group of children whose control of language warrants extra time and extra learning opportunities.

1 **Sentence structure**   When a child is asked to imitate a set of carefully selected sentences and his responses are recorded one can observe how he phrases a sentence compared with what he was asked to repeat. *The Record Of Oral Language* (Clay et al, 1983) is such a set of sentences, specially designed for use with five to six year old children. It is possible to notice what change has occurred between two administrations of this record. Children's oral language differs markedly from one district to another and from school to school. However, a good programme will be directed to the kinds of children who enter a particular school and the lower third of any class in oral language performance could benefit from extra help.

2 **Vocabulary**   *The Peabody Picture Vocabulary Test* (Dunn, 1965) is used by some junior class teachers in New Zealand as an assessment of a child's language ability. It can only be used as an estimate of intelligence when a child's first language is English, but it can be used more widely as an estimate of vocabulary control in English.

3 **Rules about inflections**   Inflections like the plural 's' and verb endings (Clay, 1982) probably provide the young reader with ways of checking on themselves as they read and the child who does not use such inflection rules in speech is not going to be able to anticipate them in print. The child with high skills in handling inflections soon begins to use these in his error correction behaviour in reading whereas the child with low skills in these may in fact lose meaning and comprehension because he is not noticing inflection errors in his reading. Such learning is not a matter of memorization in the preschool years. It has been shown to be a process of learning rules for forming plurals, for forming verb tenses, for relating verb forms to the person who is speaking, and for applying appropriate pronouns. At the time children enter school this is unfinished business and there is still much to learn.

4 **Articulation**   We have looked at conversation, at sentence structures or the complexity of grammar, at vocabulary, at rules for changing the endings of words, and now it is appropriate to look at the child's control of the articulation of sounds. Articulation moves only slowly towards perfect control of the sounds of English. Learning to pronounce the sounds of one's language is a gradual business from birth to seven or eight years (Templin, 1957). There is a shift in the distribution of scores shown by five and a half year olds to the higher scores shown by six year olds although there is considerable overlap between these two groups (Robinson, 1973). Without any particular attention to articulation we would expect most children to end up with perfect scores before they have been at school very long.

However, there are five and six year olds who would score very low on an articulation test. As with vocabulary it helps the child beginning to learn to read to have a good control of the articulation of most of the phonemes (sounds) and clusters of sounds in the language which he is trying to use in his reading. And the easy articulation of a word or sentence clarifies the sequence of its sounds (Elkonin, 1971) making it easier for the young writer to record his messages. We have found that good articulation is associated with early progress with writing vocabulary and poor articulation with limited progress (Robinson, 1973).

My first response to a child with poor articulation would be to observe carefully whether this appeared to be impeding his reaction to printed text because it might not. If it was I would want to minimize the attention to letter-sound relationships in reading for the time being. Then I would give individual help to that child at any point where confusion over articulation seemed to be interfering with reading progress.

The stories they dictate

A third way to observe children's language is to listen carefully to the stories they dictate for the teacher to write under their pictures. At first the teacher should be an accurate scribe and record exactly what the child says. As the child moves towards book reading the teacher should be able to notice an increasing control over simple English sentences for those children who began at a rather low level of sentence-forming skill. The stories that the child dictates may have language that is:

Grammatical

> The yacht is sailing in the water.

Flexible (in that he changes the story as he re-reads it)

> This is the yacht sailing in the water.

Ungrammatical

> Them together ride the bike.
> The mans are boxing on.

Like spontaneous speech

> It's a house
> and then all colours of the sun
> and then that there's all ledges around.

Like formal statements

> I saw boxing on TV.

Full of the excitement of telling

> They all chuckeded him out of bed.

Trimmed to a caption text

> Tall tree.

A record of language production

If a child is asked to tell a story about a picture, can that story be used to tell something about his language development? Robinson (1973) used a set of four rating scales. The child's story is rated on a seven-point scale for its content, imagination, structure and grammar. It is quite difficult to analyse the language a child uses as Mark's example shows.

Mark (5:6)

And then when he's got a carrot he left the door open so he's got out and escaped to school.
That one is . . . he's far away from his really home and he's going to a farm.
He meets chickens and hens and then sun goes down and he sleeps.
It's morning.
When he wakes up all of a sudden he's at school.

Robinson found that a score on one occasion for grammatical or structural features was a good indicator of the child's score on a subsequent occasion, close in time, but that this was not true for the scores in content and imagination which varied widely. Therefore judging these factors from one product would be unreliable.

Language Used in Early Reading Books

Perhaps the observation situation which is closest to the reading task is when the teacher listens closely to the sentences that the child generates as he attempts to read the easiest little books of the early reading stage. As the child progresses the sentences which he produces become more and more like the sentences which occur in text. He produces the same kinds of sentences, he uses the same kinds of vocabulary and although he doesn't get his text precisely correct he might be about 80 percent correct.

How close does the child get to the text of his first little books? It is possible to take a record of the language he uses in response to a text.

- Write down the text
- Record above the text exactly what the child says.
- Count the sentences or the captions in the text.
  Now consider these questions.

Good structure

Were his responses well-formed sentences?
How many were grammatical?
What percentage was that?

Child: *The dog is little.*
Text: A puppy can run.

Correct copy

Was his sentence an exact copy of the *structure* of the sentence?
What percentage of his sentences were close copies?
This shows that either the child can invent book-like sentences or that he can remember them because he heard someone else read them.

Child: *The dog can jump.*
Text: A puppy can run.

Self-correction

Did he revise his response without prompting?
Was the alteration
- from ungrammatical to grammatical
- from his own sentence to the text model
- of some other kind?

Child: *The dog/puppy (SC) can run.*
Text: A puppy

This is different from mere remembering. The child is probably reconstructing the sentence out of its component parts.

Talking Like a Book

Before they go to school many preschoolers will 'read' books by inventing the text. The four year old reads to grandfather and the older preschooler to the younger one by memorizing the text exactly or by inventing it or by a little of each. Some will confidently believe that this is reading while others show more insight.

One child 'read' to himself in bed while his mother bathed the younger children. He said, 'I wish I could really truly read this book for myself.' Probably he recognized that the sentences he was producing were not the same as those he had heard read to him.

Another child expressed it well when he said 'I can't read all the words but I know what they say.' He understood the message but he could not read the words.

Our use of the language we speak differs from our use of language in written form. With or without a special dialect the child's own speech habits must be modified so that he can produce sentences like those in his reading books. This is particularly so if the texts are rich in literary devices.

A new entrant came home from school and announced that he had a new book to read to his mother. He took it out of his schoolbag and 'read' it, making up a story for each page. Then he asked his mother to read it. He changed and went to play but later that evening read the book again, this time using the correct sentence beginning 'Here is a . . .' for each page. This illustrates a shift from sheer inventing from the pictures to a more controlled behaviour of 'talking like a book.' After all, who says 'Here is a...' four or five times in real speech?

At this stage of early reading behaviour this transition to 'talking like a book' is a very important step in learning. While absolute correctness of the text may not be the aim of reading at this stage, the child seems to be working on a particular challenge.

- Print can be turned into speech.
- There is a message recorded.
- The picture is a rough guide to that message.
- Some language units are more likely to occur than others.
- There is a particular message of particular words in a particular order.
- Memory or what the ear remembers helps.

With tactful guidance children make their own discoveries but they can be helped to develop and apply these concepts to the language of books in a sequence roughly like the following.

Stage 1   Print can be turned into speech

The child invents a sentence which could describe a picture. Or he writes a simple word like 'is' and proudly names it something else like 'runs.' Print and language are equated. The imperfect speech construction of some five year olds can be heard in these recorded examples of ungrammatical sentences invented for captions or simple texts.

I having a bath.	Here is blue flowers.
I sailing a boat.	Him is going.
Here rocket go up fast.	

It is also observable in the colloquial style of speaking that does not match the reading text.

Father's here	for	Father is here.
...says Mother	for	...said Mother.
I'm hungry	for	I am hungry.

Example of Stage 1

Print can be turned into speech

Reads: 'Tip' in wall story

Draws: Tip stuck in a rabbit hole

Writes: **I S**   and reads it as Tip
(After nine weeks at school)

Stage 2   A special type of talking

The child begins to use a special type of talking found only in books like 'Here is a . . .' or 'Mother said . . .' He uses only particular kinds of language structures which he thinks are used in books.

Stage 3   The picture is a guide to the message

The child invents a statement which is appropriate to the picture but which is not an exact rendering of the text.

Example of Stage 3

The picture is a guide to the message

Draws: Giraffe

Dictates: Here is Johnny the Giraffe eating the tree.

Reads: Johnny the Giraffe is eating the tree.
(After 25 weeks at school)

Stage 4   Some sentences are almost memorized

At this stage a child reads a simple book relying on what his ear remembers of the text, prompted by the pictures, and usually in sentences. His responses more or less convey the message of the text. Philippa 'read' this question from Snow White getting the words almost perfectly but Philippa could not read.

Tell me mirror, tell me mirror (Error for true)
Of all the ladies in the land
Who is the fairest, tell me who?

With a little more experience the child alters his language because he remembers hearing something from this book or one like it.

Child: *A puppy/See the little dog*
Text: Little dog.

Then he gets very close to 'reading' or saying exactly what is in his book but he does it as if he remembers hearing it (the oral language influence). The texts in the example below occur as one line per page in a caption book.

A child with a good ear for language may come to depend upon recalling what someone else has read. From his viewpoint this is using his strengths. From his teacher's perspective it is a strategy with considerable risks involved if it interferes with the development of visual strategies. For example, Paul watched his sister reading a repetitive story.

Little furry mouse
scampered round the kitchen.
But he ran back home
before the cat passed by.

Paul had a good memory for the sense of the story and was fairly accurate in re-telling it. He repeated the words rapidly, remembering the repeated lines, stopping for help, expecting it on each phrase that was new on each new page. He paid little attention to the print even when encouraged to look at the words.

Example of Stage 4	
Some sentences are almost memorized	
Text	**Response**
I like my dolls.	I like — dolls.
I like my doll's pram.	I like my doll's —.
I like the Wendy house.	(No response)
I like my kitten.	I like my kitten.
I like puppies, too.	I like puppies —
I like ballet girls.	and ballet girls.
I like pretty dresses best of all.	I like pretty dresses best of all.
Can you make a book about what you like?	Can you make a book about what you like?

Stage 5   Constructing the sentences

Now there comes an important transition which takes some experience to observe. The child combines his ability to produce sentences, his half memories for the text, the picture cues to meaning, and visual cues from letters. Putting all these together in a sequence of actions he seems to compose his response word by word.

Her mother pointed out that the name read 'Toys For Girls And Boys.'
Penny followed this along with her finger repeating the words and
locating them more or less correctly. She repeated this without help seven
hours later to her father getting the sequence and the pointing correct.

Suppose that the child is reading a basal text which uses a controlled vocabulary. (I do not like such texts but they are widely used.) The child has caught on to the fact that there are a limited number of words that can occur — Janet, John, come, look, the, up, jump, dog, here, little. The child may look at a text and pay no attention to the distinctiveness of the printed forms. He optimistically draws a response from that limited pool of words. He is 'talking like a basal reader text.' In both examples below the child uses some clue, possibly from the picture, and composes the kind of sentences that he knows occur in his reading book. Given no more instruction than the teacher's negative attention (*No!*) he reformulates his response three and four times until he gets it correct. He would prefer not to have to search for better responses, but he is learning a vital link in early reading, to search, check, reformulate, correct, and obtain some confirmation that he is right. He is not 'reading' but he is learning how to process language information. (This is not to advocate basal readers but merely to show how the child learning successfully on this type of material uses the opportunities it provides.)

Example of Stage 5			
Building a sentence word by word			
Text:	Little dog	*Text:*	Janet, look
Child:	See the little dog	*Child:*	Look up, Janet
Teacher:	(No!)	*Teacher:*	(No!)
Child:	Come and look	*Child:*	Look
Teacher:	(No!)	*Teacher:*	(No!)
Child:	Here	*Child:*	Look
Teacher:	(No!)	*Teacher:*	(No!)
Child:	Little dog	*Child:*	Look up, Janet

If a child reaches Stage 5 without paying attention to visual cues he may merely invent a book-like text in basal reader language.

Child:	*Come here.*	Text:	Here, Red.
	Red, come.		Here, Bill.
	Bill, Bill.		Come here.
	Come here.		Come here.

On any type of text, if a child composes sentences word by word and uses visual cues then he can correct an error in mid-sentence, instead of having to depend on an auditory memory for the sentence.

The linguistically able child who is using his knowledge of language as a source of cues will make 'errors' but these will be both grammatical and meaningful. One girl was thinking about meaning when she insisted that her book should say, 'The fish under the sea.' World knowledge rather than print was guiding her response.

The child's everyday speech is linked to the fluency with which he will read. Certainly he has to learn to work on new words and to predict what sounds are produced by which letter combinations. But such details can be discovered within larger chunks of meaningful language. The child who already uses a wide range of language features in a flexible manner will find it easier to work with the sentence structures in his reading book. He simply has to select the appropriate structures from his speech repertoire. The child with rich experience of books will have greater understanding of bookish forms of language and more motivation to master the art of reading.

Hearing Sounds in Words

Long before the child enters school he can use and hear the difference between words like 'cup' and 'cut' in natural speech. A child who hears and understands those words does not necessarily know that those words consist of several sounds and that the difference lies wholly in the last sound. This skill must be developed.

Do children differ in their response to learning about sounds in words? To find what segments children could hear in words some researchers asked preschool kindergarten and first-grade children to tap out the number of segments they could hear in spoken words by tapping a dowel on a table. One group heard words of one, two and three syllables (box, morning, anything) and the other group heard words of one, two or three sounds (oo, coo, cool). Results (Liberman, 1974) showed that:

- The older children did better than the younger.
- Syllables were easier to hear than sounds.
- The analysis of words into sounds developed after analysis into syllables.
- Sharp age trends were observed for both tasks with four to seven year old children.

One Auckland study showed a close relationship between high scores in articulation and high scores in writing vocabulary (Robinson, 1973). The child who can analyse his own words into their sounds seems better equipped to write those words for which he does not already know the spelling form.

The acoustic signals in the spoken word 'cup' are not the same as the sounds it contains when they are spoken separately. In the spoken word the consonants seem to be collapsed in on to the vowel and the three sounds are recoded into a single syllabic utterance. For the child to discover that the single syllable which he hears really contains three different sounds requires learning. This learning is easier if you are older. The children cannot map the printed word 'cup' which has three segments on to the spoken word 'cup' unless they become explicitly aware that the spoken word consists of three segments. In ordinary speech it does not.

The sounds of speech are a very complex code and a written alphabet is a simple substitution cipher. In speech

> we organize the phonemic segments (b–a–g) into syllables like *bag* and we overlap the segments that constitute the syllable and transmit them *at the same time*. This procedure is efficient in contrast to writing. In writing we must make the movements for one gesture and then the movements for

the next . . . in speech we move muscles for several successive phonetic segments all at once . . . Not only are the articulatory movements made with great speed and accuracy but they are organized and overlapped in very complex ways. The essence of the (speech) code is that information about two or more successive phonetic segments is carried simultaneously on the same piece of sound.

(Liberman, A. M., 1974.)

We do not articulate separate sounds one after the other the way we write them. If we make children do this we teach an analysis that is completely novel for them.

What has phonics been throughout the years? Phonics is not an immutable set of rules for relating letters to sounds. They are tricks that work some of the time, sometimes called heuristic devices, rules for locating words already known to the ear.

For many years the teaching of sound and phonic systems of decoding have been de-emphasized in New Zealand reading programmes. Single consonant sounds and other letter groups are introduced slowly in the first year of instruction but these do not receive the focal attention which they are given in many published reading schemes. What have we done? We have minimized the explicit teaching of phonics. We have taught the child a variety of procedures for analysing words into sounds, during daily lessons in small groups eager to read the story for the day. We have provided massive opportunities for the child to make his own analysis by having him read large quantities of easy material giving him prompts that guide his word-solving. And we have encouraged children to write down their ideas, even new entrants. Under these conditions most children have slowly but surely categorized the complex relationship of letters with the sound forms of words.

Unfortunately these categories are hidden 'within the child.' If our classroom practices are not leading to a slow-growing network of rules which relate sound patterns to printed forms, in some particular children the lack may not be noticed by the teacher who is not observing closely.

Inventing Spelling

To explore this vexed question further we can refer to the work of two other authorities who worked independently and arrived at similar conclusions. Charles Read (1971) made a study of preschool children who developed their own way of spelling English. From what they wrote he concluded that these children had made some kind of an analysis of the sounds of English before they had even encountered reading and a year or more before they had started school. In the word D I K T R (doctor) for example, the child recognized that the word has five segments that need to be represented. The children's spellings deviated from the standard English forms but often there were regularities in these differences.

AS CHRAY	(ash tray)	CHRIE	(try)
CHRIBLS	(troubles)	CHRUCK	(truck)

The child who produces these words and wants to spell the word truck with a 'ch' will not, according to Read, be enlightened by the teacher who tells him that 'ch' spells 'chu' in chicken. He already knows that or would guess it if he tried to write it. The close relationship between the first segments of 'truck' and 'chicken' as we articulate these sounds is what he has already discovered and it is what he is trying to represent. The child who spells 'brother' without an 'e,' 'liked' with a 't,' or 'butter' with a 'd' may be listening very sensitively to how people speak and may be recording it exactly. A phonetician might make very similar judgements.

These spontaneous preschool spellers were beginning to listen to these phonetic variations. They invented non-conventional ways of translating them into English spelling. However, Read's children were exceptional as most children do not spontaneously analyse their words into sounds and some have problems even with analysing their sentences into words.

Russian psychologists have made a close study of the child's awareness of the sounds in words (Elkonin, 1973). A good reader, according to Elkonin, is 'one who knows how to create the correct sound form not only of a known word but also of any unknown word.' Elkonin believes that 'no matter how the written word is perceived visually, whether it be perceived as a whole, in syllables, or letter by letter, the understanding is based on the sound formation of the word.' He recommended that Russian children be taught to hear the sound sequences of word forms before they are introduced to print.

New Zealand teachers would probably not wish to place a heavy emphasis on sounds as the key to reading, especially as their new entrants are only five years old. Russian children would be nearly seven years on entry to school. What is valuable in Elkonin's recommendation for beginning reading in USSR is the scheme he provides to train children to hear the sounds in a word.

In New Zealand schools reading activities would use the visual form of the word to teach the child about sounds. But according to Elkonin, this focusses the child's attention on the letters or characters. Like Liberman he believes that an alphabet is a very simplified code which does not represent the sounds of language very well. Elkonin insists that the child should learn to hear the sounds in words before he is exposed to letters. In his scheme the child is given pictures of objects. Below each picture is a rectangle divided into squares according to the number of *sounds* in the name of the object. The child is given some counters.

- The child utters the word aloud separating each successive sound with a drawled or stressed sound while placing a counter for each sound in the corresponding square of the diagram below the picture. The sounds of the word are separated and they are marked by counters.

- This activity is changed gradually during instruction. It becomes an oral analysis without the backup of counters and squares.

- Later still the child is required to carry out the analysis silently.

This procedure was used in New Zealand with six year old children who were not making good progress with learning to read and write (Clay, 1985). We found that many could not hear the sound sequences in words they were trying to write. With a training scheme like Elkonin's the children learned to analyse what sounds were in words and what the order or sequence of sounds were, so that they could write them into their stories. The sequence of sounds is what Elkonin means by the sound form of the words. From a limited number of words, say nine, consisting of a small number of sounds, many of our six year olds were able to make useful analyses of the sound sequence in words they wanted to write (with teacher help) and generalize this approach to the analysis of new words.

Liberman demonstrated that the segmenting of words into sounds is a skill that improves from younger to older children. Elkonin describes how Russian children were taught to do this. Read showed that when children take the initiative they can invent spellings in systematic ways using knowledge that they have, such as alphabet names. What does all this achieve? It forces children to carry out a splendid sound analysis of the words they want to write—a first to last segmenting of the sounds in the word. They pay attention to the sounds of words and search for a visual way of representing these.

Some failing readers are unable to analyse spoken words into sounds and many five to six year olds need special help to learn this.

Does your programme encourage children to learn this skill? If it does they will have little trouble linking sounds they hear to the letters they are learning to scan and to write.

Teachers may feel that the critical thing for the child to learn is his sounds, and they may provide an elaborate scheme for teaching that overrated aspect of reading known as phonics. They are teaching the child to go from letters to sounds. Current knowledge suggests that we may have to revise our thinking about the value of phonics. A strategy of analysing spoken words into sounds and then going from sounds to letters may be a precursor of ability to utilize the heuristic tricks of phonics. And many children may not need phonic instruction once they acquire and use a sound sequence analysis strategy.

What Read, Liberman and Elkonin are leading us towards is the insight that, given the limitations of alphabets, it may be easier if you know the sound segment to find some letter or letter group which could be the written realization of that sound than to start with the letters.

We do not find it easy to examine our own speaking. Cazden (1974) wrote that 'the ability to make language forms opaque and attend to them of and for themselves is a special kind of language performance.' How can we get young children to want to hear the sound segments in words and to search for these on their own initiative?

Carol Chomsky (1976) encouraged a discovery approach. She has suggested that children can write first and read later in school settings. From her trials in classrooms she suggested that invented spelling could easily be introduced into classrooms where child-motivated activities are valued. She has experimented with encouraging nursery school, kindergarten and Grade 1 children to try to write before they read.

> Children who write in this way in their own invented spellings receive valuable practice in translating from sound to print. This practice and experience with letters and sounds form an excellent basis for reading later on. In addition the activity develops self-reliance in dealing with print, and contributes to a do-it-yourself attitude which carries over into learning to read.

She described a first grade classroom (Chomsky,1975) where the approach which she favoured had been on trial. I have selected some extracts which capture what I consider to be the salient points.

- The teacher has been getting this message across to the children in her room in regard to spelling. 'Your judgement is good. Trust it. Figure out how the word sounds to you and write it down that way.'

- She provides a bucketful of wooden and plastic letters, a diary for each child, and many reasons to write.

- She spends a great deal of time reading to her class and discussing the sounds of words in the stories.

- They work on rhyme, beginning sounds and end sounds.

- She gets across the idea of sequence, 'What comes first? Next?' and so on through the word.

- The children's names are good to use for this kind of game, too. Names are clapped, changed and played with. In creative movement the children move to their names.

- They need a reason for writing. Writing is real and interesting when children have their own purpose for doing it. An outgrowth of this personal involvement is an independence on the child's part so that he writes regardless of the teacher.

- Using plastic letters frees up some children who have handwriting problems. They do not have to worry about the mechanics of letter formation and they can put their energies into the message.

- When children do this writing they quite naturally begin to read what they have written. They read what they themselves have written more easily than unfamiliar material.

- The children are expected to write from the start. Many can but some are reluctant to try it out at first. The teacher says she knows fairly quickly which ones are not ready and allows them to dictate their stories. Some will prefer this for a month or more. Eventually they gain the confidence to go ahead and try spelling some words on their own, according to the way they sound. 'You see their mouths moving as they think their way through the word, and you know they're on to it,' she said.

- The children's early attempts at their own spellings are often much more primitive than later productions. Here is one early story that requires the reader's attention, and it will be better understood if the reader slowly articulates what the child has written.

I MED A SBOYDR WEB ON A BRENH AND AFTR I WHT THE FILM AND I LOT AT KRAFIH.

(I made a spider web on a branch and after I watched the film and I looked at crayfish.)

The 'ch' sound is spelled with an 'h' in BRENH and WHT. Why? It is because 'ch' is a sound in the letter H (*aitch*). The child knew the letter name, was looking for a way to spell 'ch' and quite logically came upon the 'aitch.' This use of H for 'ch' has been observed often in early invented spellings.

> This hypothesis construction is an active process taking the child far beyond the 'rules' that can be offered him by the best of patterned, programmed or linguistic approaches. The more the child is prepared to do for himself, the better off he is.... After such a programme they bring to reading assumptions that they made about writing, an assurance that it is something that you work out for yourself and a confidence to go ahead.

(Chomsky, 1976)

This aspect of preparation for reading has not been wholly neglected in the past. Textbooks have treated it under the 'readiness skill' of auditory discrimination. In a global approach to the whole area teachers have helped children:

- to perceive likeness and differences in non-vocal sounds
- to perceive sound in recurring rhyming words
- to hear the words that rhyme
- to contrast them with the words that do not rhyme
- to recognize that spoken words can begin with the same consonant sound.

Such instruction has provided children with the opportunity to teach themselves a sound sequence analysis strategy. In the past it has left us guessing about some children whose reading skills do not increase despite the global auditory discrimination exercises. The Elkonin techniques make more explicit what is being learned but they should be used individually.

Sound-to-letter analysis does not reign supreme in the hierarchy of skills to be acquired for very long. The child who has learned only a small reading or writing vocabulary begins to generalize about letter-sound relationships quite early. A linking occurs of visual analysis of those simple clusters of letters with the sounds they consistently represent. Then this knowledge is transferred to new material.

> A child in the first stages of reading skill typically reads in short units but has already generalized certain regularities of spelling-to-sound correspondence, so that three-letter pseudo words (like 'zif') which fit the rules are more easily read as units. As skill develops, span increases and a similar difference can be observed for longer items. The longer items involve more complex conditional rules and longer clusters so that generalizations must increase in complexity.

(Gibson, 1965)

When the child works out a new word from two words he already knows, like 'string' from 'stop' and 'ring', he is operating on the spelling-to-sound correspondences that Gibson has written about and he has already gone beyond the simple heuristics of phonic systems. Using analogy (Goswami, 1986) he may still be leaning on his skills in the sound segmentation of spoken words, but they have a have wider application than the phonics on which we have spent so much instructional effort.

Language Handicaps

The child who has a restricted control of English vocabulary or sentence structures will have a difficult learning task at this stage because he will have to learn many new things about language. Ten repetitions of 'He is going to kick the football' may not produce a correctly formed sentence because he does not yet control that verb pattern in his normal speech.

When children enter school with some pronounced lag in language acquisition a dual attack on this problem is required. Firstly the child's language patterns are most rapidly improved by quantities of one-to-one conversation with an adult, increasing massively the child's opportunities to talk. Some means must be found of talking frequently with the child who has poor language patterns. Speech therapy is probably not enough. The teacher can help by keeping the child's need constantly in mind and making opportunities for conversation about the things the child is involved with. In addition she will need assistants, such as parent helpers, to engage in talking sessions with small groups of three or four children. Teachers may also plan activities specifically to increase the amount of conversational interchange between adult and child. Guidance along similar lines can be given to parents.

The teacher's words provide a good language model for the child to learn from but this is not enough. The child needs the opportunity to formulate his own statement, to construct his own hypothesis that this is the way you can say it in English, to actually say it, and discover from the answer he gets whether he has been understood. If he is understood, his hypothesis has been supported.

A second modification of programme for the child who has language handicaps is to continue to read to the child from interesting story books which tune his ear to literary language but at the same time simplify the material that he is expected to read. Texts which are good for average or better children will contain language which is too complex for the child with language handicaps. Much simpler texts are required and the sentence structures and vocabulary should be predictable, i.e. very familiar to that child. The sentences should be of the same kind in length and in construction as the ones the child uses in his speech. This means that the sentences would not be so drastically reduced as to be unfamiliar to him such as 'Look, John, look!' or 'See John run,' sentences often found in controlled vocabulary texts.

It becomes obvious why the child's own dictated sentences or stories have frequently been recommended as remedial reading material. What the child can produce he can also anticipate. This provides a fluency that gives him time to attend to cues and to relate several cues to one another. This is time that the retarded reader needs.

How will the child ever learn to read texts which contain more complex structures unless he is required to attempt them?

Perhaps he could improve his oral language by learning to read more complex constructions? Applied to the non-reader, or the beginning reader who is struggling, both these arguments are fallacious. His task is to learn how to learn, and in particular how to respond to literacy tasks. This can be achieved with the simplest range of reading material. Only when the process is running smoothly should his reading be considered as a means of language learning. Competent readers do learn new linguistic forms from reading English texts. We can handle complex constructions which we would never speak. The following excerpt from a daily newspaper provides an example:

Smith, who appeared in Court from the cells and had been arrested on the count, was charged that, between 3 April 1969 and 30 October this year at Wellington, having received from . . . the sum of . . . in terms of requiring him . . . did fraudulently omit to account for the same and thereby committed theft.

We learn to do such tricks after we have learned how to read. While learning to read children match the text to what their ear remembers of the oral language. Much later they learn to understand a range of forms specific to written language. Sometimes you can hear the written language patterns in an older child's mispronunciation of unusual constructions learned from extensive reading.

For the non-reader his own language patterns should be a guide to the type of text he should try to read until the reading process is well-established. Meantime his oral control over language can receive attention so that it develops not from his reading but in booksharing and in conversation.

The child's challenge is to discover how what he knows about language can be brought to the task of getting messages from written texts.

In Summary

So much occurs in oral language acquisition that supports reading and writing progress that further discussion of this connection will occur in other chapters. In the final chapter oral language is referred to as one of the early self-improving systems developed by the child. In an analysis of how learning to understand and use language interacts with all thinking and learning, Wood (1988) concludes that 'learning language involves the child in the solution of problems which are specific to language' and that further learning of oral language should have an important place in the school curriculum.

Much has been omitted from this account including the important aspects of how language is constrained by the contexts and interactions in which it occurs, how much it depends on cultural knowledge, and how classroom discourse influences the learning of the school child (Cazden, 1988).

The focus of this chapter has again been on the diversity of preschool experiences with language, and the teacher has been encouraged to listen more carefully and make some systematic observations of how her children are using language. This will help her to tune in to their progress as change occurs. In particular teachers were encouraged to listen to the transitions as the child tries to adapt the language he speaks to the kinds of languages likely to be found in his reading texts.

In his contacts with literacy activities the child may begin to play with sounds below the word level, in word play and rhymes, or in sound to letter correspondence as he tries to discover ways to write down his messages. There have not been many occasions when the preschool child has needed to do this subword analysis and I have emphasized how readily he makes progress with this level of language analysis when he becomes a writer with messages he must record.

5 Introducing Children to Print at School

Before School

In many cultures (though by no means the majority) children are initially introduced to print by the literacy around them in their everyday environments. When this is not the case the transition into literacy may need a different description from the one that follows.

We need to return to what was discussed in 'Literacy Before Schooling' so that we may trace the transition into school. Some children are fascinated by print in their environment, like special words on billboard advertisements, on television or on a packet of breakfast cereal (Goodman and Altwerger, 1980; Harste, Burke and Woodward, 1984; Ferreiro and Teberosky, 1982; Durkin, 1966; Clark, 1976). Words in a favourite story book which are well-spaced and repeated are sometimes recognized. A few children spend considerable effort in writing their names or letters to grandmother (Clay, 1987). Some push their parents into helping them to read or write. However, such high levels of attention to the detail of print are unusual rather than common.

Booksharing

Many preschool children have listened to stories and have looked at the pictures but the hieroglyphics across the pages have had no particular significance. These children are only vaguely aware that the words they are hearing occur in the books. Despite the advocacy of booksharing (White, 1984; Holdaway, 1979; Doake, 1981; Spencer, 1987; Trelease, 1982) there are few studies of how frequently it occurs, with what groups of populations, and how it is done (Heath, 1982; Phillips and McNaughton, in press). At the other extreme there are children who have never had the opportunity to see and hear someone reading. They have no children's books in their homes. Sometimes no children's books are available in their language. It is easy to believe that a child from such a background might take a few weeks to come to understand that sometimes the words spoken by children and teachers have a great deal to do with the marks in books.

Print Awareness

Some children become aware that print carries messages before they have had formal instruction. Let me take an example from a well-prepared child who was to enter school in two weeks. Penny was 4:11 and had not learned to read. She could write her name and several single letters. Yet she was quite certain that her writing conveyed messages. The postman brought her an invitation to Mary's party. She whipped it out of her mother's hand, retreated to her bedroom and then brought it back displaying the writing in the centre of the card. Her mother read it to her. For the time being she was satisfied. After her bath that night she asked for paper, saying 'I want to write to Mary.' No suggestion had been made that a reply was necessary. 'Too scrappy!' she complained about the first piece of paper she was offered. Obviously this was an important letter. 'How do you write *come*?' she asked after she was given a more elegant piece of paper. 'What do you want to say?' she was asked. 'I would like (*pause*) to come to your party.' 'Don't you want to know *I* and *would*?' her mother inquired. 'But I will have to write *come*,' she shrilled in excited irritation. 'Come' was the significant message so it was the first thing she wanted to write. She went to the newspaper cupboard and tore off an edge strip for her mother to write the copy on. When asked 'What do you want to say?' she repeated the message. It was written and she 'read' it back, the first time she had been asked to 'read' words in sequence in a sentence. She did this word for word. It was her message and she had already stated it twice. She began to write 'I' at the top right corner of the page. 'That's the wrong side,' her mother corrected. She then copied the words carefully and correctly with good spacing because she could copy letters quite well. No further help was given until she realized she had skipped the second 'to' in the message and asked for more help. She completed the task and then asked for 'from Penny.' She was only given 'from' and insisted on getting 'Penny' although she could write her own name. Was this because she could not delineate the sequential relationship of one word to the other? She asked for an envelope and copied Miss Mary B... on it putting the surname on the next line. Her mother was quite satisfied but Penny seemed to be searching for a word. 'Put (*pause*) the address.' She got a copy of this and added it to the envelope, showing concern when she thought the line would clash with the previous one.

This seemed to be a milestone. It was the first request for a coherent message to be conveyed in words to someone else and was in response to receiving a written invitation. Two promptings were given, one as to the order of words in the message and one as to the placing of the first word on the page. The episode demonstrated a skill for letter by letter copying, maintaining direction once it was established, spacing words and keeping somewhat within lines. Although she could re-tell the message exactly there was no clear awareness of 'reading each word,' no evidence that she knew that each grouping of letters had an equivalent word. There were few errors and no frustration, and the request for an address surprised her mother. The emotional tone was not one of achievement, and she did not think to display this to other members of the family. It was an important social response, like a reply to a question.

The example is important because it illustrates some of the concepts which children master in the early reading period. She knew:

- that messages could be written
- that you 'construct' the message in speech
- that the copy she asked for contained the request
- that letter follows letter in a linear sequence in copying and that spaces were important
- that the pattern of directional movement runs across two lines of print
- that one can check and correct when an error has occurred
- that letters to people have addresses.

Perhaps most surprising she went to the heart of the message first, summing up the essential information in her demand for 'come.' The episode also showed that she did not know:

- that words in a sentence have an order (wanting 'come' first)
- that the starting position on a page has to be on the left
- that the visual forms of her writing had some systematic correlation with her oral message (for although she could repeat it back she could not read it).

Children come to such concepts in different ways and at different times but an excellent preparation is having opportunities to share book experiences with adults in the preschool years and to try one's hand at writing things.

Emergent Reading and Writing in the First Year at School

The following discussion assumes that the reader already has a knowledge of how far 'Literacy before Schooling' develops for some children, and is keenly aware that there are many reasons why other children may not have become interested in literacy symbols and activities in their preschool years. Lack of opportunities to learn about these literacy concepts can happen in any child's life: the main preschool emphases may have been on boisterous physical exploration of the real world or rich opportunities to use and listen to oral language in supportive social interactions.

Lack of opportunities to learn about print does not imply deficits in the child or in his preschool culture. However there is an important implication for schools. If school entry in a particular society carries with it an expectation that children will learn about literacy, then school programmes must, at one and the same time, allow some children to catch up with preschool literacy experiences while also working with others who are building on to a rich literacy learning background. The same kinds of literacy activities can be used with all children at this time but teachers must work with the reality that the challenges of these similar tasks will be quite different for children with different preschool experiences.

Anticipation

The preschooler can already anticipate oral language.

> Betty aged five years was listening to her brother reading. He stumbled over 'he never makes mis . . .' Betty from the other side of the room muttered 'mistakes.'

What a beginning reader has to do is to discover that he can also anticipate what may occur among the visual patterns in written language. With the familiar story book the child begins with memories of the ideas that are in the book and each page triggers more memories, often of the precise language used. Some memories are already alerted before the page is turned and so the response is made more quickly. This anticipation of what may follow creates a pleasing tension — a puzzle to be solved. It is related to a skill that will be needed in reading as the child anticipates the structure of the sentence and the next step in the story.

Visual searching

A lookout in a sailing ship scans the horizon for the sight of another ship or of land. Parents searching the beach for a lost shoe scan the ground for sight of a colour or shape cue to the shoe's location. The eyes of an adult, viewing a large painting at an art exhibition, rove over the canvas fixing on one feature after another, flicking back to trace or check a relationship or a similarity and after moments of survey, producing in the mind of the observer an impression, an understanding or a reaction for or against the painting. If the adult who once knew a little Russian or French is presented with a magazine in either language he will scan a page of print in much the same way picking up a cue here and a half-understanding there and trying to link these fragments into a meaningful message. Rarely can this 'reader' get sufficient information from the text to confirm whether he is right or wrong.

The child who has looked at books from two years of age will have learned to scan pictures for meaningful messages, slowly learning how to look at books and building up an efficiency with two-dimensional representations over many hundreds of contacts (Ninio and Bruner, 1978). Parents will recall that a familiar story book is read quickly because the child expects to see the familiar pictures, comments on them quickly, and turns the page. In contrast an unfamiliar book takes longer to scan. Looking takes longer, labelling is a slower business, and understanding takes longer. This contrast illustrates the marked difference there is between seeing the unexpected and seeing the familiar.

The unfamiliar picture could be scanned by the child as the adult scans a large painting. Some features draw the attention while others remain in the background unnoticed. If something in this background is attended to, the child may focus on it for a moment or two. At the next reading that newly noticed feature may be included early in the scanning pattern.

Reading demands the analysis of a complex text by the eye and by the brain to note details which one can interpret. Some children arrive at school with far less experience in analysing two-dimensional space than other children who have had opportunities to practise this skill for some time.

A picture must be scanned to gather information and it may be scanned in any direction by complex tracking and backtracking. A printed message must be scanned in a different manner; its meaning is dependent upon scanning in a particular way dictated by the directionality conventions of written language.

Until he reached school the child was free to scan objects, people, scenes, pictures, and even books, in any direction that he chose. Immediately he becomes a candidate for reading and writing English he has to learn that for printed text there is an inflexible set of directions for proceeding across print. There are one-way routes to be learned. He must learn to go from a top-left position across to the right and then to return to the next top-left position after a downward movement and again go across to the right. For the five year old school entrant of average ability that is a challenging set of learning. We have often under-estimated the magnitude of that particular task and its particular relevance for subsequent success in learning to read and write. This directional behaviour, moving in a controlled way across a line of print, depends upon learning something about movement. For some children who have not learned a good control over linking hand and eye movements this particular aspect of learning to read may be difficult. Any attempt to relate what is said with what is seen can fall at the hurdle of not moving in appropriate ways across print.

Pairing visual and auditory messages

As a preschooler the child responded to and used oral language, learning by ear. The new activity of reading demands that he use his eyes to scan and analyse the printed text. The language and the visual aspects of a reading task now have to be related. There has to be an association of the analysed speech with the analysed shapes. This is the third area in which the child may have difficulty—pairing the visual and auditory stimuli. He may find it difficult to match the flow of auditory signals coming to his ear with the order of visual patterns on the page of his text. Specifically, he may have trouble relating the timing of the language behaviour to the spacing of visual experience.

Print carries the message

Does the child know that print, and not the picture, carries the message? According to Diack's simile (1960:130) the child at first probably has no clearer image of the print marks than an adult who looks at the pattern of branches of a tree momentarily silhouetted against the sky. We saw earlier (page 91 ff.) that Penny had discovered more detail than this by the time she entered school. The general concept that print rather than the picture carries the message was understood by two-thirds of five year old school entrants in two research studies (Clay, 1966, 1970). Within six months 90 percent of these children understood this. However, a further 2 percent still confused print and pictures as the source of the story at six or six and a half years and this made every encounter with print hazardous as a learning experience for that group. Samples of Theresa's writing given later illustrate how slow to develop was her awareness that 'print carries a message.'

Here is an example of a child who was confused about this concept. After 10 months at school he brought his book to the author and recited the text from memory. (The observant teacher can notice tell-tale behaviours like these.) He repeated the act while I covered the text using only the pictures as cues. Then he said confidentially, 'I can read that book with it closed!' and he was word-perfect. His confusion had gone undetected and no one had taught him that a picture is only a rough guide to the message of a book, that print carries a precise message, and that to read means to discover the precise messages in print on the run, by problem-solving and not by memory. He thought reading was reciting a memorized text, cued by the picture, and he was quietly proud of his achievement. That is an early byway into which some children stray. While picture cues can be a source of extra information in reading, in this case they were a source of misconception.

Fostering Attention to Print

Observe a group of children who have recently entered school (aged 5:0 to 5:6 perhaps). To what do they attend in the printed text? The five year old finds himself with opportunities to draw and paint and look at books. He is encouraged to talk about these activities. The teacher puts some marks on his drawings and these carry some message. The room is full of signs and messages among which he is sometimes able to locate a familiar one, his name.

'That says Douglas Homes!' said one boy, triumphantly, after writing a capital H.

He is encouraged to make marks with chalk or pencil and soon finds that if he adds his name or some other marks to his drawing his teacher seems to be pleased with him. She may ask him to say what he has written. In doing this the teacher is using writing activities to help the child attend to print.

It is important to foster the child's desire to explore writing at the same time as he is learning to read. Not many discussions of early literacy see these two activities as complementary. Concepts about the nature of language in print apply to both activities: what is learned in writing becomes a resource in reading and vice versa. Before the child fully understands how print carries language messages it may seem to him just like funny marks, or a string of letters, or a word with special meaning like his name. Features of the written code become more obvious to the child when he attempts to put his ideas into writing for someone else to receive, than when he tries to receive (read) someone else's ideas. So, for a time, what the child writes gives a rough idea of what he is noticing about printed language and this is because he is learning concepts that apply in both reading and writing.

The activities of early writing also contribute to the network of information that forms around a particular word so that writing information as well as reading and oral language information become attached to 'the knowing of it.'

A classroom for new entrants must be an environment in which the child becomes aware of the need for reading and writing in everyday life. At an early stage the child may know that print conveys messages without being sure what the message is. Douglas produced a drawing of letter-like forms (below) and said to the author, 'Give it to your children and learn them it because it says a lot of fings!' He hoped he had written an important message with the H's and O's on his page. He thought that print conveyed messages but what they were he knew not. Douglas had acquired a basic concept but this was a mere beginning.

Theresa entered school with little awareness of print and she learned about messages during her first year at school. When she tried to make a statement by scribbling, creating her own mock writing, she showed that she knew that messages can be written down. Theresa at 5:0 could not copy her name but she produced her own form of writing.

5:0 (Copy)

What the child writes is a rough indicator of how he views printed language. To him it may be funny marks, a string of letters, or words with special meaning like his name. By the time Theresa was 5:6 she wrote her name as two letters without regard to order.

5:6 (No copy)

When she had a model to copy she produced a string of odd letters, more or less in correct sequence.

5:6 (Copy)

By the time she was 6:0 she produced her signature without a copy. It is a word with a known sequence of well-formed letters.

6:0 (No copy)

Theresa's last example illustrates that she now successfully uses several concepts about print—letters, letter order, particular letters needed for a particular word, the use of a capital letter for a name, and the general concept that print carries the message.

After one year at school Theresa has reached the same control over her name that Penny (pages 91–93) had two weeks before she entered school. These two girls illustrate the individual differences in preparation for reading and writing that the teacher of new entrants needs to recognize. Although the examples are of writing, the concepts which they illustrate also apply to reading. (Early writing is discussed in more detail in Clay, 1975 and 1987.)

Reluctance to write

On some days the child chooses not to draw, is not inspired to print, or to point, or to talk about his work. Individual children may refuse to partici-pate in these activities for several months because of some inner sense of irrelevance or personal inadequacy. 'I don't want to do any writing today,' is a complaint from children reluctant to attend to print.

Position is important

New entrants draw pictures and talk about what they are doing. They can be asked to point to their work as they speak about it. Sometimes this is done on the blackboard but more often in today's classroom this is paper, pencil and crayon work. The 'paper on the desk' is similar to the 'book on the desk' for an inflexible young child who has problems with direction. At first the upright position of the blackboard might seem to him to be quite a different task, especially if he has to turn his body round to copy a model from the teacher's board.

If the child shows a preference for a certain position or posture when he reads or writes the teacher may need to be flexible about this at first, allowing him to do what is required in the manner the child finds easiest in order to get writing under way.

Names

As Theresa mastered her name she gained control over a range of concepts involved in attending to print. Douglas still had some way to go. A child's name has singular importance as he embarks on learning about literacy, both for the child's management of his own learning about print and for the observant teacher trying to understand his pattern of progress (as we shall see later in this chapter).

Teachers write the child's name on his work and this labelling of his drawing, of his coat-peg, of his lunch-tin, calls his attention to the distinctiveness of a name which distinguishes him from other children. This means that there is a need to choose between names by some means. It enhances his security and his self-image giving him a feeling of importance. In more than one place in the class he should have his own name on a card with big black print. He can hold it, run his finger along it, from left to right preferably, trace over it, try to copy it and contrast it with other children's names. When he begins to reproduce some features of it at home his parents will be very responsive. These primitive productions of his name have the very personal nature of a signature, his sign, which develops in detail during the year and yet is constant as an adult's signature in some respects. Children with longer names have a bigger problem.

HCIOOIOHH   CLTPOIU

Christine   Christopher

Some teachers find ways of including first names and surnames for average and better children because this introduces the child to a phrase-like structure with two component words separated in space and in sound — several important concepts.

The use of the children's names in a class activity is a useful way of developing letter knowledge. Children will use their knowledge of letters in family names or classmates' names at later stages as part of their analysis of new words. Usually it is the initial letters that catch the attention.

Programmes for Action . . .

When the child is able to write his or her own name this illustrates one important feature of how the brain works. It seems as if the writer is acting on a set of instructions or a computer-like programme which can produce the same message (one's name) but in ways that are physically very different.

> A man who knows how to write his name at all knows how to do so under a variety of circumstances and in a variety of ways. There is, for example, no-one who is able to write his name only in letters less than one inch high, or only with a pencil, or only on the blackboard.
>
> > (Fodor, 1974).

The concept involved in this learning is that the 'written form of the word' is an abstraction which can be reproduced in different ways.

. . . And Networks of Information

The information about how to write one's name is linked in complex ways to other information one has. Fodor continues '. . . my knowledge of how to write my name connects with my knowledge of how to speak my name, with my knowledge of what my name is, and so on.' A second concept involved in learning one's name is that it has a network of relationships with many other kinds of knowledge.

Such programmes for action and networks of information determine the regular features of a behavioural response without prescribing its precise shape in rigid ways. The programme for action is not necessarily a conscious plan in the mind of the performer; rather it is a sequence in which one thing leads to another. The sequence can change direction at any one of several change points. The first programmes for action are learned slowly for the child is learning not only the specific programme but also *how to put such a set of instructions together, how to store these instructions for the future and how to access the instructions when he needs them.* In other words children have to sort out what to remember and how to recall it.

Similarly the first networks of related information that cluster around a printed word (Ehri and Wilce, 1985)—the spoken word, some of its letters, how you say it, what it looks like in capital or small letters—these networks form slowly but that is because, as well as learning the word, the brain is also learning how to build such information systems about print.

Examples of programmatic actions in writing

With some examples from children's writing it may be possible to illustrate how the early responses which children make to specific features of print become programmatic in the sense that they provide a plan or scheme from which many variations can be generated. To start at zero point, some children cannot put pencil to paper either to produce 'writing' or to copy it. They seem frozen and unable to move in any direction. Then at the 'making funny marks' stage they may produce:

- formless scribble

- or repetitive forms

- or variations on letter-like forms

- and some letter forms often found in their names.

Suzanne   Tony

Throughout the first year of instruction what the child spontaneously writes tends to be a fair reflection of what he has learned to look at in the detail of print. For example the child's control over letter forms in his own spontaneously produced pattern:

l   i   l   i   l   i   l   i   l

can be contrasted with his attempt to copy the word 'Indian' on the same day.

$\qquad$ I н b ı b н

What the child generates or produces himself tends to tell us what aspects of print he has under his own control. What he copies incorrectly may tell us what is new to him. Theresa's examples showed how difficult it is for children to copy letters and how slowly this skill is acquired by some.

There is another gap which closes as the child acquires control over letters and words. It is easily observed. When a child is asked to 'Write your name' or can be coaxed to produce 'some of it', he or she can then be given a full copy and asked to write it again.

TASK 1 Write your name   **TASK 2** Copy your name

For the competent child there is almost no difference.

For the slowest children there is little difference.

In between these extremes of no skill and competence, differences are clearly observed between the products of these two tasks.

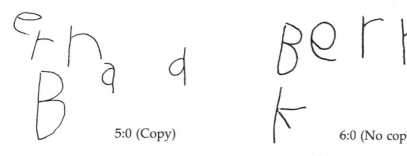

5:0 (Copy)   6:0 (No copy)

Progress is noted as the gap between production and competent copying narrows. To emphasize this point Bernard's attempts to write his name at 5:0 and again at 6:0 are given above. At 5:0 he made no attempt to produce his name and he copied without much regard for the letter-order. His letters are scattered on the page.

At 6:0 he is very conscious of the first letters in his attempt to produce both his names, and his copying demonstrates his progress.

6:0 (Copy)

The principle of order

If a child is making good progress with programmes of action which work for writing words and reading words the principle of order is not a problem; it is already taken care of. However, some children do not attend to the fact that print is arranged in a particular order.

At six years Henry was coaxed and urged to write all the words he knew. Slowly and effortfully but with confidence he wrote 't' and then to the left of it he wrote 'a.'

2   1

No further attempt at printed language could be extracted from him. This was a tentative and very limited set of behaviours 12 months after entry to school! Extra help earlier should have been given.

Henry's example reminds us that the child does not necessarily produce or copy letters in the correct order from left to right. It depends at first on what letters are salient and later upon whether he accepts the ordering principle. Early attempts to write the word 'is' often start with the 's' even though the finished product looks correct.

A child may learn a great deal about words before the ordering principle is established. One little girl wrote for her mother 'the word we had at school today.' The word was 'little.' She produced the letters in this order:

$$1 \; t \; t \qquad\quad 2 \; e \qquad\qquad 3 \; ||i$$

and her final product was spelled

$$||itte$$

It showed commendable visual memory for a new word allowing her to reconstruct the word form but her order of recalling the features of the word was not the expected one.

In writing, attention to letter order or sequencing requires a control over and above knowing the letters themselves. Familiar or salient letters will be recalled easily and the child who accepts the ordering principle must hold back his response to the familiar while he searches for initial letters rather than salient letters.

It is often easy to overlook how industrious a child has been. Despite the illegibility of the child's story at first glance (see below) it can be seen that, with great effort he has attempted to copy the story letter by letter. His control of letter forms is effortful as yet but he has a firm grasp of the ordering principle.

My daddy is a builder.

Observing Early Message Writing

Drawing is one way of expressing ideas in two-dimensional space, and children are easily led to this. A teacher may introduce a shared experience or a story to motivate this activity. The ideas expressed in the drawing can also be expressed in words to the teacher. The teacher acts as scribe to record the message in words, and models for the child how this is done. The child then has two permanent records of his ideas, the drawing and the written message. If the child also traces or copies the message it is modelled in motor activity and this forces the child to explore the detail of the print with his eyes as he works on the production.

The child's task is to discover from these examples the correlation between the ideas in the drawing, the messages he dictated and the rules of the written language game.

At this early stage the child has four ways of analysing a single message he has in mind—by drawing, saying, scanning and tracing or writing. The action sequence has been: ideas, drawing, telling or dictating, teacher writing, child copying or writing involving some further analysing. If the child returns to the teacher she may say 'Read it to me,' and he may recast his ideas in another dictated message, often different from the first in form but carrying much the same message. The teacher may make a more difficult demand, 'Read it with your finger.' Then she is demanding an integration of several responses. She is saying, 'Remember the ideas, re-tell them, find them in print, and move correctly across print.'

That integration is the heart of early reading success.

From time to time the child may lose the ideas, stumble with the language, be superficial or neglectful in his looking, or clumsy and in error in his directional movement. (Adults do not always operate in top gear either!) Only when all these activities are under the child's control and can be deliberately adjusted by him during the ongoing process of getting a precise message from the printed page will he become a reader.

Although the child is interested in books and is having stories read to him, that child's very early reading behaviours can be observed best by his teacher in relation to his drawings and early writing. A teacher should take a record from time to time of the child's spontaneous, untutored efforts and I recommend that such a record should include comments under the headings below. What can a teacher of new entrants find to say about these early efforts? Some things to be watched for can be listed.

Draws

Observe the sophistication of the child's drawing. How complicated is it or how primitive? If he has been at school for a period are his drawings becoming more detailed? I will not try to trace progressions in children's drawing that might be related to reading progress although they undoubtedly exist. Let us assume that the drawing is a creative, enjoyable activity which brings the ideas to be verbalized bubbling to the surface and which direct our attention to the emergence of attempts to write.

Produces writing

The new entrant draws and before long he writes something. It may be limited but it provides a starting point against which later progress can be checked. It should be noted that even a record which shows no writing is a record with which later progress can be compared.

Dictates

Ask the child to tell you a story about his picture and write it down for him.

Copies

If you send the child away to write some of the text, note the sophistication of his attempt.

- Is he just scribbling?
- Ignoring the story?
- Tracing over your story?
- Trying to copy your story underneath?
- Can he transcribe at a distance, from the blackboard?

Re-tells

Have the child read the story to you after a lapse of several minutes. Record exactly what he says as he 'reads' to you. Notice whether he has a memory for the story which he dictated. Listen to his language. Does he flexibly recast the identical story in another sentence? How close to reading his dictated story is he?

Points to text

When you ask the child to read his story to you ask him to 'read it with your finger.' Then you have the observation of directional behaviour available to you, and a way to view one-to-one correspondence of word-spoken with word-visually-located.

These activities provide opportunities:

- for observing the child's ability to represent ideas in words
- for the child to try to write letter forms
- for the child to read the story which indicates how well he remembers the text and how flexibly he handles the sentence
- for the child to point to it as he reads which indicates his control over directional behaviour.

The effort and industry that is applied by the child to his products and actions at this stage marks the importance of the learning.

Observation task summary

The child draws a picture. He dictates a story which the teacher writes down. She asks him to go away and write the story himself (or trace or copy or add to hers, if appropriate). When he brings back the product she asks him to read the story with his finger. A record of these observations might require a form like the one below.

Contrast the child's progress one, two and three months apart on such records. Keep a folder of these samples to document the progress of each child. One record each month would tell a story of change and development.

Draws	(Ideas)
Produces writing	(Generates written messages)
Dictates	(Language)
Copies (or traces)	(Visual analysis) (Motor control)
Re-tells	(Integration)
Points and re-tells	(Directional movement)

The next two examples show the 'bottom line' on such behaviours. They are from children who could not yet perform in all of these areas.

Deborah drew a house, a girl and flowers in the garden.
She dictated: 'The girl is going in the house' but she could not trace or copy this.

Sam drew a truck and dictated: Truck.
The teacher wrote: The truck tips the dirt.
Sam could not read that back.

If the teacher has introduced a story or shared experience she will not be surprised if Tony draws a crab instead of Goldilocks and dictates a story that interests him rather than the one that interested her.

Thoughts in Writing

What did the child actually say about his picture? At the time when children are learning to read their names they can be encouraged to speak in complete sentences about their colourful pictures. They pour out a story so fast and so idiomatically that the teacher has some difficulty in making an accurate record. From this spontaneous description the teacher writes down one or two sentences. How does she select what she will write? It must not be too long as the teacher's time is limited.

Should she copy the child's speech, 'It's a Daddy,' or should she transform it into book-like language, 'This is Father'?

The answer to that question depends upon the child's stage of progress. In the early stages if the child is expected to 'read' the text back accurately the teacher should write down exactly what that child says. This is particularly important at the stage where the child is trying to establish the link between oral and written language. If we want the child to feel good about talking, recording his language as he dictates it avoids the risk of making him feel we reject it. A little later, and in order to move a child closer to book-reading, the teacher might change the child's statement just a little, read it for him in the revised version, and reinforce him for 'reading' her version.

Should the teacher write down ungrammatical speech like 'He get a truck'? Yes; if . . ., and there are at least two 'ifs.' The teacher must decide what is the most important thing for this child to learn at this moment.

- If it is important to talk often in English the child may be threatened by drastic reshaping of his sentence and lose confidence in offering his inadequate sentences.

- If the teaching point for a particular child is to re-read with 100 percent accuracy what the teacher has written then he will do this more readily if she writes what he says despite his inadequate grammar.

When the teacher no longer needs to encourage the child to talk or read but is more concerned to increase his control of the grammar of his writing, only then would the teacher make a teaching point of his error.

A general rule at this level is to stay very close to what the child actually said. This will encourage fluency in reproduction and shows respect for the child's individuality.

How Writing Contributes to Early Reading Progress

The first explorations of print in the preschool years may occur in writing rather than reading. Preschool education places high value on painting with big brushes and bright paint to develop the artistic expression of the four year old but they should not replace paper and pencil or crayon and cardboard as additional media for preschoolers because these encourage children to take an interest in print. The child scribbles at first, in imitation of his parents' cursive writing. He may experiment with letter-like writing. Later he may want to write the names of his family members or send a letter to Nana. These may be the first steps towards reading print.

It was noted earlier that what the child writes is a rough indicator of what he is attending to in print, and demonstrates the programmes of action he is using for word production.

It was also suggested that writing provides extra opportunities for the child to gain control of literacy concepts. While a child is creating a story in print, the eye and the brain are directed to important features for the child must:

- attend very closely to features of letters
- construct his own words, letter by letter
- direct attention to spatial concepts
- work within the order and sequence constraints of print
- break down the task to its smallest segments while at the time synthesizing them into words and sentences
- engage in his own form of segmenting sounds in words in order to write them.

Information gained in these ways from writing becomes part of the network of knowledge the child attaches to familiar words.

The building-up processes complement the visual analysis of text which is a breaking-down process, and although both building-up and breaking-down processes occur in reading, the constructive nature of the task in writing is probably more obvious to the young child. It is probably by these two processes that the child comes to understand the hierarchical relationships of letters, words, and utterances. He would also be able to confirm that the left to right constraint is applied to lines of print, to words within lines, and to letters within words (see pages 126–140).

When the eye, ear and hand are jointly involved in the management of a task, each may be regarded as offering a check on the other. Writing activities can make the learner aware of new ways to check upon the language he has been saying and using. He can examine his speech in another form. He gains a new means of exploring and comparing segments of language.

We have only been considering the child's introductory transition into the world of written language. At this time it is well to remember that writing is only a rough guide to what the child's visual analysis skills are because he may well be able to see what his hand is not able to execute. On the other hand, in reading what he says is often a very misleading guide to what his eye is really perceiving. What he says is, at this time, more likely to be driven by his language experiences, what he has heard and what he typically produces. However, an absence of writing activity and no evidence of a known core of writing words after some time at school may be a signal that the visual perception of print is not being organized into programmes for seeing, producing and recalling words. At that point the teacher must think again about how to achieve a better introduction to print for that particular child.

First Steps in Classroom Writing

How can children who have limited writing vocabulary be helped to write the stories they can make up?

As implied above, teachers often begin writing activities with the child's own name, a word of high interest which provides the insight that print conveys a message. The child who can write his name when he comes to school or soon after already knows that the message consists of:

- particular marks
- placed in a particular order
- making a recognizable pattern.

In some vague and idiosyncratic way the child knows that the name is constructed out of a particular set of letters.

An approach sometimes used is for children to write what they can and want to write with no attempt to stimulate or motivate the children with preparatory activities. Children become very inventive with print and tell stories about what they have written. However, while this pretend writing has the advantage that the child is free to compose and his 'story' is not being overdetermined by some purpose which the teacher has in mind, there can be a cost in that some children develop misconceptions. Because this approach ignores for the moment that real words do have fixed characteristics it can lead some children to believe that they do not. It is fine as a starting point but to be successful it must lead to a growing control over a small vocabulary of correctly written words. Only as more and more words need less and less of the child's attention does his word-bank or writing vocabulary have room to grow. It is the teacher's responsibility to know what are the risk areas of her programme and to be alert and observant to minimize problems. A more successful approach to help children become writers and record the stories which they want to write in language that seems too hard for them is this — the teacher does the hard parts.

Another approach is to use a theme, or centre of interest around some visit or topic of study, and allow children to write on whatever aspect of the topic they choose.

Very often the urge to write comes from a story shared with a group of children, chosen by the teacher or read by a child who has authored a text, and this will often stimulate other children to create ideas for writing for themselves. McKenzie (1985) reported different activities as 'shared writing' and one of these was to have children write another version of a simple but popular story contributing to the composition as a group and enjoying the re-reading of the original and of their new version.

Everyday activities in the child's life are another source of inspiration and stories dramatised sometimes make children eager to write.

Children quickly become used to the fact that there is a time and place for writing every day. They also respond to paper and pencil being available in each activity centre and find interesting ways of putting these to use. One little boy was noticed using the play telephone, and writing down a fast food order in invented script!

At the very beginning children may play around with letters, make lists of words, repeatedly make the same words or invent new ones, hoping they say something. Making letters and letter-like forms are a beginner's occupation, but it is also an exercise in form discrimination. Playing with magnetic letters or at the alphabet table is a constructive 'writing' activity. Very soon these children begin making words.

Sometimes children prefer to have their story written for them so that they can trace it or copy underneath and this is another way to start writing, although the teacher would want to encourage independence as quickly as the child can take it, if only to save herself some time.

There are two short-cuts for children passing through the transition into formal schooling, and they are not recognized by some education systems or some individual teachers.

- The first short cut is to observe and find out what individual children can already do and use those strengths as their entry into reading and writing, allowing each child to go from where they are (rather than expecting every child to take the same steps into a standardized programme). This calls for a flexible programme with opportunities to start anywhere in the learning sequence. It is clearly demonstrated in education systems which work this way (in New Zealand, Great Britain and Australia) that both children and teachers can make this approach work.

- The second short-cut is to develop a programme that leads children towards independence in reading and writing because as the more competent children become more independent they are practising highly appropriate strategies but at the same time are freeing the teacher to give more time to the children for whom assisted learning is necessary for a longer period.

Many teachers seem to have a way of economizing on giving individual writers help that amounts to some system of collecting together commonly used words in lists (such as wall charts) which the children are expected to consult with the help of peers. In such classrooms a cluster of children can sometimes be seen discussing 'words' very seriously around such lists. This is more an invitation to problem-solve and a source of support than a demand for correctness. Of course teachers have to support children in this activity while they learn how to use such lists.

A powerful strategy for teachers to encourage is for children to use the sounds they hear in words they are trying to write, and finding letters for those sounds they hear. Since Charles Read first discovered some preschool children who were inventing their own spelling system by this means, it has been recognized by teachers as a way to become more independent as writers (for example, as 'invented spelling' in classrooms and 'hearing sounds in words' in Reading Recovery).

Organizationally it is difficult for the teacher to be everywhere at once and continually available to help with writing, but there are many solutions to this problem.

In Summary

We have only been considering the child's introductory transition into the world of written language. Children have different sets of opportunities to learn in their preschool years. A quality education system allows each child to build on his prior learning as he makes the transitions into literacy. As the teachers provide more opportunities for literacy experiences of all kinds and assist children to learn, the children come by different routes to understand many of the hidden conceptual challenges in the written code. As a necessary part of the process, children produce inventions, trials, approximations, and errors, and these provide important signals of the progressions in learning that they are making.

The learning is at first slow and there are at least three good reasons why this has to be so.

1 Children have to learn specific details about the reproducible features of each word establishing its identity.

2 In the process of doing that, children are learning how to learn words, what to attend to, and by what features each can be remembered.

3 At one and the same time children are learning how words link up with other experiences and knowledge which they have. They learn how to draw on such networks of information while reading or writing that word or other words.

Learning to read and write messages gives children information about common words from slightly different perspectives which seems to help them to understand more about the ways in which written words work.

Children come gradually to understand how print works: the slowest may find enough to challenge them for the first year of school. In the introductory stage some write only letters, others write words, and some race ahead to express whole ideas in print. First efforts are often invented, later ones copied, and as they gain more control over print children can begin to construct words for themselves. As in many aspects of living the adult's role can be to encourage the child to do independently what he may well succeed in, to work co-operatively with him on some parts of the task, and to do some of the task for the child in order to complete the whole message. This part of the production will be learned by the child at some later time.

6 Attention and the Twin Puzzles of Text Reading: Serial Order and Hierarchical Order

After their first contacts with print, children face three big challenges in the task of learning to read:

- The first is that all spoken languages have to be written down in some serial order which is arbitrary—English is written left to right and that is just the way it is.

- The second is that the information in print is organized in a hierarchy of levels—discourse or text, sentence, phrase, word, letter cluster, letter and sub-letter levels—and the reader has to know which level to attend to at any one moment to be effective.

- The third problem combines the other two—*during acquisition children have to learn how to attend to print in serial order while at the same time deciding which level of the language hierarchy to attend to.*

Yet it is not as simple as that. All this is going on while children are still constructing their knowledge of the hierarchy and what information can be gained from attending to any or each level.

Learning what information in print to attend to in what order to get the greatest payoff can only be done on whole texts and this learning underlies successful reading.

Serial Order Does Have to be Learned

Some educators have claimed that directional behaviour is not a problem to children learning to read and write. That is not the point. It is true that children learn directional behaviour easily and a series of lessons to teach such behaviour may not be necessary. The teacher does not need to teach explicitly all the things she sees children doing so expertly and for aspects of reading like directional behaviour she can 'teach' appropriate responses by clearly modelling the behaviour with groups or in individual interactions with pupils. However, it is still learned behaviour and we have to explain what children learn easily as well as what they find difficult. Teachers need to understand how this learning fits into an explanation of reading and writing acquisition.

Furthermore, I cannot agree that problems do not ever occur with learning about serial order in print. My longitudinal records have shown a gradual build-up of inappropriate behaviours in some children which persist three years later. Most of the historical concern with reversals in reading ought to have been directed to questions about the learning of serial order. The learning must be important for teachers to understand because there are marked individual differences in the time it takes children

- to gain control over these responses
- to use them consistently, and
- to reach a stage where they no longer have to give them any further conscious attention.

The interesting question here is not only how children get directional behaviours under control, but also how and when they come to use these skills effectively so they do not require attention. They use them efficiently most of the time in competent silent reading. We can assume that effective adult readers who say that they are giving serial order no conscious attention are nevertheless operating control mechanisms that tell them when a false move has occurred, because they can monitor their occasional slips such as slipping a syllable or dropping a line.

Directional Learning

So one of the early tasks for children learning to read and write is to learn what to attend to, in what order when looking at language written down. The goal of learning about the directional constraints of written English is to behave within those constraints without having to give the matter any conscious attention. Most children have almost no difficulty with this learning although it takes a little time. For a few this is one very early hurdle in reading acquisition where things go wrong. If a child's confused learning goes unnoticed he tries to respond to instruction but attends to the wrong features and uses the wrong assumptions. The teacher has to notice what is occurring otherwise all the learning that depends on serial order will be difficult—getting messages, using syntax and finding phonological information.

The child's everyday experience has actually trained him in different habits from those he needs in reading. An orange, a dog or a favourite toy must be recognized from any viewing angle. Meaning is constant when the object is small or large, is upside-down, back-to-front, or sideways to the viewer. The child has learned to recognize the constancy of objects despite their changing visual image. On entry to school he has to learn that in one particular situation, when he is faced with printed language, flexibility is inappropriate. Now he must recognize some directional constraints. Speech is sequenced in time and this is represented by print which has linear sequence and the order in English is always left to right.

A young child may scan pictures as he scans the world, from a focal point of high interest in a criss-cross of 'open search' patterns as he links up the ideas. By such a search he first locates the print of the text. Russian psychologists have been particularly interested in the development of the eye and hand searching as young children explore novel stimuli (Zaporozhets and Elkonin, 1971). They found that children attended better to the stimuli before the age of five if they traced the new shapes with both hand and eye. Most older children were able to carry out effective exploration of new shapes with their eyes alone. (See Chapter 12.)

So there is a large motor co-ordination component in this learning, the significance of which probably varies with the age of learning to read. The younger the child, the more time he is likely to take learning this directional behaviour; the older he is the easier the motor or directional learning tasks will tend to be for him.

Any complex movement like hitting a golf ball, playing a violin or reading a book must be organized or patterned. You can provide yourself with an example of this. Study the letters in each of these blocks, close the book and write down the letters.

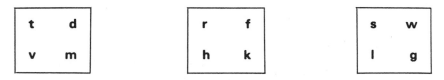

You probably wrote the letters in an order which a large number of people would follow (tdvm; rfhk; swlg). Why should this be?

When you are travelling in the car do some of the signs written on the road cause you to look twice?

WAY	BRIDGE	AHEAD
GIVE	WAY	WAY
	ONE	ONE

Our reading habits tend to make us survey letter and word patterns from top left to top right and then return down left and repeat the pattern. This can be represented schematically as:

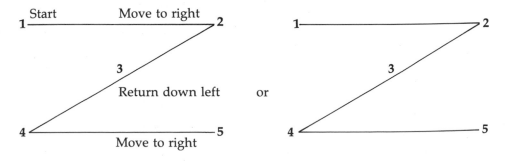

Children learn to sweep across the first part of the pattern, 1 to 2, rather easily. It takes them longer to consistently use the complete pattern in a way that is appropriate for scanning two or three lines of print. Such movements are required by the quite arbitrary conventions we use in printing our language and the adult's perception of printed messages has been trained to proceed within those particular constraints. The school entrant who has not yet learnt to read and write has not had his behaviour organized in this way. Preschool learning did not place such limits on visual scanning except perhaps the experience he may have had with books or with early writing. It is difficult to find a similar limitation on visual analysis in any other human behaviour (except reading music). Some language codes use right to left, or vertical directional patterns. All are arbitrary systems.

Awareness of Left and Right Sides

Space around us becomes described with reference to our own body's position so that we locate things as up (above our head), down (at the feet end), before or behind, to this side or that side. At two or three years the child has a basic awareness of his body when he names parts of it. Between four and six years research has shown that the child has an awareness that the two sides of the body are different from one another, although he cannot specify the difference in words. This is a sensory-postural awareness of one side as different from the other. Children with a strong hand preference may distinguish their main hand side from the other side (Benton, 1959). This is all that is necessary to master the directional schema required in written English. It is not necessary to have developed the verbal concepts of left and right unless the teacher insists on talking about directional behaviour.

If it is clearly demonstrated or modelled for the child, he can imitate the pattern, relating what he sees to his awareness of the sidedness of his own body.

Orientation to the Open Book

Perhaps the first thing that the child learns about the directional sequences for English texts is something about the placement of his body in relation to the open book. He uses a hand to locate points of interest in the pictures. To read the printed messages in English (rather than the pictures) the child must locate the left side of the first line of print. How does he know where this starting point is? Page layouts vary and text may not always occur on a left page.

In the diagram below, the arrows in A show acceptable and unacceptable horizontal and vertical movements for English text. The arrows in B indicate some of the tentative actions that children who were still learning the directional schema produced when:

- either hand was used
- on either page
- in either of two horizontal directions
- and two vertical directions.

The child must come to use only movements similar to those indicated by the solid lines and must not approach text by way of the dotted lines. If you study children's learning of this behaviour over two or three months you can see that it is more complicated than one would imagine (Clay, 1974).

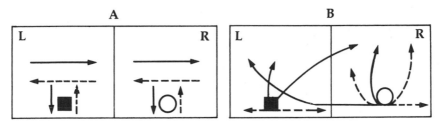

Correct (—) and incorrect (---) directional movement on left and right book pages with left and right hands.

■ = left hand   ○ = right hand

A child may be helped by a signal for a starting point like a coloured dot placed temporarily on the page

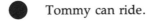
Tommy can ride.

or by a signal which indicates the left side

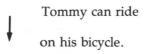
Tommy can ride

on his bicycle.

The child should learn to do without such signals or cues as soon as he has gained stable control over starting position, because the aim is to have the child (not the teacher or the publisher) control the directional schema. He will be helped to such stability by a large measure of consistency in the books and blackboard texts he reads. Careful selection of the earliest reading materials can ensure that the average to slow learning child gets practice with a top-left, left page starting point.

On the other hand the child must gradually encounter texts which vary in print formats to make him flexible in applying this directional learning to texts that begin in various positions on a page of print. Regularity makes the first learning steps easier but overall competence cannot be trained on regularity. There must be early opportunities to apply the directional schema to various different layouts.

Keeping one's place during a difficult visual task often involves locating and holding that place with the finger or hand, turning the head, scanning with the eyes, and locating with the finger. It is a co-ordinated set of movements in two-dimensional space. This pattern of behaviour is observable in most preschool children as they look at books. When they come to *read* the printed messages of books they must control both—hold their place and move across print.

If a child behaves flexibly on these inflexible directional rules of written language, and continues to think that anything goes, the relearning problem may prove troublesome. David wrote 'I am a dog.' His teacher wrote the sentence on paper, cut it up into words and asked David to make the sentence again. She cut 'dog' into separate letters to increase the difficulty of the task. David placed the cards this way:

dog   a   am   I

654   3   2   1

T	'Oh! Can you read it to me?'	
Ch	'I am a dog.' (moving right-to-left)	
T	'But you read it that way.'	
Ch	'I know.'	
T	'But you can't do that.'	
Ch	'Why?'	
T	'Because we always read that way.' (left to right)	
Ch	'Why?'	
T	'Because it's a rule.'	
Ch	'Why?'	
T	'Well if we didn't make a rule about reading and writing no one would know which way to start and which way to go and we'd get mixed up. Wouldn't we?'	
Ch	'How?'	
T	(Picking up the book) 'If I didn't know that the person who wrote this story kept to the rules and wrote this way I might read the top line like this "Engine fire the at look."'	
Ch	(Long solemn look)—'Ph.'	
T	'Haven't you always been shown to read that way?'	
Ch	'Ye—s. I didn't think it mattered.'	
T	'You are absolutely not allowed to go the other way in reading or writing. Did you know that?'	
Ch	'No!'	
T	'Well we will have to remember to go only one way and to stick to it. OK?'	
Ch	'Yes, OK.'	

T   *'Where do we begin?'*
     Child points to the right.
T   *'Where is the beginning?'*
     Child points to the right and left and looks questioningly at T.
T   *'Where shall we start?'*
Ch   *'I don't know!'*

To David, starting at either end still seemed to be legitimate. After that, every lesson began with left-hand touch-down practice. The teacher had observed the problem.

Some children already have control over directional movement on entry to school and some learn it easily during their first contacts with print. Other children have considerable difficulty developing consistency in this behaviour for six to 12 months. David's confusion was exceptional but teachers should be prepared for the fact that it can happen. Without appropriate directional behaviour children's efforts to read become a scrambled heap of cues which are impossible to untangle. To discover such children early, one needs to watch closely for specific signs of progress in learning the directional schema. It is possible that these directional skills are not given high enough priority by many teachers, especially in 'whole language' or 'real books' programmes. Like all teachers they have to ask themselves, 'Who is at risk in my programme?'

Observing Directional Behaviour

In their first year at school most children learn all they need to know about the directional rules of English almost effortlessly. We should, however, observe their progress in this aspect of reading behaviour. This may be particularly important in an instruction programme where children are attempting to respond to sentence texts without prior training on letter knowledge and word knowledge.

The first questions to ask are these:

- Does he expect to read a picture or to read print?
- Does he expect to read a left page before a right page?
- What consistency is there in his movements?

To check on the last question give the child a simple story book and ask the child to 'Read it with your finger.' If he moves his finger in anything but the appropriate direction at any time note it down and plan to observe him closely for the next few weeks. If it really was a momentary slip caused by inattention or fatigue, pay it no further attention. If it recurs treat it seriously and help the child to find a consistent and appropriate pattern of responding.

A teacher may suspect that the child's eyes are scanning in inappropriate directions or that there is a conflict between what the eyes are trying to scan and how the hand and body respond to the text. (The importance of visual scanning is discussed in Chapter 12.)

Sometimes teachers forbid pointing because authorities have associated this in older children with word by word reading and faulty reading habits (see Chapter 8). If directional behaviour is vitally important and pointing behaviour is forbidden, how is the teacher to know which way a child is surveying the page of print? She must arrange to observe such important behaviour at regular intervals when the child is reading captions or single line texts. The instruction 'Read it with your finger' provides a simple technique for an observation check and reveals an amazing variety of behaviours. Shelley read a caption text with near-perfect verbal accuracy but her finger travelled along the line from right to left.

Child: *I made a fish pond.*
          ←------------------*
Text: We made a fish pond.

Young children do not lack ingenuity in their attempts to find a track across print. They have been observed to point:

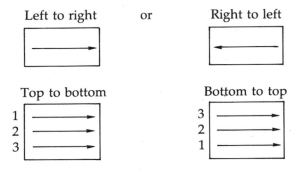

One child was observed using the centre of the book as his focus and reading *out from the centre*, right to left on a left page and left to right on a right page.

Snaking movements across a page are observed in which one line is read left to right and the next line is read right to left. This is a really economical way to move across print, a line of least effort for which there is a dictionary description, *boustrophedon*, meaning 'as the ox ploughs.'

These directional behaviours must be expected to fluctuate and increasing dominance of the appropriate movements will usually be found but some children arrive at *a consistency of the wrong habits.* They become consistent in a right to left or bottom to top approach. This will produce problems for attention in reading, and for working with the hierarchy of information in print (discussed in the opening paragraph of this chapter).

Examples of Directional Learning

Sally's success
On entry to school Sally dictated Story A and re-read it as Story B.

Story A	Story B
The other day I went in the bus with Naardi and saw Mr. Buffet's house.	I went up in the bus and I saw Mr. Buffet's house with Naardi and a . . .

She moved her finger across one line starting vaguely at the end of 'other' and drifting left to right beyond the end of the first line. Her language patterns were fine but she was not locating any visual detail in print to control her directional behaviour. Two months later she showed good control on a little book, *Round The House*. She was text-perfect, which suggests a good memory for language. She consistently moved her right hand left to right across the text on either a left or right page. Because she had an idea that a letter equalled a word she became confused trying to match a three-line text like:

> This is
> the
> window.

Three months after entry Sally's directional behaviour was securely established.

Gordon's confusion
In contrast Gordon's confusion lasted a long time and he produced some unusual directional behaviour. Two weeks after entry to school he responded to *What Goes Up* by moving his finger right to left across all five pages. He usually read a right page before a left page and pointed with his right hand. He was showing a consistent choice of 'right-sidedness' for page, for text and for pointing finger. After six weeks he 'read' text by matching a spoken word to a printed letter and this time he pointed with his left hand. The order in which he pointed to the words in a line was — 2 3 4 5 1. Two months after entry to school his little reading book was *Traffic*. He pointed left to right with his left hand and remembered the text. He *matched a letter to a word*, looked surprised at what was left over but did nothing about it.

Child:	*Here*	*is*	*a*	*car*
Text:	H	e	r	e	is a car.

On the same day he tried an unfamiliar caption book. First, he could not find the print. Then he began on a right page. On a two-line text he read only the bottom line. He read the next page from right to left. At last he gained control of the situation and read three pages from left to right with his left hand. He was learning something. At the end of one term he gained a very low score on the Concepts About Print task. The first observation of Gordon in his second term at school showed the following movements over 10 pages of a story. What is unsettling about his record is that he is now beginning to follow some directional rules but they are *his own rules*.

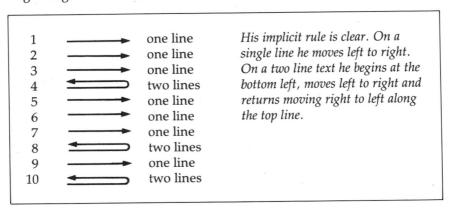

1	→	one line	*His implicit rule is clear. On a*
2	→	one line	*single line he moves left to right.*
3	→	one line	*On a two line text he begins at the*
4	←	two lines	*bottom left, moves left to right and*
5	→	one line	*returns moving right to left along*
6	→	one line	*the top line.*
7	→	one line	
8	←	two lines	
9	→	one line	
10	←	two lines	

In another month some small measure of control emerged. He read *My Brother* with only one directional slip. Just before the end of his first year at school he read an early reading book, *Wake Up Father*, with 97 percent accuracy. He used the picture for cues, matched his saying and pointing, worked well at self-correcting, used his left hand to point. For all that, his movements were not smoothly co-ordinated. It is doubtful whether any instruction other than well-co-ordinated individual tutoring could have reduced the time this learning took. Even with an individual programme it would take a long time for Gordon to learn to hold these behaviours together in an appropriate way.

Jim's problem

It is helpful to trace one child's progress in detail to see the building up of a directional and learning problem.

Jim developed a temporary reading problem. For nearly six months he seemed to have directional behaviour under control but then he spent two months practising inappropriate directional habits on his first reading books. His progress went like this.

1 After Jim had been at school for a month he painted a picture and dictated 'Jim is standing on Steven's head.' The teacher wrote down the text and he located his name and moved left to right across two lines of print.

2 Two weeks later he read a book with one line of text per page. He used the pictures for cues, slowed his voice when asked to point and moved his finger left to right. This could be counted as three steps forward.

3 Next week inappropriate behaviour was noticed. Once he moved bottom to top on a two-line text; a second time he moved top to bottom. He gave a word response to a letter and could not get any correspondence between what he said and what the text said. Two steps back.

4 Two weeks later he read the book again (see 2 above) with correct sentence structure and searching for syllable breaks in *run-ning* and *jump-ing*. Two steps forward. This was repeated the following week but now he had memorized the text.

5 After two months at school he was placed on a small reading book which he 'read' with 94 percent accuracy, moving left to right but not matching spoken words to printed words. The only word recognized was 'is.' A week later this performance was repeated but now he also recognized 'am.'

There was nothing exceptional about progress to this point. Other children do these kinds of things and sort themselves out. However Jim became more confused.

6 After the term holidays this performance was repeated but now he could not locate any words on the page.

7 He moved to a supplementary reading book at the same level, and read the text with only 80 percent accuracy moving left to right. This was a poor performance but he did locate and read five words in isolation.

8 A week later, perhaps because he was not finding solutions to his problem-solving of print, he began snaking across print moving right to left and left to right, rendering the text with 86 percent accuracy.

Directional behaviour had become a problem.

In the next two records movement across print was consistently a snaking movement and he was not learning anything new about words and responses because of this inappropriate directional approach.

9 He returned to that first small reading book and used an erratic directional approach varying his starting point page by page—L, R, L, L, R, RRLL, LL, LL, R. He said, '*Mummy bought these books. I read to her last night. She said I have to go backwards and forwards.*' He was aware that something was wrong and that he had to make an effort but he was confused and what he said probably made it worse.

10 The next week he had the directional schema under control and only made one lapse. The avoidance of a reading problem may well have been due to an observant mother who became a sensitive tutor.

What is the final achievement towards which a child is working? He should move consistently from a left hand starting point across a line of print, return down left, move left to right again, return down left and so on. With this directional movement it is important that he be able to match a word that he says with pointing to a word on the text in a co-ordinated manner as he moves left to right across print and returns down left.

Jim's records show that his most frequently used approach to print was different in three periods.

February to June he went ———▶
June to August he went ◀———
August to December he went ——▶ or snaked across the page.

And that accounted for his first year at school.

There are Different Reasons for Difficulties

One group of children who find directional learning difficult shows a general immaturity in motor behaviour which affects the learning of movement patterns.

Another group, unfamiliar with books, takes a long time to comprehend the concept that a sequence of print is related to a sequence of spoken words.

Some children settle into consistent but erroneous directional habits (perhaps proceeding from right to left) hidden from the teacher's sight because they never point to their reading and rarely write on paper. Wrong responses are learned and practised.

A small group of children practise error as frequently as they practise the correct pattern. Such alternating behaviour on a 50-50 basis either leaves the child confused or forces him to concentrate hard on the directional aspects of the task to the detriment of the visual and language aspects. In this case only close supervision will ensure that the left to right behaviour occurs more frequently than any lapses of right to left behaviour or other variants.

Children learning the left to right survey habit are so dominated by it at first that they are likely to name a series of pictures arranged in a triangle from left to right across the triangle rather than the expected sequence of starting at the top and moving round the triangular outline. After a year they use left to right survey only on printed language and outline tracing on other arrangements (Elkind and Weiss, 1967).

Children who taught themselves to read using computer-controlled talking typewriters in the 1950s (Moore, 1961) had the directional pattern controlled for them by the action of the typewriter. The children were two and three year olds. The machine only moved from left to right and at the end of the line returned to the left of the next line. The directional relationships were invariant and it was impossible to make errors. Today it is the computer (rather than the typewriter) which might provide a child with this control of the directional schema. Like the talking typewriters this may help many young children who have computer opportunities to establish the motor habits and space orientation to reading and writing described above. But it may also not help because *what has to be learned is how to personally control one's attending according to the serial order requirements of print*. We need to find out under what conditions use of a computer does lead to such control.

Teachers must observe closely until the directional schema is firmly established. It is a particular set of learning for the new entrants' teacher to bear in mind. It is important that the child knows when he is correct in reading and in writing. Somehow the learning, once established, must fade into a routine that does not call for attention.

What is mirror-writing? It is when a child starts at the right-hand side of the page and writes from right to left. Should we be concerned about this? Writing behaviour is a rather gross clue to what the child is scanning with his eyes, and directional lapses in writing continue to occur for much longer than they do in early reading. Teachers should be more concerned if the child who has been taught reading and writing for a year is still not behaving consistently in a left to right direction when he visually scans a page of print. These children must, almost inevitably, be at risk as readers. Their behaviour is disorganized and only the invitation to 'read it with your finger' reveals this.

All children show some fluctuation in this behaviour. For how long is variability tolerable? Within a month of entry to school 40 to 50 percent of five year olds in a research sample had mastered the schema in a test situation and on average the children were quite consistent six months after school entry.

Consistent Directional Movement

Percentage Pass at Five Age Levels

Age	5:0	5:6	6:0	6:6	7:0
Study 1 (Europeans only)	44	93	96	—	—
Study 2 (different ethnic groups)	53	77	84	99	99

A teaching programme which assumed mastery of directional behaviour after a few weeks at school would only be appropriate for the well-prepared school entrants. Obviously a sensitive teacher must be alert to the continuing confusions of many children with directional learning.

Helping Children Change Their Directional Responses

There is no one progression by which a child moves to control of the directional schema but there is a transition from early gross approximations to movements controlled by more and more of the detail in print.

Page-matching

A text is usually page-matched at first in that a child directs his pointing and talking to a particular page and to the print en masse rather than the picture. The child must be introduced to the marks he must attend to — black ones in his book, white ones on the blackboard. It seems impossible that a child should try to read the white spaces in a book and 'the white rivers' on the page but some children attending a reading clinic have reported this.

Starting point

As English print is read from left to right the child's first problem is to decide where to start. A child must locate left starting points rather than right ones with consistency.

The child may be able to become consistent in his choice of a correct starting position in a number of ways:

- if he sees an adult modelling the movement pattern in the same position as he will produce it
- if he consistently uses one hand
- if the messages in his book always start in roughly the same place
- and least desirable, if he has some prop (like a green sticker) which the teacher uses as a temporary means of showing the starting position.

Control over direction must become the child's control but it may have to be exercised temporarily by the teacher.

A helping hand

If a child has a firm preference for a particular hand it will be used to guide the eyes scanning the text. The preferred hand will be used on either a left page or a right page. Once the eyes have established their own left to right habit one might find the hand becomes of less importance in maintaining the response and either hand might be used to keep the place or to direct attention to some difficulty in reading.

If the child has no preference for one hand over the other, locating a starting point will be more difficult. The visual format of the pages might control his behaviour and he might be drawn to move hither and thither according to the artistic design of the pages, and the way the pictures and print are arranged.

Research shows that it is not necessary to know the words 'left' and 'right' in order to respond successfully to the directional constraints of written

English. However, the child who knows this information as well has an advantage. This preschooler demonstrates this extra control.

> Putting on shoes the child says, *'Is this right?'*
> The helpful adult says, *'Yes, right shoe for your right foot. That is your right foot and the other is your left foot.'*
> There is a long pause.
> *'This is my right hand!'*

Such leaps in understanding make the construction of a complex action system possible.

Left to right across a line

A single word caption such as 'Me' is easily located. Two words are more difficult because there is more question about where to begin on 'My Father.' A one-line sentence calls for more decisions and therefore more chance of problems. Children's first movements are a drift or sweep across a line as the whole utterance is matched to the whole movement. Some children cannot even locate the end of an utterance.

The child may point to a letter or a word at the left-hand end of the line and make uncertain movement somewhere to the right or the child may move very slowly over the first few letters or words and then sweep to the end of the line. He may move rather deliberately across most of the line and then somehow adapt to any little pieces he has over at the end.

An awareness of the right-hand end of a line is often the next focal point to develop. Children are then able to locate the first word, sweep across the rest of the line and land upon the last word quite deliberately.

Text:	I am a fireman.
Movement:	*————————>

From inconsistency to flexibility

This is a puzzling change to describe. The first approaches the child makes to printed text indicate that he is scanning it like a picture for scattered points of interest. Records of pointing behaviour reveal inconsistency. There is evidence to suggest that in the next stage of learning directional movements the child adopts a rigid pattern of using one particular hand to find his route across print. Gradually he becomes consistent, the lapses of direction disappear, his movements become surer and quicker. About this time he may begin to use either hand on either page of his book as the movement is quite easy for him and he can once again be flexible in his approach. To observe this transition the teacher might add another question to her record keeping. That question is, *'Which hand does the child use?'*

The reason for the question has nothing to do with old questions about brain control and left-handedness. It has to do with flexibility. The progress of identical quadruplets was observed during their first year at school (Clay, 1974). One was left-handed, the other three were right-handed. For the first two to three weeks of school they each showed some inappropriate approaches to the printed page. Then for many weeks each adopted a preferred hand and always used it. (See diagram, 4–6 weeks.)

Hand used to point to text
(see also page 117)

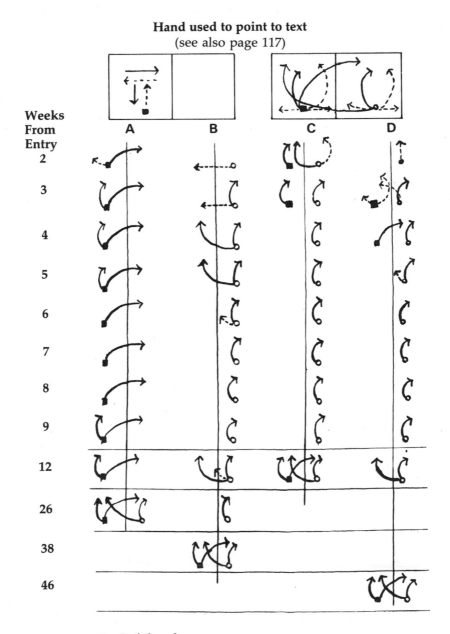

Weeks From Entry	A	B	C	D

■ Left hand
○ Right hand

One by one they began to use either hand again becoming flexible, moving away from a fixed routine. The timing of this change was individual—it occurred at 12, 26, 38 and 46 weeks respectively after school entry in children with identical heredity. It is interesting that this order was perfectly related to their rank on reading achievement; the first to become flexible in the use of either hand was the first to read successfully while the last to use either hand was the slowest to start reading. *It is likely that attention, no longer needed to control the subroutine of directional behaviour, could now be given to other learning.*

New challenges (using early writing examples)
The young learner who has established a fairly consistent habit is easily thrown by a new and unusual format or various other new factors which can enter into the reading situation. Because his directional habits are new they are easily thrown and he will be noticed to lapse from time to time in use of the directional schema under the pressures of new learning. The young child of five years may have mastered this schema yet his teacher may notice one day that he is suddenly writing from right to left. There are two observable reasons for this. One may be called 'the pancake effect' and the other may be called 'the pebble in the pond' effect.

The pancake effect
David gives a clear example of his appreciation of the directional schema as he prints his name.

At this point of achievement it is easy for the child to flip the whole pattern over—to reverse it—and, choosing a top right starting point, to carry out the movements as a pattern with all the relationships reversed. The ease with which children accomplish this may be related to Bryant's discoveries that young children can be using the background (the framing of the paper shape) to guide their responding (see page 260).

Translation of text copied from a reading book
'. . . but he liked the duck best of all.' Age 5:7

Some visual guide to a starting point, like a coloured cross or sticker in the top left-hand corner of the page, should control this temporary variability. The error arises out of a measure of control over the directional pattern and gentle coercion will 'turn the pancake' back again. This behaviour, fault though it seems, is a sign of control with flexibility.

The pebble in the pond

The other disturbance to the directional schema is also a sign of growth. One by one the child masters elements of directional behaviour. One by one he encounters new variations in the texts he is reading and he explores variations in his writing. Although he controls the directional schema in writing two or three lines there comes a day when he runs out of page. With ingenuity and economy he often spreads his left-over message around the remaining spaces, disregarding the directional constraints as the next example shows. The layout of the story *Twice A Week* is a delightful solution to page arrangement problems. The girl aged 5:1 was copying an adult's model and was not aware of the importance of spaces between words or the problem of breaks within words. She was content to begin Page 4 with the last syllable of 'paper,' continue with 'twice a week' and put her last left-over word in any left-over space.

I colour my book twice a week.

I draw on paper twice a week.

Although the directional learning is well-established, a new feature may capture the child's attention for the moment and send ripples of disturbance through the old habits. Given a little time the whole pattern will settle down again, incorporating this new feature in the old learning. Spatial problems persist in writing for a longer period than in reading.

This observation that new learning can create a disturbance in old responses which seem well-established is not so strange when one thinks about it. If learning were only a matter of adding bits of knowledge to our old stores this would not happen. When our skills are controlled by a pattern of movements or a complex set of brain reactions it is not surprising that the whole set is disturbed by adding a new component to the pattern.

Questioned about directional errors, children will frequently be able to report what they have done. After about 33 weeks at school Trevor read one page correctly, turned the leaf, began to read at the left of the bottom line and continued left to right and bottom to top without any other directional lapse. He then read six pages with correct directional behaviour. I turned back to the offending page and asked 'What did you do wrong?' to which he answered immediately, 'I read the bottom wrong,' indicating correct direction. These observations suggest that when directional behaviour is not quite a fixed habit and conscious attention is given to other aspects of the text, directional constraints can be overlooked.

Perfect rendering of the text from bottom to top sounds an impossibility. Surely the story would not make sense! In some early reading books with controlled vocabulary, texts do not have much loss of meaning even when incorrect direction is used!

Locating Words While Using the Directional Schema

How the learning proceeds on letters and words may be determined by the instruction programme. The child's attention may be directed primarily to letters, to words, to groups of letters, or to groups of words. There are two difficult concepts to be mastered by the child in this task. The first is the ordering principle of words arranged left to right, one after the other. The other is the hierarchical principle that each word consists of letters which themselves have a left to right order.

Children have to learn to observe words one after the other in faultless sequence. If we ask children of five years to count a row of objects one after the other some children have difficulty. They have less difficulty with only three or four objects and this may be one reason why a three- or four-word sentence is about right for the beginner. In the sentence 'Here is Mother,' the directional sequence is left to right and the motor sequencing one, two, three. Most children will manage the co-ordination correctly. The child who cannot point to three circles or blocks in sequence will not find groups of black symbols separated by white spaces easy.

Even after he has achieved this one-to-one correspondence in pointing to objects guided by his eyes the child may still have a problem pointing to words on a page. As this second problem is attacked he may also have difficulty finding the words in his speech. He may clump the words together saying 'apastate' when he is trying to match what he says with the text 'half past eight.' Or the child points to 'the' and reads 'the girls.' On the other hand the child might over-analyse into syllables and get two points in 'pilot' or 'laugh-ing.' Downing and Oliver (1974) explored this problem of knowing what a word is in oral language. New difficulties continue to be met as texts become more complex. There is a continuing challenge in matching new speech patterns to print layouts.

When a school entrant points to his reading text he is usually trying to match the time sequence of what he is saying with the visual survey of print in the book. He is trying to relate one signal system (speaking) to another (writing). To help the young reader with this locating behaviour publishers have made some adjustments. They have used larger print, increased spacing between lines, and increased spacing between words. Publishers who do not always like to make these concessions should be talked into them for beginning readers.

Some children come to believe that each letter is matched to a word in speech. This is an early misconception.

Text: H   e r   e   is the cow.
Child A: *Here is a   cow.*
Child B: *Here is the c———————ow.*

The first child did not solve the problem of what to do with left-over words. The second child found an unsatisfactory solution, drawing out the rest of what he has to say while he ran his finger quickly along to the end of the line.

Two or More Lines

The fragility of early learning can be demonstrated if a child who moves consistently across a single caption is faced with more than one line of text. A child who can match words in one line very well may lose control over direction when he is faced with two lines of text.

Come and play   Grandad said, 'The
on the swings.   children are here.'

In the texts above the child may just ignore the problem and give the correct response to the top line or the bottom line. He may be unable to return to the left-hand end of the second line. Perhaps it seemed so obvious that no one thought to prepare him for the new challenge.

The child may need to be introduced to two things usually treated as one:

- that we move from top to bottom of a page
- that we have to invariantly use a return sweep.

Without help the child may, like Jim earlier, try snaking left to right and right to left. Or, he may be tempted to read a bottom line before a top line, like Gordon. The next example shows the difficulties being experienced by a six year old who had been at school for a year and who had been singled out for special instruction. This child read these sentences which were arranged in two lines. He moved across two pages of print giving spoken responses that sounded correct. Only when he was reading with his finger at the request of the observer did she know where he was directing his attention.

3	2	1		8	7
Here	is	Peter		Peter	has
6	5	4		9	10
in	the	tree		the	ball

The memory for text was perfect. He read 'Here is Peter in the tree. Peter has the ball.' Both the starting point and the return sweep are problems for this child on two lines of print. All he controls is the top to bottom directional movement.

Collections of Letters Make up Words

What is a word? What is a letter? Five year olds will write letters and call them words or they may write a string of words and call them letters. The child only has to know his name and two or three other words to make correct generalizations about these basic concepts. However, many children take a long time to sort out these relationships and make some wrong assumptions at first.

(Clay, 1975)

What often happens is that the concepts of letter and word become con-fused. When one child was asked to read these three words in isolation he responded with letter names.

Child: *a's* *z* *y's*
Text: here said am

The ghost of a sound cue occurred when he responded with the letter 'z' to the word 'said.'

Another child demonstrated his concept of a word when he read his name 'Stuart.' He was asked 'How do you know?' As he pointed to the 'S' he said 'It begins like this—and it goes as far as there!' sliding his finger along under the word and ending at the final 't.'

In a test where the child had to slide two masking cards across a line of print to show the tester 'just one word,' and 'just one letter' and 'just the first letter of a word' (Clay, 1966, 1985), only 40 to 53 percent of six year olds could pass these items after one year of instruction. Such scoring reflects partly a confusion of concepts and partly the problem of establishing part-identities within wholes. Yet the directional pattern was established in 84 percent of the group who could synchronize their pointing with their word by word reading of the text.

The Acquisition of Important Concepts

Task	*Percentage Passing At Five Age Levels*				
	5:0	5:6	6:0	6:6	7:0
Matches word-space-word	48	60	84	100	100
Locates one letter	34	47	53	56	84
Locates one word	22	16	47	53	91
Locates first letter	28	22	41	56	81

Children need some help to understand that a word is made up of a group of letters. Some teachers encourage children to cup their hands around words on the blackboard. Others find ways to help children to use spaces as a cue to the word boundaries. A little attention to this 'collections of letters' concept will help the child overcome the 'letter equals a word' assumption.

At this early stage it is probably less important that the child be attending to specific letters within words. It will soon become necessary for the child to focus firstly on the left-hand letter of the word as he proceeds word by word across a line of print. Later still it will be necessary for him to attend to letters sequentially left to right across a word.

Early writing is one task where he builds words in this way. The child who can write a few letters usually gains control of left to right sequencing in his own printing before he disciplines his approach to print on a book page. In writing *he* controls the complexity and variations; in a book the author and printer do this.

One tends to assume that the simple instructions 'Look at the first letter of the word' or 'Show me the first letter of the word' are readily understood by children. To respond correctly one must understand:

- that a word is the pattern of marks made up of letters
- that a word must be approached from left to right.

Ian failed to sort out his confusions about print throughout the whole of his first year at school. He claimed that his teacher, who wrote his name as 'Ian' (which he wrote down in this way) could not spell his name. He then demonstrated that his name was spelled 'IAN.' In a bookshop he pointed to the title of a scrapbook labelled 'GIANT' and said *'There's my name,'* unconcerned about the presence of extra letters.

Trying to Match Spoken with Written Words

Children were asked to make marks with a pencil on transparent paper placed over the text of their caption book. What they said and where they pointed are recorded in these examples.

My mother   A good beginning
x x
My mother

is
x
Father is digging   Beginning, middle and end
x   X
Father   digging

Here is the horse   A letter is a word
x x x x   x
Here is the hor   se

I am a painter   More difficult than it
← ← ← ←   need be
I   am a painter

I am a nurse   Almost co-ordinated
•   • •   •
i   am a   nurse

I am a pilot   Co-ordinated speech and
•   • • • •   pointing
i   am a pi – lot

Children sometimes reject long words as words. Downing and Oliver (1974) suggest that short words of three to five letters are more likely to appear in the children's reading books and be associated with the teacher's label 'word.' On the other hand Ferreiro and Teberosky (1982) found preschoolers who rejected two-letter words as words claiming they had to have three or four letters in them.

The young child does not have a concept of the spoken word that matches his teacher's concept. Up to the age of eight years children confuse isolated sounds and syllables with words. Reid (1966) and Clay (1967) found children had limited understanding of a word or a letter and of the purposes of reading. Downing (1970) and Downing and Oliver (1974) demonstrated the child's confusion in distinguishing by ear the difference between a word and a sound or syllable in speech. Thirty children from 4:5 to 8:0 confused isolated sounds and syllables with words. It is possible that these children thought that such sounds represented 'words' that they were not familiar with.

Theory About Serial Order

It is not wise in developmental psychology to describe what happens at one stage of development by analogy from behaviour at an earlier stage. For one thing the child becomes more complex as he gains experience. However, Bruner's (1974) explanation of the development of skilled actions is remarkably informative for understanding the sequential acts in beginning reading even though he is describing how the infant learns to put separate acts into a controlled sequenced movement.

There are six stages to the development of sequenced movement.

Stage 1 The child attends to the task and performs some anticipatory actions.

Stage 2 This is the clumsy stage. A loosely ordered series of actions occur, only roughly approximate, variable and requiring much effort.

Stage 3 This changes to success with a short series of acts in proper serial order allowing for false moves, repetitions and self-corrections. There is a sharp noticeable alteration in the acts as if they had acquired a new structure.

Stage 4 Reinforcement or success modifies the action pattern so that it becomes less variable.

Stage 5 With practice the child does not need to attend to all sections of the sequence. Sub-routines are formed which the child executes with little attention. The child is freed to attend to new aspects of the task. The sub-routines can become part of a new series of acts in a higher-order structure.

Stage 6 With more practice the skilled performance becomes less variable, anticipation becomes more accurate, and speed and fluency increase because an economy of attention and effort has been made.

Learning directional behaviours and visual scanning patterns can be understood in these terms. Early reading behaviours may be thought of as sub-routines of reading activity — what the child comes to attend to visually (sentence, word, letter, features of letters) and in what order. At the same time the child learns how to switch the brain's attention within and between levels of printed information picking up essential information for the problem-solving acts used in reading texts with understanding.

Bruner (1974) discusses the role of feedback and intention in the learning sequences of skilled action, and this seems important for learning how to read.

- Within the nervous system before we act there are signals of our intended action. Our limbs would not respond to our intentions if this were not so. Because these signals occur before the action takes place they are sometimes called feed-forward signals rather than feedback. They anticipate the shape of the act yet to occur.

- Learning is also helped by feedback signals that come as the action is being carried out. This might involve hearing what one is saying, as in reading aloud, or pointing with a finger to guide the eye movements needed. Feedback acts as a control system informing us when an error or mismatch of signals has occurred.

- Knowledge of results occurs after the action is completed. Did you grasp the glass you reached for? Did you find the print signals you expected to see? Observing the results of an action leads us to anticipate the outcome on another occasion.

In performing a sequence of acts the child is helped by feed-forward, feedback and knowledge of results. At first he attends to some of these signals. But as the sub-routines are formed and linked the movements become more automatic and require less effort and attention.

Reading as a skilled action sequence presents a further problem to the child. Directional strategies and visual scanning strategies become sets of smooth sub-routines, but reading remains a problem-solving task in which the reader must get the precise message of the author. So the young reader must be 'set for diversity.' There is no one skill sequence that will cope with the task.

Reading is an active process of calling up sub-routines in ever-changing sequences to suit the task in hand. When the reader encounters a difficulty with some higher-order sequences he must be able to go back to the sub-routine in the sequence for more detailed analysis.

Only the learner can construct these action sequences. He can learn by using observed behaviours as a model. He can construct his complex behaviour from many experiences with models. He can be supported and encouraged to try and be rewarded for trying. He must, however, construct and co-ordinate the sequences. As Smith (1978) says, we merely give the child the problem; he must work out how to solve it.

Bruner's description of the learning of skilled sequences of action tells us that children have been controlling sequential behaviours from infancy. They have been practising putting constituent acts together in play and in day-to-day activities to achieve their intentions. In play they have had the opportunity to use the signals of feed-forward, feedback and knowledge of results processes, that trio of processes that control sequential actions.

From this theory of skilled action we may conclude that it will help the young reader to construct these action sequences if he is encouraged to initiate behaviour for himself.

Although the novice may know only a very few words, as long as he controls the movement pattern of one-to-one correspondence, he has created for himself new opportunities to learn. He then creates his own exposure to self-improving opportunities and activities. Each word he says is matched to each pattern of black marks separated by a white space and every now and then his eye can check that what is said coincides with a remembered word, a word in that very limited reading vocabulary of 10 or so words that he knows. The word by word technique enables him to check that his voice is saying the right word at those points where he knows a particular word pattern. In the following example he may know 'Father' and 'car' and may be content to render it this way.

Child: *Father goes to his car.*
Text: Father is   in the car.

The child is aware that the visual and vocal experiences match within the limits of his current knowledge.

Hard on the heels of such controlled, serially ordered achievement, something happens. Bruner wrote:

Here we come to a puzzle. Once the act is successfully executed and repeated with success and the constituents are put stably into proper serial order, there often appears a sharp alteration of the structure of the act used for achieving an intended outcome . . . There appears to be a re-organization of components.

(Bruner, 1974)

The new act that has been mastered soon becomes merely a sub-routine of a higher-order action. The mastering of sub-routines reduces the attention needed to regulate them so that they can be incorporated into a higher-order, longer sequence act.

Skilled action, then, may be conceived of as the construction of serially ordered constitutional acts, whose performance is modified towards less variability, more anticipation, and greater economy by benefit of feed-forward, feedback and knowledge of results.

(Bruner, 1974)

That quote seems to me like an excellent description of what happens as young learners read and write, and one which teachers could recognize as such.

The child succeeds in these serially ordered tasks if he:

- is encouraged to venture, to try
- is rewarded for trying to act on his own

- is sustained through the formative and less accurate stages of early learning
- comes to select more useful rather than less useful behaviours with the help of the teacher who gives feedback on results and knowledge of results when he is still unable to gain this for himself.

Such learning applied to reading takes some children only a short time. It takes the average child nearly six months to establish consistency in this behaviour. Observation suggests that when the method of teaching reading allows the young child to use his knowledge of the world and of language to read simple little stories for meaning, the child has a chance to establish control over the important concepts, terms, serial order, hierarchical order and position terms, and the switching of attention within and between sources of information, without losing that meaning that allows him to surge ahead once he can control and manipulate these sub-routines. Two important steps towards this are control over the directional schema, the 'left to right return down left' movements, and a left to right survey within and across words.

In Summary

A framework for attention to serial and hierarchical order

Good readers seem to learn a pattern of movements for the visual scanning of print. They must act within the constraints on movement imposed by our arbitrary ways of writing down our language. Children who learn to read from one-line sentences or captions acquire the left to right movement. Later they become able to scan two or three lines of print. Into this general pattern they build the ability to search visually word by word in sequence and later still the ability to search letter by letter or cluster by cluster but still in sequence. During the acquisition stage, directional learning can be seriously disturbed by recurrent error. Its stability is also temporarily shaken when the child tries to integrate new learning into the old schema (new letter features, punctuation, sentences running on to the next line).

Evidence of the timing of such learning was provided in a longitudinal study of 100 children and test scores on these directional variables were highly correlated with reading attainment one, two and three years after school entry (Clay, 1982). Because for most children it is not difficult learning, the attention I have paid to it may seem to stress it unduly. However, this is not so, if the aim of teachers is to both understand the learning involved in literacy acquisition and reduce learning failure.

This directional learning (and all the sequential attention needed to process information that will be part of this learning) is basic to successful and efficient reading. It is not in any sense sufficient, as later chapters will argue.

It is therefore important for the teacher to check on the control children are gaining over three things:

Check on directional movement

Check on movement across print. It can be done easily and frequently by asking the child to 'read with your finger.' Only a few will be reluctant. Note that this is being asked for only to reveal or externalize what the child is attending to. We need a situation which will externalize what the child does spontaneously and naturally when faced with printed text to help the teacher understand where the child is in his learning.

... And one-to-one correspondence

This provides the information that, within the directional schema, the child can locate words one after the other.

... And some notion of a hierarchy of information

This provides the information that the child has some primitive awareness that letters make up new wholes called words, and words make up new wholes called messages or sentences.

7 Attention to Concepts About Print

In learning to read a child must develop a clear understanding of:

- basic concepts such as a letter, word, sound, drawing, writing and reading
- hierarchical concepts such as collections of letters which make up words, and collections of words which make up sentences
- terms for position like first and last, beginning or start and end, and next, when they apply within the directional constraints of the printer's code.

Teachers cannot assume that beginning readers can isolate for attention the things the labels refer to. If they cannot and the teacher uses the terms without checking the teaching-learning interaction goes astray.

Hazel Francis (1971, 1973) confirmed Reid's (1966) and Downing's (1970) findings. She wished to trace the children's comprehension of terms teachers would use during instruction and their abilities to identify units in written and spoken language. Her study was longitudinal as she followed the same 50 children from 5:9 to 7:3. Children learned the concept of letter before word and word before sentence in her study, the two latter concepts being mastered *while the children were already reading* and derived from their experiences with written language. To the question 'What do we use words (sentences) for?' almost no child indicated an awareness of the use of words or sentences in spoken language.

The Individual Child's Attention in Small Group Instruction

Let me illustrate the problems that the very young reader has in locating what he should be attending to in the visual array.

Suppose a teacher has placed an attractive picture on the wall and has asked her children for a story which she will record under it. They offer the text 'Mother is cooking' which the teacher alters slightly to introduce some features she wishes to teach. She writes,

> Mother said,
> 'I am baking.'

If the teacher then says, 'Now look at our story,' 30 percent of her new entrant class will attend to the picture.

If she says, 'Look at the words and find some you know,' between 50 and 90 percent will be searching for letters. If she says 'Can you see Mother?' most will agree that they can but some will see her in the picture, some will locate 'M' and others will locate the word 'Mother.'

Perhaps the children read in unison 'Mother is . . .' and the teacher tries to sort this out. Pointing to 'said' she asks, 'Does this say "is"?' Half the children agree because it has 's' in it. 'What letter does it start with?' asks the teacher. Now she is really in trouble. She assumes the children know that a word is built out of letters but 50 percent do not and still confuse 'letter' and 'word' labels after six months at school. She also assumes that the children know that the left-hand letter following a space is the 'start' of a word but often they do not. She says, 'Look at the first letter. It says s-s-s-s' and her pupils make s-noises. But Johnny who knows only 'Mother' and 'I' scans the text haphazardly for something relevant, sights the comma and makes s-noises!

The teacher continues with this very short text. 'What do you think Mother said? Look at the next word and tell me what it says.' That should be easy because most children learn 'I' early but for a child who does not know the difference between a letter and a word 'the next word' will often be the next letter in 'said.' For other children who have not established left to right movement with return sweep the next word may be 'gnikab' because they are returning right to left along the second line. Still others may be conscientiously striving to decode the commas or the inverted commas before they get to 'I.'

The lesson continues and the class makes a final unison statement 'Mother said, I am cooking.' Many have focussed on the quaint letter 'k' in the middle. The teacher says, 'Does it say cooking? Look carefully. Look at the beginning. Tell me what the first letter says.' Many children may not locate the first letter. 'Does it say c-c-c-c?' Children with a budding awareness of the phonemic identity of 'k' agree heartily and they are half-right. The teacher now has reached the new information for which she designed her lesson. 'It says b-b-b-b- for baking.' Some of the children are surprised to hear that the 'k' they are focussing on says 'b' and others gain the impression that 'baking' says 'b.'

An earnest child may be found re-reading the story to himself later in the day. Matching the number of word impulses he says with the number of word patterns he sees, we might hear him read 'Mother is cooking some cakes,' and he could be very satisfied with his effort.

One could protest that if a good teacher was aware of such difficulties and was carefully pointing to the letters and words as she spoke, much of the confusion would be eliminated. That assumes rather too much of group instruction. Children are at different starting points and what is controlling their attention is hidden from our view. If the teacher examines the things she says to her class, to small groups, and to individual children she may find that she takes for granted insights which some children do not have. It was discovered that learning these concepts takes place slowly over the first year at school (Reid, 1966; Downing, 1970; Clay, 1979).

Young children lack a consciously analytic approach to speech. The use by this teacher of the words 'letter, word, sentence' was not so much an aid to her pupils' learning as it was a challenge to find out their meanings. Some children could do that; others could not.

New Zealand teachers used a set of masking cards of different sizes in their small group teaching to occasionally help children to isolate and emphasize some examples of these elements in print. The masking cards help children to segment the flow of print, isolating words and letters and locating positions like first, last, beginning and end, and the more important punctuation markers (Holdaway, 1979). The concept and function of spaces between words also has to be learned. While the message in the text was always the goal in the activity, attending to parts of the text is acceptable, *temporarily, in the service of that goal.*

There is least room for confusion when the teacher asks a child about words which occur at the beginning of lines and letters which occur at the beginning of those words. First words and first letters are complex concepts because they demand the understanding of two things at the same time, 'letter' or 'word' and 'first.' Only when the directional schema is in place does the left end of the word become a likely guess. Final words and final letters will be easier than detail embedded in the middle of a sentence, but less useful than the first letters and first words.

The puzzle in finding a word is to 'detach' that word from the whole utterance. Spaces in print help the child to segment the aural flow of words in his speech. The two sources of information reinforce each other, but first the convention and use of the space has to be learned.

A similar but even harder task in segmentation relates to sounds. As a learning task this should probably follow after the child can effectively locate word units in what he says, but need not be delayed long for the linguistically able child. Listening for first sounds in words can then be related to segmenting first letters in print.

It is not self-evident to a child that left to right movement along a line, through a book, and across a word are related. (It is not even self-evident to all teachers.) Telling the child that they are will not be sufficient. It is only through working with print, writing his own stories, reading and discovering things about printed texts, that he slowly consolidates the total network of relationships. For most children there is a gradual improvement with experience. On the other hand persisting confusions work against the teacher at every lesson, introducing noise or static into a process that should have a clear communication channel. These concepts could be mastered at the early reading stage with appropriate tuition on the simplest line of print.

An example of the simplicity of this learning can be given. Peter learns to read and write an idea down. 'Peter is here,' is his text. If his mind is working actively upon this experience he can learn these things.

Peter is here

'P' is important for my name but it is also for Paul.
(There is a need to choose between words)

Some more signs are needed. 'Peter' is not long enough.
(There is a special pattern of signs)
(Signs can recur)

'Is' is a little pattern.
'Here' is a longer pattern.
(Size of pattern can be a cue)

'Here' is like Peter but it is different, too.
(Perhaps order is important)

'P' is the first letter.
(First letter at left end)

Research has shown that children make gross discriminations before fine ones. They notice things about page layout before they notice features of words. Letter detail is noticed later still but letters near spaces, first and last, are easier to analyse than those buried in the middle of words. The order of discrimination is roughly illustrated by Catherine's attempt to write her own name.

Features of page layout	Yes, horizontal
Features of pattern	Yes, long and recurring letters
Word	Yes
First and last letters	Yes
First and last clusters	No ⟶ Catherine
Letters in the middle of words	No

Even a change in word size or in its horizontal or vertical plane can be confusing to the young learner. Simon's mother wrote in a diary when he was 5:6:

> *Stood looking at Father's truck for some time then asked if the large printed word 'SERVICE' on the side was the same as the smaller printed word on the front. He was correct.*

Each Book has its Particular Difficulties

In order to explore the development of directional behaviour the teacher must make herself aware of the order in which her preferred texts introduce difficulties of these kinds. This usually means an increase of one to two to three lines, and any unusual arrangements of texts on the page. The teacher should be aware that until children gain control over the directional schema it is easy for visual features of the text (such as colour, illustration, ornament, or print over illustrations) to draw his attention to different starting points. Even the size of the white spaces may make him suddenly reverse his directional approach or start at the bottom of a page.

Teachers should check the early reading books that they present to children and make sure that when a new problem is introduced they carry out preparation for it. The teacher should give the children a slow deliberate demonstration of the movements needed so that all children 'get the feel of it.' She should be careful to place her body, book and arm in the same place or orientation that the children will use, otherwise as a model she may confuse them.

Teachers will know from experience how the characteristics of layout and format in early reading books direct attention of some children away from the print or make it difficult for the child to find a starting point. Distractions do not bother the competent child. It is the child who is unsure who can be confused in his code-breaking attempts by the visual gimmicks which authors and publishers could avoid at least in the first stages of learning to read. Teacher-made books can be planned to challenge a particular child working on his particular concept problem.

Finding Out What Children Know

To read English it is necessary to move from left to right along a line and to return down left for the beginning of the following line. It is also necessary to read a left page before a right page and to proceed left to right along a word if the sound sequence is to match something one has heard before. This seems self-evident.

The child's movements have hitherto been unconstrained with respect to direction, and on entry to school he has to learn to relate himself (his whole body), two eyes (together), two hands (separately) to a page of print which has directional constraints. He must learn that it is made up of lines (which have direction), made up of words (which have direction), made up of letters (which have fixed orientation), consisting of particular strokes and angles.

The child who learns to read with a language-experience approach to natural language texts, works down through that hierarchy (analytically) as he learns to read his books, and up through the hierarchy (synthetically) as he learns to write stories.

After a fairly consistent habit is established the young learner is still very easily thrown by new problems, new format, and other factors that can enter into the reading situation. A teacher may emphasize something the child does not understand. Because his directional habits are new they are easily thrown and lapses in his directional behaviour will be noticed from time to time. It is not easy to maintain consistency in the hierarchical behaviour of looking at letters within words, within lines, and down a page. So the child has, for the first year or two of learning to read and write, to continually exercise control over a tendency to move in other directions. The teacher will have made a significant contribution to the minimizing of problems in the shortest time possible if she can be sure that directional behaviour is established with some consistency at this early learning stage.

Any child who has been in instruction for six months and is still confused about direction needs special attention, otherwise he may continue to confuse himself by responding with an inappropriate directional pattern as often as he does with a correct one. By practising inappropriate directional behaviour he is learning a habit that will be difficult to overcome.

At six years, from 4 percent to 16 percent of children still show directional errors when asked to 'read it with your finger.' They require immediate, special and individual attention to this problem without further delay.

If one is a young child, the learning of an arbitrary directional convention for approaching written language may be a matter of movement or placement of one's body relative to the visual field. There is a motor component to the learning. If the approach is made by eye scanning movements only, it is still a motor activity though less easy to observe. Eventually it becomes a brain scan so that during a fixation of the eyes sequential attentional scanning without apparent movement gives little sign of the motor activity which was probably necessary during the acquisition stage.

As the child addresses the open book his first orientation is that of placing himself (or his body) in the right position to get the messages from the text. He must locate a starting position and move in a left to right direction. If the text has more than one line he must learn about the return sweep action. These adaptations involve the movements of his head and pointing with the hand. Later this movement sequence becomes an efficient habit as the brain directs attention, giving little indication of the movements that were needed to acquire it in the first place. This development will be discussed in chapters 5, 6 and 12.

How can we find out simply and reliably what young children know about how language is written down? Why is this knowledge important? Educators in several countries have asked these questions in different languages and have given different explanations.

Observing Control Over Print With CAP

I was watching a five year old try to read a simple caption book. It was 1963 and I was doing the pretests for a research project. I wrote down everything the child did and said. After thinking a great deal about what I saw I took three caption books of identical format, devised some tasks that children of this age might do with such a book, and even undid the staples and turned some text and pictures upside down. I tried the new tasks on other five year olds and then refined them, using an extensive background of testing preschool children and a knowledge of what makes good and bad items in test construction as a guide. The task looked promising. Educators in the United States, Brazil, Germany, Denmark, and Israel have more recently explored this instrument in a number of ways.

Concepts About Print or CAP (Clay, 1985) has 24 items administered individually in about five to 10 minutes. The test booklet is a little story told with a picture on one page and a text on the other. The story *is read to* the child (a requirement not to be overlooked) and the child is asked to help the tester. Some of the concepts it explores are whether the child knows the front of the book, that print and not picture tells the story, what a letter is, what a word is, where the first letter in a word is to be found, pairs of upper and lower case letters, and some of the punctuation marks.

Five and six year old children have some fun and little difficulty with the form of this observation instrument. It can be used with new entrants and non-readers. It can show individual differences and how well-prepared children are for a particular instructional programme. It points the way to instruction for particular children, and it is a way of recording how the child behaves towards print before, during and after the first year of instruction. After that it is of less use except for problem readers. Their confusions about these arbitrary conventions of our written language code need early attention.

There are two forms of the CAP. If a child is to be assessed over short intervals of time, memory for what happened in the previous testing period may determine later responses, so good measurement procedures require parallel forms of a test to overcome this. The first story, *Sand*, written for children in an island country, was about a little boy digging holes in the sand and watching the sea flow in. This proved highly inappropriate for children who rarely if ever saw the sea because they lived in large cities or remote parts of continents. I searched for a more universal theme to meet this cultural objection. *Stones* was the result and in that story the little girl climbs a hill, kicks a stone, and watches it roll into a pool of water. That parallel form was the first adaptation of the CAP. I had to write a new text which was, item by item, able to test precisely the same things as *Sand*. As the *text* contains the *tasks* this was a challenge.

What Does CAP Capture?

Conventions for recording languages differ. Some languages use other scripts (Chinese or Hebrew), some use other signals (like the question mark upside down in Spanish) and the directional conventions may differ (moving right to left or from the back of the book to the front). Such recording conventions determine what follows what, and the young reader has to learn to control the temporal sequencing of attention according to these arbitrary conventions.

What is the child attending to? and in what order? If the child is attending to pages in the wrong order, to text on the page in the wrong order, to a word when he needs a letter, or to the back end of a word when he needs the front end, then it will be difficult for that child to profit from what the teacher is talking to him about. These orienting behaviours are learned over a period of time. When teachers explain things to children they cannot assume that their words have taught the child's eyes and brain to locate, recognize or use this information. There may be many reasons why children find these orienting behaviours difficult—reasons that are conceptual, linguistic, or due to lack of opportunity to learn. The emergence of this control over attention is what CAP tries to capture.

The orienting behaviours have:

- a movement-in-space or motor component
- a visual perception or looking component, and
- a mental or cognitive component.

The important question is, to what is the brain tuned? When children are young and printed language is new to them they are only vaguely aware of some features in print and they shift from vague awareness to clear understanding and even verbal manipulation as their control over print is strengthened. Then children get the items right and they come to know why they are right and they can check their decisions in more than one way. They have verbal, visual, motor and order information about CAP items. When asked how he knows he is right the competent child after a year or more of learning may be able to answer:

- because you make it this way (motor)
- because big M has points not tunnels (visual)
- because you need more letters to make a word (verbal)
- that's 'no' but if you start with 'o' it's another word that I don't know (information about order).

School entrants will test low on these tasks and will increase their scores to near perfect performance as they become readers and writers.

CAP works well as an observation instrument used by teachers to find out what children are attending to, whether progress is occurring, and what action should be taken to help the child. CAP was not intended as a test of 'readiness.' *It was not designed to predict reading progress or to measure readiness or metalinguistic awareness.* CAP gives teachers information about what the child is attending to at the time when instruction begins to create links between oral language and written language. Teachers use it to monitor progress and guide teaching.

The stories of *Sand* and *Stones* work fairly well in most English-speaking countries.

Changes for Other Cultures and Languages

Most of the trials of CAP have been with children raised in literate and print-rich environments and most were taught on entry to school in their home language. Neither of these things were true in Papua New Guinea where CAP was used in a research study with children learning English at school. Delightful redrawing of the illustration for *Stones* ensured that the children engaged with the task, and the story worked quite well in this cultural translation even though the text was still in English. Moore (1981) showed that these children did learn some of these concepts in the first two years at school but that even at the beginning of sixth grade a proportion of these pupils continued to produce errors in their understanding of first and last, and letter and word. In the years between, some of the instruction must have seemed very puzzling to those pupils. This is a clear example of where the application of a 'test' would be culturally inappropriate but CAP's value for guiding instruction could be great.

Cataldi and Nicholls translated *Stones* into Walpiri, the home language of children at Lajaman School in Katherine in the Northern Territory of Australia. Walpiri is one of many Aboriginal languages and it is the instructional language up to Grade 4 level. To readers of English the long Walpiri words look difficult. These researcher-teachers made the following changes.

1 The illustrations of the main character were changed to look more like a Walpiri child but the background landscape did not need redrawing.

2 As the Walpiri language does not depend on word order for subject/object definition substitute items were needed for the English items which changed the order of words.

Cataldi wrote, 'The children come from an oral culture and their difficulties are often not precisely explicable. If the school does not teach reading precisely (and avoid confusing the children) nothing in the environment will make up for it. A Walpiri child at Lajaman cannot learn to read outside the school.'

The common factor for these very different groups from Papua New Guinea and Northern Australia is that the children were growing up in an oral society with little opportunity to read outside of school. The use of CAP to monitor early learning is appropriate, either in the mother tongue or in the second language.

Translating the CAP means translating *the tasks, the tests, and the instructions*. Any one of these three aspects of translation may affect the difficulty of one or more items. Rodriguez (1984) used a panel of experts to assess her Mexican-Spanish version of CAP, produced to allow for dialect differences in the southwest region of Texas, for:

- the accuracy of the language translation
- the accuracy of the translation of the CAP tasks, and
- appropriateness of the instructions and texts for the culture group studied.

Iturrondo (1985) used a Puerto Rican-Spanish version of *Sand* (*Arena*) for pretest and *Stones* (*Piedras*) as post-test in a study which explored the possible relationship between story reading and the emerging knowledge of printed Spanish for a group of lower class preschool children (N=124). She matched two groups of children on CAP scores and then one group was exposed to story reading at least three times a week during four months. There was a significant difference in CAP scores at the end of the special programme in favour of children who heard the stories.

Rodriguez evaluated four versions of CAP with Mexican-American children using English directions with English print, Spanish directions with English print, Spanish directions with Spanish print and English directions with Spanish print. Her results showed the importance of the instructions. The children with the low English language scores performed better on CAP when the instructions were in Spanish whether the text was in English or Spanish, and lower when the tasks were given with English instructions. Children whose English was average or better, performed equally well in any of the four conditions. The author concluded that the concepts may be the same in English or Spanish versions *once the children understand the instructions*.

Only minor changes to the texts were necessary for both these Spanish versions, and no changes to the pictures were made. The books were easy to use with the preschoolers and the instrument seemed to be suitable for the purpose. If the two authors of the Spanish CAP's are correct in their judgements about dialectal differences for the two populations and linguists agree with them, then the need for different dialect versions for some language groups may be appropriate.

Children in the United States and Denmark were compared in a cross-cultural study by Schmidt (1982). The CAP was used in its designed form in translation. As preschoolers and after one year at school, children from the two countries scored at similar levels. However, between six and seven years children in the United States were in school and Danish children were not. Marked differences emerged at that time as a consequence of instruction. The differences disappeared after the Danish children had completed their first year of school.

Reliable Observations of Change

A reliable observation technique which teachers could use to monitor children's progress throughout the first year of school to assure themselves that change in learning was occurring would have the qualities of a good measurement device, i.e. the qualities of a good test. It would give a score which did not change much in a short period of time, but would validly record changes occurring in type, quality or level of behaviours measured.

CAP was shown in research studies to have the qualities of a good test. Firstly, it captured shifts in book behaviour that change rather rapidly over the first year or two at school. Secondly, the items used discriminated quite well. Thirdly, it had a good range for use from preschool children through to high progress readers after a year at school. Reliability coefficients have ranged from 0.73 to 0.95 (Johns, 1980; Day and Day, 1980; Clay, 1985). Correlations with reading progress have ranged from 0.63 to 0.69. Johns (1983) found significant differences among above-average, average and below-average first grade readers in the United States, and analyses of individual items revealed above-average readers superior to below-average readers on print-direction concepts, letter-word concepts, and advanced print concepts.

Designing CAP for Visually Impaired Children

An innovative modification of CAP was the development of a Concepts About Braille test (Tompkins and McGee, 1984). Sighted children are immersed in a world of written language as preschoolers but visually impaired children may have little experience with braille prior to schooling and may begin formal reading instruction without awareness of the functions and processes of reading. How could blind children be tested? The braille version was constructed to match closely CAP's 24 items and add four new items to check concepts specific to reading braille—three related to hand movement and one to identifying a whole word sign. Pictures were replaced with common household objects which had strong tactile qualities and a new text was written around these objects. The order of the items was changed, but special care was taken to retain the type and difficulty of the psychological task involved. It was necessary to avoid braille words with abbreviations within them for test items, and to choose reversible braille characters in place of reversible print letters. The reconstructed test was typed in Grade 2 Standard English Braille.

The progress of visually impaired children was compared with sighted children. Low scores at the end of kindergarten increased over first and second grade with the largest gains occurring in first grade. They took longer than sighted children to learn to perform the items and continued to improve their scores up through the primary grades. The pattern of overall development seemed to be similar in the two groups and the lag in learning could be related to lack of prior experience on entry to school (Tompkins and McGee, 1984).

What Theory Does CAP Support?

Readiness theory

When a strong relationship of CAP with the Metropolitan Readiness Test was found (Day and Day, 1980), this tagged CAP with the label 'a readiness measure,' although those authors concluded that it involved knowledge that could be acquired while learning to read (which the Danish-American comparison supported). Day and Day showed that kindergarten children in the United States had widely differing scores on CAP at the beginning of the school year and changed markedly over that kindergarten year in a programme without reading instruction. They concluded in a conference paper presented on this study, 'One could suppose that when they enter first grade and begin formal reading instruction these children will be on different cognitive levels.'

Linguistic awareness

Mattingly (1979, 1984) described the process by which children develop knowledge about the nature of their own language which he called 'linguistic awareness.' Others have included reading in this concept. More recently authors have used or discussed concepts about print as if it measured metacognitive awareness. As author I have reservations about the usefulness of CAP for answering theoretical questions in any of these areas.

Cognitive clarity

Downing and Leong (1982) proposed that children approach reading instruction in a normal state of confusion, and under reasonable conditions of instruction they work their way out of confusion into cognitive clarity. (This seems a negative way to describe the competencies of preschoolers.) They maintained that learning to read consists of rediscovering the functions and the coding rules of the writing system. The rediscovery depends on linguistic awareness of features of communication and language.

According to Downing's theory, cognitive confusion continues to arise throughout later stages of education as new subskills are added to the student's repertoire.

The theory about language of instruction

Those who have explored what children know about books by asking questions like 'What is reading?' and 'What is a word?' (Reid 1966; Downing, 1970, 1971; Dalgren and Olsson, 1986) have placed considerable emphasis on when the child can comment on the code and discuss it with the teacher. That state is, in my opinion, the end of a long set of learning about print, not the beginning.

CAP or some similar instrument with strong measurement qualities may appear to confirm several different theoretical formulations but this confuses rather than clarifies our attempts to explain what children are learning. What is needed is some psychological rationale for linking any two or more of these theories. However, CAP scores do provide a useful marker of progress for practising teachers.

Getting the brain's attention to Concepts About Print

I put a book into children's hands and as I read it I asked them to do something, to act. Most of the responses required by the CAP test are nonverbal ones to show what a child *does* with a book, not what he says about it. I assume that what is facilitating in learning to read is knowing where to attend, in what sequence, and how to pick up information perceptually. While this involves cognitive activity of a kind it does not mean that children have to deal with the problem using words.

CAP is like a screen on to which is projected the immaturity or control of a child's way of responding. It captures the child's tentative responses to books. The observation of these immature beginnings makes a vast difference to teachers because what they must do in the absence of these tentative responses is different from what they must do if the child demonstrates the behaviours.

When the child attends with hands or eyes, this behaviour may be temporarily brought to a level of conscious manipulation by teaching, and this may or may not induce a new shift in the child's concept or theory. The child is the creator of awareness, not the teacher. The child works at analysing print in such a way that the cues from various sources agree. In that analysis the child pays close attention, tries new responses, notices new features, puzzles over these, and thinks he understands. He may change his new theory within a day or so as new encounters uncover previously unseen features. Thus the route to awareness lies within the learner and the actions taken by the learner. It does not depend upon the teacher's words or the terminology of instruction. Because a child acts he comes to know he is acting and what he is acting on. He needs support and opportunity to become increasingly independent. As he reads he creates occasions for noticing more things about print. His discrimination of new features may be facilitated or retarded by the teacher.

In Summary

Children learn to read in a variety of widely differing instructional programmes. They start at different ages in cultures which have different expectations. The set of behaviours needed to profit from instruction will depend on the expectation in the culture, the age of entry to school, and the emphases in the programme.

Perhaps the visual attention processes directed to features of print before the child can read is the common factor in its contribution to several different theories. The child may have come to these attentional processes by a number of different routes. If that is so the information to be gained from CAP relates to some starting points in the slow process of shifting from vague awareness to conscious manipulation of concepts about print.

Full understanding of the language of instruction or cognitive clarity about written language are a long way down the track for the child. Linguistic awareness is a much more complicated variable than CAP can measure. It is, however, important for educators to get some control over a starting point in such an elusive process. Attending to features of print and discovering the rules of order and sequence are two such starting points. The teaching trick at first is to teach these things nonverbally rather than with explanations, to have the child sure in using them before he has to learn to talk about them. Then there is something on which to build his metacognitive awareness, should this be necessary.

PART THREE

Interacting with Beginning Reading Books

8 Problem-solving Using Information of More Than One Kind

Gaining a working control over printed language can be described as involving four sets of behaviours each governed by serial order—visual attention to print, directional behaviours relating to position and movement, talking like a book, and hearing sounds in sequences of language. As the child 'reads' his first books the teacher may observe his progressive gains in these four areas, record examples of skills as they appear over a period of three to four weeks, or test the child from time to time on tasks designed to reveal his achievements.

What the teachers can observe are the overt behaviours. From these they infer things about covert strategies or operations which the children are carrying out in their heads. If teachers observe the overt behaviours carefully they are more likely to make helpful assumptions about how the covert behaviours are operating.

Teachers also need some theory of these covert processes to guide their thinking, but it should be a tentative theory that does not lead them to overlook important behaviours when they occur, or to misinterpret them, or to deny their existence.

To read, a child has to make a time-space transformation. Sound patterns which follow one another in time have to be matched to letter symbol patterns spread out into space. The integration of skills cannot occur as long as the child is happily inventing text rather than reading it.

One child read confidently when faced with the text.

Text: So she took it to her nest to make it soft and warm.
Child: *So she took it to her hidey-hole to save it for the winter.*

This child had a great imagination and a feel for the skills required in reading but several important changes needed to occur before she could read.

The Challenge of Serial Order

When Jerome Bruner (1974) wrote that 'the study of skill acquisition must take into account the serial structure of acts' he was referring to the behaviour of infants but he could have been referring to this stage of learning to read. Children have to learn to control four sets of behaviour, with particular attention to serial order.

1 At every level of language organization serial order is critical—to obtain meaning from the order of words and sentences.

2 We saw in Chapter 6 that directional responses involve the learning of order and sequence in space and have a motor component.

3 Early steps in learning to scan print with the eyes alone require the child's visual attention to the serial order of the survey (Chapters 6 and 7).

4 The reader and writer must distinguish words one from another by their sound sequences (Chapter 4).

The mature reader has learned to control three sets of complex behaviours sequentially so that they can be executed slowly with full attention (as in an experiment), or smoothly and carefully (as in reading a legal document) or rapidly and automatically (as in most daily reading) giving full attention to the fourth area, the sequence of meaning. Controlling sequential behaviour is just as much a feature of learning to read as it is of learning to play a violin. Some children encounter difficulties in one or more of these fundamental areas of learning about serial order, and all children have to work hard to make them all operate smoothly in concert.

As soon as they begin to control some behaviours in each of the four areas they begin to co-ordinate across these different kinds of sequences giving evidence of an early integration of skills.

An Action System Which Allows for Decision-making

Observe the ways in which the child attends to print and relates each of these four sets of behaviour, one to the other. This can be called integrating the meaning and sound systems of language with visual analysis controlled by directional constraints. For success in reading all these behaviours must become part of an action system which allows for smooth sequential decision-making as the young reader moves through the messages of continuous text.

To begin reading instruction by teaching letters in isolation is to eliminate the role of serial order altogether and dodge the crucial problem.

To begin reading instruction by teaching children to recognize words in isolation is to exclude the role of sequence in all four behaviour sets—movement, meaning, sound sequences and visual attention—in all but minimal ways.

When the teacher works with a group of school entrants who are ready to discuss a new book together, this relating of one kind of cue to another kind can be encouraged. Any one child may have very few cues to use, but as a group and with the teacher's help they can discover the precise message of the text. A teacher working with a small group and a big book, or wall story, or small blackboard on which a story can be composed, models the integrated behaviours needed for text reading. By what she says, by her directional movements, and by directing attention to visual cues, or language or sounds, she ensures that the children in the group move towards this same goal. The burden on the individual child is less because the teacher scaffolds or structures the difficulty of the task and provides some of the input. This is easier for the individual child because the teacher is directing the process. It will be some time before the individual child can control all these very different behaviours at one time entirely by himself.

The peculiar patterns of children's attempts to match what is said with what is pointed to when reading text can be recorded. Records kept for several weeks would:

- provide a record of progress over that time
- help in evaluation of which kind of text experience the child should have
- allow the observation that sequenced movement across print is smoothly and easily integrated with language responses.

The keeping of such records will help a teacher to become a more sensitive observer of the child's behaviour at this time. (For running records of text reading see Clay, 1985.)

Page-matching

At first a child produces a stretch of speech as he turns a page. This is very noticeable if the book is rather difficult, for example trying to read a familiar nursery rhyme, and a mismatch will occur where the pagination breaks a sentence into two parts.

All the King's horses   Couldn't put Humpty
And all the King's men   Together again.

Learning from books with complex texts is difficult even for the intelligent child. There is much opportunity for error in trying to link what is said to what is written.

Line-matching

In the following examples the child is achieving some measure of co-ordination of language and sequenced movement. The ability to match a line of text left to right with the correct language, locating the beginning and the end of the line, is a valuable achievement. The child realizes that he must match the beginning and the end of what he says even if what happens in the middle is a mystery. One observer noted 'He cannot yet match one word in print to one spoken word but he likes to arrive at the last word on time and is confused if he doesn't.' (In the following examples x equals the number of points.)

Text: Mother is knitting.
Child: *Mother is knitting.*
Finger: xx   xx

There are many ways of dealing with the mystery and children try most of them.

Text: My baby brother.   Text: My baby brother.
Child: *My ba–by*   Child: *My little ba–by*
Finger: x   x   x   Finger: x   x   x   x

The next example seems to be based on attention to letters yet achieves an appropriate sequencing of responses.

Text: Father is smiling.
Child: *Father is smiling.*
Finger: x   x x

The child is not clear what his problem is and his record may show many of these difficulties at the same time, as the next examples show.

Letter-word confusions and syllabic breaks

Text: My big brother.
Child: *My brother –*
Finger: x   x   x

Two responses per word or two words per response

Text: My big sister.
Child: *My big sis–ter*
Finger: x   x   x   x

Correct word reading and syllabic breaks

Texts: The children are here.
Child: *The child–ren are here.*
Finger: x   x   x   x   x

Talking without pointing and then matching

Text: My big sister.
Child: *This is my big sister.*
Finger: x   x   x

Word by word

Text: Here is the dog.
Child: *This is a dog.*
Finger: x x   x   x

Matching a spoken sentence to a single line of print is relatively easy. The beginning of the line is located and a left to right sweep accounts for the rest. Rhythm helps and the repetitive language structures in some caption books facilitate this learning. One-line captions which began towards the top-left corner of a left page would create a correct 'position habit' for the directional movements required in reading. The child of four to six years adopts position habits very easily and a consistent top-left starting point is therefore preferable to flexibility of layout *until the child is able to use correct directional habits consistently*.

Examples of layout

Good   **Bad**

I am running	

	I am running

He is going to the shop	

	He is going to the shop

Mother has a red dress	and a hat and shoes

Mother	and a hat
has a red dress	and shoes

Effects of Layout

If the author slips in a two- or three- line text into the child's experience when all he has read previously has been one-line texts he has new problems. When there are several rows of print on a page this is a much more difficult task. In addition to locating the top-left starting point and making a left to right movement there is a return sweep to the next line to be mastered, a further step towards complete mastery of directional learning. A child may fail to respond. More often he will try to solve the mystery of the new situation. The one-line text:

Father is reading the paper

when written on two lines causes these kinds of problems. The meaning of the text may be familiar but the child's problem is the two lines of print. He may only respond to the first line.

	LINE 1		LINE 2
Text:	Father is reading ------------------	the paper.
Child:	*Father is reading the paper* --------	No response
Finger:	x x x x x x	

The second line may be treated in several different ways. He may:

- ignore it
- point to it in silence
- point to the first and speak to the second
- match one or two words and rush the rest
- draw out the last words until his finger reaches the end as in:

	LINE 1	LINE 2
Text:	Father is reading -------------------- the paper.
Child:	*Father is reading the pa* ----------------------- *per.*
Finger:	x x x x x x x

Sometimes the child discovers a match of text and syllables that surprises us.

	LINE 1	LINE 2
Text:	Mother is talking ---------- on the telephone.
Child:	*Mother is talking on the* -------- *tel e phone.*
Finger:	x x x x x x x

This example shows that the child is working on the problem, searching for possible solutions.

Published materials do not have consistency in the layout but a teacher can make sure that her own practice in class-made books is consistent. If there is a choice of readers then an order of preference might be:

- top left start on a left page
- top left to right on one-line captions
- top left to right on two-line captions
- slow introduction of further variability.

Word and Letter Concepts

Early readers must attend to print, scan it, respond, move to another focus point, scan and respond and so on. What visual features do children use and how do they come to match oral language responses to those features?

The experiments of the Russian psychologist Luria linking the co-ordination of motor responding with oral language provide some guide. The motor task he used was simple: the child squeezed a rubber bulb. Luria showed a developmental progression from inability to co-ordinate squeezing and speaking, to co-ordination when the pulse of the message matched the rhythm of the squeezing. He found that by the age of five years a child's motor responding could even be controlled by an instruction which did not have the same pulse as the squeezing action to be made.

The beginning reading task resembles Luria's task where the pulse of language matches the pulse of squeezing—*Go, Go* or *Press, Press*—except that the child must point and visually scan with the added constraint of left to right directional movement. He must:

- break up his produced speech into word units
- locate the visual patterns
- move in the correct direction
- co-ordinate the timing of his pointing and looking with his uttering.

Young children are trying to discover how the flow of speech can be cut into word segments. It is false to assume that the child knows that his oral sentences are composed of word units. He has to discover what the word units of his speech are. He has to break down the 'gimmethe' or 'aspastate' into 'give me the' or 'half past eight' before he can match what he says to the printed text. He learns to break his speech into words separated by pauses and tries to match units in speech to patterns in print. Sometimes he fails to find and match the words:

Text: I see the aeroplane.
Child: *I see the aeroplane go down.*

At other times he over-analyses his speech:

Text: I see the aeroplane go down.
Child: *I see the aer-   o- plane.*

Syllables sometimes confuse him as he matches speech to print. Some children get stranded for a time on the erroneous concept that a letter is a word and this example shows how confusing that might be.

Text: A   b o y.
Child: *This*   *is*   *a* *boy.*

That could teach the child wrong associations if he misreads his favourite book on several occasions and establishes the erroneous habit rather firmly.

If some unusual behaviour of this kind is observed the teacher must try to decide whether it is just a temporary fluctuation or whether the child has been practising it for some weeks. If the child is having difficulty with speech-to-print matching the teacher can increase the size of print and exaggerate the spacing. Exaggerating the spaces between words and between lines helps the child locate himself. At the early reading stage the arrangement of words on the page should force the eye to group letters within words together and detract from the possibility of grouping across a space. Thus, confusion is less likely to occur with:

This is a   boy.

than with

This is a boy.

Locating Specific Words

Although the teaching emphasis may be on the whole line or sentence rather than words, the child soon shows that he is finding recognizable parts in patterns of print in different contexts. When the child knows that a word is a pattern of marks he begins to locate the patterns that he knows. He finds first, last, and repeated words easiest to locate. They are easier for him to 'perceive.' In the text 'Here is a big house' the child may locate the first and last words, 'Here' and 'house.' In the three-line text:

> Here is my mother.
> Here is my sister.
> Here is my father.

the child may only locate 'is' in each line.

The child also locates readily those few words he has learned to write without a copy. If a word like 'this' or 'here', 'is' or 'a' is used correctly when an alternative word would have been just as grammatical, one begins to sense that the child 'knows' that word. Here is a sample of reading behaviour from a girl aged 5:2 who had been at school for two months. An observer reported that she seemed to be using cues in the following order and from the following sources.

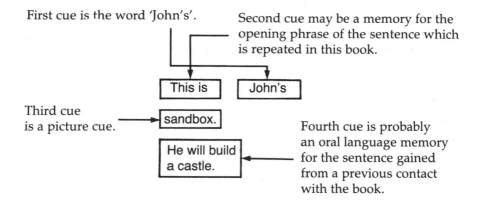

First cue is the word 'John's'.   Second cue may be a memory for the opening phrase of the sentence which is repeated in this book.

This is   John's

Third cue
is a picture cue.   sandbox.

He will build a castle.   Fourth cue is probably an oral language memory for the sentence gained from a previous contact with the book.

Marlene 'read' the caption book correctly but the recorder felt that only one word — 'John's' — was actually read. The probable sources of other cues are shown.

Notice that the child is using both language and visual cues and is relating these to past experience in order to select probable responses.She is entirely successful in repeating the precise message. This is good caption book behaviour. By 6:0 she was in the top 25 percent for reading progress.

Reading the Spaces: A Sign of Progress

When the child can point one after the other and can find the words in his speech, he still has the problem of co-ordinating the two activities, that is, making the motor pattern of his hand coincide with the word-finding activities of his ears and eyes. Would the task be simplified by eliminating the pointing? Probably not. The location of the appropriate visual pattern to be attended to is perhaps a more difficult task than pointing.

One further difficulty has to be overcome. The activities that are integrated must be maintained for a period of time during the lesson. Some children can keep at the activity once it is mastered. Others begin well, tire quickly, and their co-ordination, their locating, and even one-to-one correspondence slips away as fatigue takes over. Sometimes the fall-off of appropriate behaviour depends not on less effort but on distracted attention.

At first, children respond to caption books with the speed and fluency that is typical of their oral speech. As they develop skill in matching spoken words with print, fingers are used to point to those parts of the text that they suspect correspond to what they are saying. Fluency gives way to word by word reading. At that point the child over-emphasizes the breaks between words and points with his finger. *He has taken a major step towards integration of these early learnings when his reading slows down and even becomes staccato.* He may be thought of as 'reading the spaces.' He is demonstrating clearly to the observer the integration of these three sets of behaviour that have been described above.

The Eye Sees Word-space-word	The Voice Says Word-space-word	The Finger Points Word-space-word
Visual attention to print.	Constructing sentences word by word.	Directional rules of position and movement.

Rhythm can help the child to segment his speech and co-ordinate his speaking, pointing and looking.

Here is an example of a child whose letter and word knowledge is very limited but whose awareness of the 'space between words' is emerging.

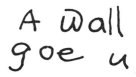

Translation: A ball goes up.

This synchronizing of skills is a high point of achievement in the early reading stage and is not behaviour to be hurriedly trained out.

Examples of Integrated Skills

These children made marks on transparent paper over their text as they read.   One-to-one correspondence of pointing and speech.

ạ bịg bọy ạnd ạ lịţtle bọy

Behaviour co-ordinated by the spaces.

'I ⁄ am ⁄ hungry,' ⁄ said ⁄ Bill.
'I ⁄ am ⁄ hungry,' ⁄ said ⁄ Peter. ⁄

Ann is up
Ann is   u — p

David is up
David is   u — p

Martin is up
Martin is u — u — p

Co-ordination at the beginning and end of lines but uncertainty in the middle.

'Reading the spaces' has been called voice-pointing. Single words are stressed and the spaces are 'heard' as distinct breaks between each word. Then when the child no longer needs to help his eyes by pointing with his finger he will, for a period, continue the voice-pointing.

Voice-pointing can be used as a signal that things are coming together. It should not be taught because it would then have no value as a sign of progress. A child could be taught to read with exaggerated breaks between words merely by listening to and copying a model who did this. We would not know whether the child was using his eyes for locating cues in an appropriate manner.

Developmentally there is usually a gradual transition in good readers from finger-pointing, to staccato reading, to light stress of word breaks, and finally to phrasing. The fast learners make this transition so rapidly that it may hardly be noticed. Slow learners may take several weeks to co-ordinate voice and movement, a further extended period for this to retreat to staccato reading and a slow gradual change to dependence on the eyes alone. If the child has passed through this sequence of behaviour we can be reasonably confident that his visual scanning patterns have become systematically organized for the reading task. On the other hand, children who appear to 'read' fluently may not be visually responding to features in the print in any systematic or precise way.

A search of observation records in one research sample (Clay, 1966) showed that three weeks prior to promotion to a 'real reading' group, 40 percent of the children had begun to exaggerate the breaks between words and a further 9 percent were children who had already passed through the stage of finger- and voice-pointing and were dependent on visual analysis alone. For 49 percent of the sample this learning took place mainly on informal texts before children were trying to read books.

One group of children had particular difficulty with the integration learning. Those children who typically reacted quickly and spoke quickly were sometimes unable to slow their movements across print to a pace which permitted the very necessary matching of speech to visual patterns. After seven months at school, one boy's record read like this.

> *Began the first page slowly matching correctly, but then speeded up, dropped pointing and invented the text with only approximate line-matching. Asked to point to what he reads he can for a brief period slow down but then races ahead and drops the movement and matching component out of the reading task.*

The aurally-oriented child whose visual attention is hard to control has difficulty discovering the 'match' between his language and the printed text. Sometimes the co-ordination is difficult because of motor inadequacies. One record carried the observation 'Pointing seems to be the stumbling block.' As long as the child cannot locate the word he is saying in the line of print, he will remain a non-reader. One week a boy's record carried the comment 'speech is far too fast for locating words.' The following week the boy complained,

> 'I can't keep up with the words with my hands.
> They're too fast' (i.e. his own speech!)

In contrast the observer's comments on a child who was succeeding with this early integration of skills were 'Word-controlled, voice-pointing, perfect matching.'

Word by Word Reading and Pointing

When are these behaviours appropriate and when do they indicate a problem? In the longitudinal, weekly records of children who succeeded in learning to read, these behaviours were present. Both pointing and word reading were useful for the beginning reader who was taught by a language experience approach. Part of the learner's task under these instruction conditions is to isolate word units in his speech and in the printed text, and match the two.

However, research studies of children who fail in learning to read suggest that the children read word by word, that they point with their fingers and that these behaviours should be eliminated at the outset and avoided. The implication is that they cause the reading failure.

Careful observation of children who are learning to read has shown that as the child makes the transfer from pre-reading books to reading books and for some variable time after that it is appropriate for the child to strengthen his locating behaviour by pointing with his hand or his voice. Once he has established accurate locating responses with his eyes alone there is reason to discard the finger pointing and to step up the demand for fluency. Word by word reading is not to be hurriedly trained out unless the teacher is certain that the child is visually locating the words he is saying. In my early research some slower children were deprived of the very props they had spontaneously discovered because teachers forbade them to use their fingers or insisted that they use only a card as a guide to the line being read.

During Transitions

Procedures that are questioned like pointing and word by word reading, memorizing the text or depending on picture cues are techniques that can be approved as long as they facilitate the development of new insights. By implication, since they are props rather than techniques to be retained in the mature behaviour system, they must at some point give way to better responses. Pointing gives way to accurate visual locating, auditory memory for text gives way to visual memory for form, word by word reading gives way to phrasing and anticipation of sentence structure, picture cues give way to semantic and linguistic cues and letter-sound relationships. It is the direction that development is taking that is vital, not the questionable procedure itself.

The persistence or reappearance of behaviour like this long after the developmental transitions should have been made may be regarded as diagnostic signs that the task is in some new sense difficult and integration of these behaviours is breaking down.

Search, Check and Error Correction

In research records of book reading behaviour, when a child was trying to read he sometimes rejected an error response and tried again. Such spontaneous self-correction was very important for reading progress.

Earlier we saw that a child not yet matching his speech and visual behaviour might be content to read 'aeroplane go down' for 'aeroplane' and not know he has made an error. A child may be vaguely aware that an error has occurred. When he can 'read the spaces' and match what he says accurately with the word patterns of his text he has several new means of detecting errors.

The Finger Signals Error

The child sometimes finds that he has more speech patterns than word patterns. 'There's no more words,' he exclaims and corrects himself.

Child: *I like my Father* (Self-corrected)
Text: My Father

If he over-analyses his speech he is then one visual pattern short in the line.

Child: *I am a pi–lot.*
Text: I am a pilot.

If he hesitates and tries again, if he reconstitutes his speech response to make it fit, a self-correction strategy is beginning to form. The child who learns to take self-correcting action because the sources of information do not match has made another big advance. This powerful reading strategy is available because the child has met the challenge of sequencing.

The Eye Signals Error

A child may utter a sentence which is semantically and syntactically possible but which is incongruous with the picture. This leads him to rephrase his sentence. Visual cues enter into the self-correction process.

Child: *Country School.*   *What's the bus doing there?*
Text: School Bus.

Where the child knows only a few words such as 'Father' or 'car' he may give a response which only checks these words.

Child: *Father goes*   *to his car.*
Text: Father is   in the car.

The visual cues and the speech responses are matched within the limits of the child's knowledge of two words. Even this knowledge can produce an awareness of error when a known word is uttered but does not appear in the text.

Child: *This is a farm.*   *Why does it say 'Here'?*
Text: Here is a farm.

Discovering errors in this way makes the child conscious of the important fact that print carries a particular message which he must reconstruct from all possible messages. It forces him to choose between alternatives, to make decisions on the basis of cues from print, from language, and from direction and position.

At this point when the new entrants begin to construct sentences word by word to coincide with the precise message of the text, they try to correct their own mistakes. This coincides with promotion to a reading book in a sequenced programme or more careful choice of books by a child self-selecting books in a real books programme. For the average child it has taken six months to learn the early reading skills. These transitions must be observed by teachers sensitively and must not be hurried unduly. They should be fostered deliberately when appropriate behaviour fails to develop in a reasonable time, after a few months at school.

Although it can lead to error, inventing is behaviour one can do something with, unlike stalling and making no response. Some children do not notice their errors. They invent the text fluently and confidently. The reader will need a kind of inventiveness when he anticipates a passage incorrectly and has to rephrase it to match exactly with the text. A shy child who is too hesitant to respond to books is hard to help, but a child who continues to regard reading time as an invitation to construct creatively his own story has completely missed the point—that reading is a matter of extracting, relating and processing cues to decode a particular message.

What is Progress?

Should the teacher be pleased with this reading?

> Child: *Mummy cooks*
> Text: Mother is baking.

One cannot tell without an indication of the direction and pace of this particular child's learning. The response is semantically correct and it matches with the picture. Perhaps the letter 'M' provided a cue, or possibly some memory of the story. In a child who had not previously used picture cues, letter cues or memory for the story, such a response could indicate progress. If this type of paraphrase has been typical of the child's responding for some weeks or months then rather than a step forward this response may represent a stamping-in or rehearsal of inappropriate behaviour.

In the early reading stage important reading behaviour is being learned. Children seem to progress in three sets of behaviour:

- visual attention to print
- directional rules about movement and position
- talking like a book

which create the conditions for learning the fourth set, hearing sound sequences and linking these to collections of printed signs. There is no reason to assume that this occurs only at the level of letters and their sounds. In fact, being able to 'chunk' information and deal with patterns while knowing every detail in the pattern would seem to be a highly efficient level of processing information.

What are the Signs of Progress?

One signal that the child is trying to integrate several different skills is that his reading no longer sounds like fluent natural speech. One may observe the following:

Very slow deliberate reading.   One little girl read, 'We have three goldfish' very slowly and then added quietly, 'I know what that says.'

Word by word reading that is correct.   The reading is controlled at the level of individual words. One child gave evidence of this. She was struggling with the recurrence of the word 'be' for the third time. She said, 'I 'get [forget] that word all the time.'

Increased use of pointing.   The co-ordination of several skills is made easier by pointing behaviour.

Unusual pauses.   It is as if the child were checking or sorting out something.

A more serious attitude   is adopted by the child to the reading task.

Overt searching and checking   are further signs of progress.

The child's response becomes controlled by the text in preference to the picture. One little boy showed an early tendency for careful checking. He expected the text to begin a sentence with 'Father.' He sounded an initial 'f' as if expecting the text to begin with 'Father' but the word was 'Mother.' He knew the word 'Mother' so he stopped, looked at the picture, found Father in the picture but not Mother, looked back at the text and said 'Mother.' Obviously his reading response was controlled by the printed form of some part of the word, not by the picture.

When the first signs are present that several behaviours are being controlled at the same time we can begin to notice examples of children trying to relate two sets of information, one to the other.

Strategies that Draw on Stored Information

The following example demonstrates integration of present experience with a previous encounter displaced in time and space. The text was 'I can ride. I can ride my bicycle.' Betty was unable to read 'I.' She went spontaneously back three pages without prompting looking for a remembered instance of 'I.' She re-read 'Here I...,' stopped, went forward three pages and read 'I come...No!' She studied the picture and said, 'I ride.' Her mother came to the rescue and said, 'That's ride but you have to read this which says can.' Betty read two lines. 'I...can...ride. I can ride...' but she was now stuck on the word 'my.' She turned back one page, asked her mother to read 'See my bicycle,' repeated 'my' softly, as if detaching it from that text and storing it in her memory. Then she turned back to the page she was working on and completed the text.

Relating a word to a previous encounter, searching for more cues, attempting to relate form to sound and succeeding, such processing of cues helps the child to categorize sound-letter relationships in ways that could be more effective than traditional 'phonics.' Even knowing for certain that you do not know the answer can be an indication that information held in memory is being checked.

The word Billy wants to read is 'were'...

- He pauses.
- He shakes his head. (If this means that he 'knows' he does not know the word, it also means that he has searched most of the words in his reading vocabulary, which is no mean achievement.)

- He tries 'went.'
- He rejects his own attempt, saying, 'I don't know that word.'

This can be contrasted with the following example.

Child: *You must see Scot home.*
Text: You must send Scot home.

The context, sentence form and some letter-sound relationships are undisturbed by the error. This causes the child no disturbance, he does not work on it, and he does not correct himself or learn from the incident.

When a text becomes word-controlled in the sense that some of the words are known to have a precise identity there is further awareness of error when a known word pattern does not match with what is said.

Child: *I . . . it doesn't even say 'I' there!*
Text: Wake up

Texts provide readers with opportunities to relate cues from several sources to the task of decoding the precise message. The integration of several simultaneously available behaviours is achieved — saying, moving, matching and usually checking.

Another type of comparison occurs in the process of self-correction as the child directs his attention to a discrimination between two words.

Child: *ride*|SC   *come*|SC   *horse*|SC   *This*|SC
Text: run| can | here| The|

Controlling Sequences of Responses

The complex, integrated sequences of behaviours in reading are controlled by particular features in the text that are recognized. At first, amid varying degrees of uncertainty, the child locates islands of certainty.

On simple one-line texts the child may respond to the dot of the 'i' or the capital M in 'Mother.' This is the hitching-post to which he ties the rest of his response, hoping that he is correct.

In the familiar story the child locates a word he knows and builds a response around it. Then the child's reading of text comes to be controlled by particular words even though he can only recognize one or two. This might be called word-controlled inventing. For example in the text:

> I am running.
> I am jumping.
> I am sweeping.
> I am hopping.

the child's behaviour may be controlled by his recognition of the word 'I' or the word 'am.' However ineptly he matches what he says with the text, at the point where he utters the word 'I' all his behaviours are co-ordinated. The child may not even know that this is happening. The first word that the child learns to control is usually his name but the next is one of the frequently occurring words in the text. One example would be 'is' which has a distinctive and relatively simple form. Or it might be a word which is fostered by the teaching programme such as 'Here.'

Is Pointing Good or Bad?

The answer to that question depends upon the child's stage of reading progress.

'Should I sweep along the line of print as I read to my preschool child?' asked a journalist father. By all means, because a feeling for the direction in which one moves across print is hard to learn when the child is young and yet it must become a habit before book reading can be attempted.

Should you ask a child to 'read it with your finger'? Yes, if the teacher wishes to observe the child's directional behaviour, the pattern of approach to lines of print, and what he might be attending to visually. On most occasions a child will demonstrate an adequate directional pattern but sometimes he will produce surprising results. My favourite illustration comes from a child who was 5:9 and who appeared to be ignoring many features of print.

	LINE 1	LINE 2	LINE 3	LINE 4
Child:	*Go go go go*	*Tim up*	*Up Tim*	*Up up up*
Text:	Go Tim	Go up	Go up Tim	Go up up up

In fact his reading was word perfect. This could only be discovered because he was asked to read it with his finger. If a teacher frowned on pointing she would not discover this handicapping behaviour (which has probably been learned after entry to school).

> Go (1)   Tim. (5)
> Go (2)   up. (6)
> Go (3)   up Tim. (7)
> Go (4)   up, up, up. (8)

A highly intelligent girl of 13 years was handed a very simple story written in i.t.a. (initial teaching alphabet). She read it very slowly, pointing with her finger. An adult given a letter in illegible writing or a smudgy carbon copy would be quite likely to locate the difficult parts by peering for a closer look or by pointing. Even good readers locate their difficulties in a decoding task by pointing. It is a common reaction for location or for holding one's place in the visual analysis of sequential material.

There are other reasons why pointing may assist the child. Children of three to four years often depend upon body or hand movement to help them learn the features of new objects while the older child of six to seven years can explore new objects with his eyes alone and without the support of his hand. What is first a visual and manual exploration of objects becomes a visual exploration only. When we introduce five year olds to reading we can expect half of them at least to benefit greatly from body and hand participation in the knowledge of new objects, shapes and forms. Some children will have a persisting need for this kinaesthetic source of information. The teacher's demand for no pointing, no tracing, only looking, is a demand which only the most able of the young school entrants can meet.

The value of kinaesthetic exploration to supplement visual information at an early stage of reading instruction has been recognized by authorities like Grace Fernald (1943) who designed a remedial programme for backward readers around this particular concept. The organization of sequential actions needed in reading seems to be particularly assisted by this kinaesthetic analysis. However, it is a means to an end, the goal being to bring the child to the point where he can carry out such analyses at the visual level only without the need to trace or feel the spatial relationships.

Reading experts have criticised the use of pointing in reading because it has been associated with the persistence in older children of slow word by word reading and a bad habit is said to have developed. Observational records of the first year of reading behaviours showed all children passing through a stage of locating words one by one, as if the identification of written with oral symbols were better emphasized by finger-pointing than by 'finger-flow' along the whole sentence. Once one-to-one correspondence was established good readers gave up using their hands as their speed of reading increased. In the author's researches most children passed through a word-locating stage but some children remained fixated at this level of behaviour.

In Summary

This problem-solving can be observed in the first three to six months of instruction for the young child who enters school between four and six years. At this time the school must provide make-up experiences in any areas to which the child has previously paid little attention.

It should provide rich experiences to support emerging literacy (in contrast to the curricula usually found in readiness workbooks such as learning colours and letters and days of the week).

It builds on the child's well-established action system that already produces language even when this language is not English, it places meaning in the centre of reading activity, it orients the child to the visual analysis of print, and it produces oral responses co-ordinated with the visual analysis.

Words seem to be easier for the very young reader when they are embedded in sequenced information, providing the text has been selected with his current competencies in mind and provided that he has been introduced to what he will encounter in the new text (see page 196).

Using searching, checking, self-correcting and confirming strategies with the goal of making everything make sense, the child can work backwards and forwards between what he knows in the visual language or oral language information, consistently building for himself all the types of phonological-visual matches that can be used to read English. Such systems include phoneme-grapheme relationships, letter clusters and their clustered sounds, orthographic patterns and their sounds, analogous parts of words, rhyme relationships between words, words within words, words combined with words, syllabic chunks (readying the child for a transition from phonic to syllabic organization of word analysis), words that are expanded by prefixes and suffixes. All such relationships, also found in the activity of writing, begin their proliferation as the early integration of direction, visual analysis and language skills become co-ordinated.

How little real guidance children got when teachers were led to believe that learning to read and write depended upon learning the letters, and learning the sounds. that letters make.

9 Choosing Texts: Contrived Texts, Story Book Texts and Transitional Texts

Many Kinds of Text

All the written texts of the home, the community, the preschool and the school have importance in learning to read.

A text as I refer to it includes the messages that children write (or compose with an adult) like

Once upon a time there was a wonky tree . . .

as well as those contrived texts that people write for children to read (the ones that do not sound like speech) like

Puff, Puff, Puff.   Jump, Puff, Jump.

and also the ones written to be read to children like the solicitors' letter from *The Jolly Postman* (Ahlberg, 1986).

Dear Mr. Wolf, we are writing to you on behalf of our client, Miss Riding-Hood, concerning her grandma. Miss Hood tells us that you are presently occupying her grandma's cottage and wearing her grandma's clothes without this lady's permission.

Any of the interactions children have with people about reading and writing using texts and many different activities provide children with points of entry into early literacy development. Consider this extensive list.

Oral language activities like

- listening to stories
- talking about books of many different kinds
- telling stories and acting them
- playing with nursery rhymes in many different ways.

Reading activities like

- responding to a rich 'print environment'
- playing with plastic alphabets
- inventing the text of a favourite story book

- following along song or poem charts
- helping to construct a language experience account of some shared event
- art, craft and drama as ways of showing that some reading has been understood (i.e. evidence of comprehension).

Writing activities like

- making marks on paper
- having one's messages written down by someone else
- all the writing done and read in class
- sharing what one has written with teacher or other children.

The list is endless and what one child happens upon is not necessarily the path into literacy for another.

Choice of Texts

Teaching approaches which ask the child to get himself to where the programme begins usually have texts and teaching materials which support a predetermined sequence of things to be learned. Such approaches are common in education systems, and they specify a particular path to success which all learners must take. They leave little choice to teachers and little flexibility for adaptations to meet individual differences.

A curriculum which allows the teacher to go to where the child is and help the individual child to apply whatever strengths he brings to school to literacy learning will allow for different paths to reading or writing acquisition even in the same classroom. This calls for organization and ingenuity from the teachers, but it also gives teachers a very important role in choosing the range of texts from which a particular child may select a book to read.

A common feature of reading programmes in schools is that they are enabling: they help children to read harder and harder texts with more and more independence. More and more they work with novel features of text without help. So somewhere in the decision-making there are criteria about a gradient of difficulty in the challenges children are facing. It is very clear in children's oral language learning that they work their way up through a gradient of difficulty as they gradually come to control the grammar of their language.

In reading, ways of working with new and unseen texts are important but are only one part of the learning to be done. As there is much to be learned by allowing children to return to and re-read familiar stories there can be free access to choosing by children among these. They look at them again in the light of new knowledge they have gained. This happens also as the child develops oral language: there is a forward thrust of new learning but it occurs within the context of using the language he already controls. Children orchestrate and refine complex ways of working with texts (literacy strategies) as they work with what they know.

Sometimes an extreme position on choosing texts is taken as in the following quote.

> There is only one criterion that needs to be taken into account when choosing books for any age child if reading is to be approached as a natural learning activity. Will the child enjoy the book? There is no need to worry about vocabulary control, type face, phonic consistency or any other problems beloved of teachers' manuals ... If the adult is to provide support, it matters only that the child should want to read that book.
>
> (Waterland, 1985)

I think care with choosing texts does matter for three reasons. Firstly, many teachers around the world have not been trained to 'provide support' of the kind Waterland takes for granted; that phrase simplifies a great deal of expertise in teacher-child interactions (MacKenzie, 1986) for which training is needed. Secondly, this advocacy does not tell us how to achieve a move to independence where the child needs little of the teacher support, and we might conclude, erroneously, that it will just come about of its own accord. Thirdly, it does not recognize the existence of confusions, false hypotheses arrived at by the child, or individual differences of the more extreme kind—hurdles to be overcome. Rather, because the adult provides all the support necessary for the child to read that text, the child's difficulties could remain unrecognized and untouched.

Today's emphasis is upon the quality of teacher-child interaction and many reasons can be advanced for avoiding the distorting and controlling nature of contrived reading texts. There is every reason to encourage teachers to learn to choose texts that will maximize the efforts of young learners, while allowing those learners some participation in the final selection.

Texts do not make a reading programme but they provide tangible evidence of some of a programme's features.

Many Kinds of Programmes

Some reading programmes give the impression that learning to read can be done simply.

- One extreme view would claim that reading was merely a matter of learning letter-sound relationships and so texts are compiled which introduce only words which contain the letter-sound relationships which have been introduced in the programme so far.

- A pendulum swing away is the view that merely providing children with well-written story books will, by itself, teach children to read. Advocates accept any beautiful books from children's literature as suitable for beginning readers, ignoring the fact that a particular child may use very simple language that is nothing like the author's or that not many teachers know how to support learning in such a programme.

- A third simplification for a school system is to buy a reading scheme from a publisher which claims to package all that is needed into its set of books and workbooks. This ignores what the children are bringing to the learning interaction from their diverse backgrounds and different opportunities to learn.

Looking beyond such oversimplification there are many ways of delivering instruction in early literacy and it is interesting to compare some of these.

- Some programmes limit what children are allowed to read (a) to what they already use in speech, or (b) to a particular learning sequence which is deemed to be the 'best' sequence. It seems to me that as children's prior experiences are known to be astonishingly variable we should be wary of teaching practices in beginning literacy instruction which limit children's opportunities to relate what they can already do to the new learning tasks.

- Some programmes are multifaceted and their 'texts' are of different kinds. For example in the New Zealand programme:
  - children's own messages recorded in their writing provide reading material
  - story books are shared and discussed in ways that allow for many kinds of child participation, and often contribute to a theme which integrates many classroom activities (These remain available for children to 'read' in different ways.)
  - language experience texts are used for group or individual reading
  - the reading books are stories selected by teachers to provide a rough and ready gradient of difficulty. The first books use language like that found in language experience texts that school entrants dictate. There is a gradual shift to more literary writing as the beginning readers gain control of their medium.

- Some programmes have a very brief 'formal' instruction period. In Denmark it has been argued that a best method of reading instruction will never be found and one will never be able to devise 'the best material' (Jansen, Jacobsen and Jensen, 1978:21). School entrants who are about seven years of age have intensive work with rather few words in the first few months of school, supported by systematic learning of letters. Then for a short period basal readers become the main educational material, together with parallel activity in silent reading. By the second year the pupils do a lot of reading from books they select and read independently from a plentiful supply of material available in the classroom. Pupils work with easy books, often self-chosen, and they use reading in other classroom tasks. Only the first year's instruction is systematic enough to talk about methods of learning to read and systematically designed materials are only used at that time.

- Some programmes have children listen to and discuss story books and introduce their children to reading through those books. Sometimes called a 'real books' approach to beginning reading this is now quite widely advocated. The responsibility for a learning plan lies with the teacher who has to know her children and her books very well. Because the teacher knows where each child is in his or her learning she can decide whether to share (read and talk about) a selected story, or to introduce it to the child who will read it with the teacher's help and prompting, or whether this child could be expected to attempt this book independently. Teacher expertise is needed in judging how to pace the introduction of new challenges to meet the needs of the young reader's growing control of reading processes. Trade story books are the main texts used.

- Some programmes which relieve teachers of a great deal of this decision-making are published sets of materials, including reading books. Usually they are prepared on the advice of a panel of experts, and they may even be trialled by teachers in real classrooms. But Pearson (1984) and Osborn (1984) have analysed some of the many problems of this approach, mainly centering on the ways in which it perpetuates conservative assumptions about instruction and inhibits innovative shifts because new ideas would not be likely to sell well. This is particularly apparent in the persistence of workbook activities. Osborn analysed a wide variety of workbooks with well-constructed tasks and then listed what they would allow students to do. They would allow them to practise details, do extra practice on aspects of reading, review, synthesize what they had learned, follow directions, take tests, work independently, and practise writing. The important omissions were creative and constructivist activities in open-ended tasks. Workbooks have to have exercises which have (a) correct answers, and (b) the same answers from every child, for quick checking. Consequently workbook activities cannot be designed to help the child to construct his own theory of reading or writing because in this case:

  — firstly, the children's answers would all be different
  — and secondly, the children would sometimes produce only partially correct responses as they slowly took hold of new learning.

Such limitation of experience is serious when multiplied by the time children spend on workbooks. The other reason for the persistence of workbooks is that they are used for managerial reasons, according to Osborn.

Text Characteristics Influence the Child's Expectations

Experience with particular types of texts can create expectations in the beginning reader and particular reading behaviours. A diet of texts with one style of writing (for example primerese) will not lead to sufficiently flexible reading strategies for the variety of texts that a reader will encounter. If we want the child to learn to read any kind of texts including literary texts and informational texts he cannot do this if he becomes locked into behaviours that work well only on a particular kind of text. Even the beginning reader needs texts that are varied in their styles.

It would be consistent with the characteristics of beginning reading texts if the young reader assumed that:

- a new line begins a new sentence
- a new sentence begins on a new line
- a new line probably requires a direct speech construction
- direct speech probably calls for the use of the 'who said it phrase' like 'said Mother.'

In beginning reading books, texts are often arranged on a one-sentence to one-line basis.

> A pig comes to school.
> A calf comes to school.
> Mary comes with the calf.
> Penny comes with the pig.

When a two-line sentence is used the second line usually begins at a distinct break in the spoken sentence.

> William the goat
> will not come.
> 'Get up, William,'
> said Michael.

When I did an analysis of the sentences of the first readers in the New Zealand *Ready to Read* series (First edition, 1963) in 1966, I found that 69 percent of all line beginnings were new sentences. The analysis also showed that a new sentence invariably began on a new line. So children limited to reading these graded readers could come to expect all texts to be like these.

Such expectations can increase fluency on a text but since these are not features of all texts they also produce errors.

Text: The children are playing
Child: *The children are playing.*

Text: with trucks and bulldozers.
Child: *Where is Timothy?* (Anticipation error)

From these examples of the effects of textual characteristics we can draw the conclusion that reading behaviours will be a result of an interaction between the child's oral language production system and certain linguistic characteristics of their reading texts not only for the features illustrated above but for many other features. When the reading book format is switched these features change dramatically and the child has lost some of the bases for making choices among responses to texts. A high-progress reader may be stimulated by the change but a low-progress reader may lose confidence because what he expects to be true of texts no longer works.

Three Challenging Ideas

Little books
We used to require that some children read a thick primer reading book for several months until they had 'mastered' it. This meant having control of whatever was between the hard covers. This approach worked for those who learned quickly but became boring repetition for those who were learning slowly.

A major breakthrough in the 1980s has been a wider acceptance of the 'little book' concept (for example *Number One*, Cowley, 1982, or *Mrs. Wishy-Washy*, Cowley and Melser, 1980 or *A Crocodile in the Garden*, Mahy, 1983). Collections of little books each with separate stories of 100 to 200 words allow the teacher several kinds of flexibility within which to meet a particular child's needs.

- She can choose stories that draw on or expand a particular child's experiences.
- She can move a child into new challenges on a more difficult text.
- She can opt for consolidation of current learning on new stories at the same level of difficulty. Then the challenge is for old learning to be applied in new settings.

Notice it is the individual child's achievements and where he next needs to go that governs the selection, not the publishers' assumptions about all children's learning. Applying these opportunities for flexibility in text selection, the teacher who has identified 10 books of about the same difficulty level may have one child read only one or two of them while another child may read five or six.

There was another gain for 'real books' programmes in the shift to easy little books. Teachers were able to move children from a book before their reading of that book was word perfect. A child does have to gradually accumulate a reading vocabulary of known words which he can recognize rapidly and does not have to work out. Only as this happens is the reader's attention freed to work on new words and solve new text problems. However, when near-perfect reading is fostered on many different texts of somewhat similar difficulty level, the challenges (i.e. new learning points) reappear in texts of about the same or slightly more difficult level. Therefore new stories in new little books provide further practice of the same high-frequency words in new settings and the near-perfect responding becomes correct responding. In addition, the correct responding is primed for flexibility: what has been learned is how to recognize those words in several different settings.

As 'there would appear to be a lag as long as 15–20 years in getting research findings into practice' (Anderson, Osborn and Tierney, 1984), one could argue that education needs a more responsive cycle of change than that. Little books and story books allow for continuous adjustment of texts to suit new practices.

Predictable texts

The word 'predictable' is often used in the reading literature to describe the kind of beginning reading books for which children can invent the text and come very close to what is written.

It can be applied to books which the child can predict from oral language. In easy first books we often find repetitive sentence structures which allow the child to predict how the sentence form will go and allow the child to make decisions about how the sentence ends. The predictability allows the child to behave like a reader. His everyday use of the language and knowledge of the world makes a portion of the text predictable. He has developed this skill already as a listener because he is able to anticipate something about the sentences of someone speaking to him. Those skills which enabled him to understand speech also enable him to understand the texts that he reads for himself. The most helpful of such repetitive books vary the sentence structure somewhere in the book, round about the time the reader is getting bored with the repetition, calling for close attention to the text, and giving the child a reminder that print cues must be attended to.

Alternatively, in addition to the predictability that comes from oral language experience, a familiarity with books provides the child with expectancies of what kinds of sequences might occur next in stories.

A third and very important source of predictability comes from the child's knowledge of what makes sense in the real world of his own experience, or in the fantasy world of books.

Predictability is a term which has also been used for some rather dull repetitive texts because, obviously, if the text hardly varies from page to page you almost know what it is going to say before you look at it.

Some authors have assumed that predictability came from many re-readings of the same book, or even from deliberate memorizing. If using information to anticipate some of the text possibilities ahead is what a real reader needs to learn to do, then memorizing strategies are plainly inappropriate. It is a better move to provide texts which encourage the use of predictability in a constructive way from the child's first encounters with texts.

I have heard children who have tuned in to the style of their basal reader, constructing texts from the controlled vocabulary they have learned to date which is, in a way, predicting what the text will say. They are not bringing their oral language, or knowledge of the world, or knowledge of how stories are structured to the task of anticipating how the text will continue; they are operating only on what they have learned about a particular type of text found in their reading books.

As the term 'predictable text' has acquired several quite different meanings, it is no longer very useful.

Learning more on familiar texts

Texts used for shared book experience can be continuously available for long periods in the classroom because they can be revisited by children who are at different levels of independence in dealing with print. If children can return frequently to re-read a wide variety of familiar material they have two opportunities: firstly, to orchestrate the complex patterns of responding to print just as the expert musician practises the things she knows; and secondly, to read those texts with increasing levels of independence.

Being allowed to read familiar material is rare in schools. Adults seem only interested in children reading unseen text. Because several readings increase familiarity teachers are wary of 'memorizing.' There is certainly little to be gained from pretending to read a memorized text but teachers who observe children closely know the difference between the child who is and is not reading. It is what the child brings to the book they read last week or last month—an awareness of plot and character, of meanings, and of language structures and words—that provides the half-recalled context for the re-reading. The reading task is still new and challenging because the child is bringing that prior knowledge to the text, and this time through the child may notice things that he failed to attend to on the previous reading.

When children are allowed to re-read familiar material they are being allowed to learn to be readers, to read in ways which draw on all their language resources and knowledge of the world, to put this very complex recall and sequencing behaviour into a fluent rendering of the text. The child is using a different kind of support from the interactive sharing of the task with the teacher. Now the support is coming from his own prior reading. That familiarity is supporting his move towards further independence as a reader. The orchestration of these complex behaviours cannot be achieved on a hard book, for then the child is practising different aspects of the reading process. Returning to easy reading is one way of developing the smooth orchestration of all those behaviours necessary for effective reading. Even fledgling readers need opportunities to put together those few responses they have already learned. Re-reading what they themselves have written is one way this can occur. Easy familiar texts they can return to is another way. Opportunities to apply new skills or knowledge just learned on one or two more books of about the same level of difficulty are all examples of revisiting the familiar.

One problem with beginning reading is that the task of the young reader is made much harder when programmes do not let him get a sufficiently large sample of the language to work with. If all he has to work on are restricted texts, and restricted texts are made up of a limited vocabulary, they are not necessarily easy texts.

Three Major Text Types

Texts contrived to emphasize sounds or words

Adults who prepare series of reading books decide what shall be taught before what. They arrange the order in which the items shall be learned. Some gradient of difficulty in the texts is based on a theory of the order in which subsets of language should be introduced to children. Often adults dissect the task logically using their own mature reading as a guide. Compassionate people have tried to make the reading task easier for the child by presenting it in easy steps. As we have come to understand more about language learning it is now clear that when contrived texts are constructed with controlled vocabulary:

- they ignore the established language production systems that children bring to reading
- they distort the expectations children have developed from listening to stories
- they do away with many of the supports that might have made it easier for the child to learn by himself.

Contrived texts are texts in which some level of language is strictly controlled. Simplification and step-wise sequences can produce strange texts. Sometimes what the author assumed about beginning reading is apparent, as this text from last century demonstrates.

> Lo! I am an ox.
> Is my ox to go in as we go by?
> (Price, 1975)

Some text writers guessed that children would find it easy to read only in capital letters, so texts like the next example were designed, operating on the just noticeable difference principle.

PAT A FAT CAT
PAT A FAT RAT
(Fries, 1963)

A text written thirty years ago controlled the occurrence of letters, letter-sound relationships, and the functions of words in sentences.

This is a hat.
It is this man's hat.
It is his hat.
This hat is his hat.
That is a hat.
It is that man's hat.
It is a hat.
That hat is his hat.

(Gibson and Richards, 1957)

The control may be of many different kinds:

1 The control may be over sounds, letters, words, spelling patterns, punctuation, syllables, sentence patterns and any permutation of these variables in combination.

2 Some units of printed messages are taught before others with a measured exposure to bits, and a deliberate repetition of bits. There may be built-in discrimination tasks to force the child to notice certain differences on the author's schedule.

3 Skills are taught additively, one after the other, in fixed sequence. The authors seem to know what should be in children's heads, and how one gets it there.

Basal readers do not necessarily have contrived texts but many in the past did. Text writers were constrained by assumptions about the learning to read process.

• Firstly, reading was assumed to mean reading unseen words and unseen texts unaided.

• Secondly, it was assumed that the reader can read unseen texts if (a) he learns the new words first, so children would need to read the new words first in isolation, or (b) he learns some way of working out what the new words could be, such as learning to decode print to words they know in their speech.

• Thirdly, if sounding out is the way to new words then these will have to be regular words.

- Fourthly, these words with regular letter-sound relationships will need to be repeated until the child can recognize them without working them out.

Attempts to control texts and learning sequences in these ways have probably made the learning task more difficult because important support systems within the language have been left out. Young children can and do learn more about the complex interrelationships within language than such programmes allow.

Does it matter if texts are contrived, based on such assumptions? For the more able children perhaps not. They may go along with all kinds of strange practices and are able to bridge the gaps between what instruction presents them with and what they need to learn. Such competent readers give the programme its credibility and seem to prove its worth. When less able children encounter difficulties the reading programme is not questioned; rather it is the children who are labelled as having difficulties.

Their difficulties arise in two ways. As set out above they have difficulty in relating what they can already do with language and with books to the new texts. But new difficulties arise as a result of specializing on such texts. Having mastered the contrived text the child who is finding learning to read a great challenge will encounter further difficulties. To qualify Margaret Spencer (1987), texts teach and contrived texts teach unhelpful things! The texts you have been exposed to will determine what you are able to do.

- If you have only read controlled vocabulary texts you will have difficulty with texts that do not control the vocabulary.
- If your texts have controlled the letter-sound relationships in words then uncontrolled texts will present problems.
- If you have only been exposed to fiction, to stories, then nonfiction material will be hard because you will not have the appropriate strategies to read it.

If readers in their first year are exposed to natural language texts which do not artificially constrain letter, letter-sound, word and structure relationships in text but try to present text that follows the natural language patterns of the child, those readers will find phonically controlled texts rather strange and possibly difficult. Children in their second year of school reading natural language and literary texts were asked in one study (Ng, 1979) to read the phonically regularized Royal Road readers (Daniels and Diack, 1954) which they read quite competently. They made comments like 'Funny way to say it,' or 'You really should say so and so, shouldn't you?' altering the text to a more natural form. Text experience determines what you are able to do and which texts remain difficult.

The materials one has been allowed to read determine, in large part, the young child's opportunities to develop and use a particular range of reading strategies. Students read easily the kinds of texts that they have had a lot of experience reading. Whether a reader finds a text difficult is influenced by the programme in which he is learning.

The less we alter texts the simpler the learning progressions will be for children who already produce oral language well. We should pay more attention to how texts for beginning readers prevent them from learning and how we can expose them to a variety of texts.

Some important checks that teachers could make with new instructional materials are these. Observe children in the process of reading or children trying to learn. Try out the material on children and stand ready to discard what does not work well. Study the match or mismatch of the text language and the language children are producing in response to the text.

Story books and a meaning emphasis

While some programmes set as their first priority that the texts carry meanings for the young reader, even the most contrived texts are not meaningless. However, when learning the nature of the written code takes precedence over meaning, it is possible to end up with texts about 'pale ale' or 'fat cats' or 'her third bird's turn' or those that have been the butt of many jokes like:

> Jump, Janet, jump.
> You can jump.
> You can run.
> You can run and jump.

If it is assumed that school entrants already understand the world in terms of their own experiences and know something about literacy and books then a story book would allow them to use their prior experience to make sense of what they are trying to do. More than that meaningful texts signal to children on many occasions that they should get more information because something is not quite right. When meaningfulness is seen to be the first priority in a reading programme, the message is more important than the words or letters which are collectively only the carriers of meaning.

Good teaching encourages the child to actively respond to the meaningfulness of the stories read to them or by them. I recently had an example of how a book written for five year olds can connect at a different level with the understanding of a younger child. Casting around for yet another story to share with a three year old at bedtime, I picked up *Mrs. Wishy-Washy* (a beginning reading book from *The Story Box* collection by Cowley and Melser, 1980) and was entranced with the reaction.

"Oh, lovely mud," said the cow and she jumped in it.	*Searches the picture*
"Oh, lovely mud," said the pig, and he rolled in it.	*Chuckles*
"Oh, lovely mud," said the duck, and she paddled in it.	*Deep chuckles*

(As reader I become aware that it is playing in mud that has grabbed the interest of my listener. Mrs. Wishy-washy scrubs each animal clean and returns to the house.)

> Away went the cow.   Away went the pig.
> Away went the duck   (Turn the page.)   *Uncontrollable*
> "Oh, lovely mud," they said.   *belly laughter*

I don't think naughtiness or winning out or any feel for a plot or climax is really part of this child's interaction even after many readings. The connection with this book and its hilarity is being able to roll in mud! The text can only teach, I decided, about things with which the child is interacting.

Learning to comprehend passages. If parents and preschools enrich children's experience by sharing many books with them children learn a great deal that is valuable for literacy learning in school. They learn about what can be found in books, and about the language of books, but they also learn about the shape and structure of stories, the kinds of things that happen in tales, and various literary devices. That they recognize the author's tricks is sometimes obvious from their comments. To learn to anticipate the language and situations found in stories children have to build up a vast experience with children's story books.

Some children do not get those experiences before they come to school for many different reasons and teachers who use a story book reading programme must provide them with make-up experiences. This sharing of books in the early childhood classrooms may be the first introduction to how stories work for some children. They cannot immediately plunge into the literary nuances which more experienced children enjoy. There is much to learn about how stories work. It is surprising how quickly they begin to use the language of books and play with the magical and fantasy aspects of stories. Given the opportunities they begin to close the gap in their prior learning.

With no instructional intent. Publishers produce a wide range of children's books for general consumption through bookshops and libraries. These books are primarily intended to be read to or by children for enjoyment or pleasure and have no direct instructional purpose. Only a small number of authors seem able to write and illustrate texts that are simple enough for beginning readers to read by themselves: authors like Brian Wildsmith, Pat Hutchins, Eric Hill and John Burningham. Experienced teachers may possibly be able to construct a gradient of difficulty from such books that would be beautifully adapted to even the earliest stages of beginning reading. However, as there is not an abundance of such texts and they are not easy to write, it is hard for beginning readers to gain enough exposure to each step of the gradient. Teachers need to supplement these materials with texts which use the children's speech or simple books constructed with such child-like usage. Two main criteria for selecting books for such a programme are (1) some books need to be easy enough for the child to learn something about reading, and (2) some need to be books from which children can learn something about how stories work.

A control over vocabulary?   Story book texts are written to entice children into the story, to bring what they know to understanding the text, to take multiple meanings and new meanings from the encounter, and to learn more about how stories can be made meaningful by the reader's active interaction with text.

Whether the story is written as a transition text or in literary language there are always high-frequency words and low-frequency words involved. Children will encounter enough repetitions of high-frequency words in texts to begin to control a 'known reading vocabulary of these words.' Both the stories below prepare the child reader for a story structure which has repeated episodes. By using the natural control of vocabulary that exists in the frequency principle in all language, 'The ghost' text escapes from the need to repeat words in strange sentences for the sole purpose of practice. The purpose of the ghost story was not to motivate the child to read the same words repeatedly but to provide a simple text which children might enjoy reading. If one read many easy stories one would read the same words repeatedly because of the frequency principle in language.

Compare the basal reader text below with its contrived repetition of words with the transition text, *Number One*, with its naturally occurring repetition of vocabulary as required by the story, and perhaps try your hand at writing *Number One* in literary language, after the style of other story book ghost stories.

Number One
It is night.
The ghost comes out of his cupboard,
out of his house, and into the town.
"Who can I boo?" he says.

Look! Here comes a man in a taxi.
"He'll do," says the ghost.
The taxi stops, and the man jumps out.
"Boo!" says the ghost.

"Oooo! A horrible, horrible ghost!"
says the man, and he runs away.
"Number one!" says the ghost.

(Cowley, 1982)

Help For The Hen
"Good day," said a hen to a dog.
"I need some help at my house.
Could you help me?"
"I can't help you now," said the dog.
"The day is too beautiful. Why don't
you ask the cat?"
"Very well," said the hen. "I will."

(Marshall, 1982)

Transition texts close to the oral language of the child

Some of the easiest texts for a child to read are the texts he has dictated. They have words that he uses, within structures which he can produce, in the frequencies that he expects. He can monitor what he is reading with a store of knowledge he already has in his head. His memory for what he said will not be exact and so he will have to do reading work as he reads or recomposes his dictated text. Such texts use the language the child already controls.

Language experience texts also have this advantage.

When adults write texts which are a close match to the way children would speak this makes it easier for children to draw on their existing oral language knowledge to predict what might occur next. The novice reader can anticipate more closely what the text might say if it is written in something like the way that he might say it. The rules and frequencies which operate in children's talk are allowed to operate in the books of the early reading programme. I will call these natural language texts.

However, it is not enough to read only natural language or language experience texts. These only work from the spoken dialect of the child. Children need book experience to read books. Book language has different forms and different frequencies of occurrence from spoken dialects. The writer has to choose language that is more explicit and express it in more formal ways to make up for not having his listener in an actual situation with facial expressions, gestures, stress and emphasis, and a chance to rephrase something to overcome the failure of his listener to understand part of the message. To become a reader and writer the child certainly needs to have exposure to the vocabulary and sentence structures of written texts and, gradually, to control the more formal usage and different frequencies of the language in books. For some children who are not well-prepared for literary texts this may not be the preferred place to begin.

Natural language texts can be regarded as transitional texts, used when the child is just beginning to relate what he knows about oral language and print to the written texts he is trying to read. While the child is trying to work out what reading is, and how he should work at it, natural language texts draw on his oral language competencies and allow him to build bridges across to more literary texts.

The 'Little Books' which give the teacher of beginning readers such flexibility in her programming for children's individual differences can be written as such transitional texts. They have many features of story books but they use the kind of language that the average school entrant would use in speech. This produces a larger vocabulary and longer sentences than those used in basal readers with contrived language. Allowing readers to use the language production system that they already control to generate possible texts gives the child control over the learning task. The examples below present contrived text rewritten in (a more) natural language text version. To make a point we will assume for the moment that the story was worth rewriting, which might not be true.

Wag bit the net.	Wag got the fishing net
"I can rip the net," said Wag.	in his teeth. He bit
Wag bit and bit	it hard and the net
and the net began to rip.	began to rip.

(Rasmussen and Goldberg, 1964)

One day Elena saw something	One day Elena saw something
that was not right.	strange. Everything in the
The forest near the mountain	forest was blue! The trees
was blue.	and the grass were blue.
The trees were blue.	She saw a blue bird in a tree,
The grass was blue.	and a blue fox chasing a blue
A blue bird sang in a blue	rabbit.
tree. Blue foxes ran after	
a blue rabbit.	

(Barnes, 1982)

The main difference at the word level is in the number of times words are repeated but if the teaching programme allows for children to re-read any story by choice with increasing degrees of fluency and independence then it is easy to see that three readings of the natural language story could provide necessary repetition of a wider vocabulary that is closer to the way children talk.

One of Margaret Mahy's stories for the *Ready to Read* series uses natural language for the child's dialogue together with some literary turns of phrase in the non-dialogue text and these two types of language together create an example of the bridging that can provide easy access to the child's oral language system, while demanding more attention to the newer forms of book language. *Crocodile In the Garden* is told by a little boy whose family have a crocodile for a pet. Crocodile is very interested in the new neighbours, Mr. and Mrs. Hedgerow. They have shiny, sharp garden tools and do a lot of work. Crocodile picked up their hedge clippers and broke them.

The story continues...

> I looked at the crocodile sternly.
> He looked at me and tried to pretend
> that it was not his fault.
> He snapped his jaws in a jovial fashion,
> and tried to whisk and frisk...
> Then I had an idea.
>
> (Mahy, 1983)

Although the dialogue in this story sounds very like a New Zealand child's speech ('Stupid croc, look what you've done' or 'Get on with it' or 'Don't muck about, hurry up!'), the language of books has crept into the text above in at least four places — 'sternly,' 'in a jovial fashion,' 'to whisk and frisk,' and 'Then I had an idea.' The book allows a child to become familiar with 'bookish' ways with words while still being supported by his own forms of language use.

Texts that facilitate this transition from oral to written dialect by tapping into the highly effective language production system which the child already has, might be of very different kinds.

- One approach has been to record children's spoken language and construct early reading books from the structures and vocabulary they use. They would read these books with relative ease but would find other books difficult. Selecting only oral language structures could deprive them of a way to move from their own oral language forms to the dialect of books unless story books were also read to them.

- Language experience materials constructed by teacher and children can use child-dictated text. As children become more familiar with story book styles the teacher can offer alternative ways of phrasing the text, and with agreement, include some more literary turns of phrase. Some teachers bring literary forms and children's language production together by having them 'write' a new version of an old story in a language experience lesson.

- Many children are well-prepared for book language by the booksharing that is a regular feature of their preschool lives. This not only builds expectancies for the kinds of language found in books but also for the ways in which books and stories work, for plots and how they unfold, and for what characters do. Even so, a text which uses natural language encourages the linking of oral language competencies to printed forms.

- Beginners who have had least booksharing in their preschool years can start reading natural language texts for themselves while, concurrently, hearing the teacher read stories and poetry. They have a dual learning task but can move gradually into reading trade story books as their ears become more attuned to the written dialect.

- If the child has become very familiar with a text by hearing the story more than once, before trying to read it he will have nearly as much control over the language as he would with a natural language text.

Texts which use language very like the child's own speech, range from a child's dictated story, through the easiest texts of single sentences commenting on a related picture, to texts composed of child-like language. Some easy trade books like *The Chick and the Duckling* contain language from which children can learn about book language and together with natural language texts they provide easy stepping stones into other story books.

Texts which support independent analysis   An important challenge to contrived texts which have been designed to make children analyse language at the word or letter level comes from the fact that children can learn to be extremely analytic of natural language texts. John was a child who was given a reading readiness test and gained a score in the lowest 5 percent of school entants. Yet his progress over his first six months at school was exceptional. At 5:6 he was fascinated with connections in print. In a programme which did not call for much work on words and no deliberate instruction on phonics, he actively looked for connections. He would say

> Look! If you cover up *painting* you get *paint*.
> If you cover up *shed* you get *she*.
> If you cover *o* in *No* you don't get anything.
> *I've* is like *drive* but it's *have*.
> That looks like *will* but it's *William*.

(Clay, 1979)

When the language and ideas of texts are predictable from what children already know about meaning and oral language they can give more attention to learning about the features of the print itself.

They can explore how words or texts are constructed without using workbook exercises. This is more likely to happen if the teacher invites or models analysis of the type demonstrated in the example. The modelling signals to the children that there are interesting things that can be discovered about the ways in which words work.

The frequency principle provides vocabulary controls   There is a consistent and inescapable control over vocabulary even in texts which use natural language. There are high-frequency letters and low-frequency letters, high-frequency words and low-frequency words, high-frequency sentence types and low-frequency ones. The high-frequency words occur often and the least frequent words are controlled out by matching to something like the children's speech. Every linguistic unit has its frequency value.

The powerful and pervasive contribution of the frequency principle to predictability in speech and in texts, provides us with a sense of the kind of thing that is likely to occur next. This helps us to maintain reading fluency. It also means that children will be exposed to many repetitions of previously introduced words. As a result of many opportunities to read easy texts children are quite likely to discover the regularities of features in frequently occurring words. This awareness can be sharpened if the teacher calls attention to the idea that words are constructed just as sentences are constructed. The child's experience as a writer links cumulatively into such learning.

Texts for slow progress groups   While creative, varied or flexible approaches to writing and reading seem appropriate for average and high progress readers, slow progress readers have great difficulty discovering the regularities in a rich reading environment. The optimum reading environment for the brightest and best pupils could inhibit progress in the poorest achievers.

If I am working with children known to have severe limitations or poor experiences with learning to read I expect the first interactions of child and text to occur on natural language texts that are close to the way that child speaks. The child will most readily generate that kind of language. The first thing that comes to mind will be those language forms he uses in speech. The best checks on whether he is right will come from his personal check with the language he knows so well. We can use his knowledge of language to prop up the early reading responses.

However, from the beginning we can share more literary kinds of texts with him as we seek to enlarge the range of text language he can read. For such extension he will need book experiences. A child used to hearing stories will anticipate book language, the story schema, the plot and character features, and the structural devices used for effect. The child without this preparation in the same programme will need more preparation for reading texts in the form of story sharing, either before reading particular stories or as a general foundation.

For the poorer readers there is reason to make the regularities so obvious that they trip over them in the same place on several occasions and then again in a somewhat different place for several more occasions. Regular contact with familiar material in familiar contexts (achieved easily by being allowed to re-read familiar texts) will suit the slow progress reader better than trying to force on him a flexibility on many varied texts which he is not yet ready to operate.

Strong cautions must be stated, however, over the selection of simple material and regular or controlled materials for slow progress children. While complex and varied texts may defeat these children's efforts to read, materials of a limited or controlled type will only develop habitual responding for that type of material. This learning will not transfer readily to more complex texts. For a slow child if the regularity of the texts is increased at any time to facilitate correct responding, a variety of language structures should be reintroduced as soon as the new skill is established.

Teaching with Transition or Story Book Texts

There is a danger that the agent of change in reading acquisition will be seen to be the texts when the focal issue is 'What kind of teacher-child interaction accompanies the reading?'

- Firstly, the teacher has a role which is to be a party to the interaction of reader and text supporting and discussing as the need arises.

- Secondly, careful observation by the teacher of individual children as they read, and some record taking from time to time, keeps her in touch with the changes that are occurring in children.

- Thirdly, introducing a new text to the reader giving an overview of the story is an important orientation to the task which the teacher can give.

- Fourthly, what the teacher does as the outcome of the reading is important. If the reading is near-perfect and independent, the text was easy for the child but presented little challenge. If the reading seemed to result in little understanding then the text was probably too hard or the child poorly prepared by the introduction to read it. More support work by the teacher was implied. If the reading was fluent with successful problem-solving and perhaps some residual error, it presented the child with some learning challenges. Observations and evaluations of this kind lead the teacher to what book choices she helps the child to make, and what kinds of interactions she herself engages in with the child.

When Margaret Spencer (1987) wrote *How Texts Teach What Readers Learn*, I cannot believe that she intended teachers to think that the text alone would teach the beginning reader and that there was no role for the interactive support of an adult sharing the activity and helping the child to venture into new territory. Her title has many meanings and these should be 'unpacked' by teachers in discussion.

In the teacher-child interaction the child is encouraged to take on more and more independent problem-solving. He is taught how to monitor his own reading, to check on himself, to use his oral language as a resource, and to use people and sources around the classroom as his print resources. In these ways he gets many opportunities to learn the regularities of print, *and the exceptions at the same time*, contrasting the one with the other.

What children are actually learning is hidden from the teacher's sight. To make responses to the child that are of most value the teacher has to have a fairly accurate model of how that child normally solves his problems. Fortunately, with a little training the teacher can become a sensitive observer of children's progress. The teacher can observe many overt reading behaviours which tell her how well the child is working on print, what kinds of cues he is using, and what kinds of 'rules' and relationships he is learning. The teacher has no reason to become a sensitive observer if she expects texts all by themselves to produce readers.

In the early reading stage the wholeness of the story text provides the child with support. He begins by generating a text to fit the story, the illustrations and the teacher's introduction but not without attention to words. After reading some words in several different settings he comes to know them in isolation. Checks must be made that this is happening and that the child is gaining a control over his particular reading vocabulary because this frees him to attend to new features of print. Learning to read is a matter of progressive shifts of attention to novel features in text.

The child can be expected and required to monitor his own reading. At first he detects errors of meaning or sentence structure by reference to his oral language system and when they occur he is expected to try to solve the problem by reading work. He may have to seek more information or help. Gradually the child begins to detect errors because of what he is learning about the visual forms of print, and their relationship to the sounds of his spoken language. In this way his monitoring behaviour is enriched by new strategies for working on the information in print which go beyond his oral language control.

The gradient of difficulty problem is helped by having many texts available at any one level of text difficulty. Careful record keeping and a good observation record of a child's accuracy on a previous reader could be the basis for accelerated promotion of a child through several levels of text difficulty (see Chapter 10). If the child is accelerated in this way careful checks should be made on his progress in the ensuing weeks. Some children never recover their balance after well-intentioned but unwarranted acceleration.

Changing a child from one type of text to another (natural language story to a contrived text with regular phoneme-grapheme relationships) will force that child to attend to new features previously neglected. This could make the child's reading more flexible for, according to Bruner's argument, such changes might stimulate the child to formulate more generic rules about the nature of written language. Only a teacher who was a sensitive observer of reading behaviour should try that manipulation deliberately, watching what happens. In real education situations children often encounter such switches.

Shared reading

As teachers moved to using real books with beginning readers they made a new discovery. The teacher could use the same book with children at different levels of learning but she would work differently with the children on different levels (see *Reading in the Junior Classes*, 1985, a teacher's manual which accompanies the *Ready to Read* books).

The problem of sharing a book with a group of children in a classroom, however small the group, is that the typical trade book can be shared at the level of pictures but not at the level of text. In New Zealand schools the practice grew up of teachers choosing some story books for their memorable quality, high interest and special satisfactions in language, to be made into large versions of the originals with big print that allowed every child in a reading group to see the detail of letters and words. Enlarged text made it possible for a group of children to participate in the pleasures of the story being read to them and at the same time enjoy a clear view of print detail. The text of the enlarged book was an exact copy of the original. The layout of the original trade book guided the format. This helped the children transfer back to the original small book for reading to themselves at a later time. The texts were illustrated but not necessarily elaborately, sometimes by the children themselves. Teachers selected from a range of papers — brown, white or coloured — to make the books. Usually the paper was doubled to add lasting quality and light cardboard covers back and front helped to protect the pages. They were assembled so that the pages were turned and the text read with a left page before a right page. The book was stapled together down the spine with heavy duty staples often bound with book cloth for extra strength.

Many publishers now produce big books (to match smaller story books) and these are used by teachers in small group instruction.

When the teacher wants a group of children to share a story she takes a text which is beyond the reading level of her reading group and, in the manner of the lap story, she introduces it to the children in a way that the discussion calls up most of their prior knowledge that could be directed to this story. Then she reads it allowing for reaction, comment and discussion. At some time she re-reads it with re-telling by the children. Then the story is available for children to browse through, to recall the story by the pictures to discuss with classmates and to request to be read again.

Experiences with story-telling provide an exciting entry to narrative, and are important experiences in their own right. They have special advantages too. They can be used by parents and teachers in situations where there is a shortage of story book literature in the child's familiar home language.

Guided reading

At this stage the children are capable of doing more of the reading work and while the teacher helps them to recall, and problem-solve, and learn about new features in print, she does not share the reading of the story as she did in shared reading. With individual copies of the story the children might sit in an informal group in front of the easel with the teacher seated on a small chair to one side, or they might all be grouped around a table. All need a clear view of the teacher's worksheet or blackboard.

The teacher introduces the book differently from in shared reading. She goes over some important features of the plot, the characters, the language and the concepts. She aims to help children to recall any knowledge they might have to relate to this story. She gets them to help her paraphrase what they think will happen, and the children's reading will then allow them to find out whether their predictions were good ones. During some form of group reading or individual silent reading of the whole story (to keep the plot intact and contributing to the children's thinking) reading work might need to be done on the teacher's large worksheet or a small chalkboard. Some ideas might be recorded here—the characters' names if they are difficult, a phrase or two, a repetitive rhyme, a word or two. Such focussed guidance is brief and temporary, and might occur before, during or after the story, whenever clarification is most helpful and least interfering. In *Reading in the Junior Classes*, how the teacher works at guiding reading appears under the headings:

> Before the reading — Choosing the text
> Before the reading — Selecting a purpose
> Introducing the reading
> During the reading
> After the reading

with particular attention to how the teacher questions the children. That book suggests that 'Children come to know reading as a process of actively reconstructing meaning' and as 'a process of predicting one's way through print.'

However, the reader's reconstructions and predictions are embedded in processes of finding, checking and cross-referencing information from several levels in print (letters, words, sentences and phases of the plot) and operating error detection and self-correction processes on the reconstructions of meaning. So the teacher might also help children to problem-solve a difficulty, or focus on a new feature of print, or make links with things already known, or note another instance of something discovered on a previous occasion. These are only brief detours and children quickly return to the main task of reading the text mostly by themselves. It is preferable for the whole story to be read by each child —certainly not a page today and a page tomorrow, and not a page for Johnny and a page for Mary.

Independent reading

If teachers are always raising the difficulty level of texts to face children with new challenges this must mean that whatever their stage of reading acquisition children could need support and encouragement from their teacher. However, it is possible for them to gain some measure of independence on their tasks at any level, even the novice readers, if the tasks are appropriate, introduced well, and supported at first by interaction with a teacher. Reading for understanding and reading independently are possible at any stage of learning to read, and opportunities should be provided every day for this to occur.

Nevertheless, there is another sense in which the reader becomes an independent reader. The last four chapters of this book are about the child slowly building up the strategies he needs to be an effective reader by carrying out 'reading work' on reading and writing texts and ending up with a system of behaviours which expands itself, i.e. a self-extending system. This is a repertoire of responses which allow him to become better at reading or writing every time he reads and writes. He did not have all those strategies when he began to learn to read but now he is able to approach new texts with very little support from the teacher. He needs less sharing and less guiding, although both types of teaching interaction are still appropriate for texts which are beyond his present independent level. The final chapters of this book relate to independent reading and how the teacher might interact with its development.

A Gradient of Difficulty in Texts

The following discussion about gradients of difficulty applies only to the years of reading acquisition when the learner is building a production system that allows him to read and to learn by reading. In Denmark and New Zealand (see earlier) teachers pay particular attention to a gradient of difficulty in the reading materials in the first one or two years of schooling. While the New Zealand programme is for five year old beginners and tries to harness the children's knowledge of oral language to the task of learning to read, the Danish programme is for seven year old beginners and has something in common with the basal reader approach for the initial teaching of words, letters and sounds but in that country they move away from basal readers during the first year of school (Jansen et al, 1978).

The child who has already taught himself how to construct the utterances of oral language has worked through a gradient of difficulty in that task. We do not understand how young children focus on the most useful and most general aspects of language and gradually build the exceptions and more difficult rules into their use of language but they have been shown in research studies to move through very similar sequences. There is clearly a gradient of difficulty in what they are choosing to attend to in the fully formed language that they hear.

Most school programmes have provided texts for children which start with very easy texts which gradually increase in difficulty. There have been many discussions about what makes texts difficult—such as vocabulary loads, insufficient repetitions of new words for learning, non-regular letter-sound relationships when the child is trying to apply a phonemic analysis, layout of text, absence of meaning. Writers of texts have manipulated these variables in many different ways to create gradients of difficulty in texts which somehow 'match' children's learning.

A gradient of difficulty in series of reading books may occur for three main reasons.

- A sequenced introduction of what has to be learned, like letter-sound relationships or a controlled vocabulary, creates its own gradient of difficulty by insisting that the child move through the predetermined sequence.

- In programmes with many little story books developed on several levels of difficulty, the gradient of difficulty has often been determined by the writers or publishers, hopefully after extensive trialling with children to find groupings of books which those children found easy, more challenging and most challenging. This approach accepts the criteria that a book is difficult if children find it difficult and easy if children find it easy.

- A third approach to a gradient of difficulty accepts the criteria of children's learning response determining the difficulty level but recognises that what is easy or difficult will vary from district to district, from school to school, and from child to child. Teachers make lists of the books they have found useful levelled in some approximate way according to how successful they have proved to be with the children. Experienced teachers carry in their heads knowledge from children's responses to books and are able to 'level' a new story book against some benchmarks they have built up. They have an internalized gradient of difficulty for reading texts. New teachers have yet to gain that experience and they need guidance as to how they know their children are gaining in control over texts. They need to search for benchmarks. It is most useful for teachers to collectively discuss the levelling of texts and to share their knowledge and experience to provide some gradient of difficulty among the books they like to use in the reading acquisition stage with their particular school entrant populations.

If all this discussion sounds somewhat approximate it is intended to be. A gradient of difficulty, established by any means whatever, is going to be wrong for a particular child. A difficult text is a text which is difficult for a particular child. An easy text is easy because a particular child can read it. What ought to be a small challenge to a child who has just completed one book may turn out for him to be an impossible leap into the novel. *Gradients of difficulty are essential for teachers making good decisions about materials they select for children to read but all gradients are inevitably fallible.* They cannot be right for individual children and yet a programme cannot work efficiently without them.

There is an exciting enthusiasm among teachers in some countries today for teaching from story books but this is often associated with a strong disregard for any gradient of difficulty in the texts used. Any levelling of books is seen to be unnecessary and an impediment to learning. Perhaps such teachers are really using their own astute observation of children and knowledge of story books to teach very effectively without an apparent 'gradient of difficulty.' However, many children learning to read will be confused without assistance from some form of a gradient of difficulty in reading books. How do new teachers build up a sensitivity to what makes a text appropriate for particular children at a particular time? A minimum requirement is discussion among teachers about books and which ones suit which children at about which time.

Children who are having difficulty understanding a reading task have particular need for some assistance from the texts they work with, and appropriate sequencing of texts in an individualized programme calls for a great deal of understanding by their teachers of gradients of difficulty in the texts used.

In Summary

Most reading instruction programmes have assumed that children can learn to read on contrived texts which are controlled in many different ways. A different way to learn to read is more comparable to oral language acquisition. The child is provided with texts that relate to what he already knows about language and about the world. Then teacher and child work together on the story. The child is required to problem-solve as much of the text as he can. His problem-solving is supported. Help is not withheld; rather help is regarded as teaching. The test of progress comes when he can problem-solve his way through the whole text independently using cues from language and from print and maintaining a high level of fluency. The criteria of progress are not whether the child can read unseen text, or what new words the child can decode without assistance. The criteria are whether the child can read the texts he needs to read in his education with a problem-solving approach which

(a) allows him to understand the passage, and
(b) makes his reading strategies more effective.

Some texts are more facilitative than others in allowing this problem-solving to occur.

10 Progress on the First Reading Books

On Entry to School

An eager child making a good adjustment to his new school should quickly engage with its programme. This should happen whether he is well-prepared for literacy or not. The difference between the well-prepared and the less well-prepared child will be the level at which he begins his engagement. *It follows that a starting programme should be so designed that it provides for engagement of different children in different ways on different levels from the beginning.*

What children have already learned about literacy is the springboard from which they dive into the school's instruction. What the child has already learned about literacy in the preschool years determines what the child can respond to in the school's programme. Children are not moving to a point in time when they can suddenly take aboard reading and writing (which is what the old idea of 'readiness' suggested); each child is slowly and gradually adding to what literacy concepts and behaviours they bring to school. There is, then, no point in waiting—for maturation, for informal learning, or for the child to get to where the teacher wants to start. The best way to get a process of cumulative learning under way is for the teacher to go to where the child is and help the child to build some kind of useful interactions with books, print and writing, whatever his starting point.

One child could choose to 'read' a simple book with one-line text and write a story about his drawing on his first day at school while another might look at picture books and make some strange marks on paper. The teacher needs to provide a range of such activities so that in the next few weeks she can observe the child and discover where his current strengths lie. Many publications in the last decade which have described literacy learning in early childhood help teachers to understand what prior knowledge the child is demonstrating and what his preferred kind of interaction seems to be.

As well as different starting points a teacher must be prepared for different rates of progress that are *not* indicated by the level of performance at entry to school. What the child can do when he enters school will only be a good indicator of how fast he can now learn if all his preschool experience had allowed for optimum print-oriented learning. Since almost no child will have had opportunities to learn in all areas there is no telling how the pace of taking on new learning could change if the programme starts where the child is, provides large numbers of opportunities, and responds to the child's pace of change (rather than his level of performance on some entry test).

The Shape of Progress

If we were to plot the heights and weights of five year old children on a graph we would find that they scattered around an average in something like a bell-shaped curve — a normal curve.

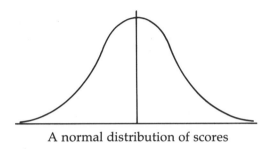

A normal distribution of scores

For beginning reading or writing the curves of attainment are different. At some point in the child's history a decision is made that he begin to read the written language. Usually it is society that decides and in some countries like New Zealand, England and Scotland it is around five years, in the United States around six years and in various European countries around seven years. Because school entry in New Zealand occurs at one particular age (the child's fifth birthday), research studies in that country show clearly how the curves of progress change after entry to school, plotted against age. An idealized form of that progress appears in the next figure.

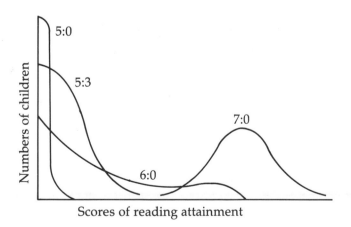

Scores of reading attainment

Only a few children can read on entry to school so the great majority are clustered around a score of nil on tests of word knowledge and writing vocabulary. Children move away from this no-score or zero position at different rates. In the past this has been attributed to intelligence but there is a good case for regarding this as a result of prior knowledge about print activities which children bring to school. The children are faced with learning in new areas and they bring their past learning to bear on it. For most children at this time the formal acts of reading and writing are new or novel behaviours acquired under formal school instruction for which past experiences can be very relevant.

If novel learning is open-ended, continues for years and is cumulative in type, as in learning reading vocabulary, a normal curve of scores will emerge after a period of instruction as with the seven year olds above.

However, if the learning is a closed set of learning like letter identification or letter-sound relationships, the curves move through three phases like this.

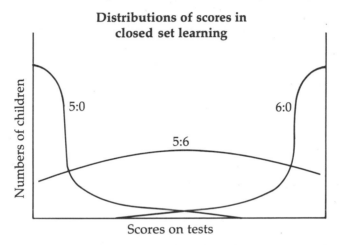

Distributions of scores in closed set learning

If the learning is a skill or series of skills that moves from awkward discovery in the early stages to smooth automatic and rapid responding like directional behaviours or visual analysis of the symbols used in print, then the learning curves are difficult to plot but would be recorded as high levels of slow processing with frequent error dropping off to hardly noticeable levels of processing executed rapidly with only a rare slip from efficiency.

The kinds of indications of progress that teachers might monitor, like words or letters or sounds, have changing shapes to their curves over time, differing from programme to programme according to programme emphases. The ages of peak achievements would differ depending on this and also on the age of entry to school.

A Study of the Spread of Achievement in the Third Year of School

Most schools have some way of linking retention or promotion to the quality of progress that children are making. In very few classes can children be taught across an extremely wide band of achievement. If children get too far behind, the slowest are retained to repeat the work another year. If they get too far ahead they are double promoted into a higher class to be young among older children. Even so most classes have to deal with a wide band of achievement—probably wider than is highly efficient for the organization of teaching or for child learning.

In a random sample of 29 Auckland schools, Wade (1978) checked on the promotion histories of 1195 children aged 7:2–8:2 tested in July-September, the middle of their third year in school. Children who were seven years of age were spread from non-reading to advanced levels of reading. This is a situation to be faced by any educational provision or programme.

Looking at this from the teachers' or schools' viewpoint he found 567 children were clearly at or above reading level for class and 396 were on the low side of average and would make the appropriate level for class by the end of their third year. That totalled 963 children or 80 percent of the children making satisfactory progress. A further 131, or over one in nine were slow progress readers to whom the teacher would have to devote extra time and effort if they were ever to be independent readers. There were another 101 children or one in 12 who were still beginning readers already reading 18 months or more behind their average classmates.

Looking at the cultural makeup of the children not doing so well we find two non-European children for every one European in the low progress groups and two Europeans for every one non-European child in the high progress group.

If there were ways to provide for better progress for those 232 children who have low progress for age the payoff would be considerable in terms of educational effort, economic investment and long-term insurance about a sense of self-worth.

Interventions would have to start early rather than late. Good quality first teaching would be the place to start. Sensitive observation and monitoring of progress by all classroom teachers in the early childhood years with appropriate instructional changes would be a second step, and an early intervention programme with enough power to get a high proportion of those children to independent status in reading and writing would be a third step.

Follow-up of New Entrants in this Third Year

Children whom I studied intensively during their first year at school between 5:0 and 6:0 were retested at 7:0 and 8:0 and the relationship between their early progress and later outcomes in reading skill were reported as correlations. If we consider that a correlation of 0.60 or above indicates a moderate to high relationship between two kinds of behaviour which are changing rapidly and are two years apart in time, then this follow-up study which used tests of word knowledge as criteria of reading progress has some very consistent results.

Relationships of Reading Progress at 6:0 With Later Status
at 7:0 and 8:0

	6:0 Word Test	7:0 8:0 Schonell R1	7:0 8:0 Fieldhouse NZCER
World Test at 6:0 with—	—	.90 .80	.88 .83
Book Accuracy and Rank at 6:0 with—	.93	.80 .69	.77 .72
Letter Identification at 6:0 with—	.84	.86 .81	.80 .83
Concepts About Print at 6:0 with—	.79	.73 .64	.69 .70
General Intelligence (S. B. 1960)	.55	.54 .48	.50 .55
Metropolitan Reading Readiness at 5:0 with—	.55	.49 .45	.43 .48
Self-correction rates averaged 5:0–6:0	.67	.61 .60	— —
Error rate averaged 5:0–6:0	.85	.78 .77	— —

1 Word tests at 6:0 ranked the 83 children available at follow-up in the same order, more or less, as tests at 7:0 and again at 8:0.

2 Book Rank at 6:0 based on running records of the graded reading books was also highly related to later reading status.

3 Letter Identification at 6:0 was also a clear predictor of later status.

4 Concepts about Print scores at 6:0 had a stronger relationship with later progress than might have been expected since, once mastered, these would have little further contribution to make to progress.

5 Individually administered tests of general intelligence correlated 0.5 with later reading achievement which does not indicate a close relationship.

6 Reading readiness scores at 5:0 had lower relationships with later progress than any other variables.

7 The rate of error generation and the rate of self-correction in the first year of learning to read were related to reading progress two years later.

The lower predictability of the readiness test scores suggests that children's 'readiness' has been changed by the programmes of their schools and their later reading achievement does not rank them in the same order as the original scores at school entry. Some performed better than predicted and some performed worse.

A pessimistic note is struck by the consistency in rankings after 6:0 years coupled with widening in the range of achievement. In relation to their classmates children were in much the same ranked positions at 7:0 and again at 8:0 as they were at 6:0. The schools' programmes had served to confirm rather than alter the six year old rankings. The range of achievement had widened but few children had changed their ranking.

We usually reassure ourselves by saying that children differ in ability, that ability differences lead to different rates of learning, and that in our good educational programmes a spread of achievement is to be expected. It is found in every system.

Analysing results of this kind leads one to wonder if it really has to be that way. Evidence we now have shows that literacy learning begins at home in the preschool years and some children come to school without having had those opportunities to learn. There is a strong likelihood that schools that blame poor progress on poor abilities and comfortably accept different rates of progress, may be creating the spread of abilities which we now have in the manner of a self-fulfilling philosophy.

The question then arises as to whether another outcome is possible and that is what the Reading Recovery programme is testing out on a large scale in New Zealand, Australia and some parts of the United States. The purpose of the programme is to alter the progress patterns of the bottom 20 percent of children between 6:0 and 7:0 after a good first year of school in such a way that correlations like those in the last table might be much *lower*.

The Amount of Reading Done

Observation records of book reading were taken at weekly intervals for the 100 children in the Auckland research study and the amount read varied with the progress a child made because the better readers spent a higher proportion of the year in the book reading stage while the poorer readers spent much more of the year in the preparation stage.

Each observation record tallied the number of words read. The reading usually consisted of a very simple book of up to 10 pages or part of a larger book, but always a whole story was read. This was estimated to represent roughly one-sixth of the child's reading experience per week.

Using this estimate we may say that the child making high progress (H) read something in excess of 20,000 words in his first year of instruction, the child in the second quartile group (HM or High Middle) read around 15,000 words, the child in the next quartile group (LM or Low Middle) read about 10,000 words, and the low progress child (L) probably read less than 5000.

Number of Words Read in Weekly Observations
(First Year at School — medium case of each quartile group.)

Progress Group	Words Read	Estimate of Words Read per Year
H	3 570	20 000
HM	2 601	15 000
LM	1 680	10 000
L	757	5 000

The H and HM progress groups were known to be reading and printing at home to a greater extent than LM and L children which would tend to increase differences. Such differences in the quantity of reading might have been expected but their size is interesting. The figures probably reflect the amount of teaching time spent with each group. Teachers may protest at this claim but it takes longer for a child to read the books that have more text. One suspects that when a child fails to respond to the initial efforts of a teacher to get him started on reading and she begins to think of him as a slow developer, there is a natural tendency to devote time to those who are responding and to find an excuse in the maturation concept for letting others come in their own time. Slower children may well benefit from a break with traditional timetabling and the opportunity for brief reading periods twice or even three times each day.

Slow progress children also need many more opportunities for independent reading than they usually get. In our concern to move them into more advanced texts we often reduce the opportunity they get to practise their skills on easy material. High progress children have such opportunities. A wide selection of materials suited to the lower level of skills of slow readers should be available.

Organizing for Prevention

Administrative and staff commitment to a concept of more equitable provisions and an attempt to reduce the numbers of children who make slow progress during the first year or two at school will involve the following.

- Considering the importance of the first year of instruction for shaping an effective versus an ineffective behaviour system, the staff for these early classes must be very thoughtfully selected.

- Classes must be small or we are going to generate inefficient behaviour systems, because teachers must be able to interact with beginners, noting their confusions, and supporting their tentative attempts.

- First year reading progress should be carefully monitored by sensitive observation accompanying each stage of teaching (Clay, 1985). Time for observation must be available. Although the techniques are simple, teachers will have to be taught to use them, and encouraged to develop ways of using them.

- As each child reaches a particular part of the school's programme—perhaps one year into school, or as he turns six or seven years—his progress is checked. If this check is made on or around a birthday it is staggered throughout the year and this would mean that individual assessments could be carried out at any point in the school year. If it is obvious that the child is making satisfactory progress this survey need not be detailed.

- A flexible and experienced teacher, well-versed in teaching individuals and especially qualified in a wide variety of approaches to reading instruction, must be available for intensive and sustained re-teaching of the children making the lowest progress in their second year of school.

Recording Reading Behaviour

The teacher of new entrant children needs less prescription of what to teach and more opportunity for sensitive observation of precisely what her children are doing, so that she can acknowledge a small-step learning gain with enthusiasm. The teacher has to know what direction the learning or development of individual children is taking. She must foster a delicately balanced integration of early skills.

How does a teacher know when a child is failing to progress to a better quality response if much of action is 'in the child's head,' implicit and not expressed in some overt form? A teacher knows the developmental progress of a child:

- if she knows the child well
- if she has some records which catch current behaviour in such a way that it can be referred to some weeks later
- if she sets aside time for observation periods when she pays close attention to precisely what individual children are doing.

The teacher, like the child, will become more articulate about the behaviour observed as a result of doing this.

Knowing what to look for, remembering to arrange to observe it, and making some record of behaviour, are the means to improved observation by teachers. The unlined exercise books which children use in some schools for their drawing and printing activities provide an excellent record of the child's development in creative writing. Each day's activities need to be dated because a child may not move from left to right through the book. Blackboard examples of the child's work do not provide a record (although they could be sketched). Reading very simple books or daily drawing and writing activities provide much opportunity to observe what a child is doing, but only cumulative records allow an accurate assessment of the direction of progress.

Once the child is reading a book a running record can be used as an observation technique (Clay, 1985). It can be employed when a critical decision about promotion from a book or class has to be made, or when reasons for slow progress or error behaviour are being sought. Explicit standards can be recommended. The child is clearly ready for promotion from a book if he reads it at or above the level of one error in 20 words (95 percent accuracy). This standard is too demanding for children who are taking a long time to learn to read and if these children read with one error in 10 words (or 90 percent accuracy) a teacher may consider this satisfactory. Below that level of error most children find it difficult to use meaning as the main check on what they are reading and they attend to analysis of print without making sense of the text. (See Footnote.)

Change to a new book can be of two kinds: (1) to texts of a similar level of difficulty but a different story so that the child has many opportunities to put together all that he is able to do; or (2) to a slightly more challenging text. The child is always ready for more books if he reads a text extremely well or from memory, because it then becomes more difficult to help him to observe more detail in the highly familiar text. Of course that text remains part of his familiar reading material which he returns to for pleasure. Reading only highly familiar books would not challenge the reader to reading work which in turn builds a more powerful set of strategies (see Chapter 13). Parents' observations demonstrate this point.

> *Just rushed in from school and said he could read 'The Fire Engine' and recited it off by heart.*

> *Terence said tonight that he has read the same book at school all the time. It is called 'Early in the Morning' and he is very put out because he doesn't get a new one. I told him it must be because he doesn't know it all properly.*

So there are two main types of gain from reading. The first is enjoying easy reading and familiar texts and having the opportunity to orchestrate a network of decision-making strategies in fast, fluent responding.

The second gain is being challenged to problem-solve some difficulties in a text of about the right difficulty because this results in learning new things

---

FOOTNOTE: If desired a reading rate can also be observed, although I would consider this to be justified only in research studies. After a warm-up on three pages the child's reading of a page is timed with a stop-watch. Take three such records per day per child and the total number of seconds is divided by the number of running words in the text.

about print which in turn gives entry to harder texts. It is not the quantitative gain of another level of book or a 'good' accuracy rating that counts, but the new insights about print that the child has learned during the reading of the book, plus the practice gained in operating on print in suitable ways.

A running record of reading behaviour will show the teacher whether the child is actively sorting and relating cues. It is important for the teacher to think beyond the obvious fact that a child has 'learnt a new word' to what kind of benefit the child can derive from that learning to apply to new texts.

Any time a teacher needs to 'eavesdrop' on a child's processing of text that child should read to an observer those pages of his reading book *for which his teacher has prepared him*. The reason is simple. At this early stage of learning to read unseen material will not give good observation records of processing behaviour, and that is where a running record makes its best contribution. An orientation or introduction to the story provides children with a means of checking on their own reading. Being slightly familiar with what is to come enables the child to do 'reading work' of better quality than novel texts, and that is what the observation needs to capture — how he can work on a text. It is possible for the child to read a whole 'little' book of up to 20 pages (with alternating text and pictures) at one session. The most strategic observations to make are all the oral responses to the written text, including true report, error, attack, repetition, self-correction, and comments on words and letters.

Records are often spoiled when a child omits or invents large sections of a text, and this is more likely to occur on a novel or unseen text.

Some tolerance must be allowed for the time it takes to bring a group of children from a 90 percent to 95 percent accuracy level on a new book, from a day or so to one week, assuming that other books and familiar reading are also being read in the same period. This might be because a particular child is trying to adjust some aspect of the reading process and is struggling at a personal hurdle, or it might be because one child needs more opportunities to practise and consolidate new learning than another.

To achieve objectivity in records of reading behaviours it is necessary for the tester to be a recorder of behaviour and not a stimulus to behaviour. All comment, teaching points, helpful replies, leading questions, and pointing guides have to be dispensed with entirely during a reading observation. A guiding maxim is 'Record now; teach later.'

A Cumulative Record

Records of children's progress through a gradient of text difficulty kept by new entrant teachers will show the horizontal/vertical tendencies of children's progress. The direction of change over time between any two points at which checks are made is important.

Graphs of reading book progress plotted against time at school taken, say, every two or three months, will locate

- children who have been unable to move out of the early reading period
- children who are making excellent progress
- children who have moved out of the early reading period and back into it again.

The graphs which follow (pp 214–215) record weekly observations of reading behaviour of four different groups of children. Along the vertical axis is a scale indicating the level of the reading book the child is attempting. Across the horizontal axis is the time in weeks.

A Cumulative Record Including Accuracy

More informative records would be provided if accuracy counts were made for those children who sound like poor readers and/or those who have largely horizontal records, not moving up into texts of a more challenging kind.

If the class teacher were to take a running record of the child's reading and to work out the accuracy level with which the child is reading, important additional information would then be available. In the previous graphs, weekly observations of reading behaviour were recorded and checked for accuracy. Open circles and black dots distinguish readings above and below 90 percent accuracy. By taking one reading group per week she could cover her class in a month, or once in two or three months whichever she chose. She could plot on a graph the reading book level with an accuracy check.

The graph of 5:0 to 5:6 illustrates that some children established accurate reading very early and showed no change from this; some records show fluctuations between accurate and inaccurate reading; and some records show a sudden switch from inaccurate to accurate reading without subsequent relapse.

The graph of 5:6 to 6:0 illustrates that some children were promoted progressively on books without reading accurately; and some children with inaccurate but rising records began to read accurately towards the end of the period. Others did not.

The graph of 6:6 to 7:0 illustrates that some children who could not read accurately were being moved rapidly through books of increasing difficulty; and mixed records with filled and unfilled circles persisted.

Overall the graphs illustrate that a check on accuracy makes it possible to locate children with consistently unsatisfactory records whose needs are not being met by the teacher and the programme even though they are being moved up through a gradient of text difficulty. It also permits us to locate children who are reading with uncertain accuracy, that is, children whose behaviour system is running roughly. Presumably they have needs which are not being met. They are basing their decisions on inefficient cues. They

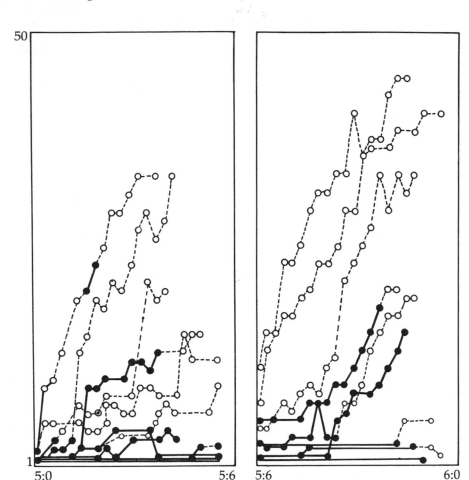

are being moved too fast, prepared inadequately, have insecure strategies, or poorly organized behaviour, or they may have faulty concepts of what is required. Most serious of all, children with vertical black records are being forced daily to practise errors, to use inefficient strategies, and to build habits of responding on this poor foundation.

The Quality of Teacher Judgement

The young child increases his control of oral language by creating texts (what he says) for which his oral language system works well and into which he injects his frontier attempts to extend his control. I think it is the same in reading and writing. Learners do what they do well, and supported

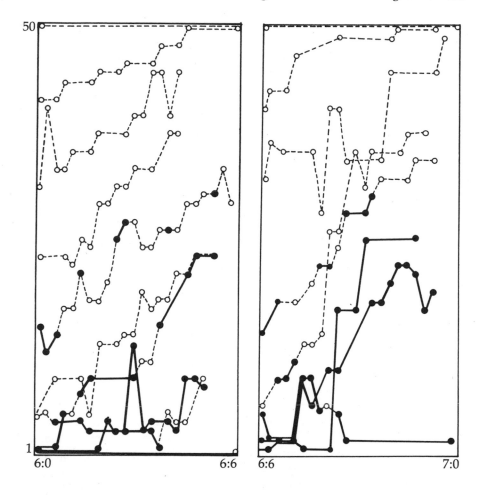

by this context they go beyond the control they already have. *Therefore the reader needs the kind of text on which his reading behaviour system works well.*

Around this limitation we can read stories to children, we can share reading with them, we can introduce stories and let them do what they can with them, but at the heart of the learning process there must be the opportunity for the child to use a gradient of difficulty in texts by which he can pull himself up by his bootstraps: texts which allow him to practise and develop the full range of strategies which he does control, and by problem-solving new challenges, reach out beyond that present control (see the final chapter).

Teacher judgement about texts is very important. The judgement that a child needs to consolidate new learning on a text of similar difficulty to one he has just read, or alternatively that the child is ready for a more difficult text, is a highly skilled one, and the graphs provide evidence that those judgements were often correct in the children I studied.

A teacher who thinks that a child is able to skip three or four steps in a gradient of difficulty is proven correct when the child masters the book easily in a short time at somewhere around 95 percent accuracy. By the same token, her judgement is sometimes wrong and she has some new decision to take. Flexible movement on texts to achieve consolidation of new skills or challenge on more difficult texts is desirable but can only occur as a result of sensitive observation of the child's behaviour and what that behaviour implies.

Fluctuations in performance, large leaps forward, movements backward in text difficulty to consolidate or recapitulate, are movements to be expected under satisfactory conditions of instruction. The characteristics of a satisfactory record would be predominantly forward or upward with consistently accurate reading but with fluctuations.

However, reports of observations in classrooms in many education systems have shown that movement of children through texts may not stem from sensitive observation of the child's reading behaviour but can arise:

- because a particular reading programme says that a gradient of difficulty is not important
- or because, alternatively, rigid attention is given to the sequential steps in a reading programme
- or merely to interest the child without having regard to his achievements
- or because there has been a change of class and the child is fitted into an existing group in the teacher's plan
- or because the end of the school year is approaching
- or for some other administrative reasons.

In none of these cases are the teachers' decisions determined by what the child is currently able to do. Without sensitive observation of reading behaviour teachers' judgements of appropriate challenges along a gradient of difficulty are liable to be unsuitable.

One further point should be made. One can trace in such records that teachers' decisions become more appropriate as children move up the scale of difficulty. It is at the early reading stage where fluctuations are greater and the ups and downs more pronounced. Drops in the effectiveness of the child's reading behaviour system are less readily predicted and sudden gains are surprising. Two different explanations can be offered and both are thought to be operating concurrently. The child's behaviour is difficult for the teacher to observe in the early reading stage and she may have a little more difficulty knowing what his current skill is. In addition, there is evidence to suggest that the child's behaviour is being organized at this point in time into an efficiently functioning system, and it is possible for him to make big gains as he discovers new ways of linking some aspects of behaviour. The reading behaviour system can suddenly improve in efficiency.

The conclusion from this is that more time and more care will be needed closer to the beginning of reading than will be necessary once a satisfactory behaviour system has been established.

Even at this early stage the failing child, if not detected, may practise bad habits daily until they are firmly established in an inefficient system for processing cues. However, there is evidence to suggest that if we actively support partial correctness rather than negate it as wrong, learning will proceed at a faster rate. It takes a well-trained person who knows a great deal about possible routes to success to be able to effectively support partial responding in reading. Adults do this naturally in speaking to the pre-schooler because they respond rather consistently to meaning, even when the child produces a partially correct response. Perhaps 'helpers' could effectively use a similar approach. Nevertheless, the teacher needs to attend closely herself to the early changes in reading and writing behaviours of her new entrants and to support shifts in the child's attempts which are moving in an appropriate direction.

However, this is not what usually happens. Until the child demonstrates clearly to the teacher that he can read in some organized way she is more inclined to let him browse, listen to stories on tape while looking at a book, or let parents or parent helpers work with him.

Individual and Group Instruction

The term individual instruction refers here to one child taught by one teacher. (There are many programme variations called individualized instruction which do not refer to teaching interactions with an individual child.)

Although it may be ideal it is almost impossible for the teacher of a class to teach children individually on their own particular choices of books (although I know of some teachers who try to do this). The difficulty which group and individual instruction share but which is so much more acute in individual instruction is keeping the rest of the class gainfully employed while the teacher interacts with a single child.

For group instruction this can be achieved in a variety of ways. Helpers may supervise other class activities while the teacher works with a few children, or there may be team-teaching arrangements. Children may work at reading or re-reading on teacher- or child-selected activities or on creative activities which are an outcome of reading, inspired by them, and which provide evidence of the children's understanding of what they read (Clay, 1986). Good teachers avoid mere busy work like workbooks. There are various ways of getting extra helpers for those other children (such as parent participation, team teaching or peer support) but the best solution is to make as many of the class independent readers and writers as soon as possible because then they can, by definition, engage in independent learning activities.

The greatest challenge to the teacher, and the busiest time, is during the early reading stage. In many classrooms a small group of children share a story with the teacher and work together on some aspects or features in the print, and this is a satisfactory introduction, with children reading the story individually to the teacher after this.

Allocating time for some one-to-one instruction will always be necessary and this is profitable expenditure of teacher time for it allows for directing the teacher-child interaction to a particular child's needs. Such focussing can accelerate learning that takes longer under conditions of group instruction for some children.

Questions of Classroom Grouping

Should teachers work with groups or individuals?
Practices differ. In British schools the emphasis is on individual children interacting with the teacher during reading. In New Zealand it would be quite common for a teacher to be managing four levels of reading groups each of six to eight children, but memberships of these groups change often throughout the year according to rates of progress. In some American classrooms group membership would be set by a readiness test which determines which children stay together during the year because children are working through a sequenced curriculum.

There are some important questions teachers should ask as they work with children in groups. In the United States there has been a strong and justified critique of grouping as 'tracking' children, preventing children making poor progress from getting opportunities to interact with rich texts, among other things. However, a wholesale move to whole class teaching fails to solve the gradient of difficulty problem, unless we assume that on a particular text the teacher gives little time to the competent readers and large amounts of time are spent interacting and sharing the reading task with poor readers.

What are the characteristics of a reading group that works for learners?
Children in a group are likely to be of mixed age and widely varied in general ability but they will have in common somewhat similar reading behaviours *at a particular point of time.*

When and how does regrouping occur?
This is the key question. If reading is dependent on cumulative learning then classroom groups must be changed according to the rate of individual progress of children. A teacher cannot establish her reading groups at the beginning of the year and keep them intact throughout the year. If she does then she is not addressing individual differences, and not responding to differential rates of progress or allowing for different paths to the same goal. Somehow her practices are locking children into fixed rates of progress.

What is certain is that children will show different rates of progress not related to their level of performance at entry to school but related to the programme's potential to engage them in useful learning.

A fast learner should move forward to a high group reading texts more appropriate for that child. A child who needs some consolidation of new skills can move to a new group just beginning a text on the level he requires but different from the book he just struggled with.

Regrouping may occur because a survey of aspects of reading has been conducted (Clay, 1985) and revealed some surprises. Some children can handle texts more independently than the teacher supposed and others may now be showing confusions that she could not have anticipated. Grouping must be responsive to the effects of learning during the year and not predetermined by entry characteristics.

Regrouping may occur because a teacher, sitting beside one child to listen to him reading, inobtrusively takes a running record on a scrap of paper and discovers that the book is far too easy for the child.

Why would a teacher give the child a harder level of text?

The teacher would judge that the child's whole reading process is ready for new challenges and, although uncertain about what or how the child will learn from a harder text, the teacher changes the level of difficulty, increases her helpfulness and observation, and supports the child's renewed effort to learn.

Why would a teacher select a book at the same level of difficulty?

Before a story becomes boring, highly familiar, or signals to the child lack of success and lack of progress, it needs to be changed. Here the value of having many different short books that are somewhat equivalent in vocabulary and difficulty level becomes apparent. To avoid the situation of reading that old book yet again the teacher shifts the child to a new story on which he can consolidate the skills not yet quite under his control. New discoveries are possible as the child is now attending closely again to the new book. Interest is stimulated, known skills have to be applied to novel text, and there is another opportunity to learn to orchestrate the reading behaviours in a total reading situation.

How does a teacher work with a group?

Children's attention would be drawn by the teacher to some familiar texts — story, poem, song or language experience text — some of which are read. In New Zealand classrooms one might see the following procedures.

- A new text is introduced with attention on understanding the story in some holistic way.

- A small blackboard is used to solve errors or work on difficulties as they arise.

- Children are encouraged to find their own errors and do something about the mismatches of information.

- Teachers encourage word work in many different ways: for example, by grouping initial letter words in lists — shaving, shouted, shop; by inviting children to discover a new word by analogy — went, by, bent; by working in similar ways on a particular word to draw attention to its construction; or by brief but necessary word study of a new, difficult or forgotten word. *This is a temporary move from text to detail and the group return to the whole story.*

- Teachers take these opportunities to observe closely what individual children are saying and doing.

- Many opportunities to return to this text are devised for the individual, pairs, a group of peers or a teacher-led group which allows the child to re-read that story several times.

Progress on the First Books

The length of time children spend with a reception or preparatory or new entrants' class teacher will depend upon the organization of schools in a particular education system. Variables like age of entry, type of programme, and level of print awareness may be important. Frequently a defined part or whole of the calendar year is allocated to this transition by education systems.

This could be determined by the child's entire pattern of engagement with the school and particularly by his progress in literacy learning. For if we take preschool exposure to literacy learning seriously so that children are allowed to build on to the competencies that they bring to school, then schools have to make some choices.

- They can kill time for competent children while they work throughout the year with the least well-prepared who have more ground to cover.

- They can move with the competent children and retain the low achievers to repeat the first year again since the preparatory class has not prepared them adequately for the following year's work.

- They can group and regroup children throughout their first year of school according to their level of engagement, responsive to the changes in their learning and even changing their classes to place them with children at their level of challenge.

It is rare to find a field programme which aims to take the third option, and almost beyond the realms of possibility to find a school system providing extra and better teaching in order to accelerate the progress of those who might have missed out on some of the preschool preparation for literacy and be having some difficulty making the transitions and trans-lations.

I will use one New Zealand study to illustrate these points but practices have changed in more than two decades and the description is not a current one. One hundred children were studied in 1963–64 in five different schools. In some sense the movement of children was governed by the calendar. No child was book-reading on entry to school but most children were in daily direct contact with simple book material and language experience materials within five to seven weeks of school (Clay, 1967).

So the assumption was that children would be able to interact *in some way* and at some level with text material on entry to school. This suggested an awareness that early reading skills have to be learned on printed texts and are not acquired in play with blocks and puzzles.

Exploring writing was regarded as related experience and was introduced to the five year olds in the first week of school. Such practices must be accompanied by observation of the ways in which different children interact with text reading tasks, whether they are well-prepared or poorly prepared. This must be observation of *individual* children. All may be introduced to the world of print but the teacher's teaching goals for particular children should already begin to differentiate according to these observations of the child's current interactions with texts.

Stories were being read to children daily but the uniformity with which teachers introduced all children to reading very simple story books for themselves was interesting. While all children were introduced to simple texts on entry to school the timing of their transfer into more difficult story texts was different. There was a range of three to 21 weeks on language experience types of materials before children began to attempt to read books.

At first glance that seems to reflect the time it took children of different abilities to master early reading skills but when one looks in more detail at the 'promotion patterns' through a gradient of texts, some important questions arise. Are some children being hurried unduly through their books as the end of the year approaches? Was the low progress group being adequately prepared for their books, for they spent as much as nine whole weeks on the first reader level? Could the teacher have given these children more individual attention? Would more help and support have brought about more rapid change?

These are questions about classroom groupings for instruction and the extent to which assumptions about these facilitate or constrain progress which the children can make.

The progress of a successful reader

The description that follows is an account of close to optimum learning in a programme which valued text reading for meaning. This is not to say that this reader did not have a bank of known words and considerable phonological segmentation skills. Listening to her read or taking careful records of reading behaviours rarely showed any overt evidence of processing at the letter or word level. No experiments were conducted to externalize such knowledge.

The child to be used as an example was well-prepared by her preschool experiences and was the middle child of the top 25 percent of a research sample (Clay, 1966). I will call her Helen.

Helen entered school at five years. Her adjustment was good and she settled quickly. She had high intelligence measured by an individual test and was at the lower limit of the superior group (I.Q. 118 to 128). She mastered left to right directional behaviour within three weeks of entering school. She was given a simple reader after five weeks, she self-selected a preprimer of an American basal series after nine weeks and read it very well with some knowledge of words, some detection of errors and the use of several cues to achieve a precise response to the text. At 11 weeks she had moved out of the reception programme and was placed in a new class and promoted to books listed by teachers as at the first level of difficulty.

She moved slowly through the lower levels of the gradient of difficulty provided by the teachers and she read many different books. When she had been at school for six months Helen read a new story every week and each book had more text in it. She read fast at the rate of one word per second. Her accuracy level on a book two to five days after it was introduced was about 95 percent. Her responses were therefore both fast and accurate for her level. On easy material Helen produced errors which she did not notice because she read so fast that her voice was outrunning her visual checking skills. At other times she was quick to detect error because it was very obvious in her otherwise accurate reading. She absorbed new vocabulary readily.

Helen had effective text reading strategies. She was accurate on her first responses making one error in 37 words and with her self-corrections she successfully corrected one error in three. She was satisfied only if her response was highly probable within the meaning and syntactic context. To achieve self-correction Helen's major strategy was returning to the beginning of a line or sentence. She did not read ahead to gather context; rather she took a fresh run at what had gone before. Helen's knowledge of structure (syntax) in English guided her responding. She substituted words that could have occurred in English in that position 76 percent of the time. She repeated lines to confirm correct responses.

On new words Helen's main strategy was not to sound out the word. After a rapid search she seemed to decide 'I cannot read that one' and she asked to be told. She problem-solved the word when it recurred in the text after that. Her errors showed letter-sound associations 50 percent of the time.

In summary, she had completed all the levels of reading preceding the move to much longer texts and heavier new word loads by the end of her first year at school. She had fast efficient techniques for extracting a sequence of cues in a text sequence. She expected her sentences to be meaningful and highly probable. Letter-sound awareness was paid less attention than the structure of language in sentences. Sound associations were not used overtly very often.

The top 25 percent of children in the Auckland research study could not be expected to make better progress under any reading scheme. They enjoyed reading and writing, they were proud of their attainment, they made the transfer to longer stories and books effortlessly, and they read fluently for meaning. An analysis of their efficient self-correction behaviour showed that they were working for meaning. These children needed a short time on a book, absorbed new vocabulary readily, quickly detected errors, corrected themselves effectively. They used meaning and grammatical or structural cues effectively. Perhaps they could have learned, with a little extra effort, to give even more attention to features within words and to search for many kinds of information in print. By the time they can approach extended texts independently they need to have a range of ways of solving new words. These good readers appear to do their own analysis of the relationships between words (analogy) and between print and sound even when the instructional programme does not stress these, but teachers can encourage this by appropriate questioning.

How did less successful readers respond?

The reading behaviour of Bob, a child who made average progress in this research group, differed in many respects. He took 16 weeks to master left to right directional behaviours. He 'read' many simple books in his seventh to twentieth week at school, and further preparatory books for six more weeks. He was then promoted to the first text level for 'real reading' and was already attempting to correct his own errors spontaneously as he read. He completed half as many steps in the gradient of text difficulty as Helen (above) did in her first year at school. At 6:0 he was where Helen was at 5:6. He had read about the same amount of text material in one year as she had read in six months. He made errors once in every 10 running words and normally read with about 90 percent accuracy. He corrected one error in six, and read at the rate of one word every 1.5 seconds. Thus, as well as taking twice as long as the high progress reader to cover similar ground, this average child made more errors, read less accurately, engaged in less self-correction, and habitually read half as slowly. This pattern of behaviour suggests not merely a slower pace but a learning experience that differs markedly from that of the high progress reader. Nevertheless he seemed to be making progress along the same trajectory as Helen, once he got through the necessary transitions and translations.

Children who made moderately good progress seemed to have the right approach to reading but had not yet constructed such reliable bases for sampling cues and making decisions as their high progress peers. They needed to pay more attention to visual form (bearing in mind that initial letters probably are the ones which help to classify words in a maximally useful way at this level). They needed to use sentence structure to anticipate what might follow and to learn better use of cues for checking on their predictions. More time could be spent building up expectations for the words that might occur next (and that would happen in today's classrooms). As a group this moderate progress group was hurried through the reading books at a pace which the children could not always sustain and one improvement to their instruction might have been to hold them a little longer on texts which helped them to consolidate efficient responding and to offer more opportunities to reread familiar texts. Also teachers must be prepared to accept a temporary drop in fluency as legitimate when a child is trying to use new kinds of cues or information in the on-going activity.

The low progress group

The middle child of the slow progress group was Tony who was also given a simple book in the seventh week of school and also took 15 to 16 weeks to master directional behaviour. By the end of a year he had been moved through three levels of text reading but he had had a succession of unsuccessful experiences with books. He made one error in every three words, usually read with 60 percent accuracy and corrected one error in 20 words. Yet he was trying to read at the same pace as the average child, one word in 1.5 seconds. Over the long summer vacation he forgot a great deal more of the limited skills he had learned than children in the higher groups. His foundation for future progress in reading was basically unsound.

Some children in the slow group had pronounced directional difficulties which had to be overcome before they could begin to respond appropriately to texts. In the first year at school the lower half of the children did not do much reading and perhaps two reading periods a day could be organized for them. High progress children will create more practice for themselves in the classroom and at home. Slow learners will not. Probably this is just as well because low progress children need close attention from a helpful tutor to support their few correct responses. They are often right but do not know that they are right. As they try to read they destroy the semantic and syntactic context with their error behaviour and they need help and encouragement to put the fractured utterance together again. Rhyme, rhythm and memory for the text are legitimate props for these children. Special attention to the predictability of their texts and reading environment is also important. Good introductions of the simple texts they read will support their efforts.

Time has passed and educational change has occurred in the New Zealand education system. The classroom programmes for the first year of school have become more oriented to emerging literacy, to the importance of oral language, and to sharing children's story books with children. A new series of story books have been specially written to stress meaning as the most important aspect of early literacy learning.

But, in addition to those changes, there is now a programme which children like Tony get which is individually designed and individually delivered to accelerate his progress by starting from where the child is and moving along the most accelerative path for him bringing him as close to average band performance for his school as possible. At the time of writing in 1989 between 10 and 20 percent of children (i.e. those who are the poorest performers in this low quartile like Tony) are getting supplementary and better teaching in the Reading Recovery programme. It is better teaching because teachers have special training and work one-to-one with children's learning needs. After one year in a good first programme,

- when teachers can be almost certain that the trajectory of progress for a particular child is deviating markedly from the successful children in her programme

- and when teachers can reliably identify children who are at the lowest levels of literacy performance without false categorization

extra help is provided to bring these children through the transitions into literacy learning. For all but a few this seems all that was needed. A very high proportion are able to engage with the mainstream of their classroom programme as a result of this help which comes from daily 30-minute lessons lasting 12 to 20 weeks.

Children must be given time to engage and to show how they can respond to classroom programmes. The unreliability of observations and the sudden shifts with new insights that children make have to be allowed to occur. By the end of a year at school New Zealand children are six years of age, and that has been used as the time for teachers making judgements about who are the children with the lowest literacy achievements, despite good first year programmes. A range of literacy achievements is surveyed and the children selected for special help are the lowest performers, not excluding anyone for any reason.

What is the Child Learning?

In some programmes the answer to that question is quite clear, because the programmes are designed to teach a particular sequence of skills. The materials and the curriculum make highly visible the learning that the programme intends to develop. As we have seen in previous chapters children who are successful in such programmes will in reality learn many more skills than the programme specifies. Such learning is overlooked when the value of these highly controlled programmes is assessed.

When children are not learning from a planned sequence in a basic series but on a variety of texts, what progress do we look for? Any method of instruction will selectively stress some aspects of the mature reading process to the neglect of others. What aspects are taught in a programme where the children read real books, write creative stories rather than complete planned exercises, and use texts which do not have clearly marked gradients of difficulty? Can one ask of these programmes, 'What are the skills being fostered?'

Firstly there is usually high dependence on oral language skills as a source of responses, to support fluency by creating expectancies of what might come next, and for developing checking strategies rather than traditional word-attack techniques.

Five years olds begin by 'reading' sentences. The use of detailed visual information tends to be learned very slowly over the first year of instruction. The children develop considerable facility in error detection and correction as a result of checking strategies but analytic methods of word-attack for new vocabulary are not used overtly and do not appear in the records of even the high progress group. If there is a lack of attention at the subword level this might become particularly noticeable when children move to longer texts with a heavier load of new words, and more multisyllabic words.

The skills learned in the first six to 12 months at school are many. Some that might be listed are these.

- Directional control appropriate for print.
- How to draw upon and use background experience.
- Using pictures as an aid to reading print.
- Using some conventions of print.
- Searching for meaning.
- Taking risks (on the basis of available information).
- Word by word reading.
- Re-running for various purposes.
- Cross-checking two types of cues.
- Self-correcting following recognition of errors.
- Confirming attempts in an alternative way.
- Using some letter-sound relationships.
- Using first letters.
- Using word endings.
- Correcting medial sounds.
- Using letter clusters.
- Getting to new words by analogy with known words.
- Building a vocabulary of high-frequency reading words.
- Building a vocabulary of high-frequency writing words.

It is perhaps more helpful to cluster what the child is learning under the heading of the type of activity he could be engaged in in the classroom.

1 From hearing stories read
The child learns more language in discussion, more book language, a range of new vocabulary, more about how pictures cue meaning, more about story structures that help with understanding how stories work, more about the enjoyment to be found in books.

2 From shared reading
As the learner tentatively joins with the group in reading a story he is supported for trying, predicting, confirming, self-correcting, spotting visual cues, recognizing print, and learning to sample cues in effective ways. Texts may range from the most enjoyable story books to very simple books but are not just word labels on pictures.

3 Language experience activities
These allow the child to produce stories, construct his own texts, read

them to himself or to others, use familiar words, meanings and structures and focus on the constructive task of making a book or telling a whole story. So much is familiar that it is easy to give attention to cues and relationships, to controlling the total act in a fluent but well-managed sequence.

4 Writing

This places more attention on visual graphic forms, the order and sequence of letters, on knowing a word in every detail, on the relationships of sounds to letters both regular and irregular, and on how to relate ideas to written forms.

5 Reading books

On familiar texts the young reader practises the orchestration of this complex set of achievements calling up information to support a strategy of self-correction as and when needed. On new texts or new aspects of more familiar texts the young reader can put to the test his range of word analysis strategies.

This is a reasonably large number of things to learn to control in the first few months of school. The fast movers work through the skills listed above, the average readers make good progress, and the slow progress children work on the early skills on the list.

At its best the behaviour fostered is very similar to that of a mature reader except that the child has a very limited number of specific responses to a few sources of text information. Development should be in the direction of more responses, finer discriminations and greater flexibility.

This approach is appropriate for young children who come to school with relatively mature and stable language skills which can provide a good anchorage for new learning. On the other hand it is essential experience for children who come to school with less advanced language and world knowledge. For both groups visual discrimination of what carries information in print is new learning and will probably be learned slowly. Similarly, the sound segments of words are something that most children will have paid little attention to in the past and this learning may also be acquired slowly.

A programme which uses story texts in this way does not appear to build in a clear, sequenced introduction to the analysis of words and letter-sound relationships. Two major reasons given for avoiding such sequencing are that they draw the child's attention away from the leading role that meaning ought to play, and that they complicate the task for children who make slow progress. On the other hand critics have claimed that because such skills distinguish good and poor readers, these poor readers must be instructed in the skills as the major focus of their programme.

What these critics have overlooked is that it is possible to direct children's attention and learning to the analytic aspects of text *during* the reading and enjoyment of real stories. That is, of course, what good readers are doing on narrative or informational texts. It is also easy, when the child is writing, to teach him about *hearing and writing sounds and clusters* in ways that the child can relate to his reading of texts.

Planning for Maximum Success in Early Literacy

A programme starting at different levels
It is logically possible to design a programme limited in vocabulary, in the letters used, in regularity of letter-sound relationships, or in regularized spelling so that learning is fed systematically into the child's experience. The curriculum is defined: you start here and go to there.

On the other hand the early reading programme which allows the child to pick up a particular fragment of knowledge about print which he can recognize, and extends his response from there, utilizes the prior knowledge of the child to best advantage in classroom instruction. This recognizes that children differ in abilities and in prior learning about literacy. They arrive as new entrants having had varying degrees of opportunity to use that potential to the full, as a result of very individual sets of experience. The children's talents may be under-developed or highly fostered by their preschool environments. They have formed interests and have learned to be selective in the stimuli that catch their attention. If the most interesting word that a child can first learn is his name (or that of a family member) then children move off from very different starting points—i.e. different knowledge of the alphabet and print.

Such a programme would have to allow children to enter instruction at different levels.

Observing precisely what children are doing
Having a good programme for a large class of children is fine, but unless the progress of individuals is followed it will result in (1) survival of the fittest, and (2) good readers who get better and better, and poor readers who get poorer and poorer. Individual differences will emerge as the fast learners master the learning tasks in a few weeks while the average and slow learners take much longer. Those who can will learn and teach themselves more and more. Those who struggle will develop some confusions, some false concepts, effortful processing and handicapping strategies. When it takes a long time for a child to develop consistent directional behaviour, say six months, he will already have had many opportunities to practise wrong responses. The fast learner who has mastered the habit early is saved from such error practice. That example may be indicative of what occurs in many aspects of early reading and contributes in some way to the 'Matthew effect' (Stanovich, 1986). Slow learners cannot be pushed with undue haste into learning new skills which they need to build slowly, but there are dangers in leaving them practising poor procedures for prolonged periods. One might even suggest that six months of muddlement is more than enough to create poor readers out of school entrants with average or superior intelligence. Certainly some intensification of help and supported learning should be

initiated for the child who has made little response to literacy experiences after six months in school.

More help and more books to read

Both undue haste and prolonged delay can be detrimental to the child's progress *once he has begun to try to participate*. Teachers can improve the quality of their decision-making if they make careful records of literacy behaviours (Clay, 1985), organize for some individual teaching time for those making the slowest progress, and treat early reading and early writing as reciprocal processes helping the child to use one set of learning to support the other. Research now questions whether training perceptual skills on pictures and geometric forms does carry over to reading progress. Perhaps the translation is harder than the original reading task!

The sets of learning observed during the early reading stage are fostered by contacts with written language. The visual perception of print, the directional learning, the special types of language used in books, and the synchronized matching of spoken word units with written word units will only be learned in contact with printed language. There is a strong case for saving learning time by supporting the immature child in reading tasks on simple story books and giving him more time and more help in a more controlled, detailed and structured way in his areas of weakness.

If a child shows low performance in any or all of the four sets of behaviour—directional learning, visual scanning for information, hearing sounds in words, or the language aspects of the task—it is consistent with much research that his new tasks, reading and writing, be approached through as many sources of information as possible so that strong skills can support the strengthening of weak ones. Rather than leave the child who is poor in language playing in the developmental group for extra time, he needs the introduction to early literacy activities that other children get, but for more time, and with closer teacher interaction. He also needs more attention and enriched experiences in his areas of weakness so he can learn to produce the new behaviours. It is pointless to wait for them to blossom without tutoring and support.

PART FOUR

The Deep Structure of Success: Reading Strategies

11 Behaviours Signal a Developing Inner Control

This chapter discusses *observable* behaviours which seem to signal a developing inner control. While I assume that reading involves a system of perceptual and cognitive operations, teachers can see only the outward, observable signs of these.

The discussion applies to the reading acquisition stage of any instructional programme which has been designed to encourage children to read independently.

When the young reader is able to read class-appropriate materials with almost no need for teacher assistance, this is often described as reaching a level of 'independent reading.' What is the nature of this independence? What signals its existence? What acts as its control system? What are the processes used by an independent reader? What gives independent reading its forward thrust? Such questions provide the theme of the last four chapters of this book.

Sensitive Observation While Teaching

Teachers can become astute observers of reading and writing behaviours and skilled at producing responses which advance the child's learning. In doing this they become more articulate about child behaviours, and what they may mean (Clay, 1987). Observing reading behaviour informs a teacher's intuitive understanding of cognitive processes and her teaching improves. *She has a way of gathering data during teaching and she has a way of keeping her explanations of her teaching in line with what her pupils actually do.* So every teacher builds a kind of 'personal theory' of what the surface behaviours in reading imply about the underlying cognitive processes.

It is my suggestion that teachers can become sufficiently expert in observation to use what they see children doing as a way of checking on their own theories. My argument is not that reading behaviours can provide us with an adequate explanatory theory of reading, because cognitive operations are clearly involved. The first part of the argument is that the observation of surface events (reading behaviours) guides what teachers do and that systematic observation (the collection of data) will increase quality of teaching. The second part of the argument is that the teachers' reflection and planning should change as they search for better explanations of how children are producing those behaviours. Teachers who are good observers of their students have a means of refining their personal theories of what it is to learn to read.

Much discussion about instruction has been directed to getting correct performance, as if learning to read depended on an accumulation of correct responses. However, many of the child's early attempts to read are partially right and partially wrong and, like parents talking to a little child, teachers need to make a facilitating response to the half-right, half-wrong response of the child at a particular moment in time. They must respond to gradual shifts in less than perfect performances. (A good analogy is with the less than perfect language of the two year old which gradually shifts to the control of the four or five year old.) The child passes this particular point in his experience only once. What does the teacher have to know or do to make the most of it?

When children are novice readers their cognitive processes used for reading are 'in formation,' undergoing changes from less expert to more expert. Available theory rarely addresses this problem. Explanatory theories in cognitive psychology usually address questions of mature and expert functioning or expert subprocesses achieved by young readers: they rarely address questions of *continuous* change over time in immature processing. Yet that is what reading involves at the acquisition stage. Sensitive and systematic observation of behaviour is really the only way to monitor gradual shifts across imperfect responding (and research in oral language acquisition has demonstrated this).

Sensitive observations of particular changes in the behaviour of individual children (linked to some explanatory assumptions) are helpful to the practising teacher. However, it is asking too much of the class teacher of 20 to 30 children to carry in her head the particular learning history of each child during the past two or three weeks. Yet this is what the mother talking to one preschooler remembers! It is helpful for the teacher to have some systematic observations to refer to and to guide her responses to the half-right responses. She needs to be on the same track as the child and systematic observations of how the child is working with texts from time to time provide the teacher with necessary information.

Treating behaviour (what the child is doing) and cognition (what the child is thinking) as explanatory alternatives is not helpful for understanding teaching interactions. Both teacher and child exhibit behaviours and both operate on cognitions. The teacher has a general theory in her head about children's responding. This is a theory she should check against what she is able to observe and infer from the individual child's responding, and which she should be prepared to change if the two are in conflict. So although reading behaviours are only signals of the inner control over reading that a child is developing, they are important signals which teachers should notice and think about.

Signs of a Developing Inner Control

1 Using language

Reading involves messages expressed in language. Usually it is a slightly different kind of language which is found in books. Most children bring to the reading situation a fluent oral control of their mother tongue. This consists of an unconscious control of most of the sounds of the language (with some ability to manipulate these orally in rhyming, inflections, invented words, and new vocabulary), a large vocabulary of words standing for meanings and relationships that are understood, and cognitive strategies for constructing sentences. The child's speaking is generated by an inner control of language which is being expanded by our conversations with him. One can 'hear' the child's oral language in his early attempts to read and write.

2 Gaining concepts about print

Reading also involves learning certain concepts about print, concepts that the skilled reader is not even aware of because he responds without apparent attention to them (to the direction, spaces, formats, punctuation cues and general features of texts). Pick up a Chinese, Thai or Hebrew text and explore your own concepts about print! Preschoolers in a print-filled society learn some of these concepts from the print in their environment so that they come to school quite well-informed. There is no reason for children in orally oriented societies to pay much attention to print until they enter formal schooling.

3 Attending to visual information

Reading involves visual patterns—sentences/groups of words/syllables/ blends/letters—however one wants to break the patterns up. The reading process appears to be so automatic in skilled readers that it is only by drastically altering the reading task in experiments that we can show how adults scan text to pick up cues from patterns and clusters of these components. The reading acquisition task is to discover what the significant patterns in print are. Children begin to explore the visual patterns of print in very personal ways and from very different starting points. (Features which they are attending to are clearly evident in their attempts at early writing.)

4 Hearing sounds in sequence

Reading involves knowing about the sound sequences in sentences, in words, in syllables, and in letter clusters. The flow of oral language does not always make the breaks between words clear and children have some difficulty breaking messages into words. Children find syllables easier to locate; they have greater difficulty breaking up a word into its sequence of sounds and hearing the order in which those sounds occur. This is not strange. Some of us have the same problem with the note sequences in a new melody.

Four different kinds of behaviours have been described above, all of which children need to control when they try to read texts.

Language was put first because language has two powerful bases for prediction: its structures and its meanings. The child uses these skilfully before school. A third language base exists in the sound system of the language which the child uses but which has only been accessible for conscious manipulation in activities like rhyming and the use of inflections.

The concepts about print were mentioned because although this learning soon requires little attention from the reader it cannot be taken for granted in the early stages of learning to read. It is sometimes the source of some fundamental confusions. Concepts about print govern the child's attention to print, acting as a road map for directing that attention and other behaviours (Clay, 1989).

The visual analysis skills were mentioned because visual cues are basic for correct, fluent functioning. Skilled readers tend to use as little visual knowledge as possible, scanning for just enough information to check on the meaning. The beginning reader must discover for himself what visual cues are helpful in reading, and when and how it might be safe to use partial information. If we are forced to explore the features of some unfamiliar scripts (to read place names in Japanese, for example), we begin to appreciate what the beginning reader's task is like.

Print-sound relationships used by the reader are varied and are not limited to letter-sound associations. All readers tend to work in chunks or clusters if possible. To operate sounding-out behaviours two kinds of analysis must be brought into strict co-ordination:

- an auditory, temporal analysis of the sound sequences in spoken words (hearing sounds in words)
- and the visual and spatial analysis from left to right of letters or clusters of letters in a written word.

Order is the major cue in this co-ordination. However, it is important to note that readers usually check this information with other sources to see if they have arrived at a meaningful conclusion. Letter-sound associations on their own will lead to unreliable pronunciations. Novice readers are able to anticipate a word from a few letter-sound cues and more competent readers are able to check out details when they are uncertain because both types of readers are drawing on other sources of information such as their control of language and meanings.

Reading acquisition involves the accessing and integration of these processes and there are undoubtedly other component processes which are not easily observed in everyday oral reading. After only one year at school the high progress reader has an inner control over these sources of information in print, can manipulate or cross-reference any of them, and can operate with high accuracy and high self-correction rates (Clay, 1967). With meaning as both guide and goal, the reader checks what he thinks the text will say with visual information, and by carrying out analytic manipulations. This young reader has several alternative ways of functioning according to the difficulty level of the material. If he cannot grasp the meaning and check the print with higher-level strategies he can use any of several lower-level strategies. A teacher observing and thinking about the reader's behaviour can build some theory of how the child is working on the task 'in his head.'

Expect Different Reading Behaviours in Different Programmes

Common descriptions of reading 'methods' like 'look and say,' 'teaching sight words,' 'teaching phonics' and 'a whole language approach' are gross caricatures of the programmes actually delivered, and merely highlight particular emphases and advocacies. Reading programmes cannot and do not teach just sight words, or phonics or some strange thing called whole language. One has images of some machine delivering the words of a text one on top of the other in the sight word task, or always having to read at the letter-sound level, or never analysing below the whole story level. Such labels applied to reading programmes are also extremely poor characterizations of what a reader does as he reads. Reading is more complex than these labels imply.

How do these labels come about? What are the different emphases among teaching methods? A language is organized on several levels: phonetics which distinguish speakers of different languages and dialects; phonemes which change meanings within words; syllables, words or morphemes; phrases, sentences, and larger paragraph or story units.

In the early stages of learning to read one way in which we 'protect' children from complexity is by the controls we exercise over texts. Every device has been tried — control over letters or sounds or words, or symbol-sound relationships (as in the initial teaching alphabet programme) or sentence structure. People have advocated the use of capital letters only, or lower case letters only, the inclusion or exclusion of quotation marks and other punctuation, and increases in the size and the spacing of print. Control has been exercised over the content to interest children.

In using these controls adults are preselecting what the child will have an opportunity to learn and therein lies a danger. Three examples of the effects of preselection are these.

- A teacher who uses an approach that is as close to children's literature as she can get may not give children an opportunity to learn how to take words apart to discover known components.

- The child in a graded phonics programme may not learn that there are images and expressions to be thought about in reading. A code-cracking mind-set may exclude a sensitivity to literary nuance or the use of sentence structure to anticipate what might occur next.

- If we build our reading books with the language that children use we may prevent them from extending their vocabulary by reading (Chomsky, 1972).

Adults decide which of these levels of analysis shall be the entry point and major emphasis in the first stage of a reading programme, and in what order the learner shall pay attention to other levels. Written language can be approached from any of these levels. Beginning with letter-sound relationships and moving to words is called a bottom to top sequence. Alternatively, they might begin with reading stories and, aided by the meaning, come to analyse the word and letter-sound relationships as they encounter the need, a top-down approach. Another starting place is with words, moving both down to sounds and up to phrases or sentences. And children could begin with writing letters, words and messages, all at the same time!

That seems straightforward. However, interactions between levels begin early and are central to effective performance. Most high progress readers can be noticed interrelating information from more than one level of information in print from their first attempts to read, and they get better and better at doing this.

Because of the high value of interactions (being able to relate one level of information to another level) it is not easy to work out which starting point is best by any logic, argument or appeal to research. There may not be a necessary sequence for developing the component processes. Starting points and emphases may not be critical issues. If the mature reader requires a flexible control of *all* processes the important outcome of the acquisition stage would be a flexible and developing control of all necessary processes. We should be wary of any advocacy likely to get in the way of such flexible control.

All this is the focus of the analytic-synthetic debate between those who want children to work with whole messages and analyse the details within these, and those who want children to gain control of the letter-sound details and build or synthesise words and messages out of these. Programmes control what children have the opportunity to learn. Different programmes provide different learning opportunities. Therefore research on what children do when they read will reflect what children have been given the opportunity to learn. In particular the teacher's classroom observation research will reflect reading behaviours constrained by that teacher's programme. The effects of programmes are widely ignored in reading acquisition research.

What is usually forgotten in this debate is the developmental fact that the little child learning to speak does not learn all his sounds before he uses words, nor does he know many words before he knows sentences. He is immature in his control of language, in his cognition, in his visual perception, and in his motor activities. Despite these immaturities the child gradually improves in his control over each one of these aspects of oral language. The best approaches to instruction in reading and writing acknowledge such a way of learning.

Teachers become very committed to their personal theories about methods of instruction; they defend them passionately at times, and resist their revision. My position is that there are costs and risks *in any programme emphasis* and the only defence is to be fully aware of what these risk areas are. For example:

- comprehension might be de-emphasized
- reading vocabulary might accumulate slowly
- mean reading age or grade level may rise but the slowest children may be left further behind.

There are always costs in any choice of emphasis and some that are not so often thought about during the implementation of an educational change are these.

- Literal interpreters may look for meaning in single words and miss the meaning in word relationships.
- Speed may be fast (or slow) and constant rather than varied and flexible.
- Reading vocabulary may be learned in lessons but not be something the child extends independently while reading.
- Accuracy may be perfect but the significant question is what strategies can the child use on a slightly harder text?
- The age at which independent reading is possible after which children learn primarily how to read by reading may vary widely from one programme emphasis to another.

Obviously the texts and teaching used in a programme will lead to different behaviours emerging in different programmes. And the novice will learn to operate on print in different ways.

Do such programme differences matter? The child may not be able to transfer what he learns on contrived texts across to reading narratives. What he learns from reading narratives will only partially prepare him for reading information texts which have many new ideas and less support from story structures. Programme differences also alter the sequences in which components are learnt. What is taught earlier may help or hinder what has to be learned later. Most important of all is the stress that the teacher places on component skills (i.e. what she gives her attention to) because some children come to believe that for them what the teacher stresses is what reading is!

A Little Evidence

A study of spelling errors by Margaret Peters (1967) reported that learned differences showed themselves clearly in types of spelling errors that children made. In the schools she studied in Britain three groups of children in (and I quote) 'look-and-say, phonic, and i.t.a. programmes' were compared. All three groups had been rigorously taught by teachers and head teachers who were totally committed to the method used and were heavily prejudiced against other methods. To bring out the differences clearly one would have to describe the error categories that Peters used. However, in brief, the differences in method or medium seemed to train the children to attend to words in different ways. Children:

- may attend mostly to one type of cue in the text (visual, or meaning, or structure)
- may use a particular strategy for working on the text such as word sounding corrected by meaning, or meaning corrected by word analysis
- may remember what they learn in different ways.

I am particularly interested in another finding reported by Peters. When she divided her sample by intelligence into a broad average group with IQ's 85 to 115 and a bright group above IQ 115, Peters found these differences held only for the broad average group. For the group scoring higher on cognitive tasks, differences due to teaching method or medium vanished almost completely. Does this mean that some children are better prepared to overcome the problems of the programmes we deliver?

When programmes focus on some components of the reading process rather than others then it follows from Peters' finding that the broad band of average children seem to be good learners of what their teachers want them to learn, and the more able children acquire more than the programme offers.

I carried out a pilot study to explore the differential effects of programmes during a visit to Scotland in 1972. With the help of local reading advisers I was able to work in four schools, each of which appeared to be committed to a particular teaching programme for reading which might be summed up as having separate and focal emphases on phonics, sentence makers (as in *Breakthrough To Literacy*), language and story experience, and a word emphasis. I studied the children's skills after three months at school and one year later. The different programmes did produce differences in patterns of subskills.

- After three months at school children making good progress scored well on the subskills emphasized in a particular programme.

- In the second year at school subskills that were not emphasized or were neglected in the programme showed the highest relationships with reading progress.

For example, in the second year in School A with an emphasis on phonic instruction, it was the measure of Concepts About Print that showed a high relationship to reading progress. In the language experience programme it was the Letter Identification test. Results like these suggest that when a teaching programme pays minimal attention to a particular skill, those children who make good progress are those who gain that skill in spite of the programme, or in addition to what the programme teaches. *This neglect hypothesis* is worthy of research. I offer it only as a hypothesis as this study was only a pilot exercise.

Harris (1976) warned that variability in reading tasks and purposes must be kept in mind if we are to train flexible readers. He warned that careful, systematic and detailed reading instruction can become counterproductive. It is based on learning associations and not on gaining strategic control. Word learning can be of this kind. It may be too difficult for the reader to become flexible and adaptable if he has overlearned the programme emphasis. This is the risk in any programme. Our enthusiasms act like blinkers: they give us tunnel vision. We select our course, measure what is important to us, and give practice to habituate those skills we value. Any programme can become counter-productive if children are helped to habituate only a narrow repertoire of reading behaviours, no matter how effectively we teach.

Guthrie (1973) reported from research that a good reader can build the subskills of reading into a single process so that the components of the process become mutually facilitating. The poor reader, on the other hand, had a number of disconnected and independent subskills. Perhaps in Guthrie's study the better readers (highest 50 percent) transcended any limitation in the programme and discovered for themselves other useful things about written language. If this were a likely explanation then, in evaluating any scheme it would be important to look at what is happening to the lower 50 percent of readers.

The role of the teacher is complex. Board studied what instruction does to children in the DISTAR scheme, a basal reader (a Sullivan linguistic approach) and a language experience approach. He found that instruction does not seem to interfere with the components of the cognitive model being constructed by the best readers, and the average readers also learn to read well enough, but that the poorest readers tend to be doing exactly and only what they are told. The more structured the programme the more effect this had. Board identified these struggling readers as instruction dependent.

These results from Peters, Guthrie and Board may all imply differences occurring at the level of 'the developing inner control' of reading rather than merely at the level of learning particular behaviours. For the poor readers it is as if the items are entered in the computer without a programme for getting from one store to another. In the good readers the strategies for accessing and changing the information source are also available.

When a programme controls what children are 'allowed' to learn, placing strong emphases on some things to the neglect of others, then it will constrain children's functioning. It follows that theorists arguing for a particular starting point or emphasis must go on to show how and when all the other processes which good readers use (such as comprehension in a decoding programme) can survive the initial emphasis and become part of the reading behaviours of the less competent readers.

Checking on the Effects of Programmes

If one were to try to study the effects of programmes on the behaviours of readers, how would one go about this? Let me explore this at two levels.

Firstly, for the teacher in a particular school, what would this mean? Teachers commonly keep some record of the levels of test scores or reading ages that their children are reaching, often from a word recognition test. This involves an assessment at one point of time of a level of correct responding reached. It is a measure of outcome or product, but not of the process of getting to such outcomes. However, if a teacher is a sensitive observer of the reading process she will want information from text reading and how that is changing over time, and other information from the processes of writing and spelling. Will time permit this testing? The teacher could decide to follow a small number of advantaged new entrants and an equal number of disadvantaged new entrants through the first three years of their schooling, say a minimum of 10 of each.

Her problem will be to find assessment procedures that are adequate to measure the processes used by children for picking up information from the various levels on which language is organized—a letter identification test, a word test, an early writing test, an oral language test, a test of letter-sound relationships and concepts about print. An analysis of the child's reading behaviour as he reads a book is required to tap the orchestration of strategies. The teacher's biggest problem will be to think of tests for the aspects of her programme which she does not consider to be important, but in reading about new ideas that other people are trying she will encounter measures of those things. I believe that testing for the things that a programme has not emphasized is extremely important if we are to understand the effects of programmes. They should be included in the battery of observation instruments.

Even within the first six months of school this approach will produce material of interest—she will find results that need to be talked over with colleagues. After a longer period of time she should begin to notice which components of her programmes her school's population do particularly well on. She should notice that the good readers do things she never really paid attention to, and that the poor readers do not. This would be an example of my 'neglect hypothesis'—that good readers learn more than the programme teaches. This observant teacher might then devise ways to add something to her programme for the low progress readers without changing its nature. This happened in New Zealand recently when interest in improving letter recognition led to alphabet corners where children choose to use letters in a variety of ways during the developmental period in the classroom timetable. It could support a current concern in that country, expressed by Nicholson (1986), that children need to build a store of known words. The challenge to New Zealand teachers if that claim is true is how to give emphasis to word reading in a way that does not change the basic thrusts of the programme with its emphasis on the orchestrated problem-solving of meanings. (I suspect the solution is already available where good writing programmes exist but that the link between these activities and detailed word knowledge is very rarely recognized by reading researchers.)

In a larger and more formal study of the emphasis in a curriculum for a school district, very careful consideration must be given to the selection of tests because some tests favour progress under some programmes. We are not looking merely for those which will confirm our biases but for a range of tests that will reveal the biases of our programmes. Also, like other aspects of child development, reading behaviours change as the child moves through a programme. In some components the children move from no score through to perfect scoring after about two years. This happens in letter identification which is a set of learning which one can master completely. Other knowledge, like direct recognition of words in one's reading vocabulary, is open-ended. There is a rather complex patterning of such components of the reading process in the first two or three years of instruction and any evaluation of it must be designed with an understanding of the shifts that might occur within the programme of instruction that has been adopted.

Observing Behaviours in a Story Book Programme

The child who begins to read his own dictated text

David is five today.

written by the teacher under his picture on his first day at school has several options. He may try to read using letter-sound relationships which he has to group into clusters or syllables, regroup these into words, and regroup the words into phrases, linking the phrases into the sentence.

On the other hand if the child begins with the message, i.e. the sentence, he can take in that sentence, its phrase structure, word elements and parts of words all at one time. He reads the sentence practising its structure, meaning, words, sounds, intonation, and punctuation. He can take time to pause and study any feature on any level of linguistic analysis, and relationships between levels remain intact. *The child can work on several levels of analysis on the run guided by a single reconstruction of what the sentence is about.* If the words and sounds in the text tend to occur in the frequencies in which they are found in his oral language, this helps him to predict what is likely to occur next. According to Kenneth Goodman (1970):

> We have understood the importance of using the learner's own experiences in making charts for early reading for many years but we have not sufficiently understood the importance of using the child's own grammar, phrasing and vocabulary.

First concepts

The child who is to begin to read on sentences must quickly become aware of several features in written language.

- He must appreciate the directional pattern of movement needed to read English. There are three stages to this learning: (a) left to right sweep across lines; (b) word-space-word matching within the left to right sweep; and (c) letter analysis left to right across a word, within the word-by-word analysis, within the left to right sweep across lines.

- He must realize that the language he speaks is related to the written English he is trying to read and is a valuable source of cues.

- He must become aware that there are visual cues which he can use.

- He must actively search for cues from different sources, check his own responses, and correct his own errors.

With these concepts the child can 'read' in the sense of the following definition of reading.

(1) Within the directional constraints of the printer's code (2) verbal and (3) perceptual behaviour are (4) purposefully directed (5) in some integrated way (6) to the problem of extracting a sequence of cues from a text (7) to yield a meaningful and specific communication.

Emphasis is on the on-going, sequential, message-grasping process. Development in the first three areas can be observed on the early reading books and one can predict that children whose records show these behaviours are likely to make good progress. Cues must be searched for at all levels of language and used in some elementary form to problem-solve.

Conversely, readers can gain word recognition scores equal to norms by the end of the first year of school and yet be omitting several aspects of the behaviour described above.

What behaviours are acquired in those making good reading progress?

A willingness to choose between alternatives

The beginning reader may, and often does, 'read' his first book by a low level strategy of approximate memory for sentence, page or story. His memory for oral language is driving the process. There is nothing wrong with such a starting point if it leads on to the development of new behaviours. However, some children with good oral language continue for their first year to produce only approximate responses to the text, apparently unaware that it is the author's message which he, the reader, has to arrive at. Like the preschooler's complex puzzle or the adult's solution to the crossword, there is a solution that is the best fit! When a child realizes that there is only one oral response equivalent to the text he develops a need or willingness to choose between alternative possibilities. The child then has a vague awareness that he must work to discover the best-fitting response. That is an excellent beginning.

Behaviours on very easy books

This always depends upon the child's prior experience and the amount of teacher assistance that is available. A child may:

- move with some consistency across print within the broad directional constraints of written English, left to right and return down left
- produce a nearly perfect rendering of a one-line text under pictures
- match speech and text word by word and space by space with some accuracy using hand or voice to synchronize the matching
- locate a few familiar words on the basis of cues although he is vague about what these are
- expect what he reads to sound meaningful and sensible.

Children's performance is varied and fluctuating; adequate responses appear and disappear. Gradually the responses become more controlled and accurate, although it is not always the most appropriate consistency that is arrived at.

Writing and getting to new words

Children will usually bring to school some writing behaviour which the teacher should know about. Given opportunities they will form letters, write words or sometimes begin with brief but whole messages. A class environment which creates the assumption that children will write will have writers. There are many ways in which the teacher can foster the exploration of print and act as scribe or co-author messages which children compose. The class should expect child authors to read messages to them from time to time and they should find messages all around the room.

To write messages the children must come to terms with the distinctive features of letters which make any one letter different from all others. They will learn about words, and the importance of letter order. Their letter formation will be extended by the writing they do and their repertoire of known words expanded. If they are encouraged to be independent and to say the word they want to write slowly, to hear its sound sequence and to try to write it, children begin to believe that there are alternative ways of getting to new words that do not depend on memorizing the spelling.

As the core of known words builds in writing, and the high-frequency words become known, these provide a series from which other words can be composed taking familiar bits from known words and getting to new words by analogy.

By the time the list of core words a child controls grows to about 40, the writer controls most of the letter-sound associations of the language, plus the most frequent and regular spelling correspondences, and will have an exemplar of each in his 'known' vocabulary. Writing as it accumulates provides the phoneme-grapheme correspondence practice that children need to work with to form a solid foundation of both reading and writing skills of the more analytic kind.

Cross-checking at the level of text

The teacher may soon notice that the child seems to be cross-checking different kinds of cues across the text during fluent reading of a simple book (see Chapter 8). The child checks a character's name with the picture, re-reads the line when the number of words spoken does not tally with the number pointed to, comments when a singular noun suddenly becomes a plural, or that a phrase is repeated three times. The reader works at synchronizing the visual, directional and speech aspects of reading and this is evident in rather deliberate word-by-word reading and in self-correction strategies.

What factors can interfere with this co-ordination and linking behaviour? In a complex activity such as reading, strong responses may mask a weak aspect of behaviour. The record of a boy aged 5:6 with fast fluent oral language and poor motor and directional learning, states

> *Depends on picture interpretation and story invention. Does not use auditory memory for the text. Points rarely and then only with a sweeping movement along the line. The speed of his oral response prevents any linking of speech to visual forms.*

Later the primitive beginnings of cross-checking at the level of text seems to be indicated by this record for the same child aged 5:10.

> *Has slowed his response and does some visual matching with a few known words. Slips readily into old habits of fast inventing.*

He has slowed his response and checks a few words he knows as he 'reads' the whole text.

It is easy to miss or misread these behaviours which imply cross-checking one source of information in text with another. Newly learned responses are unstable and do not occur consistently so that the new behaviour appears and disappears. So:

- directional control which guides visual survey from left to right may lapse, and give way to invention, or

- reading controlled by a small recognition vocabulary may lapse into auditory memory for the text, or

- a fast reader, capable of word by word reading, may speed up to a rate where motor matching is impossible, or

- the fluency possible with auditory memory may be dropped as the child begins to search for cues in the text and to read word by word, or

- as a child tires his capacity to work with relationships across stretches of text tends to break down.

It seems unlikely that a prescribed sequence of learning could be devised to bring about this delicate meshing of several activities because it must be dependent on the strengths and weaknesses of individual children who differ markedly. Each child would be working out these behaviours on different samples of experience: prior experience, school experiences and out-of-school experiences. Learning conditions for the individual child must facilitate the potential to be flexible in meeting textual challenges. In many programmes flexibility and interactions of different kinds of information are left to chance.

Good observation by a teacher captured this description of behaviours which points to an emerging control over relationships at the level of texts for a five year old in the first months of formal instruction.

> *She is improving on reading some words, not confusing so much and adding less. As word-by-word correspondence has improved, self-correction is beginning to appear.*

If teachers are taking running records of text reading at widely spaced but somewhat regular intervals and have some way of knowing that their children are moving into more and more complex texts, they may be able to capture this cross-checking at the level of texts in the analysis of errors and self-correction behaviours in those records.

Discovering things about the written code
While children are enjoying the reading of stories there are many things about the written language code that they gradually come to control.

Learning to identify the letters of the alphabet and concepts about print are two sets of knowledge which are gradually built up while reading stories. They are highly related to success in reading. Full awareness of these two sets of learning would not ensure reading, but a gain in one leads to gains in the other.

Although the everyday speech of the child is important for successful reading, language skill does not ensure reading success either, as there are other things to be learnt. Oral language creates appropriate expectations which narrow the field of possible responses and make final selection quicker and more accurate. Goodman (1970) wrote:

The ability to anticipate that which has not been seen . . . is vital in reading, just as the ability to anticipate what has not yet been heard is vital in listening.

This applies to the anticipation of meanings but it also applies to knowledge of how sentences are constructed (grammatical structure) which facilitates fluency in reading because it helps the child to anticipate what comes next.

Habitual responses to the directional requirements of printed texts are a prerequisite for reading progress. Directional behaviour can be observed in these early stages if the child is asked to 'Read it with your finger.' It seems to take a developmental course from a sensory-postural awareness supported by a pointing finger, to voice-pointing in word by word reading, and then to visual survey only. The sensory-postural habits must be learnt before the child can perform successfully in reading but the conditioning of visual perception continues over a long period as the child learns more and more about orientation and patterns of print. Even in older children errors may result from the difficulty of scanning a single line at a time. For the text

> from a nest long . . .
> had been reared

the child reads 'from a near . . .' gathering and integrating cues from two lines.

Two different trends emerge
There appear to be two different types of change occurring.

- Some behaviour related to direction and visual perception is learned in a conscious way, overtly, but should retreat to a level of habitual response which facilitates fluent responding. It should be allowed to retreat in its own time and not be forced too early.

- Oral language skills have to be used in new ways in the new activity and the manipulation of language has to become more and more explicit, conscious and considered as the child reads more difficult texts.

A search for differences
Awareness of a few letter or word characteristics permits the child to search actively for differences, similarities or identities between what he says and the text. Knowledge from writing experiences can help with this. Differences are by far the easiest to detect because they need only be different in one aspect or detail or dimension. Identity must establish a correspondence in every respect but children can detect errors on occasions when they cannot supply the correct response. One can hear the doubt or uncertainty in their voices. They should be praised for such awareness even if they need to be helped to the solution.

How does a reader check for identity or difference? How does he select from his stock of responses the significant ones to match the input signals?

Comparison of visual form. If a word resembles another in visual form they may be judged to be identical, for example '100' for 'too,' or 'It was round' for 'I saw round—'.

Comparison of parts. Parts of words may come to be identified with that word, for example when 'is' is recognized by the 's' alone this could lead to an error with 'as.'

Abstract or coded comparison.   An arbitrary group may be learned as when the forms 'Q, 2, and q' each represent an arbitrary, abstract whole which is made up of the sounds /kw/ or when the words 'dog, DOG, and Dog' are known to be the same. Once the groupings have been learned there is no essential difference between these and other perceptual reactions.

Children search for difference and identity by each of these methods.

The child at first will tend to use either visual or language cues, neglecting the alternative source, but as the reading behaviour system begins to take shape the child's errors are likely to show a marked increase in substitutions which match the text word in more than one way — sense, structure and visual cues. The word has several identities — orthographic, phonemic, grammatical or semantic — which can be checked one against the other.

Increased attentiveness to cues

The learning tasks for the remainder of the first year relate to developing new ways of discovering cues in the text and increasing accurate responding. A small amount of error or an occasional prompt in a predominantly correct text leads the child to notice new differences. A large quantity of material read fluently will allow many opportunities for new discoveries to be made.

When the child reads a new text an appropriate question is 'What new feature(s) about print did he notice for himself today?' A teacher cannot introduce the child by lessons to the thousands of possible cues in print. The teacher's lessons orient the children to the types of features they can use and good readers find a range of exemplars through self-discoveries.

The child who knows very few letters or words but who is actively searching for cues and confirmation will make more and more perceptual comparisons. He increases his own attentiveness to finer differences in print and in language. Here is an example of this behaviour near the beginning of book learning.

Text: Fish swim in the sea.
Child: *Fish swim in the water.*
         No. That's not water. It doesn't begin with 'w'. S (letter-name) sss (letter sound) *sea* (self-correction achieved). (He initiates re-reading.)
         Fish swim in the sea.

(McKenzie, 1986)

This child is using meaning (substituting water for sea), finds and recognizes a visual mismatch, initiates a search by letter name and then by letter sound, keeping hold of the meaning, finds the solution, and initiates a 'whole text' reading. This child already reads with a flexible approach to text processing, and has a good balance of visual skill and language prediction.

Such increased attentiveness to print is by no means inevitable. A child who has been repeating the text of the first book many times may know the text by heart and not yet realize that there are visual cues in print to help him. His long contact has served to make him inattentive to print.

There is an advantage in using texts rich in cues. In the initial stage of learning to read a teacher cannot easily find a baseline of common experiences or strengths among children who have idiosyncratic experiences. Experience is individual and private, particularly for the young child. Meanings common to a group are gained only with extensive experience. A text, rich in information sources, is likely to provide cues that suit a wide range of beginning readers, touching the experience of different children in different ways.

The immaturity of the five year old and the instability of the early learning lead to the firm conclusion that material rich in information is more appropriate for communication than material that has been controlled and regularized down to the just-noticeable-difference level.

Discovering new words and new features of words

The child who has learned how to use cues to work out new texts for himself shows considerable enthusiasm when he works out a new word successfully. He finds this activity rewarding and reinforcing.

When a book is interesting this encourages continued participation in the reading situation. Such reinforcement of an interesting activity will increase the likelihood of responding without any assurance of accurate response. A close check on the learner with praise for responses of good quality is very necessary in the early stages of learning to read. Once the child learns how to search for cues (information in the technical sense) the reinforcement lies in the agreement between all the signals in the code and the child no longer requires so much outside help to confirm whether his response is right or wrong. Only at times of confusion is that necessary. The activity of making all the cues fit, of eliminating any misfit, is rewarding to the child if he succeeds. MacKinnon (1959), who observed groups of children working together, reported that the children showed great enthusiasm when they solved a new word. They said the word with stress, often repeated it aloud, and sometimes clapped their hands.

Children differ in the devices they use to extract cues from print placing varying dependence on:

- letter analysis
- syllabification and clusters
- little words in bigger words
- visual analysis by analogy
- syntactic and semantic information (or context).

Pupils must acquire a variety of approaches and develop flexibility in dealing with new words and although they may learn to use several of these devices to some degree in the first few months of beginning reading, development in word discovery techniques goes on for many years.

The mature reader may read a phrase as a single unit or he may read a word sound by sound. He can use cues from large chunks of print or language or parts-within-wholes. Good readers after one year of instruction show a similar flexibility and awareness of parts within wholes. Poor progress readers are more specific in what they know and more rigid in what they can do with it.

Substitution strategies: not mere guessing

When a child omits, inserts, or changes words he seems to be using strategies that keep the activity going. Sometimes these are looked upon as 'indiscriminate guessing' or 'not seeing words.' For the child they serve useful purposes. They lower the risk of senseless reading or the effort of prolonged searching or the embarrassment of 'failure to respond.'

Substitutions are worth recording during reading for subsequent analysis. They tend to be prompted by the child's oral language usage so the teacher can often tell whether the child is drawing on his knowledge of oral language if she listens closely to the substitutions he is making or reworks what he said from a 'running record' of text reading. Substitutions can also show that the reader is making good predictions of what could occur next in a sentence. Because predicting what comes next is an important facilitator of fluent reading, the teacher would be wise to support this behaviour. Questions she might ask are:

- Does it make a good sentence? (Grammatical expectation)
- Does it make sense? (Semantic expectation)
- Is he merely juggling words?
- Is he afraid to search? Has he been in a hurry or has he been criticised for self-correction? Is he so lacking in confidence that he dare not try to search for cues?
- Is he confident enough to say 'I don't know' and can he expect acceptance and help? Or will he feel less conspicuous if he flings in any word?

To reduce the use of inappropriate substitutions for words in the text the child must be taught some additional means of gaining cues and checking his responses. What these should be can only be decided by analysing the substitutions that a particular child is currently making. In addition the child must feel that he will not be hurried, harassed or criticised because he searches at length or because his efforts are eventually unsuccessful. The willingness to search and to choose between alternatives must be preserved. The child who gives up searching becomes the problem reader.

Re-reading

To confirm a response the young child tends to re-read a word or a word group. Repetitions may be a check upon correct responses. Most frequently young children return to the beginning of a line or a sentence. This clears away the memory of any previous error. It helps the child to recall cues which he had forgotten because of a long delay at a difficulty. It allows the child to use relationships between words as cues. It may arouse memories which were not activated on the first run. If re-reading succeeds it places the correct response in its correct matrix of association so that sound patterns, grammar, intonation and meaning are all correct. This should make for better responding on subsequent occasions.

Teachers believe that children can and do read ahead to complete the semantic context. There was little evidence in my research that *beginning readers* do this, and the previous paragraph gives many reasons why the strategy of repetition of sentences is more adaptive for the stage of early reading.

Re-hearing: oral reading

Oral responding may have a critical role in facilitating the mental processing of new or difficult information for several reasons.

Firstly, saying words and sentences aloud resulted in greater ability to recognize and understand written words and sentences among beginning readers in a research comparing oral and non-oral approaches. Mature readers will also read aloud when the text is difficult increasing self-stimulation. This would suggest that oral language must play a supportive role in reading behaviour.

Secondly, data available on self-correction behaviour suggests that young children respond, hear their errors, and correct them. As reading skill increases, this thinking aloud, after an error has been made, disappears and with it observable self-correction. The behaviour of trying out a response, rejecting it and finding a better attempt has probably become a set of processing carried out covertly in the brain. Because at an early stage errors are heard by the child and fed back into the processing activity of his brain he may become able to mentally correct his errors. If this hypothesis can be further supported in research then oral reading may be a necessity to get a feedback system working.

Thirdly, as the reader gains control over reading simple texts he gives more attention to reading work at the word level. Oral reading allows for whatever articulation of word components during word-solving is necessary to sharpen phonological awareness for that particular solution.

Finally, oral reading remains important as the only situation the teacher can use to observe, check and reinforce appropriate reading behaviour in the first few years.

All these arguments would suggest that oral reading is an aid to learning at this level and not something to be minimized lest it create slow readers.

Perceptual or cognitive operations

Downing (1967) described the child as a code-breaker who consciously breaks up his words into sound units, who finds simple, rational relationships between spoken language and letters, who appreciates the logic of the connections and who is possibly encouraged to reason by the reading task. He believed that children have ability to appreciate and benefit in 'empiricism and reasoning.' According to Downing, the child needs to be taught problem-solving techniques to consciously break the code of written English.

Spache (1963) would not agree. He supported the view that reading responses are not made at the level of conscious awareness even by older readers.

> In all probability the reader is seldom aware of the particular type of context clue which aids him in deducing word meaning. He hardly recognizes whether the word meaning was clarified by some structural aspect of the sentence, by his own inferential thinking or by some other types of clue.

MacKinnon (1959) studied children learning in a group teaching situation which seemed to make the working out of cues more explicit. The group of children rarely allowed a reader to make an undetected error, forced him to make choices from among the group's suggestions, and increased the pressure to be right, therefore to preview rather than review material.

By actively engaging in search and check the child seems to become more aware of what he is doing. The reader pulls himself up by his bootstraps as it were and as a result, gradually becomes aware of how he is behaving. However, the highly analytic, conscious processes do not operate in fluent reading. It is as if the child reads text in ordinary light, and momentarily turns a spotlight on a problem. Over time it is the new challenges in text that get into the spotlight. Earlier problems can now be handled in the ordinary light.

Self-monitoring and self-correcting

These activities provide important behavioural signals of inner developing control. They appear early and persist as the best indicators of inner control in oral reading. The teacher must encourage the child to monitor his own reading and encourage self-management. These activities are discussed in Chapter 13 as they clearly belong with issues about a particular aspect of the reader's developing inner control—the kind of strategic processing that the reader is developing.

Towards the End of the Acquisition Stage

In my New Zealand longitudinal study of changes in processes, the high progress reader after one year at school had fast, efficient techniques for reading continuous texts. Directional behaviour was established very early and so was an expectancy for meaningful, grammatically probable sentences. During text reading, letters and sounds did not appear to receive as much attention as syntax, and sound associations were not used overtly.

This early behaviour for good reading of continuous material had changed by the third year in school. Two studies reported on the progress of these older children. In the first, Williams (1968) studied a group of children who had been at school for two and a half years and from six Auckland schools. Most were good to excellent oral readers. They read with accuracy, solved unknown words, corrected errors, and read at a comparatively fast rate.

The most powerful cues in their reading came from oral language. The errors made by good readers seemed to occur as a result of pressures from context (grammatical and semantic). They predicted from the previous text what the following text would say. Poor readers made more errors, misusing visual cues. Their errors were more often cued by letters and were less contextually and grammatically adequate.

Complementing these findings, Clay and Imlach (1971) reported a study of pitch, pausing and stress which showed good readers at this age pausing at punctuation points, after whole phrases and sentences, but poor readers stopping and stressing a word at a time and often a syllable at a time. Their reading behaviour was well-organized at the letter, syllable and word level, but they were not working across text at the phrase or sentence level.

At this age, 7:6, the good readers in New Zealand were well beyond the basic reading series and were relatively independent readers. They had increased their speed and they paused less often. Oral language expectations for grammar were used but the children also predicted from semantic cues. Synonyms for the actual words in the text were selected which also matched the first and last letter sequences. Reversals rarely occurred and phonic attack was rarely used. Rapid re-reading was a good strategy. Self-correction was a good indicator of a problem-solving approach and an attentiveness to the vagaries of printed language. The good reader was able to operate on large stretches of language at the phrase and sentence level and even on cues that held across sentences.

For any teacher who has doubts about this holistic approach to learning to read or write, let me state one thing I am absolutely certain about. If you have children who read and write texts it is extremely easy to make them conscious of any component process you feel is important using material they have just read or written successfully. It is extremely hard to help them with component processes on material that is too difficult for them to read.

Signs of Independent Reading Work

It is the aim of most reading programmes to bring children through the beginning reading scheme to a stage called independence in reading. The independent reader reads; the more he reads the more he improves his reading achievement (Stanovich, 1986). Why is this? A quick and unthinking answer might be that he is repeating the words so often that they are becoming part of his automatic responses. That can be only part of the story. For his responses do not only get speedier and more correct. He also becomes able to read more difficult text. What accounts for the rise in level of performance? How does he improve his own skill and pull himself up by his bootstraps?

The child reading to himself knows when he is more or less correct because 'one of the beautiful advantages of reading sense is that it provides its own feedback' (Smith, 1978). One way to describe this independence is that the child has learned how to work out new parts of messages for himself. He finds this activity rewarding. Once the child learns to search for cues to a word the reinforcement lies within the reading process, in the agreement he can achieve between all those signals and messages in the code. He no longer needs as much outside help to confirm whether his response is right or wrong. The activity of making all the cues fit, which is the challenge of the task, and eliminating any misfit, is rewarding to the child who succeeds.

Any or all of the behaviours discussed in this chapter may be evident in the independent reader. Three additional characteristics of the reader's behaviour may be noted:

- The child can work on more difficult texts more or less on his own, with a few appeals for help.
- The searching, checking, correcting activities proceed rapidly, efficiently, and usually covertly; observing oral reading you see only the outcome of the processing.
- The problem-solving, when it can be observed or when the child talks about it, uses high-level strategies like analogies, personal rules, hypotheses, and tentative solutions awaiting further information later in the text.

Does the word 'decoding' capture the essence of independent reading? It is commonly used in this sense. Jessie Reid (1973), thinking about the young readers in four studies where error behaviour was analysed, said they were using 'predict and check' in many cases as a substitute for letter-sound decoding, in situations where their print knowledge was inadequate. These intermediate skills enable a reader to use prediction to narrow the field of possibilities and to reduce the decoding load.

> It may well be that a great deal of the hold-up with poor readers resides in their inability to perform such cognitive acts as suspending judgement until more information is processed; modifying a first guess (or hypothesis) in the light of further information; transferring information from the short-term to medium-term memory, or fusing information from different cognitive systems.

> (Reid, 1973)

Independence in reading is not achieved by learning letter-sound relationships. It is a much larger cognitive enterprise relating to thinking and understanding, and governed by feedback and self-correction processes.

The teacher has to do less teaching of the independent reader. Meek (1982) suggested that the teacher has made herself unnecessary. She provides the structure, the time, and she acts as a resource but the child pursues a large amount of the activity by himself, pushing the boundaries of his own capacities as he tries more and more material of increasing difficulty. The inner control is in place driven by the challenge to find meaningfulness in the sequence of messages. Strategies designed to pick up information and extract messages control the observable reading behaviours. It will be argued in Chapter 14 that these strategies also expand the system.

In Summary: Signs of an Inner Control

This chapter has discussed behaviours that can be observed and from which we may infer the formative stage of an inner control over reading which eventually makes for reading with little outside help. At this point we should summarize what we can observe the beginning reader doing as he presumably processes information from any one of several levels in texts and cross-relates such information, learning from the experience.

There are various ways in which printed material can provide cues. If the reader decodes the following sentence he could then analyse how he solved it. What were the cues used?

Lxttxxx xxx xxx xxx xxly clxxx xxed xxx rxxxxxg xxrds.

In 'reading' that sentence the adult reader is helped by knowing:

- the letter symbols
- the sounds of English
- the frequently used function words of English and their patterns of occurrence
- the pronounceable sequences of English words
- the sentence patterns of English,

but the final acceptance of the message is governed by its meaningfulness. He not only knows that language varies in the distribution of letters, words and structures but he is familiar with the full range of variation along each dimension.

At first the child is producing a message from his oral language experience and a context of past associations. He verifies it as probable or improbable in terms of these past experiences and changes the response if the check produces uncertainty. The oral language achievements of the linguistically average child provide relatively stable responses which can give some success in predicting what a text will say and when an error has occurred.

At some time during the first year at school visual perception begins to provide cues but for a long period these are piecemeal, unreliable and unstable. This is largely because the child must learn where and how to attend to print. Slowly the first sources of cues from experience and from spoken language are supplemented by learning along new dimensions such as locating or directional behaviours, concepts about print, letter knowledge, word knowledge, hearing sounds in words, letter-sound associations, and pronounceable clusters. As differences within each of these dimensions gradually become differentiated the chances of detection and correction of error are increased.

However, it is not inevitable that under the support of oral language habits visual perception will proceed to more refined knowledge of letters within words. Some children maximize the importance of oral language and fail to attend to the visual cues. Seen in perspective the child's oral language skills make an excellent starting point since they provide a set of well-established stable responses. Adequate learning must proceed in the direction of more and more receptiveness to visual cues which must eventually be a critical component of the reading process. They cannot play a major role in the child's decisions about texts in the first year for many children can only discriminate half the letter symbols and letter learning is not yet complete but they have become a critical source of information by the third year when they govern the ultimate choice of word.

This description of behaviour change during reading acquisition is difficult to test with traditional research designs which deal with the comparison of averages for children grouped in wide age bands. The research strategy needs to be longitudinal and based on individual progress to capture the changing balance of reading processes and skill components.

- One reason for this is that points of entry vary from child to child depending more on past learning and attentional factors than on what instruction tries to direct attention to. Therefore a stage description of early reading progress that assumes all children can progress through the same learning sequence is not likely to provide an adequate instructional theory.

- A second reason is that the first words or text features to come under control will produce the rapid perceptual responses in other texts that sustain the meaning while newer words are analysed. How a child will 'read' a *word* is more a matter of how long the response has been around in the child's repertoire than what skills or strategies he has.

Cross-sectional research designs reporting the averaged performance of children who are at different points in these acquisition transitions does not produce a picture of real achievements or a description of the processes by which the changes occur. By analogy with colour-mixing we end up with a muddy brown view of the primary hues that went into the mix at different stages.

More than thirty years ago language acquisition researchers found that the longitudinal study of the changes in children's behaviour as they make progress provides more valid descriptions of a developing inner control of oral language than other methods. There are some parallels between language acquisition and reading acquisition here for the guidance of research and theory. However, literacy research rarely studies the reading process in formation by recording changes over time in individuals.

12　Visual Perception Strategies: One Kind of Inner Control

The Importance of Visual Analysis

The visual analysis carried out by a reader is one kind of inner control that seems to be either hard for teachers to observe, or easy for them to ignore.

> The study of perception is, perhaps, the most difficult area of psychological inquiry to justify to intelligent people. They are prepared for the answers to psychological questions to be bizarre or convoluted. What they are not ready for is to be confronted with an investigation where they detect no psychological question at all. Informed that our interest lies in 'seeing' they simply fail to see any psychological substance to the problem at all. Much of the difficulty stems from the apparent immediacy of skilled perception. Looking, seeing and recognizing seem indivisible. So effortless is recognition that it is difficult to regard it as the outcome of complex problem-solving operations.
>
> (Henderson, 1984)

Henderson expresses the problem of this chapter well. Those who work with young children in the acquisition stages of reading need to think about changes in perceptual learning about print at this time. An increased awareness of visual perception is what is needed, rather than any change of instruction.

A useful analogy can be found in the visual perception aspects of driving a car. Imagine the complexity of driving and making judgements about your car speed, the speed of the car in front, and the speed of approach of the car behind you, seen through the side or rear vision mirror. At the appropriate time you slow in response to what you see ahead, decide to apply the brake, but as you do you watch the car behind to make sure that it is responding to your braking signal. Visual perception is guiding most of your behaviour and you are making several decisions one after the other, in sequence, and very rapidly, mostly on the basis of visual information.

This all occurs on your way home from work along the route you usually travel. Your mind goes to that problem that arose at work and when you arrive home about 15 minutes later you realize that you have a probable solution to the day's problem and you remember very little about the drive home. Now your driving could not have been carried out without decisions being made—how fast you will travel, where you are on the road, the need to negotiate turns, to avoid other vehicles, to slow or increase speed, to respond to traffic lights, and the characteristics of other traffic such as speed, density, position on the road, and change of direction. If you had not taken in all such information, processed it effectively, and made appropriate decisions it is doubtful whether you could have arrived home without having an accident. The journey was completed without noticeable allocation of attention. Yet it involved active perceptual search for information, the use of information from several sources, and taking a series of decisions. *You were monitoring, evaluating, and correcting on the basis of visual information while your conscious attention was on something else.*

When you were learning to drive you probably only used some of the available information. As you gained experience you learned where to direct your attention, what information to seek, how to interrelate it, and how to decide more quickly. If necessary you adapt your driving to the need to pick up necessary information. You use not only visual information but also sound signals from the engine or passing traffic, and memories of past encounters and past solutions. All this 'processing of information' about driving which needs little attention in the competent driver does not just 'happen.' It has to be learned. The novice driver has to be sensitized to important types of information and must become able to selectively attend to the necessary information at the right time. Most learner drivers get better during instruction, but they continue to improve as a result of doing all these things *on their own* after their driving lessons have finished.

Learning to read is very like this. There are many sources of information in print, and the beginner attends to only some of these. The reader is sensitized to different sources of information and selectively uses these to make decisions as the need arises. Familiarity with some simple processes frees the attention (but not the brain) for attending consciously to new sources of information while at the very same moment using information taken in perceptually and/or brought from somewhere in the brain. Parents, teachers and interested others seemed to find it difficult to take into account the part that is played during reading by perceptual information that is used without apparent attention or effort.

Perceptual Learning and Reading Acquisition

Perceptual learning has not been comprehensively reviewed since Eleanor Gibson's 1969 book on that topic, according to Aslin and Smith (1988). Those authors suggest that interest in this area waned, firstly because researchers uncovered the impressive perceptual competencies of young infants, and secondly because the perceptual tasks which researchers gave to young children were found to be strongly influenced by cognitive and language factors.

The perceiver has to:

(a) detect relevant stimuli
(b) discriminate them from other similar stimuli, and
(c) identify the stimuli.

The perceiver has to direct his attention as he

(a) selects what to attend to
(b) breaks up the patterned stimulus into parts, and
(c) transforms or integrates the information.

Children have good control of visual perception in learning about the world from infancy, and can solve problems using visual information (Bryant, 1974). However, this does not mean that they come to reading and writing equipped to immediately use the visual information in print. The visual perception of printed language is a special task which involves several sources of sensory input and many stimulus interactions at any one time. It consists of a large set of new learning taking a little time to master. Perceiving printed language is improved with practice but it is an effortful process when stimuli are novel. Exposure and specific learning are both necessary.

Adults faced with the task of reading a language written in a new script (say Hebrew, or Russian) find the discrimination of symbols, one from another, calls for close attention and much effort. Some symbols become familiar, and then slowly and with learning, the identities of others separate out. Gradually over time the whole set of symbols is learned. The information is processed slowly at first but gradually the reader becomes more efficient at arriving at decisions about identity.

The human perceptual system is highly flexible and sensitive to the effects of experience either via general exposure or specific learning.

(Aslin and Smith, 1988)

The statements which apply to visual perception in general can be applied more specifically to a child learning to read and write who has:

(a) to discover what information exists in print
(b) to learn how to search for that information
(c) to handle multiple sources of information and make decisions
(d) to work sequentially with sets of information (to decide, for example, which of two possible pronunciations of the word 'object' to choose).

It is necessary to do these things rapidly and efficiently, and to be able to correct for an earlier wrong decision.

If the learner already knows letters (the set of symbols), this is a good start for the new task. If he does not then he can learn letters at the same time as he is learning other kinds of new visual information.

Information at the front and back end of words is easier to 'see,' the first letter gains prominence once directional behaviour is established, patterns of letters become recognizable in groups, length of word is an important clue — there are many more sources of information in print than just the original set of letters (Bruner, 1957; Haber 1978).

The child who reads well effectively searches for different sources of visual cues in print, makes decisions using this information, and shifts rapidly to using chunks or patterns of information because this is highly efficient. This seems to be as easy as seeing a view through a window, but even this viewer must direct some level of attention to picking up information. In the beginning the learning requires attention and effort.

Learning to apply visual perception skills to print is more complicated than just mere looking and snapping the image into the brain like a photograph. Learning must be undertaken and reading work is involved in coming to locate and recognize patterns and sequence of stimuli. The letter identification scores of children aged 6:0 (after one full year at school) showed a higher relationship with reading progress at 6:0, 7:0, and 8:0 than any other variable investigated in the Auckland research. Correlations ranged from 0.80 to 0.86. The exact nature of this relationship is complex but the child's visual scanning of letter forms and his manner of labelling or categorizing each one to establish its identity as different from all others is important learning. One can say that because the child reads his letter identification improves and vice versa. High progress readers learn many new letters for every letter identified by the low progress readers so that entrants who do not differ markedly on this variable at five years show increasingly wide variability as the first year progresses.

Visual Analysis of Continuous Text . . .

It is possible that looking at the subskills of reading in minute detail may never allow us to construct a theory of the complex act of reading. Information theory researchers have experimented with letter perception, word recognition, eye movements and scanning and have related their findings to more complex systems of behaviour like reading. Common sense suggests that their findings should relate to the teacher's task. In my search for theoretical explanations I accept Haber's position that:

> to be properly called a reading task, there needs to be a continuous visual language context from which the reader wishes to extract meaning.

(Haber 1978)

In other words, there needs to be a text in front of the eyes before it is possible to have reading occur. Tasks like the presentation of (single) letters or words, matching pairs of letters or words, naming sequentially presented letters or words, identifying or matching non-alphabetic symbols, or recognition of letter sequences which are not lexical items in the language are skills but they are not reading.

A theory of text reading cannot be studied in experiments with single letters or words. Learning how to direct attention and what information to search for in order to make a decision is learning that is best done on information-rich texts. Learning how to hold on to the message being processed while searching for information at another level (in words or letters) can be done effectively by young children on stories.

Some of the information in text which supports reading cannot be obtained by attending word by word. The linguistic feature called 'cohesion' (which describes things like the way pronouns refer back to particular nouns, or the way subordinate clauses relate back to their main clauses) provides support to message-getting at the text level (Chapman, 1983). Another type of support arises from the availability of redundant information in printed texts (Smith, 1978). Language codes give listeners and readers more information than they actually need, because the same message is often coded in more than one way (Haber, 1978, 1981). To give a simple example, the written question:

'What are you thinking about?'

signals a question in three ways — it begins with a question word, it changes word order from 'you are' to 'are you,' and it has a question mark. This means that the reader can ignore some of that information and still understand that a question is being asked. Of greater importance redundancy allows the reader to check one source of information against another and so confirm an earlier perceptual judgement. (Redundancy is discussed further in Chapter 14.)

If texts are rich in complex relationships across various levels of language organization then a very important question at any stage of acquisition is 'To what is the learner attending?' For, while the teacher is talking about one source of cues, the learner may be directing attention to quite different features of the book. During acquisition the learner has *to learn what can be attended to in text*, and how to access that information. The visual characteristics of the text which the brain is attending to are not directly observable, but they are something for a teacher to puzzle over. As a guide she can use behavioural signs of what the eyes (or the pointing finger) appear to be attending to.

... And Focussing in on the Features of Print

Dividing attention

It is not clear how the reader of text attends to the message and yet, when necessary focusses in on one of the other levels of information in order to sharpen the choice of words within the messages. This is a very skilful thing to do, a division of attention. He has to select a source of information likely to help his decision-making, and direct his attention only briefly to that source, keeping the message in mind.

Exploring the detail in word and letter patterns

Little children have to learn to recognize real objects, pictures and symbols. Their eyes move across a surface as they scan in some systematic way to see whether there is something they have seen previously. As they become familiar with a particular pattern which recurs they survey it in some systematic way.

Faced with the challenges of beginning reading the child develops a scanning sequence that is appropriate for printed text, and practises this scanning pattern until it becomes habitual. While he engages in the formation of this scanning process, he simultaneously learns more and more about the detailed patterns in print. However, it takes the learner several years to explore all the details in word and letter patterns, and locate quickly

- the smallest details that make a difference
- the patterns within patterns
- and the largest patterns that one can operate on without risk of error.

Children do not need to learn all the symbols in the writing system *before* they can proceed to reading stories. On the contrary, once they have learnt a few letters they usually have a procedure for learning letters and they can learn the remainder while writing and reading. And their skill in working with this perceptual information probably undergoes changes for the first three years of learning to read, even for the best readers (Clay, 1970; Gibson 1975).

What visual units are used in reading?

While experimenters are still exploring this vexed question and programme constructors are jumping to conclusions, the literature on early writing has captured some useful evidence about what young children are attending to.

Even two year olds notice two things about print—that it flows in lines across pages (so they produce scribble streamers) and that there are isolated bits (so they repeat circles, crosses, and other favourite signs). Before long one or two single letters emerge, or even the child's whole name (give or take an error or two). The next big transition is a phonological link to speech but to make this the child must begin the task of trying to find the bits or patterns in print that might match with his speech. Young children's writing samples show that in no particular order they are giving attention to punctuation signs, to spaces, to groups of marks and breaks, to similarities among letters, to flexibility with directional rules starting anywhere on the page and then to behaviour within the constraints of the directional schema. (This progress was dealt with in Chapter 6.)

The visual units recognized by a young reader may be any of these—features of letters (dots or tunnels or tails hanging down), letters, or clusters of letters, or words, or repeated phrases, or orthographic features like spaces and punctuation and arrangements of text in short lines, or illustrations. Although programmes may emphasize letter, sound or word knowledge, the young reader uses whatever he finds practical in the complex task of working on texts. Simple story texts allow the reader to learn a flexible use of a variety of visual units.

When children are paying attention to print detail they read slowly with effort. As their reading improves they spend less time searching for visual information, their speed of reading increases and their error rates fall. They direct less attention to familiar vocabulary, they process more information at each fixation point and changes continue to occur in their ability to recognize patterns. Juola (1979) related this to an explanation of how we form the units which we use as we read. It is unnecessary and inefficient to use more detailed information or smaller units if a larger unit is recognizable.

At any point in the learning sequence the child may learn wrong associations, form inappropriate categories or 'find' regularity which is not a characteristic of the code. *Whatever method is adopted for teaching reading, some children will stray off into strange procedures at some point.* About 25 percent of children, those making the poorest progress, pay too little attention to letters, word patterns or print features while they are trying to read stories.

Whenever a reader's visual perception of print is at risk he needs two sets of processing behaviour which reduce the risk of error occurring.

- He requires procedures and information that will allow him to detect and correct his errors.
- He requires several ways of solving a problem so that when the visual perception aspects of learning cause error, another approach to problem-solving is possible (for example language prediction).

In the physical and engineering sciences, when a process involves risk, safety factors and error detection devices are built into the controlling system. These are also required in a complex task like reading text.

Sources of Information: Direction

The pictures in children's story books may prepare a child for reading in that they arouse interest in books, add content to an impoverished text, and stimulate recall. Pictures allow freedom to scan in any direction and do not induce any directional habits unless perhaps when they are in a strip cartoon.

The child's attempts to read cannot be matched correctly to the printed text unless he is attending to the correct position when he says a word and is proceeding in the correct direction as he completes the sentence. Any learning about any visual units must depend on which part of the text he is attending to. Left to right movement across a line of print is usually established by the time a child has been in school for three to six months.

The movement or scanning patterns required in reading may be learned in the specific context of a particular book but will become flexible so that it can be applied to any page of print, in new contexts, and in different planes. Running off the appropriate sequence of directional behaviours on any page of print should not require conscious attention because this detracts from the attempt to extract the message from the text. Children need to pause to scan word patterns or letter forms without loss of place or message.

Sources of Information: Orientation is Important

The child who overlooks the detail of orientation will make errors on letters which, if reversed or inverted, could become a different letter. A study of letters (Dunn–Rankin, 1968) found four groups of letters which tended to produce confusions. These were:

1 e, a, s, c, o
2 f, l, t, k, i, h together with y
3 b, d, p together with o, g, h
4 n, m, u together with h, r.

This does not account for all the confusions that can occur. For some reason Dunn–Rankin excluded j, q, v, x, z from his survey. Other authorities have confirmed the y and k confusion, perhaps because of their angular characteristics and in addition have noted how the I i l L 1 set is a very confusing one as 'I' may be read as the number one.

After six to 12 months, when the young reader is familiar with many letters and can discriminate between similar words on the basis of several letters, orientation errors are less likely to happen. Mastery of letter orientation is achieved gradually, spreading into the second year of instruction.

What is wrong when a child makes errors of orientation? These may merely be a sign of incomplete directional learning (which is the way they tend to be treated in mathematics when numbers are turned around). They are common in children's reading and writing during the first year at school and the child should have the benefit of a year's experience with reading and writing instruction before errors in letter orientation are taken as signs of possible problems. Of course, during that year the child will be provided with many opportunities to work on constructing correct models.

Some children who seem to ignore orientation of confusable letters do have the knowledge to make the distinctions but do not seem to use that knowledge when they should. A gap exists between what can be done and what is actually done. They just do not generate that behaviour although they are capable of it. In this situation the teaching task is not to introduce them to new learning but to entice them into actively applying what they already know.

Sources of Information: Letters and Categories of Letters

To the literate adult the task of recognizing letters seems extraordinarily simple but:

> this illusion arises from the fact that, at this higher level of development the operation occurs by then as abbreviated, generalized, perfected and automatic mental behaviour which requires no effort and causes no problems . . . learning a new skill cannot and consequently must not start from its final form . . . but on the contrary proceeds by consistent changes of its first forms to its final mental form.
>
> (Elkonin, 1971, 559–560)

Learning how to scan for letters embedded in print, or producing them in writing, are, in my opinion, more significant learning gains than being able to name the symbols of the alphabet or give their sounds. It is a matter of knowing a letter as a distinct entity rather than whether you can pin a label on it. What we have overlooked for too long is the fact that *before a child can attach a sound to a letter symbol he has first of all to be able to see the letter symbol as an individual entity different from other symbols.*

Letter identity

Letters are the components by which words are differentiated. Children have to learn to perceive the symbols of the alphabet. Each letter must be contrasted with every other letter so that thousands of discriminations are made initially on some basis that works for a particular child and probably not like any of the systems which adults think of. At the earliest stage this is not phonetic learning or alphabet learning or even key word learning. It is something inarticulate and unsystematic that works for an individual child.

Calling a letter something which distinguishes it from other letters is giving it an identity even when that identification is of an unexpected kind. One child spelled 'big' as 'b-i-gigglygoo'! The 'g' had an identity distinctly reserved for that peculiar form. Whether he makes the discrimination first on the basis of alphabetic names, sound equivalents or some rather personal association like 'the first letter in my brother's name' is not important.

Durrell (1958) found that six year old children who learnt to read successfully in the first year of instruction had acquired a large amount of letter knowledge prior to entry to school but there were wide individual differences. He found early skills in letter knowledge a good predictor of early progress in reading, during the first year of instruction. Knowledge of letter names and sounds does not, he claimed, ensure success in acquiring a sight vocabulary but lack of knowledge produces failure. It seems that letter discrimination is a necessary but not sufficient skill for reading progress.

When should children be introduced to letter learning? As soon as the child is encouraged to write his name his attention is being directed to letters. Often the first two or three letters that occur in his name become distinctive because of these efforts. Most five year olds studied in New Zealand research were recognizing words by the distinctive features of particular letters or by particular associations such as 's' in 'is' or 'Delwyn's little 'd" (see page 276).

After a year at school individual differences range from Grant—who regarded 'G' as his name and who would presumably respond to all words beginning with 'G' similarly—to Jimmy who could tell you all the alphabet names, all their sounds, a set of words beginning with each letter and other interesting details if you had the time to listen. How can instruction work with such a range of individual differences?

Gradually the child who is making these discriminations more or less accurately develops more than one system for identifying or distinguishing letters—phonemic, alphabetic and visual. He then has little residual 'trouble with symbols.'

Whatever the method used to teach reading the child will pay attention to letters. This is not to say that he must learn some letters before he reads some words, but he probably will. Even when he appears to recognize a few words he may only be noticing a particular letter or feature. Mothers' diaries of the home activities of a group of research children over their first year at school suggest that much spare time was devoted to letter learning at home when this was not an activity stressed by the methods used at school.

'Asked for name letters to be printed and started to copy them.'

'He copied over large print in the newspaper with a crayon, showed it to me and pointed out some similar letters.'

'He showed a little friend how he could write his name and copied her name after his.'

'Wrote his first name in sand very clearly without anything to copy.'

These children considered the exploration of print a serious business.

As with directional learning, if there is some reason for a child's finding difficulty with making discriminations about letters, waiting will do no good. Some aids must be devised to assist the child to establish some letters as recognizable, distinct from similar signs. We cannot hand the child who has difficulty our basis for making the discrimination. Instead we should *arrange for him to make successful discriminations* on whatever basis is viable for him and through successful practice allow him gradually to systematize this knowledge.

Plotting the gradual gain in control
The visual discrimination of each symbol, one from another, is a large learning task and the accumulation of skill is slow and gradual over the first two years of instruction for children who begin school at five years. Chil-

dren will be reading and writing while still extending their control over letters. Karl writes his name as 'Kpnl,' points to the 'n,' says 'I got that wrong,' but fails to see the 'p' is also wrong. In some programmes too little attention has been paid to the size, complexity and particularly the gradualness of this perceptual discrimination learning.

The graph below describes the progress of a group of children on a Letter Identification Test. The solid line shows the scores of Sample 1 at 5:6, and the two broken lines show the attainment of Samples 1 and 2 at six years of age. Most of the children have mastered most of the letters but a few of the children have low scores. In contrast the solid line shows that six months earlier at 5:6 only a few children had mastered all letters whereas many children had a lot more to learn. Sample 1 at 5:6 had an average score of 26 letters known. This group represents the progress of one particular research sample (Robinson, 1973). In another school with different teaching emphases the children might be slower or faster in learning to identify letters and the graphs would take a different shape. The 'change over time' is easy to see if there are at least two sets of results taken from the same children at two different times.

Distribution of Scores on Letter Identification Test (total 54)

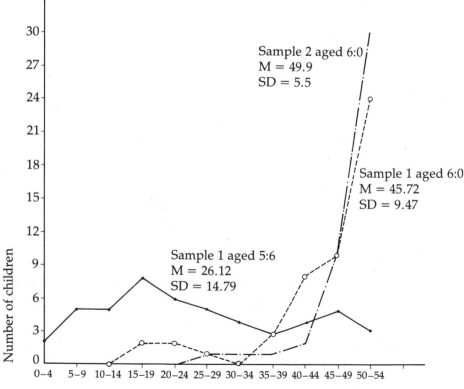

Sample 2 aged 6:0
M = 49.9
SD = 5.5

Sample 1 aged 6:0
M = 45.72
SD = 9.47

Sample 1 aged 5:6
M = 26.12
SD = 14.79

Number of children

Raw scores

At the end of the first year at school some letters were much more likely to be known than others. The reasons are many and various. Some occur more frequently than others, some have a distinctiveness of form, some capitals and lower case letters are virtually the same.

Whatever the approach to beginning reading a major learning task for the child in the first year is learning to identify as distinct entities the letter forms commonly used in English orthography. The discrimination of letters one from the other is only partially acquired after one year at school and further development must take place during the second year. It is a large set of learning which takes place slowly over a long period of time as new forms are successively distinguished from known ones. In their second year at school children should not only complete the mastery of all letter identities but they should discover names and sound labels for most letters. They then have several different means of identifying letters. This knowledge can be gained while reading and writing. *Teachers need only check for gaps in this knowledge and teach deliberately those names and sounds that are providing to be elusive or difficult for individual children.* This means specific attention to the particular difficulties of individual children.

Reading instruction could be designed to produce high scores for letter identification early in the first year of learning to read but naming letters in isolation is not the difficult part of the task. *It is extracting information from embedded letters while reading for meaning that is the challenge, and the real learning goal.*

The low scorers need special and individual help.

Categories of letters

At first glance it seems like a simple task to remember the letters and to produce a response in speech or writing. There are, however, qualitatively different ways of achieving this. At the most abstract or flexible or generative level a letter which we intend to produce can be written out in a variety of forms and settings,

and the correct form of a written letter can be produced by a variety of action sequences.

It is really a matter of grouping symbols into categories. While some symbols change their meaning by reason of changed orientation others change because fragments are removed (h, n; o, c; w, v). Upper and lower case letters vary, cursive and printed scripts vary, font types vary. Overall, the visual constancy permitted and not permitted to each letter in the alphabet is arbitrary, capricious and illogical. All this is independent of any letter-sound irregularity. For the child, the game is really one of categories. Which forms is he permitted to group together as similar? He learns the arbitrary features of the printed code gradually.

Sequences of letters

Research shows that adults who read English report a string of letters flashed on a screen in an order which has been trained by their reading habits. They have an organization of behaviour which leads them to attend to and report the letters in serial order from left to right. How soon after instruction has begun does this behaviour appear in children? The answer is not simple but, by and large, it appears within six months for children who are good at learning to read and has not appeared after 18 months in children who are failing to learn to read (Clay, 1970). Only children making good progress can, if need be, survey words in a controlled way letter by letter, left to right.

A research test of concepts about print indicated clearly that a child taught to read under the New Zealand syllabus notices features of lines of print before he notices word order within lines and well before he can detect errors of letter order. The ability to pay close attention to detail deep in the middle of words while continuing to use other cues correctly is apparently a difficult task for a child taught to read on little story books.

A child finds the beginnings and ends of words easier to 'see' than features embedded within sentences or words. The spaces help him to locate and perceive the letter at the edges of the spaces.

lineorderiseasierthanwordorderwhichiseasierthanletterorder

That example is interesting. Most people are able to locate the familiar word units within it but what is disturbed by the deletion of spaces seems to be the sequential eye movement across the line. It is as if left to right movement is helped by the spacing. In particular, it may be that re-scanning or checking behaviour is most disturbed by the deletion of spaces. I suspect the capital letter at the beginning of a sentence is of similar assistance to the eyes in the scanning of a text.

The child who is writing stories must give his attention to detail in every part of the word as he learns to construct patterns of letters in left to right sequences. The child at first produces strings of letters. In the accompanying 'illustration and story' it is interesting to imagine why the child wrote what he did. He knew certain letters (d, i, p, A, l, f, e, M, D, c, h, T, a) but he also knew other important things about sequencing letters.

- Letters that follow one another are usually different.
- Letters can recur together like ll or first and last, as in (did).
- Capital and lower case letters occur mixed together but lower case predominate.
- Words are of varying lengths (did, PAll7M, DeliqadM etc.)
- The word concept seems to be indicated by the enclosing of groups of letters — (did2).
- There is even a hint that vowel and consonant relationships are sensed.

Before the child can write a sentence he is already becoming aware of factors which are important about the sequences of letters which can occur in English.

Although the beginning reader knows that letters follow left to right across a word he makes errors of omission and substitution as he writes, concentrating on forming the letters and forgetting about their sequence. He often loses his place and his patience in the complexity of the labour. At this stage an error in letter sequence in the child's writing is caused by the immaturity of the skill and the complexity of the task.

Lewis Carroll was using another kind of knowledge about letter sequences when he wrote English-like nonsense words, like *jabberwocky* and *mome raths*, and that is that some sequences are permissable in a language and some do not occur. If adults are given a selection of letters and asked to write down what letter is likely to follow they frequently write sequences of letters which have a high probability of occurring in English. Young children learn something about these predictable sequences as their experience with written language increases.

> *Copying words from a book John chose only those in capitals from the titles. He concentrated hard while other children danced to a record. He burst into tears when he was interrupted and lost the sequence he was following. He is usually very patient. Shown the place he resumed the job and finished it.*

Seeing letters embedded in words and text

Readers do not have to respond to all letters in a word to 'read' it correctly. They only have to recognize enough cues to distinguish it from other words that might occur. In this sense they can go straight from a simple recognition of letter, cluster, or word to the message. The child has only to notice some new feature to distinguish a new word from all other known words.

Discrimination of letters in isolation is not the task required of the reader. He must identify them when they are embedded in text, and attend to the sequence or order of letters. Here are some examples of diary entries written by mothers on letter difficulties.

> *My biggest gripe is the way the home readers vary in the way they print their letters, every book is different and Brent finds great difficulty in sorting out the words because of it. I feel that the books should be of uniform nature starting with the very simple, and not chopping and changing as they are doing now.*

> *Has improved out of sight with his words but finds the different ɑ a and ɡ g very confusing. In the new books they are easier to read. Also gets stuck with capital letters at beginning of sentences.*

However, there is some evidence to suggest that most children are helped by being introduced to variable print and variable letter forms (such as capital and lower case) early in their programme.

Capital letters are very salient and eye-catching in texts but only because they stand out among the lower case letters. For slow learners some reduction of the variety is justifiable and probably helpful on a temporary basis. Authors of some early reading books have, somewhat arbitrarily, made drastic adjustments and omitted capital letters, quotation marks, and other such symbols. Like controlled vocabularies this may in the long run be unhelpful.

A study of how reading behaviours change between 5:6 and 6:0 explored a large number of tests and how they were related to reading progress. Robinson (1973) discovered in that study that the number of words a child could write with prompting but without help—that is the number of words he knew in every detail and which he could produce from within his own head from memory or by construction—was highly related to early reading progress. This seems to underline the suspicion that when the reading method calls for analysis of letter and word detail within sentences the complementary process of learning to write words and building words out of letters and sentences out of words is a very important activity.

Sources of Information: Analogy Using Clusters of Letters

Eleanor Gibson (1965) reported an experiment to discover how long after beginning reading children begin to anticipate words in terms of clusters of letters which they expected to occur together. She used real words, pronounceable non-words and non-pronounceable words.

Real words	Pronounceable non-words	Non-pronounceable words
RAN	NAR	RNA
TEN	ENT	NTE

From her results she concluded that soon after beginning reading most readers tried to read nonsense words by using clusters of letters.

While new entrants are reading and writing their first stories they are building up a vast amount of visual discrimination learning which is vital to subsequent progress. Such learning is not only occurring at the level of single letters. The child who is learning to differentiate letters one from another, and to associate letters with sounds, will, at the same time, be using larger building blocks—clusters of letters or sounds. Psychologists describe this as working with 'chunks' of information. These terms have technical meanings but they are correctly related to dealing with clusters of signals rather than single letters.

Goswami (1986) examined children's use of analogy in the beginning stages of learning to read with nine carefully designed experiments. She asked these questions.

1 Would young children be able to use an analogy strategy to get to new words in reading or did they have to be close to Piaget's stage of formal operational thinking before they could do this? Analogy was clearly a

useful strategy in addition to visual and phonological coding and it was available from the very beginning of reading to five year olds. Even non-readers used analogy to 'read' non-words.

2 Could an analogy strategy be the link between early skill in rhyming and later skill in reading and spelling? Words that rhyme share common sound patterns and these categories often map onto words with similar spelling patterns. The results gave some experimental support to the possibility of this link existing.

A further interesting outcome of this research was the finding that inappropriate analogies are made more frequently in spelling than in reading. There is no way to check whether you are correct in spelling but in reading text there are syntactic and semantic sources of information which can be used as checks.

Teachers use analogy intuitively in their interactions and prompts to young readers for getting to new words and they also use it in classrooms as a method of introducing new words in small group teaching. To attempt the new word 'goat' or 'spring' teachers may ask children to read two 'known' words and work out what the third word would be.

boat	goat
go	flower
goat	float

Without overtly segmenting the sounds of the words many children who are familiar with the first two words have no difficulty deriving the last one. Children manage this approach better if they have a store of experiences with print before such teaching is consciously and systematically introduced in lessons.

Sources of Information: Coding a Sign in Several Ways

Another instance of letter probabilities that good readers 'know' quite early in their schooling is that certain letters can say several sounds —

as 'a' does in Father, am, said,
or 'o' does in Mother, oh, on.

Not only do they know that some letters have a range of sounds but they also learn 'before long' that within that range some occur more often than others, that is they have probailities of occurrence. Advocates of the special initial teaching alphabet (i.t.a.) thought they had simplified the child's task by writing each sound with a different letter sign. This is not the way that English operates and may have distorted what the young reader needed to learn.

Some research suggests that if a child must ultimately operate in a flexible way on such confusing patterns as the spelling of English he should learn such flexibility from the start. Other research would emphasize that the child learns best when his experiences are consistent and from these he can move to flexibility. In a sense both positions are probably true. The high progress reader needs only a brief period of consistency before he learns to operate in a flexible way. The slow progress child needs the consistencies of his environment increased. Knowledge of the sequential probabilities of language are 'hidden learning' which is not readily observable except perhaps in a child's attack upon unknown words. The child who is failing to learn these probabilities is easily overlooked.

Sources of Information: The Perceptual Span

Rayner (1985) reviewed research on the perceptual span in reading and concluded that a reader sees from three to four words down to a single word in one fixation depending upon the techniques used for testing. He emphasized that *the crucial question is not how much the reader sees in a single fixation but what information is used during a single fixation.*

Different types of information can be gained from different parts of the field of vision during one fixation. The perceptual span for semantic information appears to be rather limited to one or two words but information guiding the eye movement to its next location may be 14–18 characters to the right in English and a similar number to the left in Hebrew. This is interesting because it shows that the perceptual span is asymmetric and biassed in the direction from which useful information can be obtained. This must be learned by the child who is learning to read. The area of effective vision during an eye fixation appears to extend from the beginning of the currently fixated word (but no further than four characters to the left of the fixation) to about 14–16 characters to the right of fixation.

To Check on What Children See

Observe attempts at early writing
One way to observe children's visual scanning of letter forms is to observe them when they are writing (Clay, 1975, 1987).

Observe how a particular child remembers letters
A child may be able to discriminate between letters quite well even when he cannot name or write them. It is easy to check on this visual analysis.

One child was shown a picture of a horse with 'h' under it. She said 'horse' and then added 'a stick and then over.' She traced the letter in the air. Shown the letter 'C' she said 'cat' and then 'c' (letter sound), tracing it in the air.

After further explorations of this technique I began to test young children for letter identification in this way, particularly those children who were unable to give a verbal response to letters.

The standard procedure I selected was to show the child a picture, turn the card over to show a single consonant sound and ask 'What is this?' I accepted a letter name, or a sound or a word that began with the letter. I also accepted a drawing in the air. Children who found it difficult to remember the word to go with the picture or to name or sound the letter were often able to write it in the air either with their eyes closed or with the card turned over. They had some kind of representation of the letter in their minds and this could produce a response in movement but not a response in language.

Teachers can use this technique:

- to locate children who cannot analyse letter forms
- to find out which letters a child does attend to 'in his mind's eye'
- to test whether letters currently being taught have been visually scanned.

The following sample of behaviour was gained from a child who had been at school for two weeks. Shown a display of letters she selected a lower case 'd.' Asked 'What is it?' she made no response. Spontaneously she wrote it in the air. Then she looked at me and said, 'That's Delwyn's little 'd',' a reference to her sister's name. That was learned at home. She then selected 'm,' traced it in the air, and whispered m-m-mouse. That was learned at school. Then she selected in turn 'i, k, s, c,' and gave them their alphabetic names. That was the limit of her skill and she paid no more attention to the letters on the table. Two weeks later this child was tested with the alphabet and at one point as she was tracing one of the letters in the air with her eyes closed she said 'Me can see my finger.'

It is common when children are asked to write the letter in the air for them to close their eyes as if trying to see the letter as they follow out the movement pattern. This is an interesting confirmation of a link between the motor and the visual aspects of early reading skills. This writing in the air seems to be easier than writing on paper.

Observe the child's grouping of letters

In the early stages of learning letters the child may deal with the diverse array of letter forms by grouping similar letters together. Researchers have tended to say that children make errors when they do not distinguish between forms such as 'n' and 'r' and each of these from 'h.' Recast in a more positive form this behaviour could mean that as a first stage in learning the child forms only a few categories. From such gross classification of sameness, new distinctions will emerge.

A three-piece puzzle

Letters have a constant position. Before a child comes to school things like toys do not lose their identity even if their position is changed. So a bucket is a bucket whether it is upside down or right way up or on its side. One of the things a child has to learn in writing is that letters change their identity if you turn them around the wrong way. This learning is contrary to his experience in the past five or six years. That is a very difficult thing for the child to learn. What have been called reversals might be looked upon as behaviours found in a child who believes that shapes have constancy no matter what their orientation. That is true for objects in his environment so why should it not be true for letters that he is learning? For me this seems the simplest explanation.

Examples of Problems With Letter Sequences

A three-piece jigsaw was made of each child's name and each child was asked to make his own name. Most succeeded after six months at school but these three children were having more difficulty than most with this letter sequence problem.

pɹ	ნo	uo	Go	rd	on
on	Sh	ar	Sh	ar	on
Ca	en	rm	Ca	rm	en

A three-piece puzzle

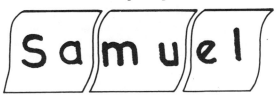

To test this awareness of the constant position of letters I have used a three-piece puzzle. All the vertical sides have identical curves and so they can be fitted together in any order and even inverted with the bottom at the top. I divide the child's name into three groups of letters. (It was my guess that three pieces of puzzle is sufficiently difficult at this stage of development.) If there are only three letters in the name, such as in Kay or Jon, then one can go on each piece of the puzzle; if there are nine letters then three can go on each piece. The principle is that the child's name can be constructed with the three-piece puzzle that can fit together in many ways.

There are many possible arrangements of the puzzle. When the child places the letter groups in correct order and correct orientation he is probably selecting correctly only those ways that are appropriate for printed material. So we have another chance of checking on his conceptions about print.

The task is confined to the use of the child's name for a special reason. It is not a test of reading skill, and the aim is not to find out which words the child can read. The task aims to reveal something about the visual scanning the child is applying to the task and his name is familiar and likely to be of high interest. By using the child's name we are using a word which he learns relatively early even if it does take him some time to know all its detail.

Which name is yours?

Write the child's name with a capital letter and lower case letters, then write it in reversed form (mirror image) and then in inverted form (shadow image). Scatter these three versions of his name around with about six other names (too many names will make the task too difficult) and ask him to pick out his name. In the earliest stages he will tend to pick out his name in any of these three forms, normal, reversed, or inverted. Perhaps he is judging from its initial letter.

As time goes on he will reject the 'wrongly printed' words and come to choose only the name in correct orientation as his name. This task would be a poor teaching device for school entrants but it is a useful discovery task. We cannot be quite sure what the child is looking at or what is guiding his choice but we can demonstrate with it when his behaviour is appropriate for the reading task.

Observe eye movements

One study observed children in a controlled way looking at their eye movements while they read to their teachers. High scores of eye-on-print behaviour were related to reading progress and high scores on eyes-wandering were related to slow reading progress. The eyes-wandering children moved their attention to the illustration, to the teacher, to the floor, to other children, perhaps searching away from the book for cues rather than scanning the print for cues (McQueen, 1979).

It is easy to pick up from the turn of the head and the shift of the eyes whether the child is scanning the print before he gives a response to text.

Test letter identification

A more systematic check is made when capital and lower case letters are presented in random order with the instruction 'What do you call this?' The child is credited with a pass if he gives

- an alphabetic name
- a phonemic equivalent
- a word beginning with the letter.

He is not credited with a pass if he notes correctly a letter in the middle of a word or identifies it as the last letter, for example the 's' in 'is.'

A teacher may wish to check the range of letters that have been taught so far. However, if she presents a wider range of letters than she has already taught she will probably discover that the child knows more than she has taught him. This saves her some work.

After one year at school the full range of letters, capital and lower case, should be checked to see that the gradual accumulation of letter knowledge is going well. When children are given a letter identification test of lower and upper case letters in non-alphabetic order they should be allowed to give their preferred response to the letters.

And study the answers
This checking yields information on the number of letters correctly discriminated, the dominant mode of identification, and the common confusions for any one child. It showed that the average Auckland school entrant in 1963–64 knew very few letters at school entry and that letter identification increased in importance for reading progress throughout the first year of school. When children were asked 'What do you call this?' the majority preferred to use alphabet names for 40 percent of the capital letters and 34 percent of the lower case letters read correctly. Sounds were given for only two percent of the capitals and one percent of the lower case letters. The limited use made of a word beginning with the test letter (16 percent for capital and 11 percent for lower case letters) is surprising since the teaching method directed attention to initial letters. At six years most children could identify 28 of the 54 letters tested. By seven or eight years one could expect nearly perfect scoring from all children (Clay, 1966). Later research has suggested a more rapid learning of letters (Watson, 1980).

Children's Responses to Letters

Age	Total Correct		Alphabetic Name		Sound		Word Beginning	
	Capital	Lower Case	Capital	Lower Case	Capital	Lower Case	Capital	Lower Case
5:0	8%	3%	6%	3%	0%	0%	1%	0%
5:6	35%	21%	18%	12%	2%	2%	15%	8%
6:0	58%	46%	40%	34%	2%	1%	16%	11%

Multiple categorization
This research showed that when instruction did not stress letter or phonemic learning, high progress readers had a mean letter score of 50 symbols after one year of instruction. They were able to give 50 letter names, 50 sounds and 50 words beginning with the letters, on request. They showed not only that they could distinguish almost all the symbols, one from another with-

out confusion, but also that they could categorize each letter in several ways, multiplying their effectiveness for rapid responding or for checking a response. This *multiple categorization* suggests a flexibility and a competence which makes mere sound associations seem somewhat meagre. The alphabet or the sounds are mere labels which are the tip of the iceberg, used to represent all the stored information about each letter symbol. Even when their letter identification became over-learned and habitual it continued to be enriched by building more extensive associations around these letters.

The New Zealand children's preferred responses were, firstly, alphabetic; secondly, words beginning with the letter; and lastly (and decidedly least preferred) the sound equivalents. This does not indicate poor teaching, nor does it necessarily imply that children did not have phonic knowledge. It suggests that children found the alphabet an easy and economical way of identifying the visual symbols, one from another.

Using the Concepts About Print test
In the Concepts About Print test (Clay, 1985) there are four important items that provide information about visual search and scanning. They are the items that ask the child to find what is wrong with disoriented print.

- Can the child detect displaced lines?
- Can he see that the words have been re-arranged?
- Does he notice when the order of the first and last letters is changed?
- Does he notice when the arrangement of middle letters is changed?

Those four items represent a steep gradient of difficulty, a gradient of noticing, a gradient of visual scanning strategies (Johns, 1980). Many experiences with print are needed before a child will be able to pass a more difficult item. As an opportunity to observe what a child is paying attention to, those items are very useful.

Facilitating the Visual Perception of Print

As children read story texts and write their own messages their teachers can guide and encourage them to learn about the detail of print, and discover many kinds of visual units in print. Some things to consider in making this approach effective are:

- there is an art in doing this to gain maximum benefit without spoiling the story read or written
- there is a requirement on teachers to know whether children are increasing their control of the various kinds of visual information in print in systematic ways
- some kind of check on this at appropriate intervals can replace tedious and unnecessary workbook training exercises and letter and word learning drills with extensive experience of reading simple stories.

Does attention to environmental print lead to reading?

Preschool children respond to print in their environment and reading is said to begin when children are able to identify stop-go signs, labels on cereal cartons, and the names of fast-food restaurants (Downing and Oliver, 1974; Goodman and Altwerger, 1980; Harste, Burke and Woodward, 1984). It is argued that acquiring these print-meaning associations enables children to begin learning about the graphic system for recording language. Print and non-print distinctions are made, the print is recognized outside of its original context, and parts of the signs become recognizable on their own.

Other researchers would argue that this is not enough and that *in order to begin reading*, children must acquire prerequisite skills such as letter knowledge, phoneme segmentation skill, and left-to-right orientation to print. It is assumed that these skills must be acquired in the classroom unless supportive family members read to children, teach letter names and answer questions about print (Chall, 1983; Gough and Hillinger, 1980). Ehri and Wilce (1985) argued that if children are to shift attention from environmental contexts to the print itself they need to master the alphabet. Because this is a difficult task involving the discrimination of more than 40 shapes one from another and each with an arbitrary name or sound, these authors argue that acquisition requires explicit instruction and practice and is not picked up simply through exposure to letters.

Ehri and Wilce (1985) and Masonheimer, Drum and Ehri (1984) do not appear to have a model of an active constructive learner in mind (Wood 1988). It is not only by external intervention that children explore the features of text.

It is certainly not true that children do not begin reading and writing until they have mastered directional behaviours, phonemic segmentation and all the letter knowledge. With a little knowledge the process can get under way, and using this small amount of knowledge children discover many new ways to work on printed language, and expand their control as they do this. The narrow concept of delaying real reading until the teacher has given them prerequisite information does not match with the way control over reading expands as a product of trying to be a reader.

What does emerge from careful experimentation in this area is that not all children will inevitably go from environmental print experience to reading by themselves, and that interactions with an 'expert' will be helpful. It is the kind of interactions that is debated. One kind involves learning meaningless, arbitrary names and sounds as a prerequisite. The other kind of interactions use what the child is already attending to in text, and the story that is meaningful to him, as the means of keeping him at work on the long acquisition process.

Minimum contrasts make learning tasks hard

Children find it easiest to distinguish letters with the maximum of contrast at first. This is a good teaching principle. They must gradually learn the minimal differences for discrimination within sets of similar letters.

Relatively little research has been done on the legibility of print and layout for children. Conventionally, the type size in beginning reading books is larger (14 to 18 point) and the space between lines is generous. Lines are usually short (20 pica). Reviewing all the literature in this area Tinker (1966) concluded that all-capital print is extremely difficult for adults to read and that lower case print is overwhelmingly preferred. It may be assumed that children will react similarly when the majority of their reading is of lower case texts.

Teachers of beginning readers have observed that an exaggeration of the spaces between words and between letters within words assists children's discrimination. It is possible that publishing layout could reduce in some measure the learning problems children have with visual discrimination. Some teachers make large brown paper books with simple texts in five centimetre letters. Children span their hands across the large word patterns using gross motor patterns rather than fine co-ordinations. There may be perceptual advantages in using such large print for brief periods.

Exaggerated spacing of words, letters and lines can be a help and publishers of the very first reading books have to be convinced that this is necessary. Starting position on a page could be consistent in the early books and could be cued by some standard sign. A reduction in type-face variations for beginning readers is important as is elimination of any features which confuse one letter with another. Increasing the spacing between phrase and clause breaks or before constructions like 'said Mother' would be justified. It would serve the same purpose as limiting lines to full sentences as is frequently done in beginning books.

Writing letters of the alphabet

It would be reasonable to hypothesize that writing letters contributes to learning about them. It is recognized by researchers that seeing letters embedded in text is not as easy as seeing them in isolation. When the child is writing he is forming letters singly one after the other and at the moment of formation has an unimpeded view of each letter. If the child's early attempts at creative writing are handled sensitively this provides for that focus on letters without undue emphasis on these letters.

A series of experiments was conducted with children learning to write Russian letters. Children encounter many difficulties in their attempts to copy words even when they have a model. In the Russian research study children were taught by three different methods.

Just having a model.   The experimenter wrote a letter in front of the child and gave him general directions to copy it. More than 50 presentations were required per letter for the average child to achieve mastery under this condition.

Children gained the skill of writing correctly each letter on which they were trained.

A model plus instructions. In addition to the above the experimenter indicated all the basic points of the contour and an explanation of the shifts from point to point. The verbal guidance is what psychologists call orienting, focussing attention on the significant features and actions. This method reduced the training sessions to 10 per letter on the average.

Children were able to write unfamiliar letters but whatever they had learned was unstable and sensitive to changes in the surroundings such as a shift from book to blackboard or to lines of different width.

Model and directed search. The most successful training encouraged the child, independently, to identify supportive points by analysing the presented model for himself. The average number of training sessions per letter was then reduced to four.

The children trained in this third type of programme shifted to writing unfamiliar letters in varied settings without much difficulty.

> Thus special organization of the orienting-exploratory activity in situations of activity is an important condition in forming motor habits in the preschool age (under seven years).
>
> (Zaporozhets and Elkonin, 1971)

These authors maintained that for the mastery of movements the child's observation gradually refined *the image of the action being copied*. Attention was directed to the sequence of movements in the action to be learnt, not to the product of that action, such as the letter written.

Apparently the child learns something of great advantage in his future progress when he is allowed to organize the sequential steps in his own learning for himself. Learning with only a model might be called permissive—the child is left to do it in his own way and those who can, succeed. Learning with a model and directed search might be called guided learning in that the child is helped to attend to the significant moves in the skill but is allowed to put it all together in his own way. In the guided learning approach, like Type 2 above, adults tend to talk too much, using words which may confuse the child and overcontrolling the organizing of the task.

Bruner discussed a model like the directed search part of the Russian experiment. Drawing on his research with infants organizing skilled actions, Bruner (1974) arrived at some general principles that have surprisingly useful explanatory power for children entering school and beginning instruction in reading. The child's preliminary level of skill dictates what he can utilize from a model of new behaviour and what he can carry out in imitation. The child should be encouraged to venture, rewarded for venturing his own acts, and sustained against distraction or premature interferences in carrying them out. The learner needs opportunities to carry out intentions, and to initiate and sustain action. How does the child modify an action he is in the process of carrying out? He gets feedback at each stage of the movement and he gets knowledge of results. Environments must be supportive and challenging, but the changes made by the child to the organization of the skill come as the result of feedback he himself generates during the process of initiating and organizing the behaviour.

When sequential action is difficult

A standard reference text among Soviet psychologists and educators (Zaporozhets and Elkonin, 1971) on research in early child development deals with the perceptual processes from birth to seven years and it reports that three to seven year olds cannot visually isolate elements of a complex form without appropriate training. Children who cannot indicate the elements that make up a complex figure can do this after a series of practical exercises in which they actually build a figure from the elements using different forms. The children then begin an analysis of the figure by purely visual means, anticipating in the process the paths traced in their practical activity. These experiments have described a series of changes that occur in the ways a young child explores new objects and forms, by hand and by eye. The child builds up a series of routines, and sub-routines are combined into more complex patterns.

Hand exploration of a hidden object

1 At three years hand movements resemble grabbing rather than exploring.

2 At four to five years the child explores gropingly with the palm of his hand.

3 At five to six years he explores with both hands but not systematically.

4 At six to seven years he carries out a sequential exploration of the entire outline of the figure with his fingertips.

Eye exploration

Changes were also observed in eye movements recorded on film during the perception of an object.

1 At three years eye movements are few and attention is frequently diverted.

2 At four to five years there are twice as many eye movements.

3 At five to six years the eyes appear to pursue the contour of the figure.

4 At six to seven years eye movements outline the figure and also dart across it.

During the latter stages of this sequence the exploratory eye movements become successively shorter, the pausing or fixating takes less time, and attention is paid to the more informative characteristics of the object.

There is an interesting in-between stage when the child visually scans the figure but uses some movements of his hands also, movements which model the figure's form at a distance. It is as if the hand movements organize and adjust the process of visual exploration of this object.

Later still the eye movements observe the entire contour of the figure and perceive its properties in detail.

After more experience a quick glance directed to one particular characteristic of the object enables the child to activate the entire 'internal' model of the whole object, leading to an instantaneous judgement of all the qualities of the perceived object.

In summary then, research has shown that the three year old explores objects and forms manually by touching, manipulating, tracing with fingers and turning things over. The four to five year old uses both touch and visual exploration together to investigate shapes, supporting one with the other. By six years many children can systematically explore forms and objects with their eyes alone. Such visual exploration involves a type of motor skill (Zinchenko and Lomov, 1960; Zaporozhets, 1965; Lynn, 1966).

Manual activity aids visual learning

On entry to school it will help the *slowest* children to have their hands guided through a manual analysis of forms or letters. Teachers who guide the hand of a hesitant new entrant know this. The average child at this stage will benefit from information about print coming to him from both hand and eye. He may be able to discriminate better the shapes that he can handle or make movements with, rather than the ones he can merely look at. Learning to write directs his attention to letters in a particular order and forces him to work sequentially at the survey of print. The writing he is copying should be in front of him where he can trace or feel it, not across the room, vertically on the teacher's blackboard. The most advanced five to six year old children will be able to depend on their eyes alone when they enter school. This would seem to give them an advantage but it is not necessarily so. It is more difficult for the teacher to check the effectiveness of the child's survey of print when he is a fast, visual learner.

While most will learn to organize their behaviour and attend to print in an orderly manner following the directional schema, some will attend in a more varied way with right or bottom starting points on pages of print, or right ends of lines or of words, or selecting unusual middle features. These behaviours are not normally observable by the teacher. They can become established habits that are difficult to change.

Children who have difficulty with the exploration of new forms can be trained to follow the contour of a figure sequentially. In the formative stages of this behaviour the exploratory movements of the hand perform a key role. The eye registers and pursues the movements of the hand. In the later stages of training the eye can solve the perceptual task and systematically inspect the form's contour without the support of the hand.

Complex tasks

Much learning is 'overdetermined' which means that we have probably arrived at new learning by (a) many routes at the same time, or (b) in several alternative routes experienced singly but all giving the same sort of message. It makes learning difficult for some of us if instruction tells us that there is only one way to learn this. Those who devise curricula can make tasks difficult by oversimplifying them.

In Summary: Learning How to Access Visual Sources of Information While Reading for Meaning With Divided Attention

The heading is a mouthful but that is what the reading acquisition task is when children are learning to read on story texts.

If it is difficult for adults, including teachers, to grapple with the 'hidden' curriculum of perceptual learning, it would not be surprising if they were not able to respond to the particular child's learning challenge at a particular time. A prescriptive curriculum may be the result of such uncertainty and perhaps that is the reason why some education systems come to believe that children have to know their letters *before* they begin to make reading and writing responses.

Other observers, seeing children doing a fine job of accumulating letter, word, reading and writing skills from a more general approach using real books and story writing, can overgeneralize the extent of the success and claim that all children will get there if they are supported in these activities. They resist any checking on the progress as philosophically a mismatch with the freedom to develop.

As both these positions must seem, even to the lay person, unwarranted, it is surprising that the middle road is so seldom advocated. Using observation of what the child can already do and is at present trying to do, the sensitive teacher can interact with these activities taking the child towards the prescribed curriculum not via arbitrary exercises but through activities that are meaningful and enjoyable. This teacher must know all the possible routes to the end goal and have regular ways of checking that each child is on course even though the courses may all be different.

The teaching may have to go the child's way to the teacher's goals. The teacher can support the child's ability to construct his own knowledge. The child did this in oral language and can do it in early writing (Goodman, 1990). Why is it assumed that he cannot do this in reading also? The necessary extra is that the teacher observes sensitively, records progress and interacts supportively to achieve forward movement.

To inform her day-to-day interactions with individual learners the teacher must observe very carefully what her pupils are trying to do. She must employ simple discovery techniques to check on any aspect of learning that cannot be readily observed: the learning of the movement patterns, the spatial concepts, the sequential survey of words and the detailed survey of letter features. The child's writing behaviour provides opportunities to observe his spatial concepts and demands attention to letter and word detail as a complementary activity to reading. Whether the method has a decoding, or word, or story emphasis the visual perception of the symbols is an essential part of any learned association with sounds or spoken word. However, the child does not have to learn to recognize all the symbols of the writing system *before* he can proceed to reading stories.

Visual perception of textual features is certainly part of the inner processing system from which the reader generates reading behaviours. The beginning reader has to give attention to visual information as well as the language and messages but gradually becomes able to use visual information without much conscious attention, freeing more attention for the messages and language of the text and for novel information which expands the system. More than that, visual perceptual processing occurs without much attention, freeing the reader to attend to messages. Visual analysis may need conscious attention to support some problem-solving by deliberate cognitive processing.

The relationship between the cognitive processing which is generally conscious and apparent to the reader and the rarely conscious perceptual processing was described well by Bruner (1957, 1974). His theory placed cognitive and perceptual processing on a single continuum of problem-solving and decision-making. Within that theory it is possible to encompass the reader's conscious message-getting activities, the conscious search for and analysis of other types of information, the necessary vigilance, and error detection processes, together with the highly practised perceptual responding which requires so little attention.

13 The Development of Processing Strategies

Independent Reading Requires Strategic Control

We have considered the changes that occur in a child's literacy learning in the first three years of school. A 'typical' school entrant is not a reader on entry to school but has learned some preliminary reading and writing behaviours which have been labelled 'emerging literacy' (Morrow and Strickland, 1989) or early literacy (McLane and McNamee, 1990). At entry to school the child does have an impressive cognitive system for understanding and producing oral language and teaches himself more about language every time he speaks.

Such a child moves into the school's programme tentatively but by the end of the third year has a major degree of independence in reading such that he is really teaching himself more about reading every time he reads. For the most part he works in familiar territory, building up varied experience, and problem-solving minor challenges as they arise. As the child gains some control the teacher lets him manage more of the processing until he is carrying out all the 'reading work' independently. By that time he is not only directing the reading of a text but is also directing his own learning and needs only occasional guidance from his teachers, parents, or peers.

To trace this development in this book I explored the knowledge that children bring to school and how this undergoes changes during the transition into formal instruction. Established competencies in oral language and new learning about print, texts and books were examined and three processing challenges emerged. These were:

- controlling directional behaviours
- directing attention in a serial order appropriate for print
- understanding the hierarchical relationships that exist in printed language between letters, words, and longer stretches of text.

Children trying to read their first simple story books are attending to these three challenges. They are also bringing together information from several sources — information about meanings and language structures, visual information in print, and a growing awareness of the links between print and the sounds of language.

Without trying to control the vocabulary of simple texts we can be confident that the frequency principle in language will ensure that the reader meets familiar words many times and will meet new challenges within the context of those familiar words. Instruction can manipulate the balance of challenge and familiarity to make the child's task easy or hard.

In the last two chapters I have been developing the argument that we can observe reading behaviours which are early signals of a developing inner control over the reading task. The visual perception of print is one aspect of such inner control. In this chapter we examine another important component of that inner control — the strategies the reader initiates

- to search texts at any level of text analysis
- to select some sources of information for momentary attention
- to make choices among possible responses
- to monitor the meaningfulness of the resulting 'reading'
- to detect and correct error when necessary.

Strategic control over what one can do to problem-solve novel text is central to the reading process. More than that, strategic processing may well be the major determiner of the common observation that those who read well get better at reading (Stanovich, 1986).

Word Attack is Not Enough

It is necessary to deal briefly with the common misconception that learning to read only requires a child to learn to 'attack' words using a knowledge of letter-sound relationships. This skill is assumed to make the reader independent, in that he will be able to work out what new words say. Some of the arguments as to why this is probably not so are reviewed in this section.

Increases in reading achievement have been equated with increases in word knowledge. According to the concept of 'word attack,' knowing the letter-sound relationships will result in children sounding out new words which will somehow enter the reading vocabulary and empower the child to read more difficult texts. 'Word attack' is conceived of narrowly as sounding out, which has in turn been equated with a need to know one's sounds. It is possible to argue that word knowledge, word attack, a sounding out strategy, and knowing one's sounds, are four different things, the last making only a small contribution to the first.

This view of how the reader increases his control over texts is held by professionals and nonprofessionals but despite wide support it has problems. Only a few will be discussed.

- Children who learn to read on texts in a 'whole language' programme will be heard to make errors, correct them and learn new words without any sign of sounding out.

- Despite the care with which teachers teach (and children learn) letter-sound relationships, some children are not able to read more difficult texts.

- A sounding out strategy does not explain how a reader (usually an older reader) can read a new word with a measure of understanding supported by the text but may mispronounce it if reading aloud.

The regularities of print-sound relationships will help a reader to work out the pronunciation of a new word only if that reader has heard that word before, can identify it from the 'sounding' out, and if it is not an exception or a member of a different set of regularities in spelling (Smith, 1985).

There is mounting evidence that sounding out is not enough. Some of the arguments are these.

1 **A wide range of phonological information**　Research has shown that the good reader uses not just the sounds of letters but phonological information from several levels of language. He can provide phonological identities for letters, diagraphs, clusters, syllables, prefixes and suffixes, root words, phrases, and nonlanguage strings. He will select a larger rather than a smaller unit for efficiency and may check one source of information against another. Occasionally his word-solving will be done at the letter-sound level but not only at that level. As reported earlier (page 273), Gibson (1965) found children in their first year of reading instruction who made use of clusters of letters which were always found in the same position in a word and which did not vary in pronunciation. (For example, not many older children have difficulty with '-tion,' irregular though it is, and 'ing' is a cluster which beginning readers rarely segment further.) The functional units young readers use can be one letter but may be three or four. Such clusters function as units which organize perception as soon as they enter the 'reading vocabulary' or 'writing vocabulary' of the child. By comparison single letter analysis is slow, requires more learning, allows for more error and is more difficult to re-instate as a word. The larger the pronounceable units a child can discover and use, the less learning effort will be required. Phonological awareness is involved but rarely phonics or blends.

2 **Text reading behaviours**　Descriptive accounts of what children do as they read texts (Clay, 1967; Weber, 1970; Biemiller, 1970) produced evidence of other ways in which children work on text, like predicting, checking and self-correcting.

3 **Information sources in texts**　Other insights came from information theory, with analyses of how we use the multiple sources of information embedded in texts—syntactical, orthographic, visual, spatial, frequency, transitional probabilities, and redundancies. The reader can attend to information in print on many levels—the continuous text or discourse level, the meanings, structures, words, part-words or letter clusters, and letter-sound levels. Phonological information of various kinds is used in analyses of words and in checking processes but single letter-sound relationships are only one of these sources of information available to readers.

4 **Meaning**　From both linguistic and cognitive psychology sources there came a new emphasis on the role of meaning as a facilitator of reading, not merely a product of it, and a new understanding of how the knowl-

edge we gain of the world around us through experience helps us to give meaning to new events, to language, and to texts.

5 **Early writing** Despite the claims that children need to use phonological strategies of the single-letter word-attack kind before they can read new words, a researcher will rarely hear any sounding out behaviour that goes beyond the first letters or letter clusters of words *if children have not been specifically taught to do this.* On the other hand such behaviour may be heard much more frequently, and beyond first letters, when the same children are trying to write texts. Learning phonological identities of letters and letter clusters in the context of trying to write a message and trying to get down a new word which is in your language repertoire but which you have not tried to write before is the meaningful, analytic task that some theorists have been calling for (Stanovich, 1987). It is important to continually think about the interplay of early reading and early writing.

In the face of these discoveries, how one learns to read can no longer be reduced to learning letter-sound relationships. If the young reader is to work effectively on different kinds of texts he needs to have experience of texts of different types, for reading with understanding is more than reading words. It is possible to read all the words correctly and still not to get the message. New words are added to a reading vocabulary by reading them successfully and the processes by which this happens are many. Sounding out need not be the first or even a major strategy because once the child has *read the new word aloud two or three times, its phonological identity is available to him for closer analysis.*

There is evidence to suggest that rather than knowledge about letters and sounds always preceding learning to read, the reverse can occur. We will think differently about the sound of a word as a result of having read it or learned to write it. Familiarity with alphabetic writing induces a more analytical awareness of the phoneme contrasts in speech (Morais et al, 1979). For example, an impression of orthography sometimes accompanies our attempt to understand a spoken homophone in English: we may think of the spellings 'sales' or 'sails' when we hear the sentence 'Yacht sails are down.' Similarly, we may refer briefly to the visual forms 'crews' or 'cruise' when we hear the sounds spoken (Henderson, 1984).

Exploring the role of phonological awareness in reading acquisition with experiments cannot specify its role in instruction. This is partly because other important sources of awareness and segmentation are not taken into account. It is also because the experiments do not tell us how children use phonological information conjointly with other sources of information and in various ways. This is not to say that the experiment with its tight controls is not an important way to uncover contributing factors. It is just difficult for the experiment to handle change over time in partially correct responses contributed to by several other sources of information.

Attending to Many Sources of Information

Visual information was discussed in the last chapter. It is important to refer here to three language-based sources of information.

It is the assumption of the following discussion that there are many strategies which a novice reader can initiate to problem-solve the challenges of new texts. The reader uses understandings of what can happen in the world (meaning) and language knowledge (of words, structures and sound sequences) and several approaches to phonological information from oral and written sources. He mediates the appropriateness of possible responses through attention to visual information. Observation studies reveal a young reader who works very actively on the information in texts. What makes him more able to do this without assistance (independently) is being able to initiate or call up a range of different strategies over which he has a flexible control.

Bringing meaning to text

Meaning is the most important source of information.

It is a source which lies outside the text in the sense that it depends upon what the reader is able to bring to the text. Research and practice show that a good introduction of the text to the reader before he attempts to read it will make the task easier for him. The reader:

- brings prior knowledge to the text
- carries out reading work in order to make sense of what he is reading
- and uses meaning as his ultimate check that all is well.

The most important test for the child to make is 'Does it make sense?' because if it does not then there is clearly some more reading work to be done by the reader until it does!

Sharpening phonological awareness on texts

High progress readers operate as if they know the regularities of letter-sound correspondences although they may not be able to verbalize these. Will the discovery of rules be automatic for all children given sufficient reading and writing experience?

In one experiment of learning to read Arabic words, some English-speaking adults taught by a whole-word method analysed the component letter-sound relationships of Arabic for themselves but some did not (Gibson, 1965). Individuals may vary markedly in the degree to which letter-sound relationships, simple or complex, are induced *without specific instruction* as they learn to read.

When a programme is built around story-reading some children appear to read the stories well enough but may not become analytic of print and create phonological identities for letters and parts of words. To ensure that this occurs teachers will call attention to these *within the context of the story* when they are introducing or discussing texts with individuals or groups. As the teacher shows the print form and draws attention to particular letters or clusters or analogous words and pronounces the feature normally, she models that it is both interesting and important to attend to the ways in which letters form into words.

If her pupils are also composing their own messages in daily writing and working towards independence in this activity it is hard for them to avoid being phonologically analytic about words.

Both these types of learning opportunities do not force the child to deal only with single letter-sound relationships but allow the reader or writer to work with any size of phonological cluster as one of several ways in which to solve texts. Perhaps it is important not to refer the child to an arbitrary scale of associations of letters to sounds but to some phonological knowledge that he has. Thus analogous letter-sound or cluster sound experience becomes the reference point, not 'the sound of that letter.'

Using syntactic information

The previous discussion has acknowledged meaning and phonological levels of language information. Grammatical knowledge which allows the child to construct sentences and predict which way a sentence might go is a third kind of language information which children use. We do this kind of predicting as listeners when we follow the speaker and often almost finish his sentence for him. The child has the same kind of control over syntactic prediction at the level of his own language usage.

Most theorists and many research studies agree that readers use language prediction skills (Tumner, in press) and use 'context' to solve words. It is commonly asserted in books about teaching reading that 'the context' provides the child with cues and that he must learn to 'read for meaning.' The terms 'context' and 'meaning' are not precise enough for teaching. If, following errors, teachers ask 'Can you say it that way?' or 'Does it make sense?' children answer the questions in different ways. They treat the first as a grammatical question and the second as a semantic question. Context may be seen as semantic or grammatical context (and arguably, both at the same time.)*

Faced with a meaningless set of printed symbols the child does not lack ingenuity in making his predictions but, as the following examples show, error behaviour can illustrate *the kind of information not being used*, and sometimes the semantic relationships are kept but the grammatical ones lost, or vice versa.

(a) The picture is misunderstood (no semantic correspondence).
   Father is ringing up on the phone.
   Father is shaving.

   I am tired.
   I am waking up.

---

* The third important meaning of context in education is the situation within which the whole activity occurs.

(b)   The meaning is retained.
        I will wash the car today.
        I will hose the car today.

        Father is razor blading.
        Father is shaving.

(c)   The word is of the same grammatical category.
        They all chuckeded him out of bed.
        They all pulled   him out of bed.

(d)   The word sequences are grammatically equivalent.
        I will go and get lunch.
        I will get   lunch.

(e)   One word is altered to agree with another error.
        We go   for the bread. Mother's looking.
        He goes   for the bread. Mother looked

These examples suggest that it is not sufficient to complain that a child is 'guessing' instead of 'reading.' Obviously some guesses are responses to sources of information in the text and some take more information into account than others. One can conceive of some errors being better than others depending on which relationships one prefers to stress. Some writers about reading have stressed the importance of semantic context, others have stressed the letter-sound relationships, and these two viewpoints have been the source of much chicken and egg debate over teaching method. Currently reading experts advocate that both aspects be prominent in any reading programme.

My analysis of 10525 errors substituted for text by the research group of 100 children (Clay, 1968) produced these important facts. The total errors were subdivided into single word errors and sequences of words substituted.

- Five year olds being taught to read anticipated the class of single words which should occur next in a sentence for 79 percent of the occurrences. That means they usually replaced a noun with a noun, or a verb with a verb as the previous examples show. Why would this happen? If they made a series of errors in sequence this figure was lower (58 percent of the occurrences) but if these two types of error behaviours are combined children followed the syntax of the language in 72 percent of their errors (or 7674 out of 10525 errors).

- Those same five year olds who predicted the syntax of the book's sentences quite well only matched their errors of the text on letter-sound correspondences in 41 percent of the single word errors when the criteria of correspondence favoured higher scoring.

The summary table below shows that the grammatical context was a significant source of cues to the young reader (remembering that the readers were

Error Analysis

Substituted a word of the same grammatical class.	5 035 examples 79%
Substituted several words in a phrase of the same grammatical structure.	2 639 examples 58%
All grammatical substitutions.	7 674 examples 72%
All letter-sound correspondences in single word substitutions.	2 388 examples 41%

taught by one particular method on a particular set of texts). Semantic categorization of errors was not included in this study. I concluded that the child's control of sentence structure was most important in assisting his attempts to read transition texts (texts that were close to the spoken language of the children). Contrived texts which are regularized by imposing letter-sound controls or vocabulary controls run the risk of reducing the support from grammatical cues.

Although only 41 percent of the substitutions showed any letter-sound correspondence by six years other New Zealand studies have reported visual information being used as often as language cues by the third year of instruction showing that learning was proceeding in an appropriate direction.

Help for the reader may come from phonological, grammatical or semantic aspects of language. In reading acquisition texts the messages need to be simple, but simplification should not remove rich sources of information in the text which the novice may need to draw upon. If a text contains a full range of language cues there is more chance a particular child will be able to direct some prior knowledge to that text; if the control over one set of features, such as phonology, dominates we have set a task which requires the child to bring only one particular set of language knowledge to the problem-solving.

Having Opportunities for Independent Solving

A flexible use of many sources of information allows the independent reader alternative approaches to problem-solving text. Teachers' manuals for programmes using language experience or simple story texts suggest that independence in reading texts that are information-rich depends upon a flexible use of a range of skills like these.

- Anticipating a possible sentence or discourse pattern.
- Using prior knowledge of the world.
- Using prior knowledge of stories.

- Using previous experiences with print.
- Recognizing most of the salient features of most of the words.
- Using two known vocabularies, from reading and writing.
- Using clusters of letters from known words to get to new words.
- Getting a new word by analogy with a known word.
- Using analysis of sounds or clusters of sounds.
- Using picture cues.

Initiating a search of any of these sources does not occur in isolation. One source (say predicting what kind of language structure could come next) can provide support for completion of the task while the child works out something new about letters and sounds. *A useful assumption is that the teacher can allow the child to catch on to any information source that will help in any order.* A steady growth in the ability to use every source of information in the text is essential to meet the challenge of each new book.

In this section we consider in some detail the scope for learning more about reading while reading by considering four kinds of responses:

- Correct responses (no error having occurred).
- Repeating correct responses (confirming checks).
- Errors, no solution having been found independently (but with prompting from the teacher for further independent solving).
- Self-correction (errors corrected without prompting).

Correct responding may have involved the reader in independent solving but it tells the teacher or researcher nothing about the kind of processing children were engaged in. Confirming checks are of interest, and errors provide the child with opportunities to do some reading work like self-monitoring and self-evaluation. An examination of self-correcting processes suggests one way in which a forward thrust and increase in control can emerge from what is initially an error.

Correct responses

Correct responses are the goal of most instruction and yet they receive little attention from teachers. Correct responses usually result from peak performance in information sampling but we cannot tell how the child got to the response. They tell us very little about the reader as a processor of information because the processing is covert.

A correct response fits all the sources of information in texts like the last piece of a jigsaw puzzle. The reader may only use one or two bits of information to confirm this fit but could check all the information if need be. Because the message is understood by the reader he receives positive feedback for whatever processing he did. Good readers have so few errors in proportion to correct responses (see below) that they are able to use the main sweep of structure and meaning as primary sources of cues. Novice readers making good progress do make many errors and they build error-correcting strategies to deal with them (Clay, 1967, 1969).

Confirming checks

Children repeat correct responses as if to confirm what they have said or to test out their surprise at the way the text went. Mature readers experience similar surprise with wordings which have two meanings. These repetitions must be seen as examplars of the searching, monitoring and checking strategies used by the reader.

Error rate

It would be consistent with much that is written about reading to argue that the rate at which errors are made causes success or failure and that merely selecting appropriate material will enable the child to perform above a level of 90 percent accuracy.

In my longitudinal research studies in Auckland (Clay, 1982) teachers were carefully extending or supplementing children's experience as seemed appropriate, and progress was, overall, extremely good, but there were large differences in the *rates* of making errors in the observation records over the first year of instruction.

- Low progress children made one error in every three words.
- Low middle groups made one error in every eight words.
- High middle groups made one error in every 15 words.
- High progress groups made one error in every 37 words.
- The best readers made one error in every 100 words.

Because the better readers read many and longer texts compared with the poor readers, their errors were a small proportion of what they read. Error was embedded in long stretches of correct reading. There were patterns of information against which a stray error could be tested. It could be argued that the low progress children did not have enough correct responding to support them and allow them to learn from their errors.

Sources of error

Errors will occur when the child needs some better ways of sorting the incoming messages from text. In other words they will occur during the processing of information. My view of the teacher's role is to decide how to be most helpful to the child who must enlarge and extend his strategies in-the-head for picking up and processing information. (It *does not involve a requirement to be accurate*.) If the teacher can increase the effectiveness of those strategies they will in turn generate further appropriate behaviour. However, much teaching and most programmes encourage teachers to teach items of information.

Some of the reasons why errors in processing occur are suggested below but the list cannot be exhaustive.

The child fails to search   Mere inventing of what could occur in the print provides teaching opportunities to direct a pupil to some worthwhile search for features he knows and can use as checks on what he is saying.

Insufficient information is picked up. Error could result from immature oral language habits:

> I are running   for   I am running

or from the pick-up of visual information:

> at the   for   after

or from slow learning of unfamiliar word forms:

> cupple   for   cuddle

or from failure to anticipate the probabilities of the written language of the book:

> Here's   for   Here is

Interference   Error may result from interference when strongly competing ideas rise to the 'tip of the tongue' and obscure the correct response. Competing responses may be thought of as words of similar meaning (quick, fast; look, see) and words of similar syntactic relationship (run, jump, look) or words which represent opposites (right, left; up, down). The competing pair 'was' and 'saw' frequently fit the grammar of the sentence, fit the meaning, and have identical letter components:

> Martin was the boy.   Martin saw the boy.

These two words are distinguished by directional cues and by letter-sound relationships but the child may not have learned to use these cues.

Masking responses   Error may result from a frequently practised response masking or preventing the use of other responses. The beginner who accepts 'M' as the equivalent of 'Mother' will produce mistakes with a word like 'Martin.' The common speech error of using the plural 'are' for the singular 'am' in 'I am' blocks the use of the correct response in early reading for some children. This type of error often stems from oral language habits and tends to be eliminated as behaviour comes more and more under visual control and letter-sound relationships begin to be established.

Practised or systematic error   Errors may be learned by systematic practice of wrong responses, often resulting in confusions. For most children systematic error tends to be short-lived and is corrected in a few weeks if new material is presented. When a child is held on a book that he repeatedly reads incorrectly he may be practising his errors. Working on boringly similar material invites the reader to become a juggler of possible words rather than a reader of actual words. Reading mostly to oneself, or to another child, if either child is weak on error-correction techniques, is inviting this systematic practice of error. An example of systematic error is given below. A boy who had been at school seven months reads a preprimer of a basal reader, a very limited text probably contributing to his confusion. (Many children are reading texts in basal readers which are not much better than this extreme example.)

Child:	*Oh Tim*		
Text:	No Tim		
	Oh jump		
	Go up		
	Oh jump Tim		
	Go up	Tim	
	Oh jump jump jump		
	Go up	up	up

This is likely to train the response 'Oh' for 'Go' and 'Jump' for 'up.' If the child, regarding this behaviour as successful, practises it over several days or weeks and nothing occurs to create any suspicion of misfit then he is learning systematic error responses.

The need to learn more about cues   Error may reflect ignorance of the cues that could be used. Until he has mastered the reading process the beginning reader is, by definition, ignorant of many sources of cues which cannot all be introduced to him at once. The child who cannot distinguish 'fireman' and 'fire engine' is ready for a further advance in word and letter discrimination.

A reader may not initiate a search   Error behaviour may result where a child who can read does not search effectively even though he may have learned the appropriate cues. He is too precipitate in accepting a wrong response as suitable or in saying 'I don't know.' Children who fail to search also fail to learn how to use cues effectively and do not develop error-correction techniques.

Effort to read fast   Errors may result from an increase in speed of reading to a point where it is beyond the subject's capacity to process all the information or apply all the error checks, so that errors are overlooked during otherwise fluent reading.

Change in type of text   If the type of text changes markedly from that which the child has come to expect, he predicts wrongly. Too rapid promotion on books can produce this kind of response. A change to a different series of readers in which the language has different regularities (phonic regularity, natural language texts, controlled vocabulary texts) may increase the occurrence of errors. Such a change may at times be used intentionally to force the child to attend to some new features of print. This might apply to a good reader who neglects to use the phonological knowledge that he has. However, for children having difficulty learning to read, drastic changes in style of text are not suggested. They need the firm foundation of what they already control as a launching pad for learning more about the information in print.

Teacher attention to error

What happens when teachers attend to the errors that their pupils make? McNaughton's analysis (1978b) shows that teachers provide two types of information for children.

- They ask questions or give prompts about how to get to the correct response.
- They give a correct response.

If a teacher delays prompting or helping until the child has read to the end of the sentence readers become more efficient than if she attends immediately. Immediate attention:

- restricts the child's opportunity to self-correct
- deprives him of post-error content
- restricts the kind of help she can give.

McNaughton suggests that most errors which are not self-corrected should be attended to but, if more than one error in 10 is occurring, it may be important not to attend to those errors which hardly change the meaning at all. This is an adjustment because of the high cost of too much attention to error. It is most important that the teacher's statements should be brief so that the pupil can keep his attention on the contextual cues.

Teacher attention to error provides her with an opportunity either to direct the pupil to her way of thinking about the sequence required by the reader, or to help the pupil become more independent at solving such difficulties. Her questioning and discussion can be item-oriented or strategy-oriented. *She can emphasize the error, or the opportunity to problem-solve.*

Reconsidering a Response

Miscues are partially right and partially wrong

A correct response in reading fits neatly into a matrix of relationships at all levels of language organization and with all the associations of visual perception that the reader has learned. If we rename errors 'miscues' this emphasizes the fact that an error response may fit a number of these relationships but may be incongruent with one or more. Thus, in the common five year old reading error 'I are sleeping,' the parts of speech, word order, verbal meaning and first letter correspondences are retained but word agreement and letter-sound correspondence could produce in the reader the awareness that something is wrong.

When something seems to the child to be a bad fit he frequently pauses, and then searches for more evidence against which to check his response.

Often he cannot solve the problem although he knows that it exists; if he is successful in his search he finds and adds into his processing other important information.

This searching, finding and adding to the partially correct response to achieve a correct response may prove to be very important in explaining how the effective reader learns more about reading while reading (see Chapter 14).

Prompted corrections: a teacher's call to search

The major heading of the previous section was 'Having Opportunities for Independent Solving' and the following discussion suggests that while teacher interactions could be directed to reducing such opportunities they can prompt active processing strategies.

It is common for teachers to accept the partially correct miscue with positive comments like 'That makes sense but . . .' or 'It looks like . . . but what does the first letter say?'

When the teacher calls for the child to search for more information she may ask a general question or one which directs the child to a particular cue source. The call to search may ask the child in a somewhat general way:

- to find the error
- to try some alternatives
- to look at visual cues
- to sound parts of the word
- to make a choice
- to be flexible and change the response
- to be self-sufficient in solving the problem.

Teachers in Clay's (1967) research were asked what they said when a child hesitated or stopped when they were hearing children read individually. Some of the useful things teachers said they did were:

- Wait, giving the child time to process cues.
- Tell him, when the word is too hard for him to solve.
- Help the child to read back a little for context.
- Use questions to guide his thinking.
- Say 'Look for something in the picture that starts like this.'

Such teacher behaviour is consistent with that advocated in the 'Pause, prompt and praise' procedures widely used in parent or teacher remedial work with children (Glynn and McNaughton, 1985).

Other teacher responses also call upon the child to 'do reading work' but with more attention to a particular strategy.

- Give a word known to the child starting the same way.
- Emphasize the beginning sound.
- Say 'Get your mouth ready for the first sound.'

Teachers also said they used procedures which I would consider unlikely to develop processing strategies like flash cards (in which the teacher has no control over what the child is attending to), and going over a word again and again until it was correct, which invokes memorizing processes of storing and recalling an image. Perhaps useful for gaining quick access to what one knows, such procedures do not provide opportunities for the child to build a flexible repertoire of strategies for picking up, sorting, checking and cross-checking the information in a text.

Children who need help may develop ways of controlling the teacher to get her to intervene and give help. They look up at her, look away, wriggle, ask for help. One child said w-w-w for any word and told her remedial teacher that it usually got her the help she needed! So children's responding can be very controlling of the way teachers respond, and teacher demands can be very controlling of how children will be allowed to respond. An important question is, are there opportunities and help for the child to work independently on texts?

A strategy encouraged by teachers

Some teachers try to train children to miss out problem words in their reading and go to the end of the line or sentence in order to complete the meaning and so solve the word. Yet research (and day-to-day observation) shows that despite this training, young children at the acquisition stage spontaneously return to the beginning of a line or sentence to solve their problem. One can guess at the reason. The syntax or structure of the sentence which establishes the relationships between words is frequently destroyed or changed if words are omitted. Syntax, as we saw in the error analysis above, is one source of information which supports early reading behaviour. Teachers often demand that children try to read ahead long before they have the competence to benefit from this tactic; it works well with competent readers, and it could work when children are reading familiar words in new stories. However, if the child's inclination is to return to line or sentence beginning and catch up some more information to solve the troublesome word, it is doubtful whether we should insist that he adopt the more artificial strategy of reading on.

Reconsidering a response: trials and self-corrections

Confirming checks, mentioned earlier, are one type of attempt by the reader to reconsider a response. The young reader who monitors his own reading provides us with evidence that he searches for cues and cross-checks between sources of information. Such 'reading work' often turns the partially correct response into a correct one. Even beginning readers can be self-correcting some of their errors. Errors provide the opportunity to learn to detect their occurrence and to attempt to correct them. An acceptance of some error behaviour is implied if we are providing opportunity for self-correction to occur.

Meaning usually provides a signal to children that they are right or wrong. However, children know that from time to time in their lives they encounter things that are totally novel or things they do not understand and they come to accept a degree of nonsense in their lives. Sooner or later, they think it will fall into place. Consequently they will accept a 'near enough' result at times.

The novice reader must become aware that there has to be a neat fit of language and visual cues in reading and writing almost all the time and if he monitors this he will know when things are not quite right. Three conditions create or facilitate this awareness.

- There must be time to discover that all is not well.
- There must be permission to work at the problem.
- There must be encouragement to discover something for themselves.

Most children who notice a mismatch have the need to get rid of the dissonance or irritation. The child may be seen to do one of these things.

- Return along a line of print — to the sentence beginning, or several words, or only one word.
- Make several attempts at a word.
- Show signs of dissatisfaction with puzzled looks, verbal complaints, using a finger, or making appeals for help.

These may occur because the language patterns and visual patterns are not matched in number, or because the visual form of the word is clearly not the one being spoken. The reader takes another look at the word or another run at the sentence.

In self-correction, by definition, the child failed to use some information, noticed some mismatch, picked up some additional information, and put together and achieved a correct response. We should be interested in this overt, observable process in the young reader. It could be progressive, lifting the reading or writing competencies of the young reader. On the surface there is one more successful reading of the word. In fact much more has occurred. When the child solved the problem of the initial error:

- monitoring his own behaviour was reinforced
- the signals he used to detect the error worked
- searching for new information paid off
- the new information was noted and used
- producing alternative responses was successful
- checking alternatives and choosing between them worked.

In correcting the error, the child practised monitoring, searching, generating, checking and choosing processes and they were all reinforced because success was contingent upon them. In addition the signals of error, and the new bits of information previously neglected, also contributed to success. During this cognitive activity the reader is sensorially open to new possibilities (Bruner, 1957) and the event seems to have high tutorial potential, but the tutoring is entirely self-tutoring.

A closer look at self-correction

Unprompted, children often correct their own errors (see chapters 7 and 8). They stop, return to the beginning of a line, and try again. Sometimes they comment aloud on their problems.

When you hear a child read, do you notice those errors which a child makes but corrects through his own efforts? When I set myself the task of recording all the reading behaviour a child produced, it became noticeable that some children were working very hard at correcting their own mistakes (Clay, 1967, 1969). It was a natural occurrence in the act of reading for beginning readers. Self-correction appeared early when only a very elementary knowledge of reading has been achieved.

If we give the new entrant interesting simple books which encourage him to construct stories out of his oral language habits, and if we observe carefully, we soon find the child searching for information in the book which will confirm that what he is saying is in fact on that page. Pictures, the general shape or pattern of the print, a letter he recognizes, any of these may provide some measure of confirmation that he is on the right track. In fact, self-correction behaviour appeared in the records of 90 percent of a research group three weeks before their promotion to book-reading (Clay, 1967).

When the child sets himself a goal to choose a particular word to fit all the available cues he develops search and check procedures which have been described by many writers about perception and thinking. High progress children in the research study used cues from several sources — meaning, grammatical structure, letter-forms, and letter-sound relationships — and if children sensed disagreement between their first response and some of the cues, they searched for a different response which would resolve the problem.

- A child alert to meaning reads 'Dad, let me paint you' and exclaims, 'Hey! You can't paint you!'

- A child who observes visual pattern reads 'said' for 'shouted' and protests 'It hasn't got the same letters as "said."'

Usually children who thought errors had been made went back to the beginning of a line, wiping the slate clean as it were, and tried again. They were often successful on the second or third trial. The courage to make mistakes, the 'ear' to recognize that an error had occurred, the patience to search for confirmation — these were the characteristics of children who made good progress in their first year of reading. Although the child's detailed knowledge of cues may be rather limited and poorly learned, confirmation is obtained when cues from several sources are checked one against the other. If such a process is successful the child is likely to become aware of new ways in which he can discriminate between words. He learns at those very points where he makes an error that he recognizes.

Some very intricate self-correction behaviour occurred in the research records. The observations showed that a child who was aware that 'something was wrong' went back over the line or tried several responses until the error was corrected. Signs of children's dissatisfaction with their own responses were frequently noted. They stopped, looked puzzled, complained, repeated the line, or ran a finger along a word. An unsuccessful attempt at self-correction can be quoted as an example.

A high progress reader aged 5:6 came to the text

'Look after Timothy'

and worked at the word 'after' in this way:

— *It wouldn't be 'at,' it's too long.*
— *It wouldn't be 'hats'* (which was semantically appropriate but linguistically awkward).
— *It wouldn't be 'are,' look, it's too long.*

The problem was unresolved and the child left it. Three pages further on the word was read correctly without effort.

It is exceptional for the school entrant to be able to state what he is doing in this way, and the verbalized reasons for his decisions may not be the significant ones. In the above example the expressed reasons for dissatisfaction with the possible responses were size and meaning, but it should be noted that two of the three attempts correctly categorized 'after' as a word beginning with 'a,' and all three have at least two letters in common.

Of 10525 errors in the Auckland research (Clay, 1968) self-correction occurred spontaneously in 26 percent. The top 50 percent of children corrected one in every three or four errors while for the low groups the self-correction rates were one in eight and one in 20. All groups used self-correction but the better readers used it more effectively. Half the self-corrections (52 percent) was achieved by returning to the beginning of a line and most of the remainder by repeating a phrase or a word. Self-correction rate was more closely related to reading progress scores in the first three years of instruction than either intelligence or reading readiness scores.

Even so, self-correction is a useful sign only for a short period. It emerges towards the end of the early reading period and later it disappears as good readers change from solving their errors aloud after they have been pronounced, to working out the problem silently before the error has been vocalized. This change to pre-processing is illustrated by the child's comment below.

Child: *Bill.*   *I nearly said 'Peter' there.*
Text: Bill

Errors and self-correction are considered in the next figure.

• The low middle group attempted to use cues but they made so many errors that it was difficult for them to recognize when they had made a correct response. They showed low effort and bewilderment before complex stimuli.

- The low group seemed to make little effort to relate anything to anything. They seemed to be 'waiting for the light.' They never seemed to know when their behaviour had been appropriate.

Both these low groups need their reading individually supervised with frequent praise for correct responding.

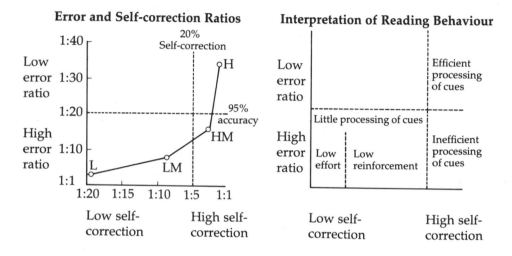

Error and Self-correction Ratios   **Interpretation of Reading Behaviour**

The young reader is able to respond to dissonance or consonance between any aspects of language—phonological, grammatical or semantic—or with visual information. A reader may become conscious of a difference between what he has said and one of several messages from the text when

- the response does not make sense in the sentence, in the story, or with the pictures
- the response makes sense but some visual feature of the print is incongruous with the response given
- the number of locating movements of hand and/or eyes does not match with the number of words spoken.

Each of these incongruities forces the child to consider alternative ways of expressing his ideas. This establishes a need to choose between alternatives and the child develops an awareness that there is a precise identity for the word in the text which allows for no difference between what is said and what makes sense. In time, a smooth predict-and-check procedure is established, using phrases and sentences as the units of meaning. The competent reader is, however, able to check his response in a more detailed way to resolve a conflict, down to the visual discrimination of individual letters if need be.

Earlier, the significance of the ratio of error to correct words was discussed and now it is clearer why this is a factor in reading acquisition.

- The child who is reading for meaning responds to error with a search for more information.
- He may try to cross-check cues from movement, from visual and from language sources.
- An awareness that identity consists of agreement in all details keeps the search alive.
- As he searches and checks, more and more detail in the print attracts his attention. He is sensitized to more of the interrelationships in language which can provide cues and checks.

He has developed some ways of learning from his errors, of getting to information he had overlooked and testing its importance.

High progress readers made many errors which gave them opportunities to develop effective search and check procedures. Long stretches of correct reading with a full measure of grammatical meaning and story cues provide a rich backdrop to error when it occurs. Children then become progressively better at self-correction. For a long time we have recognized that the proportion of error in reading is important and authorities recommend that the child read with 95 percent accuracy. A higher error rate blurs the matrix of cues. The child becomes confused and instead of a progressive gain in skill the activity becomes non-progressive. There is scope in the very complex activity of reading for much error behaviour, and a good defence against this is strong error correcting strategies. These strategies can be developed by the young child who is still in a stage of intuitive rather than logical thinking. As children respond they gradually become aware of what they are doing and become able to employ analysis at a conscious level. None of the error detection and correction devices were very accurate at the level of the very first reading books but working in concert they were useful.

The argument is not that errors are bad and correcting them is good. That is simplistic. The argument is that errors provide opportunities to become aware of mismatches in redundant information in texts, and when they trigger self-correction processes which involve reading work it is the work done to problem-solve errors which has high tutorial value for the reader.

After Two Years of Instruction

Children from six Auckland schools were studied in their third year of instruction (Williams, 1968). Their average age was 7:10 and mean I.Q. 102. They read three to five short passages of prose graded in difficulty from the teachers' supplement to the six- to 12- year levels of the Ginn readers (Russell, 1966). A detailed analysis of their errors showed some interesting facts about the cues the children must have been using.

All were guided by the sentence structure and word order to some extent, like the younger children. A strong trend was still noted for the substituted words to be of the same grammatical function as the text word, indicating that many children are influenced in their choice of word by the grammatical structure of the sentence. Readers were guided by the sentence pattern leading up to the error. Results varied with the quality of reading. The best readers had 80 percent grammatically acceptable substitutions, the average readers 70 percent and the low progress readers only 62 percent.

Of course meaning was also involved in error behaviour. Of all errors, 80 percent were acceptable within the meaning of the story for the high progress readers, 65 percent for the average group and 54 percent for the low group. The good reader matched his attempts to both sentence structure and meaning in 80 percent of his trials. For the average and low progress groups their responses were more often matched for structure of the sentence than for meaning.

Do children's errors indicate that they are using letter-sound correspondences to guide their attempts? Overall, in this sample, there was almost no overt, observable word analysis or word attack used by children in this study. Audible analysis of words into syllables or sounds was noted in only 5.5 percent of the errors or attempts. In a further 6 percent of responses there was a delay of such a degree that the recorder was able to assume private solving taking place before a successful response was given. Thus only 11.5 percent of word study could have been phonic or syllabic in the sense of conscious manipulation of phonological elements. (However, all the reading was oral and therefore realised in phonological forms.)

Williams analysed this 11.5 percent of error which might have involved word analysis behaviour into:

- syllabic attack as in *sur-faced*
- compound words as in *can-not*
- letter-sound combinations as in *sl-a-sh-ed*
- mixed letter and syllabic attack as in *w-ait-ing*.

Of these four types syllabic attack was the most common, even at this young age. The group most likely to use letter-sounding was the high progress group. However, they also used larger clusters of letters than the low progress groups. These findings are consistent with research findings on pronounceable units (Gibson 1965).

Nevertheless, perhaps the child responds unknowingly to letter-sound correspondences as he makes his guesses. An analysis of all the single-word errors for letter-sound correspondence showed that 87 percent of the children's attempts involved some letter-sound correspondence with no marked differences between progress groups. These figures are high compared with 41 percent quoted earlier for five to six year olds. Beginning letters or clusters were the same in 80 percent of the errors, indicating a high degree of matching choices to letters. Last letters or clusters matched in 53 percent, showing fairly well-developed attention to inflections and suffixes.

Minimal attention was being paid at this stage to medial letter groups. The focus of attention appeared to be initial concentration on the left end of the word, then a quick visual sweep through the central section with sustained attention on the final element.

Errors of position or order, often called reversals, accounted for only 2.5 percent of all substitutions. Left to right sequencing behaviour appeared to be firmly fixed as a major convention in reading. First letter groups or first and last letter groups provided cues, with medial sections of words receiving less attention.

A high progress reader at this level makes few errors. When he does fail to solve a word and match it exactly to the text there are four chances in five that it will fit the sentence grammatically, and that it will be meaningful in the context, and nine chances in 10 that it will match some of the letter-sound features of the word. The attempt will probably correspond with beginning and ending sounds but not with those in the middle.

High progress readers at this level read faster than the high progress readers in the first year at school, but low progress readers of both groups read at the same slow pace. The high progress reader gathers his cues and selects his responses at a fast rate, but he also adapts his speed at a difficulty and after an error. The slow reader has less flexibility and reads slowly word by word.

The skills of the average and low progress readers in these three aspects of cue gathering—grammatical, semantic and letter-sound correspondence—should be developed and strengthened, in that order, and emphasis on sounding out or syllabic attack limited to a breakdown technique and not the sole approach to words.

At the third year of instruction half of all the successful attack on words involved self-correction behaviour—that is, it arose out of an error which was noticed by the child so that he searched for more cues and solved it. Most of the self-corrections involved going back to repeat a single preceding word or returning to the beginning of a line. Rates of self-correction varied with reading progress, being one in three errors for the high progress group, one in four for the average group, and one in eight for the low progress group. When the language pattern of the errors was an acceptable one, syntactically and semantically, the likelihood of self-correction was greatly reduced.

Repetition of correct text which had occurred in the records of the first year reading appeared again in a kind of confirming check of the correct response. Repetition occurred when the reader had an expectation for a response which conflicted with the letters he was about to read and when the words were not a language pattern that sounded natural or acceptable to him. The teacher can look upon repetition as an indication of efforts to search for, check and confirm responses.

These findings seem to indicate that high progress readers are gathering cues from meaning, grammar, letter-sound relationships and cross-relating these in an active process of search and check. The average and low progress readers use fewer types of cue, make less effort to relate these, and do this processing less accurately and more slowly.

A second study of children in their third year of instruction looked at pausing and stress behaviours (Clay and Imlach, 1971). One of the first things a remedial teacher may do is to encourage her pupil to 'read the punctuation.' Nothing destroys the meaning more rapidly than droning through the phrases and punctuation marks, pausing at points which break up the syntactic groups and the sense. This study showed that good readers paused after phrases and whole sentences at punctuation points, but poor readers stopped and stressed a word at a time, and often a syllable at a time. Even when the words were familiar they punched them out with even pitch and heavy stress as if grouping had no significance. Good readers appeared to gain in speed and understanding from anticipating whole stretches of text and checking visually whether their predictions were correct. Good readers were operating at the sentence and phrase level. They could move to the word level when necessary, and could use letter-sound correspondence to distinguish between similar words or to analyse new words. The low progress groups seemed unable to use cues beyond the syllable and word level. They were over-committed to the idea that reading was word recognition and sounding out.

Acquisition Means Continuous Change in Reading Processes

To repeat an earlier simile, any correct response in reading fits a matrix of relationships in a sentence like the pieces in a jigsaw puzzle. A mismatch along one or more dimensions of this matrix produces errors. A child may use cues from more than one source in selecting a response and when he is conscious of some disagreement in the cues he begins to search for an alternative response.

A word's identity can be checked at the level of sounds or letters, and in this limited sense those authors who stress the learning of letter-sound associations and sounding-out operations as the essence of reading are correct. The rules of consistencies which relate the sounds of the language to the letters, however unsystematic, are the ultimate reference for the precise pronunciation and discrimination of many written words. Yet, when good readers read, 95 percent of their reading activity shows little evidence of this analytic behaviour.

Efficient reading can be described in terms of Bruner's (1957) definition of perception. Some primitive identification of print is made and some expectations of what will follow are aroused in the reader in the form of probabilities arising from past experience with oral language and with reading. These expectations narrow the alternatives to a few which can be checked against a young child's limited knowledge of reading. This knowledge is initially based on a limited awareness of cues. It is the nature of the language code that several sources of cues converge in the case of the correct response to produce consonance rather than dissonance.

The child gradually learns to respond to more of the rich sources of cues in the text, to search actively for the cues, to relate one to another with greater precision and to increase the accuracy with which he makes his decisions about what to notice and what to ignore.

On familiar material, anticipations can be made and checked on the basis of a few cues without undue risk of error. A detailed search is only made on unfamiliar material or when some error seems to have occurred. In keeping with Bruner's account the following behaviour outcomes might follow from such a detailed check.

- An increase in sensitivity if the choice is near to being correct, causing a closer look.

  Child: *hot   top   tap*   (Self-correction)
  Text: tap

- A decrease of search in that direction if the choice is not close to that required.

  Child: *Look   and*   (Change of direction)
  Text: A fire.

- Stop searching if the input fits.

  Child: *tractors*   (Fits within the child's ability to discriminate)
  Text: trucks

- A gating or filtering system to stop further searching.

  Child: *here is*   (*Oh! 'is' is not there. Too bad!*)
  Text: here are

Research suggests that the good reader manipulates a network of language, spatial and visual perception cues and sorts these implicitly but effectively, searching for dissonant relations and best-fit solutions. Many sources of cues allow for confirming checks and act as a stimulus to error correction. Habitual responses will be continuously emerging as the result of successful performance.

Tuning in to continuous change

Teachers make reasonably accurate assessments of what their pupils are familiar with and what their pupils do not yet know. To improve the quality of their teaching interactions they need to know more about (a) what strategies the children are using to bring some currently novel features of text into the field of the familiar, and (b) what strategies they are using to reach out further into new territory. They need to be able to interact helpfully in the reading work being done by the child.

Standing back from the detailed analysis of responses, the teacher should ask what evidence there is that the child is engaged in reading work, checking back and forth across his knowledge bases, problem-solving his way through text independently, and in ways that point to an advance on his more recent responses and likely to increase his reading of even more difficult texts.

Two major questions for the observant teacher to ask are:

1 What evidence can I find that the child relates his other language and real world experiences to this reading task?

- life experience?
- story experiences?
- familiarity with this story?
- with an earlier part of the story?
- another word known in a different context?
- other experiences with letters or symbols?

2 What evidence can I find that the child responds to visual and phonological cues and to serial order at the

- letter level
- cluster level
- word level
- word group level
- sentence level
- plot or story level

on text of this level of difficulty?

It is assumed here that reading work will consist of using all knowledge of language across its different forms. Language learning in one area (for example, reading) will draw upon and reinforce learning in another area (for example, speaking or writing). This has been recognized in Language Arts curricula in American elementary schools, and the teaching of English in British and Commonwealth countries where programmes have tried to work with the interrelationships across all forms of knowing language. From the beginning of a child's instruction there is encouragement to search for such interrelationships. Language Arts people seem to assume that using a knowledge of oral and written language and a knowledge of the world, children carry out operations on texts which are just adequate for reading the more difficult bits. To do this children engage in reading work, a deliberate effort to solve any new problems using familiar information and procedures. *The model assumes that the child is constructing his own language system and his reading strategies and his writing production system.*

By observing the day-to-day interaction of teaching and responding — correct responding, partially correct responding, prompted responding, and unsolved errors — rather than merely the correct responses on tests, teachers can guide the gradual build-up of effective independent strategies as part of the young child's reading response system.

The Importance of Strategic Control in Reading Acquisition

At school entry, prior learning must be transformed into useful ways of dealing with a new medium, print, which has its own special features. Of necessity, education in groups calls for a new measure of independence and initiative from the child learner, greater than that demanded in the preschool years. I have argued that the successful beginning reader demonstrates a strategic control over literacy activities which enables him to learn to read by reading. Is this a concept of practical or theoretical importance?

1 Early intervention

One reason why the first two years of instruction may be critical for learning to read is because this is the formative stage of efficient or inefficient processing strategies — the means by which the child picks up and uses the information in print.

Visual exploration, visual scanning and visual pick-up of relevant information in the symbol system of printed language are first-year learning tasks of major importance which have been neglected because they are difficult to observe and record. Language skills are very important for reading progress but cannot be applied productively to the task unless the child learns how to direct his attention and explore the text with his eyes.

If the processing strategies function effectively the child reads with little error and adds to his experience with text with each new exposure to the task. If the processing functions ineffectively the child establishes ways of working with print that limit his further progress, and the processing strategies become hard to change.

For example, an exaggerated attention to words, stressing the word units and separating them by pausing, is both a sign of problems and a creator of problems because it makes it difficult for children to use information at the level of meanings. For meanings lie in stretches of text, not in the isolated words. A second example reported by researchers is that good readers have both reading and writing vocabularies but the very poor readers have meagre writing vocabularies. They 'know' words in some narrow way. Good reading depends upon rich sources of information and strategies to search back-up resources when the obvious links fail.

The significant question at any stage of progress is not 'How much does he know?' but rather 'What operations does he carry out and what kinds of operations has he neglected to use?'

At this time we begin to produce our reading failures by allowing some children to build ineffective processing strategies which limit what they can do throughout their school careers. As older readers they are difficult to help because they are habituated in their inefficiency and because their processing behaviours are hidden from view. In the terms of the computer age they have been poorly programmed. They wrote the programme and we do not know how to get into it.

2 The evaluation of programmes

There are probably risk areas in every instruction programme. This seems to me to be inevitable for three major reasons.

- Any programme includes decisions about the order in which children's attention shall be directed to information in text. The programme order may not be ideal for one child. Not all programmes or teachers are able to allow an individual child to get to independence in reading by a different route and therefore there are likely to be children at risk in any programme.

- Teachers will have a personal theory about how children learn literacy skills but because they do they reinforce positively those children whose behaviours match their theories (the ones they expect to see) and they try to prompt and guide other children into the same sequences.

- There are many aspects of reading behaviour for which, as yet, we have little understanding. These include the analysis of visual features that children carry out, how they learn to select the critical information to yield fast responses and how they learn to operate on the redundancies of language.

For these reasons, and probably others, every programme should be analysed so that potential risk areas can be identified. An implication of choosing any programme is that we build in checking procedures, insurance activities and recovery opportunities (Singer, Samuels and Spiroff, 1976). Teachers need to organize their teaching to retain the advantages and minimize the risks, providing real alternatives for individuals at risk.

3 Relationships to current theories of reading

Phonological awareness.   A main thrust of experimental cognitive research on reading in the 1980s has been towards how the brain learns about and manipulates phonological information in print. Stanovich (1987) called it a success story. A key variable in learning to read had been identified as phonological awareness. Directing attention to only one source of information used by the reader of text can produce problems. Phonological information may be seen as a key variable but so are meaning, syntax, and visual information. Teaching a key variable can distort a complex process unless its learning becomes patterned with other key variables and opportunities are provided to work on the interplay between variables.

A dual-process model of mature reading.   The dual-process model of mature reading assigns a major role to letter-sound associations. Supported by a large body of research data and several theorists, it has been summarized succinctly by Henderson (1984). According to this model there are two ways in which readers can derive sounds and meaning from print.

In the dual-process theory it is assumed . . . a lexical route allows the retrieval of a word's meaning and phonology by means of direct, orthographic addressing of the lexicon . . . (and) an alternative, segmental translation route utilizes spelling-sound translation rules to assemble the phonology of a word without lexical consultation.

(Henderson, 1984)

The dual-process model then postulates these two alternate routes used by readers, one drawing on direct visual perception of the orthographic form and the other using spelling to sound translation. Harris and Coltheart (1987) caution that the dual process theory of reading is a theory about reading words in isolation.

However, the dual-process model leaves reading *acquisition* with all the unsolved problems of how such a dual-process comes into existence (i.e. was constructed). The developmental psychologist Elkonin warned that 'learning a new skill cannot and consequently must not start from its final form,' and I would argue that the dual-process model describes only higher mental processes which are probably the abbreviated, generalized, perfected and automatic behaviours of such a final form, to use Elkonin's words. I favour an hypothesis which assumes that the novice uses many different strategies to draw on his stores of knowledge and problem-solve the meanings of texts and that, over time, reading experience 'shakes down' in the main for the mature reader into the two major strategies of the dual-process theory.

So even if we accept for the present this dual-process description as the end state of mature reading *and that it might be applied to the reading of texts*, there are dangers in using the theory of mature reading to guide acquisition as Elkonin warned. For example, teaching programmes derived directly from statements about the dual-process theory could drastically reduce opportunities for the child to carry out reading work by using what he learns in writing to solve reading problems and vice versa. Writing one's own messages can contribute to the analysis of words sound by sound or letter by letter but also gives the child experience with the whole word within its language context as he re-reads his story. To which aspect of the dual process in reading would such activities contribute? Surely to both with a great deal of 'to-ing and fro-ing.'

My interpretation of available research and theory is that reading behaviour becomes organized into a complex system of strategies for cue-finding, cue-using, choosing, checking, and correcting during the first two to three years of instruction in a way that sets the pattern for subsequent gains in skill. Conceptualizing the critical learning in reading acquisition as the development of such processing strategies to access information and problem-solve new words and messages is consistent with a view of mature reading as a simple dual-process activity. Each process could be the outcome of what

Elkonin described as abbreviated, generalized, perfected and automatic behaviour. One would expect to find that young successful readers demonstrate processing behaviours on problems under conditions that make text reading difficult and that poor readers do not have a range of strategies available to them under such conditions. While good readers continually move new vocabulary into the realm of 'abbreviated, generalized and automatic behaviours' using both lexical and phonological processing, poor readers operate compensatory mechanisms (Stanovich, 1980) which may solve the immediate 'reading of text' but seem not to extend the range and efficiency of their strategic systems or rapid access to old learning.

For both practical and theoretical reasons the concept of strategic control does warrant further investigation and development.

14 Extending the Inner Control

It has been argued, and tested in practice through many replications in an early intervention programme called Reading Recovery (Clay, 1985), that during reading acquisition children have to engage in 'reading work' (a general term for what we cannot see them doing 'in their heads'). They solve text problems by using their theories of the world and their theories of oral and written language. They cross-check in their heads which options are most likely. Teachers encourage and support such processing, and expect readers to carry out 'reading work' by any means they can to problem-solve the challenges of new text independently, with minimal help from others. This reading work can be *heard* in the early stages of reading progress as the child reads orally but it becomes a silent process.

In preceding chapters many factors have been discussed which are involved as the beginning reader learns to process the coded information in text. A question in search of an answer is still how does the reading of one text lead to being able to read a more difficult text? How does a good reader learn to read by reading? A possible answer to that question is that the behaviours, the inner control, the visual perception and the in-the-head processing learned in the reading acquisition period become part of an interactive system of strategies which work in some way that empowers the system. Once a reader is using a set of strategies which enable him to monitor his own reading and check one source of information with other sources in a sequential solving process then engaging in these activities serves to extend the potential of the reader to engage in more difficult activities and he assumes the major responsibility for learning to read by reading (Smith, 1978). This has been called a self-improving system, that is, a response system which extends its own capacity, (Clay, 1979b; Holdaway, 1979) or a bootstrapping process (Stanovich, 1986). More specifically, this could be characterized as a self-extending system of literacy expertise, as the act of reading expands the range and effectiveness of strategies which the reader can bring to the task, and the size of the practised response repertoire upon which he can draw.

This chapter will relate the discussion of the last three chapters to the development of such an interactive system.

The Formative Period

Preschool children explore stories and early writing in ways which lead into what they do at school. Some children have more opportunities to do this than others. However, few children will solve all the problems of learning to read and write on their own and most will use the support of a teacher in the acquisition stage.

This acquisition period, corresponding to about the first two years of schooling, is characterized by formal instruction. When adults formalise this learning they make various assumptions about the nature of the task. For instance some educators see this period as a time when children should learn to break the code. Some believe that comprehension of texts can be set aside for a time while children are taught sounds and words. In contrast the discussion in this book describes programmes with quite different assumptions. Children can focus on comprehension from the beginning under certain conditions.

Briefly, they read texts that are meaningful to them (such as stories). They read texts which use language that is close to things they would say or are learning to say (and not the stilted, reductionist primerese of controlled vocabulary texts), and they have high levels of interaction with teachers who help them to develop a variety of strategies for working with texts. They gradually take more control and responsibility for dealing with the 'hard bits' in the texts they are reading.

It seems reasonable to suppose that the first years of formal instruction will be critical ones for the formation of such a network of strategies conducive to literacy learning. Developmental psychologists have reported that perception (auditory and visual) and cognition (thinking and problem-solving) change markedly between five and seven years in all children. Schooling must profit from, and contribute to, these changes. Visual exploration, visual scanning and visual pick-up of information in print are first-year learning tasks of major importance for the school child often neglected by educators and researchers because they are not easy to observe or record. Language skills are very important for reading but can only be applied to literacy tasks if the child learns where to direct his attention as he explores the text with his eyes.

In the normal course of events the first two years of instruction may set the pattern for subsequent gains in skill because that is the time when reading becomes controlled by newly developing strategies which initiate, search, select and check on the reader's attention to print, and his pick-up and processing of information.

The constructive learner

Cognitive developmental psychologists have applied the terms 'active construction' by a 'constructive learner' to many of the child's activities — seeing, searching, remembering, monitoring, correcting, validating, and problem-solving. They examine how the carrying out of an activity builds more competence in the activity. According to Deardon (1984) such gains are not accounted for by the empty vessel metaphor in education, nor do they fit with the 'growth from within' model of child development. He argued that views of child development which referred to

- learning from activity
- self-directed learning
- and learning by discovery

were closely related to the growth from within model but did not account for two recent bodies of knowledge:

- that the child is affected by what follows what he does
- that the child is a constructor of his own experience.

Deardon concluded from the above analysis that some styles of teaching might facilitate learning consistent with becoming independent learners and some styles might impede such learning.

As children try to understand what their day-to-day experiences mean — the social, narrative, informative, literary, aesthetic or linguistic meanings — there may be ways of interacting with the children that enhance these experiences. In the specific case of emerging literacy there are ways of encouraging a search for meaning in their experiences with print. As children search for meaning in print they are able to notice new things about words or print or messages, constructively linking these to other things they know. There are ways of instructing or learning which foster such responses and other ways of instructing or learning which limit opportunities to do these things.

The child's contribution to learning

There has perhaps been too little discussion of how the child actively contributes to his literacy learning. Our thinking about individual differences in reading has been dominated by our attention to differences in abilities like levels of intelligence and prior language knowledge. We have expected literacy achievements to correlate highly within those ability levels. This deserves some attention.

The child enters the classroom equipped to learn language and able to do so by methods of his own (Chomsky, 1972). Before the child comes to school he has already learned how to learn by making responses and getting feedback about its appropriateness. He has developed a complex differentiated internal representation of his world. He has strategies for remembering, grouping, problem-solving. He has constructed a complex system of language rules which enable him to understand and produce the sentences of his language. He builds these rules by a process that is still not very well understood but his language learning is innovative and rule-governed.

There are many things about learning to read which the child must teach himself because we do not understand them (Smith, 1978). Three examples are given.

- The child has to discover for himself the distinctive features of print that govern the discrimination of letters.

- The child has to discover for himself the sources of redundancy in written language (Smith 1971; Haber and Haber, 1981). This knowledge is not accessible to us at the level of conscious manipulation. We acquire it and use it without awareness of what exactly we are using.

- The young reader has to learn to use eye movements which jump across print in just the right sequence of moves to make smooth reading of the message possible. The early reader focusses on a word at a time but soon becomes a phrase reader. How does the eye learn how far to jump?

There is also the problem that no matter how well we observe the behaviours of young readers we cannot ever know the nature of what generates their reading behaviour at one point in time. We can only infer something of the ways in which 'the generating system' is changing from detailed records of responses to texts. There are critical aspects of the formative period in learning to read which we may never fully understand. Perhaps as in the oral language learning of the preschool child, it is just as well that we have not tried to teach these things we do not understand. We can be instructors in those areas where we know what the task involves, but in other areas we can only act as someone whom the child can consult (Smith, 1985).

Understanding Reading Processes

Reading, like thinking, is very complex. When you think, all you have to do is produce the responses from within you. When you read you have to produce responses which interpret what the author wrote: you have to try to match your thinking to his. When you think you do not think in single words but rather you find sequences of words which express sequences of ideas. Similarly reading involves sequences of ideas.

Most people are familiar with the old game 'Twenty Questions' or 'Animal, Vegetable or Mineral.' Reading is very much like that. The smartest readers ask of themselves the most effective questions for reducing the uncertainty; the poorer readers ask trivial questions and waste their opportunities to reduce uncertainty. They do not search for information in effective ways, and they have not learned the complex relationships between items of information and strategic activity.

All readers use information from the text about:

- the sense
- the sentence structure
- the order of ideas, words, letters
- the size of words or letters
- special features of sound, shape and layout
- and special knowledge from past experience.

This is true of the competent five year old on his first reading book and of the efficient adult. The reading acquisition task is to build the inner strategic control that allows the reader, with the greatest efficiency, to relate information within these levels, and across these levels, to remembered information, on the run and without loss of meaning or fluency. When instruction directs students to conscious manipulations of letters, sounds, or single words it turns their attention away from such important developments.

Observable reading behaviour provides evidence of all the things teachers have always thought it did—knowing words, getting meaning, using a sense of story, and working on unknown words in some way. It also includes directional behaviour, recognizing letters or pronounceable clusters, working to get the word sequence right, reading fluently, and locating and correcting error. Such behaviours signal that, inside the child's head, other kinds of activity have possibly occurred like:

- anticipating what could follow
- searching for more 'information' in the print
- self-monitoring, evaluating and correcting processes
- linking to prior knowledge
- lining up a new item with an existing general rule and perhaps extending that rule.

The inner control of reading allows the reader to extract information in the text from any known source and to use such information to prime and guide inner strategic activities. During the reading acquisition phase the novice reader is not only learning words or letter-sound relationships but is also learning how to use each of the sources of information in texts, how to link these to stored knowledge, and which strategic activities make 'reading' successful.

The good reader manipulates language, spatial and visual perception cues, and categorizes these efficiently, searching for dissonant relations and best-fit solutions. Familiar responses become habitual, require less and less processing and allow attention to reach out towards new information that was not previously noticed. While reading the reader can construct larger chunks or units of information out of smaller ones, or break large units down into smaller ones for closer examination.

The following quotation from Wood (1988) outlines this view in a more general form. He sees such expertise as characteristic of human information processing, and uses reading and chess as examples.

> . . . expertise in an activity is reflected in processes of attention, perceptual organization and memorization. What an expert is able to perceive as she observes an event that draws on her expertise is more organized, memorable and meaningful than that experienced by a novice. Put in other terms, the expert's 'speed of encoding' is faster than that of the novice. Basically, this term refers to the time taken by an individual to perceive, analyse and respond in some task-appropriate way to a perceptual event. So, the 'speed of encoding' of Grand Masters confronted by a chess configuration is faster than that of novices . . .

Slow encoding speeds when novices try, say, to read a word, take in a mathematical problem or even attempt to 'count' the number of objects in a small set, place limits on how much the novice can assimilate and memorize. The capacity to *perceive* and the ability to *perform* are, in such tasks, two aspects of a single process — one which, so to speak, follows a 'spiral path' in development. As the child becomes practised in acting upon some component or components of the task, her actions become increasingly automatic (though it has to be admitted that we do not yet understand the biological processes that make this possible). However, developing 'automaticity' means that the child no longer has to consciously *attend* to the practised elements of her task activity. 'Automated' actions may be performed without the need for constant monitoring or awareness. As some aspect of the developing skill is automated, the learner is left free to pay attention to some other aspect of the task at hand. She 'perceives' more and can concentrate on perfecting some other feature of her performance. So the metaphorical spiral grows in diameter as expertise develops.

(Wood, 1988)

What about phonological awareness which has received much attention in recent research? One possibility is that the phonological awareness that reading researchers have measured and reported can be an outcome of reading successfully. Readers can gain this knowledge effectively as a result of operating strategically on print. Its sources lie in oral language, and it exists prior to entry to school but not in a form needed by the reader. It is developed further during discussions about easy story books, in reading aloud, but is also developed by the child's early attempts to write messages because writing is, by its very nature, a segmentation task. In school it develops in tandem with orthographic knowledge about the printed code. My assumption is that the reader/writer can most easily become articulate about phonological aspects of reading when he is already making use of them, that is once he is reading and writing small stretches of text. One need not teach him phonics in order to be able to read, but could use what he is able to read and write to develop the articulate awareness of phonology and print, on many different levels, which the good reader needs. If a teacher of reading can make it easy for the child to be successful at getting messages from texts, this is the experience out of which the child will be able to construct inner strategic processes including phonological processes.

If children succeed in sorting out what the reading and writing game consists of, they extend their response repertoire every time they read and write in three major ways.

- They are introduced to new vocabulary and new expressions which hover in the memory waiting for the next encounter.

- They apply old knowledge to new texts so that what they already know about words and texts is arranged in different ways to transmit a new message.

- They pick up extra information about something that was difficult on a previous occasion and solve it easily at this encounter.

When the children are reading successfully they are free to direct their attention to novel features of texts. As their experience with words expands in range they have an increasingly rich store of prior experience to back up their problem-solving. They develop effective strategies for getting and acting upon information about new words, language, and meanings. And the strategies for problem-solving that are used on novel features of text strengthen every time they are used. In this way, using what is known on new problems extends the system.

An ineffective processing system in formation

Processing may be efficient or inefficient and the pattern may be set for gains or for failure. Education contributes to reading failure if it allows (or encourages) children to use ineffective strategies for literacy learning at this time. As the risk of encountering difficulty with this complex task is high, *every programme of formal instruction needs to have ways of dealing with that inevitable risk for some children.*

For myriads of reasons (and many of them have to do with events in homes or in schools), some children begin to build inefficient literacy systems. As they try to meet the instructional demands they become more and more confused about where to direct their attention, they remain unsure about how to apply what they know to the new tasks, and the doors to problem-solving on novel texts begin to close for them.

It has been traditional to think of the low progress reader as a child who learns slowly, who needs more time. But if we have a concept of early reading as a time when an effective read/write processing system is in formation then some low progress readers may be constructing an ineffective processing system. What would be its characteristics?

The low progress reader or the reader 'at risk' has few resources to fall back on. He tends to only operate on a narrow range of manipulations. He may pay no attention at all to visual details and rely on what he can invent from his memory for the spoken text. He may disregard discrepancies between his response and the words on the page. He may be looking so hard for words he knows and guessing words from first letters that he forgets what the message is about. The low progress reader may be producing responses in a haphazard way guided by odd rules or by no rules at all, and he may have no way of checking on their correctness. The risk is that inappropriate responses might become habituated and automatic when they are practised day after day, and become quite resistant to change as early as 12 to 18 months after entry to school. Two outcomes are possible: the problems may be straightened out in due course; or this may be an ineffective processing system in formation. If the system functions inefficiently the child establishes habits of inefficient processing of information with each exposure to the task.

I believe that it is important to allow school entrants time and opportunity to learn in a good programme before identifying those 'at risk' of building an inefficient processing system. However, it is important to take a long, hard look at reading and writing behaviours after one year of instruction in order to prevent problems and provide help. At this time we should ask questions about the quality of the inner control that is developing. The best person to make such a check is the class teacher. Each child having difficulty will have different things he can or cannot do, different confusions, different gaps in his knowledge of meanings, of letters, and of words, and different ways of operating on print. The class teacher can then adapt her teaching to these individual learning needs.

An intervention programme

A few children do not succeed even with such individual attention from the class teacher. An intervention programme especially tailored to the needs of each child in this small group in a one pupil one teacher situation may be needed to supplement a classroom programme. The aim of such an intervention would be to ensure that a child does construct an inner control of reading processes.

Such a programme offered at the end of the first year of school has been shown to recover children who are becoming confused and struggling, by giving them individual instruction which accelerates their progress and allows them to rejoin the average group of their class (Clay, 1987). Why should we wait until the child has been at school one year? Why not begin earlier? There are several reasons.

- Children on entry to school will have different levels of ability and will respond to school programmes at different rates.

- Children will have learned different things from their preschool experiences. Their knowledge will differ in type and quality and they will need to learn many things in the first year of school as a background to later progress in reading.

- Children take time to learn to work in social groups and this social and emotional learning is vitally important as a foundation for success in school.

- Predictions of 'at risk' children improve once children have had an exposure to learning and false identifications made prior to school are reduced by providing the children with opportunities to learn.

Extensive experience with an early intervention programme (Clay, 1987) convinces me that we begin the production of our reading failures by allowing some children to build inefficient systems of functioning in their early literacy programmes and failing to provide them with the support they need. They struggle with the reading and writing activities of the classroom.

As older readers they are difficult to help because they have developed inefficient behaviour responses for finding, using, checking and correcting the information they get from print. If we can reach a better understanding of the complex strategies developed by successful children in reading we have every chance of helping other young children develop those strategies.

Existing Self-improving or Self-extending Systems

The self-improving literacy system which children develop in this period is not the first they build. The preschool child is the creator of a very powerful system which generates and extends his control over language (Karmiloff-Smith, 1979). Oral language was discussed in Chapter 4. This is a system which a child contructs through his conversations with people.

This child constructs another cognitive system which allows him to make sense of the world. He uses information, his own experiences, probabilities of occurrence, schemas of what kinds of things happen in particular contexts and a keen awareness of what human beings are likely to do, all directed towards understanding events around him (Donaldson, 1978).

The model of literacy instruction discussed in this book assumes that formal education can and should capitalize on these two existing self-extending systems and that one of the school's tasks is to help the child build a self-extending system for literacy which includes reading and writing.

The powerful preschool self-extending systems which get better with each interaction with the physical and social world of the child do not ensure that the learner can and will develop a self-improving system for literacy learning. We have plenty of evidence that some children who talk well and make excellent sense of their worlds, acting intelligently upon them, do not always develop an effective literacy learning system. Perhaps this occurs because formal instruction, unlike conversation, has been too intrusive without being sufficiently observant of the learner's confusions.

A Literacy Learning System

Items versus strategies?
Reading and writing are often assumed to be the end-product of learning many items (letters, sounds, letter-sound relationships, words and parts of words). So we have two popular explanations of teaching reading—one based on teaching letters and their sound equivalents, and one based on teaching words. However, my experience in longitudinal monitoring of progress of the first year of instruction was that letters, sounds, words and word analysis were accumulated gradually over time *because the child learned many different ways of working on print*. This suggested an alternative model of

reading acquisition in which what the child acquired was not merely a set of information but a network of strategies for operating on or with text. It assumes that in order to read with understanding we call up and use a repertoire of strategies acting upon stores of knowledge to extract messages from print. Reading and writing acquisition involves the active construction of that repertoire, with comprehending having a central role. The learning of many items is a by-product of such learning. So in both reading and writing children learn a host of things:

- the aspects of print to which they must attend
- the aspects of oral language that can be related to print
- the kinds of strategies that maintain fluency
- the kinds of strategies that explore detail
- the kinds of strategies that increase understanding
- the kinds of strategies that detect and correct errors
- the feedback control mechanisms that keep their reading and writing productions on track
- the feed-forward mechanisms (like anticipation or prediction) that keep their information-processing behaviours efficient
- and most important of all how to go beyond the limits of the system and how to learn from relating new information to what is already known.

Learning of this kind depends upon children being active processors of printed information and constructive learners.

A network of strategies
Consider the changes that occur in a child's literacy learning in the first three years of school. Imagine the child is not a reader on entry to school but certain preliminary reading and writing behaviours are emerging. What the child does have is a very impressive system for understanding and producing oral language.

The child of average intelligence with a typical preschool background and experience moves into the school's programme, gets help and by the end of the second or third year can manage most of his reading without help. This independence is demonstrated when he reads texts of appropriate difficulty level on which he can operate as a problem-solver using meaningfulness as a guide and searching for information and relationships which give order to the complexities of print and therefore simplify it.

In earlier chapters of this book the formative stages of a network of strategies to be used in reading were introduced. Summary reference will be made here to these topics already discussed.

1 Reciprocal gains.   While the child has only limited control in writing and in reading he can be encouraged to search for information in either reading or writing, establishing reciprocity between these aspects of learning about literacy.

2 Controlling serial order. When the child comes to control the directional schema required for print and to segment his speech into words and part-words, he is able to operate on the problem of matching serial order in space (print) with serial order in time (speech).

3 Problem-solving with more than one kind of information. This occurs on the first attempts to read simple stories, when making sense of the text, using oral language, knowing about print and controlling serial order come together under the child's control.

4 Acting on information. Working often on reading stories and writing messages the child develops programmes of action for working with print and begins to cluster information of different kinds around particular words which are 'known' in several different senses.

5 Using visual information. The child provides the teacher with signs that he is using visual information from the text effectively.

6 Using phonological information. The child provides the teacher with signs that he is using letter-sound relationships, singly and in clusters.

7 Searching, checking and correcting. There is behavioural evidence that the reader is searching the print, checking and correcting his own reading without prompting.

8 Drawing on stored information. The child is also searching inner stores of information and checking information in print with this prior knowledge. He is obviously controlling the sequencing of his problem-solving and decision-making. An inner control is in formation.

9 Categories, rules, and probabilities. With or without prompting from the teacher the child appears to form categories and rules about features in print which he applies with some success to novel text and he works with some sense of the probabilities of occurrence.

10 Signs of independence. Providing the teaching allows room for the child to assume control of the task, the child applies all these types of learning with increasing independence to increasingly difficult text.

We cannot assume that we know what all those strategies or operations are. Some are general cognitive processes for which we have many theories and research analyses (like using past experience stored as memory schemas, or using auditory information to read visual language), and others relate to current research questions like 'how do we extract information from texts?'

No specification of sequence

It is probably implicit in the idea of a dynamic network of strategies that we are unlikely to ever have a sequenced specification for teaching acquisition strategies. The complex outcome could presumably be built up in many different ways. On the other hand a classroom teacher can make systematic observations of children gaining more and more control over more and more difficult texts and gradually taking over an independent control of learning to read by reading, and learning to write by writing. As the child becomes more independent the teacher's role changes from helping the child to acquire a network of strategies that works successfully to providing opportunities to expand and extend the range of texts across which that system can operate.

The terms 'network' and 'literacy strategies'

Teachers of literacy acquisition need a language that deals with literacy strategies. It might be argued that these are general cognitive processes which are not specific to reading, but there are particular challenges in making them work on the coded messages in texts and only some children accept those challenges without help. As mentioned earlier most children find it difficult to use their existing strengths in the service of literacy without some support and guidance from teachers. The significant question at any stage of progress is not 'How many items (letters, sounds, words,) does the child know?' but rather 'What operations can he initiate and carry out and what kinds of operations has he neglected to use?' Answers to those questions can guide the teacher in her prompting and questioning of the novice reader.

The learner is gaining a strategic control over how external and internal information is dealt with in the brain. By means of a network of unobservable in-the-head strategies the reader is able to attend to information from different sources (for example, reading and writing, oral language and visual learning, meaning and phonology). The good reader can work with both internal and external information and make decisions about matches and mismatches in his responses. A dynamic network of interactive strategies allows the reader to change direction at any point of the processing path.

How could this processing generate greater achievement? Supposing the meaning of 'broth' in 'She gave them some broth without any bread' is 'old' knowledge and the child produces the response 'soup,' then a visual check for 's,' or a phonological check of some kind, may signal a mismatch. Reading work is called for. What the child will now learn depends on what strategies he tries, and what the teacher does. The child's attention is on the features of the text that are new for him.

This reading work clocks up more experience for the network with each of the features of print attended to. *It allows the partially familiar to become familiar and the new to become familiar in an ever-changing sequence.* Meaning is checked against letter sequence or vice versa, phonological recoding is checked against speech vocabulary, new meanings are checked against the grammatical and semantic contexts of the sentence and the story, and so on. Because one route to a response confirms an approach from another direction this may allow the network to become a more effective network.

However the generative process only operates when the reading is 'good,' that is, successful enough to free attention to pick up new information at the point of problem-solving. An interlocking network of appropriate strategies which include monitoring and evaluation of consonance or dissonance among messages that ought to agree is central to this model of a system which extends itself.

Active Processing: The Power of Strategies

This book is not the place to trace the nature of a self-extending system in writing which I assume exists but which is a concept needing further exploration. The focus here has been on reading, always assuming that whatever is done in writing should be thought of as a resource for reading acquisition, and vice versa.

It is helpful to recall Bruner's (1974) account of infants learning to organize an early skilled action and compare it with the young reader trying to get some order into all the things we expect him to do. Imagine a young baby trying to reach a small piece of apple placed on the table in front of him. Bruner described a period of prolonged orienting behaviour as the child regards the desired apple, making movements and sounds that get him no closer to the apple. There follows a period when new behaviours appear but not in an effective order and without result. Having first clenched his fist he flings out his arm and knocks the apple on the floor. Trying again but still with clenched fist he approaches the apple cautiously and makes gentle contact with it but an essential piece of the behaviour is in the wrong order. He cannot pick up the apple because he first closed his fist. A new effort is made, this time with open hand, but the execution of the movements is clumsy and the infant does not get the apple. On the next trial, with each segment of the sequential action in the correct order and under reasonable control, the child gets and eats the apple. Notice, however, that success on that one item is nothing compared with the long-term infant-serving strategy he now has for grasping objects he wants. It is the strategy, not the apple, that is the powerful acquisition.

In addition to the concept of strategy the above account illustrates that control must be gained over sequences of behaviours. When the infant is faced with the novel situation,

- there is increased anticipatory behaviour (such as random excited movement of the hands)
- some behaviours occur but not necessarily in an order that works
- after several attempts the constituent acts come together in a workable order
- the behaviour is less variable, uses less effort
- the behaviour pattern becomes efficient.

During this learning there may be a sharp alteration in the structure of the act. Such alterations can be of several kinds, according to Bruner.

- Some sub-routines can be practised without carrying out the whole act, and they may become efficient before others.

- A sub-routine may be dropped from the act because it is no longer a necessary part of it.

- An initial first pattern of action may be displaced by a new routine, a drastic change over the earlier pattern, yet still allowing the old pattern to recur. In this case a higher order pattern has taken over.

Although there are undoubted risks in reasoning by analogy from the behaviour of infants to the learning of five and six year olds I strongly suspect that re-organizations of this type occur in reading and await description. For example, a shift in phonological processing is probably necessary if the young reader is to manage the multi-syllabic texts of the third and fourth year at school which call for the handling of many unstressed syllables. Again, there are obviously shifts of some kind that enable the child who reads aloud relatively slowly to become an efficient and faster silent reader.

We find ways of dealing with information while keeping very little in mind, according to Bruner, and we increase our powers by converting bodies of knowledge into generative rules for thinking about the world and about ourselves. The learner acts to reduce strain and confusion by limiting the amount of information received and the search for prior information needed to understand the incoming message.

More about strategies

We cannot have a definitive description of what the child does in his head as he reads. We can observe how the child works over texts as he reads them. From his behaviours we can get hints of what he is looking at or what is being related to what. We observe him reading texts, watch him go back and try again, and hear him correct himself unprompted. Some of this behaviour stems from the problems of controlling attention to sequential information in texts; other behaviour arises from a failure to pick up necessary information. We can examine the words the oral reader utters for their syntactic, semantic or visual appropriateness. We can observe behaviour that tells us he is monitoring his own reading. We have ways of knowing whether he understands what he is reading.

Bruner (1957) defined a strategy as a decision process which involves a search for discriminatory cues that will code the stimulus into appropriate categories. That is one way of describing the mental activity initiated by the child to get messages from a text during the acquisition stage of reading.

Strategies are variables we need in order to explain the differences between people who all get the same solution to a problem but by different solving processes. They also explain the work we do to shift from uncertainty to certainty when we look at an object which is hard to identify (for example a highly magnified object or a photo taken from a misleading angle). The eye and the brain scan the object and its context, and memories of past experiences, searching for cues that will reduce our uncertainty.

A different example would be when, in a telephone conversation, we 'hear' a ridiculous piece of information which does not fit with what preceded it and seems out of place. Working over it we decide that we misheard and that the actual message was a different one. Information is often lost in sound transmission and we are forced to construct possible interpretations from the incomplete signals. We engage in constructive cognitive activity, perhaps use words to point up characteristics, search for and recall a particular memory, weigh up the evidence, perhaps discard one possibility, choose between other possibilities discarding some, and so on.

Strategies can describe the operations we carry out when we try to memorize or recall information, and our ways of doing this tend to be highly practised, very efficient, and hard to analyse. We manipulate information and we do it in ways that can differ from one person to another. How do you solve an anagram? or a mental puzzle? or a verbal puzzle about travelling east 40 km and then south for another 40 km and after several more such turns where are you?

Strategies are ways of working to locate information, or to work on information, or to relate it to things already known, or to transform it by some known procedure, or to produce a possible interpretation and a response. The child needs a reason to attend to novel features of print before he can develop a strategy for getting information and using it. Soon he begins to understand something of how to work on such material. Knowledge of a few items plus a useable strategy will help one go beyond the information that is already stored in the head and allow one to respond correctly to another novel item. *A few items and a powerful strategy might make it very easy to learn a great deal more.*

The kind of strategy discussed here is 'in the head' (in contrast to many overt behaviours fostered in teaching programmes). It has strategic control over how external and internal information is dealt with in the brain. It is a critical concept in an explanation of how we learn to read by reading, or how the bootstrap effect operates to allow the good reader to get better at literacy tasks. The acquisition of appropriate strategies could explain how such a system extends itself.

Redundancy and strategy

The reader is helped by the many sources of information in language plus additional sources in orthography (see Chapter 12).

In reading instruction based on story books the child can estimate not only the kind of word likely to occur (either from the meaning of the story or from a knowledge of sentence structure (syntax) or from the probabilities of words within sentences), but also groups of words or phrases likely to occur. The reader has more information available to him for word-solving than if he were dealing only with the information in a single word presented in isolation. The reader usually samples only some of this available information, sufficient to satisfy him that there is nothing inconsistent in the information; no mismatch has occurred. Text carries redundant information, more than the reader usually needs to attend to.

Some examples of the ways in which texts provide redundant information are the following:

1 Redundancy among the visual features in letters provides more information than the reader uses (merely dotting 'i' and crossing 't' eliminates confusion with all but 'j' and 'f').

2 Word length is used in text reading along with other information, probably not alone, to signal syntactic features at the limit of the perceptual field.

3 Printing conventions carry signals—capital letters, punctuation, paragraphing. Young readers come gradually but quite quickly to operate on such information in text.

4 Languages place extraordinary restrictions on the possible positions particular letters may occupy in words (i.e. on the distributional frequency of different letters and on the sequential combinations of letters and rules). Knowledge of this kind of redundancy is acquired as reading is acquired, and facilitates rapid responding.

5 The rules of grammar also impose severe restrictions on the permissible sequence of words in sentences and with experience in reading the reader increases his knowledge of these restrictions which increases speed of responding.

6 Other sources of syntactic information are:

- When single words have multiple meanings each meaning may be a different part of speech.
- Syntactic information may be represented in more than one way as when the WH question (when, where, why, who etc) also ends with a question mark.

7 Many sources of information arise from semantic links between parts of the text, from the author's style, from experience with genre and different types of text (narrative, descriptive, scientific), or from cultural restrictions or other knowledge of how the world works.

Haber's (1978) account helps us to understand the interaction of the reader with the redundancy in the text. Firstly, he says that redundancy refers to the relationships among the elements in the text that are predictable or specifiable. In this sense redundancy resides in the text itself. However, only particular types of redundancy can be claimed to exist in letters, or words. Knowledge of spelling rules cannot be applied to random letter strings, and knowledge of syntax will not help the reader to read single words. If the reader is reading from story texts there are many potential sources of redundancy to support him.

Secondly, there is the question of how much redundancy is available to the reader. This depends upon the extent to which the reader can make use of the redundancies in the text. Learning how to do this must be one of the important aspects of reading acquisition.

Thirdly, the reader can interact with a text in different ways. If read by an expert on the topic a text would carry more redundancy than the same text read by a non-expert. An introduction to the topic would make the reading task easier for the non-expert. Allowed to read the text a second or third time the non-expert would have more access to the redundant features of the text. Yet the expert would, on the basis of his detailed knowledge of the topic, still have greater access. Some of the many sources of redundancy in texts are discussed by Smith and by Haber.

Haber and Haber (1981) concluded that the normal adult reader resorts to letter identification for problem-solving (as distinct from rapid recognition) only when more general hypotheses about syntax and semantics have failed him and that these more general hypotheses or expectancies require context for their generation. A very important conclusion to be drawn from their arguments is that the meaning or rule extraction processes cannot be learned from studying subcomponent parts or processes in isolation. *You need a context for a subcomponent in order to derive rules about its probabilities of occurrence.*

Strategies Which Maintain Fluency

Using the oral language system

Reading instruction in the past has paid too little attention to the language learning which preschool children have already achieved. All that we have learned about language acquisition has had little influence on the practices of early reading instruction. It is true that story-sharing in the preschool years, and more recently experience with nursery rhymes, have been related to progress in reading but these connections have been specific to the activity studied. Few have argued that the entire language production system which each preschooler has constructed as a user of language is an efficient action system and rich resource upon which to base instructional procedures (Cambourne, 1988). Smith (1978) and Clark (1976) argued for the appreciation of all the learning the child brings to school. Smith wrote:

> Two things are perhaps surprising about the skills and knowledge that a child brings with him when he is about to learn to read: the sheer quantity and complexity of his ability and the small credit that he is usually given.

(Smith, 1971: 223)

The study of language acquisition since the 1960s has been rich and varied, and has raised questions of how such complex behaviour can be learned by little children. In a short but comprehensive book which over-views language and speech knowledge, Miller (1981) summarized a massive research and publication effort in this way.

At birth a child utters sounds reflexly to express emotions, much as living primates do. Shortly thereafter we see the appearance of gestural communication, under voluntary control. Then gestures are accompanied by spoken names for objects pointed to or reached for; the names become progressively differentiated and become independent of the gestural system. These words are soon combined, though with little respect for word order. As utterances grow longer, recognizable syntactic patterns are adopted to organize them. Learning the inflated vocabulary of modern industrial society continues into adulthood — if, indeed, it ever stops.

(Miller, 1981: 120)

Miller then goes beyond vocabulary and syntax to consider recent gains in our understanding of children's conversation and the role of language in thought. Current thinking in these two areas are worthy of close examination because of their potential to contribute to teacher-child interaction in the first years of school.

Conversation . . . is a co-operative interaction: participants must agree on the topic, they must take turns in developing it, and their contributions must be intelligible, relevant and truthful.

(Miller, 1981: 121)

Conversation is governed by conventions. Only one person speaks at a time, the gaps between speakers are usually short, and there are sets of rules for taking turns. Children have to learn these conventions, and it is clear that, as the speaking conventions vary in different language and ethnic groups, children coming into their first classroom may have learned different conventions for conversation (Cazden, 1988; Au, 1984). Stressing the importance of such learning Miller summarizes its main dimensions.

The value of co-operation in accomplishing tasks of importance to individuals and groups is fairly obvious although the way we actually use language to establish co-operation is often subtle and indirect. Less obvious, perhaps, is the kind of co-operation required to hold a conversation at all. Not only must conversationalists co-operate in turn-taking but speakers must wish to be understood; they must co-operate to make their contributions informative and germane to the hearer's interests by anticipating the hearer's problems with anaphora and deixis and by laying the groundwork for what they want to say. And hearers must wish to understand, they must co-operate by drawing all the inferences that follow, not just from what the speaker says but also from the speaker's presumed wish to be understood.

(Miller, 1981: 134)

If conversation is to succeed each participant must co-operate by observing the maxims to be intelligible, truthful, relevant and informative (Grice, 1975). To be informative and relevant the speaker must introduce new information by relating it to familiar information. Miller suggests that if a child asks what a zebra is, an adult may answer that it is a horse with stripes, thus assuming that the child knows what horses are. In some parts of the world with zebras, but no horses, the introduction could be the other way around. The human mind works often by analogies and will relate something new to something already known and familiar. Reasoning by analogy is probably our most fruitful source of hypotheses about any intellectual problem.

Speakers make listeners contribute. Here then is one link between language and thought which led Miller to conclude his book with the comment that 'human language is surely our richest source of evidence about the nature of human thought' (p. 145). It is also an important link to understanding what is read.

Understanding what is read

An earlier chapter dealt with the ways in which 'texts teach' and it is only necessary here to review briefly. Texts to which children can bring interpretations, and texts which are close to children's oral language use, give them power over the learning tasks. Language experience materials would also use their oral language competencies if dictated by the child or composed co-operatively by a group.

As the child approaches a new text he is entitled to an introduction so that when he reads, the gist of the whole or partly revealed story can provide some guide for a fluent reading. He will understand what he reads if it refers to things he knows about, or has read about previously, so that he is familiar with the topic, the vocabulary or the story itself.

If the reader thinks this is being too helpful to the learner, consider again two people in conversation. Understanding will not develop between them on the topic of conversation unless one of two things happens — either the speaker checks or keys into the prior knowledge of the listener, or the speaker creates the scenario by way of an introduction so that the speaker can understand.

The child's encounter with text may be brought to a new level of understanding if he follows the reading with some kind of expressive output — not comprehension questions or workbook exercises but something which calls upon the child to show he understands what was read like recasting some aspect of the story in art, or construction, or acting or re-telling.

Understanding provides for future predictions

Understanding what you read today and the ways in which the meanings were expressed give the reader prior knowledge for reading at some other time. To that prior knowledge and past experience the reader applies well-controlled language strategies like prediction, anticipation, and hypothesis testing (Smith, 1975; Goodman, 1970; Wildman and Kling, 1979). Smith (1975) wrote:

> I believe that reading is impossible without prediction and since it is only through reading that children learn to read it follows that the opportunity to develop and employ . . . prediction must be a critical part of learning to read.

> (p. 52)

Faced with text the brain is confronted with many possibilities. A decision must be made. Decisions take time and the greater the number of alternatives the more time is required for the decision. Prediction in this sense does not mean predicting the word that will occur; it means the prior elimination of unlikely alternatives. Those possibilities that are unlikely are set aside and the possibilities that are highly likely are examined in the light of the information available. Such a procedure is efficient, it is supported in part by understanding what is being read, and it is strongly supported by the reader's knowledge of the syntactic alternatives and restrictions of the language.

Strategies Which Detect and Correct Error

Self-monitoring
Children must be given the responsibility to monitor their own text behaviour, guided by meaning. This mainly involves pausing on the part of the teacher or parent as if expecting the child to solve the problem (Glynn and McNaughton, 1985; McNaughton, Glynn and Robinson, 1987) or prompting them to check.

Self-correction
When good readers aged five to eight years read text orally they follow an error response with a spontaneous self-correction with ratios of 1:2 and 1:5. The behaviour is overt and recordable in everyday reading. It can be prompted and manipulated. It can be increased and decreased by teacher response and variation of text difficulty. It is a strategy deliberately developed in one early intervention programme, Reading Recovery, because the children are taught to do what good readers do.

Overt self-correction behaviour emerges early in instruction, changes over time and disappears between seven and eight years. A summary graph from weekly observations in the first year of school showed very different outcomes for children in different achievement quartiles. The high progress group made many errors but these occurred within large quantities of correct responding so they had plenty of opportunity to self-correct. Self-correction behaviour summed over the first year of school correlated moderately with subsequent progress at six, seven, and eight years at the 0.67, 0.61 and 0.60 level with standardized reading tests. (See the graph on page 306.)

Self-correction can only be expressed as a ratio because the opportunities to self-correct are determined by the prior production of an error. A criticism of attending to self-correction behaviour is that because *it* depends upon the prior occurrence of error it cannot explain anything that a study of errors would not explain. However:

- teachers and parents can be led to teach more effectively by attending to self-corrections than by attending to error behaviour

- what happens at a self-correction calls for explanation, because the behaviours suggest different cognitive processes from those that occur with an uncorrected error.

Self-correction works on perceptual through to cognitive levels. It starts with a vague awareness that something is wrong. With the accumulation of successful reading experience, self-correction can come to be a more precise conscious cognitive process that can be verbalized but is less often heard as the child becomes more competent. Therefore self-correction occurs and has an instrumental contribution to make to progress long before it can qualify to be a metacognitive activity.

Self-correction is probably an example of one strategy the use of which extends the inner control. When children read texts of appropriate difficulty for their present skills (i.e. at or above 90 percent accuracy) this gives enough support from the familiar features of text for attention to shift to novel features of text, enough time for reading work, without losing the meaning. For it is the meaning which provides the context in which the word is embedded, the basis for anticipations of what comes next, and the signals of possible error that trigger a checking process. These active constructing and checking processes ensure that readers will learn more every time they read, independent of instruction.

As children read they engage in a deliberate effort to solve new problems with familiar information and procedures. They learn ways of operating on print using what they know to check on their estimations of what the novel features of text say. They learn how and where to search for cues, how to cross-check information, how to get confirmation. They cannot do this within a one-dimensional word-solving technique like sounding out words, but must go beyond that strategy if they are to 'know' whether they are correct.

Self-correction in such activity can be seen as an outcome of a control process in which by monitoring, the child discovers a mismatch of information and engages in problem-solving, resulting in an overt self-correction. But there is more than this involved. The self-correction process is also progressive and cumulative because at the mismatch the child initiates a search for missing information and *finds or attends to features previously ignored*. He may not notice any new features of a correct response which fits perfectly into its textual slot. On the other hand when an error occurs and is self-corrected, it is not an impossible task for the reader to be aware of what was wrong and what brought about the self-correction. By definition self-correction occurs when everything that is necessary for the solution is available.

Self-correction is only one illustration of processing activity. But it allows us to be more explicit in thinking about other processes which may occur as the child reads text correctly. For example he may not have direct access to a word, and so he may use covert processing and read the word correctly. Or he may read correctly yet be aware that the correct responses still do not make sense *to him*.

The problem-solving process of making all sources of information fit together confirms new responses made by the system.

When the child is given some introduction to a story, which he then reads for meaning, then monitoring his own problem-solving could lead to extending the system because:

- success will be confirmed by meaningfulness
- the use of the problem-solving strategies will be reinforced
- new features and information are highlighted because of their contribution to the solution
- new discriminations are made
- the check includes an outside frame of reference beyond the reading task—in the meaningfulness in the real world.

In this particular problem-solving encounter the reading behaviour system can be affected either by the addition of new data or by the enhancement of the strategy for making such discriminations, but most probably by both. Success improves performances on text of the same level of difficulty but also extends the capacity of the system so that the strategies can be applied to a text that is more difficult.

As some successful reading responses will also be the result of problem-solving and checking, the active learner has more daily experience with such activities than records of error and self-correction behaviours alone will show.

What constrains this kind of activity? Self-correction is reduced if contrived texts are used, if the instructional theory does not permit errors to occur, if the teacher does not allow time for self-correction and intervenes immediately at an error, or if children are taught to depend on a dominant strategy such as sounding out in single phonemes.

Self-correction is hampered if the child has a limited language system to draw on, if the child has trouble attending to the visual learning required to cope with print, or if the child adopts a passive rather than an active, 'constructive learner' approach to the task. (Instruction can induce passive learning, Johnston and Winograd, 1985.) It does not work well until the child has adopted the directional schema of the written language because there is too much confusing information available.

As self-correction could be held to play an important role in the construction of a self-extending system, it is important to explore some problems and questions about it.

This examination of self-correction illustrates how it could operate as both a controlling and extending process. A testing question is how do 80 percent of children learn to read in programmes which take little notice of such behaviour? Research has shown that good readers learn more than the programme teaches and they presumably have available to them more information than the programme specifies (and more information than assessment measures). Even on highly contrived texts children work hard at self-correcting. As the child gains a wider reading vocabulary writers are able to write more 'normal' and less contrived texts so in basal reading programmes texts may improve somewhat after the first two years of instruction. Many children survive on texts which are severely controlled because their active, constructive approach to learning is hard to subdue.

Why did self-correction seem to disappear in my studies of successful readers? To make self-corrections children first return to sentence or line beginnings and there is a gradual shift closer to the point of error until the child tends to produce only the first phoneme of the error before correcting as if the post-processing of the early reader is shifting to pre-processing strategies which run off very fast even at points of difficulty. The shifts in self-correction behaviours are

- from overt to covert
- from slow to fast
- from after the error to after the first sound of the error response
- from long stretches of text involved in the self-correction to only local information.

Self-correction provides a window on active processing during the early acquisition stage of reading but is not often heard as the competent reader gains in skill. Silent reading provides no such window into the processing that is occurring.

In summary, self-correction provides one example of when and how a self-extending network of strategies might be observed or studied, and some support for explanations which have to do with positive feedback or agreement. Although the observer cannot tell precisely which cues the child used to generate the error or the self-correction, the behaviour sequence tells what is ignored in the error response and the self-correction tells what extra information could have been attended to to get the correction. So an error response with a mismatch of information is noticed by the reader (conflict) and self-correcting activity is initiated. By definition the result of a self-correction is agreement between all sources of information in the text.

Strategies for Problem-solving New Words

A model of reading acquisition which defines reading as working on continuous texts with the story as the focal point of attention describes word-solving in somewhat different ways from a theory that regards reading new words in isolation as the significant activity. In this book, attention has been on an analysis of what children do when reading texts, and no specific attention has been paid to words in isolation. Observations of children reading stories suggest the following.

- Competent children choose most often to ask someone who might know the word.
- They make an estimate supported by the text and often get it right.
- They make estimates which are errors, detect them, and correct them. In this processing their search for relevant information to resolve conflicts among competing responses is a tutorial highpoint in which they are instructing themselves and (by definition in self-correction) arrive at the correct answer.
- They select rapid or slow processing to facilitate the pick-up of necessary information.
- They direct full or divided attention to selected features.
- They choose either precise search of detail or partial sampling of enough cues to solve the problem.
- They derive unknown words by analogy from known words.
- They partially sound the words and complete the solving by using meaning.
- They sound the word in parts and link to known words.
- They sound the word and are unable to link it to any prior knowledge.

As with many other aspects of literacy learning the learner may make progress from any particular point in a number of directions. That is what creates the complexity and flexibility of the processing. For example the outcome of reading a new word may be a direct link to a known meaning and way of pronouncing that word. Alternatively it may be recognised only as partly familiar and like some other known word, in form. Or it may be held in limbo, a new word which will need to be encountered in other settings before a network of information becomes attached to it.

Is the Child Attending to the Processing?

Developmental psychologists have studied how children remember. What do children do when they are told to remember something? One interesting discovery is labelled by Flavell (1982) as the 'production deficiency.' A young child may be able to rehearse a list of numbers or words if he is required to by the instructions that he is given but left to himself he does not think to do so. He does not seem aware that he, himself, can relate one area of knowledge or one cognitive strategy to another. John Flavell (1982) and Ann Brown (1981) have written extensively of the importance of how the child orchestrates these strategies. Does he try to use what he knows? Can he use them when they are appropriate? Does he know what the task is about? Does he look? search? try to remember? Does he predict? generate? hypothesize? plan? select? check? monitor? test? change? recycle? recheck? Although the child has these subskills, can he orchestrate their use to obtain the message in the text?

Many of these strategies are already available from cognitive development in the preschool years and are highly practised. As the child tries to apply these established strategies to learning about print he may find he has to learn to attend to what is happening, and he may take some time to gain a working control over those strategies he needs for problem-solving in reading.

Conscious attention during successful reading can be predominantly on meaning. Teaching a child to expect reading to make sense provides him with an easy-to-learn signal that processing is necessary. At the moment of making an error a child reading for meaning will notice it. To continue, the reader has to take some action. At this moment he is observing his own behaviour very closely because he will have to decide which response he should retain and which he should discard.

As the beginning reader searches and selects in rough and ready ways he must carry out two further types of self-regulatory action. He observes his own behaviour and he assesses his own behaviour. Has he solved it? Has he got it right? Do all the angles of this piece of the jigsaw fit in that particular slot? His search ends when it makes sense within his knowledge of the world.

In using the processes of self-observation, self-assessment and self-reinforcement, the young reader discovers new features of written language, new instances of things he learnt earlier, new relationships, and best of all for fluent reading, new short-cuts to storing and retrieving information. The child's contribution is considerable. Teaching methods with demands for meaning draw upon strategies that were there before the child began to read, they also help the child to slowly but surely come to know how he can make predictions and self-corrections, and how he can weigh the evidence and make decisions. The good reader is able to attend to his processing strategies if need be although many times they may be employed without conscious direction. The competent children resourcefully cast around all their experience to find cues, strategies and solutions. The appropriate questions are: What do I know that might help? How do I know this? What can link up with this? Is the message still clear?

The Reader Constructs the Strategic Control

Many of the long-standing debates in education pivot around the issue of whether teachers teach learners or learners teach themselves. There are some important secondary issues. If what children learn is directly a product of what teachers teach, then when a proportion of the children get it wrong is that the fault of the teachers? Alternatively, if children teach themselves and teachers merely arrange the opportunities, how do we explain the lack of progress in children who fail to teach themselves? Theories of disabilities in the field of literacy have developed to account for these problematic cases. It is possible that many of the 'disabilities' are a product of our willingness to believe that they should exist.

Only the child can develop strategic control over the experiences and information coded somehow in his brain and governing many of his behaviours. (Even behavioural theory had to have a concept of reinforcement history which was particular for individuals.) No teacher can manipulate those strategic activities in any tightly controlled way. There can be no teaching programme to engineer this control because it is a product of the idiosyncratic past history of the learner.

However, many children do learn to read in prescriptive programmes in which the teacher decides what shall be learned, in what manner and with what result. Even under these conditions children do develop self-extending systems. As learners they accept the external control as the track that leads into the activity, but gradually they work out relationships between the programme's requirements and other things that they know and can do. Very soon they are initiating moves within the teacher's system, and making new discoveries which are not being taught. To the teacher it seems that the prescriptive programme is working well and children are learning what she requires. That they are also learning to strategically organize and manage their own reading processes is fortunate because no prescriptive programme can hope to capture the intricacies of literacy processing.

Research suggests that there are some children who meet the teacher's requirements, taking each step as she introduces it, timed and paced by the limits of her prescriptions (like not being allowed to read ahead of the set pages prepared for today's lesson). They are not able to see how this relates to their successful problem-solving in other activities. They seem to do what they are being taught to do without adding a self-improving component to the learning equation. They continue to be paced by the teacher's prescriptive activities.

It is likely that those who make the poorest progress find it difficult to follow the teacher down the track prescribed. They get confused because they do not add for themselves what the teacher has left unsaid. Willing though they are to meet school requirements, nothing they do seems to match what is demanded.

One account of how children can be rescued from such poor progress operates in the Reading Recovery programme. Children read and write different texts and teachers attend to how the children operate and whether they are actively working on the information in print. If the child can be supported to do something effectively for himself then the Reading Recovery teacher withholds her teaching. She does not reveal how the word could be learned unless the child shows that he has no way of relating anything he knows to that word. If the child begins some reading work (that is, he actively searches and tries to find some solution to his problem), the teacher must sensitively follow, support, prompt, help, and assist the child to find a correct solution in the most independent manner. (On the other hand she will very quickly intervene when she recognizes unproductive moves she has seen fail in the past.)

The best British infant schools have been admired for the teacher's ability to act as a facilitator or consultant to the child and not as a didactic expert.

> Where the teacher's expertise really counts . . . is in knowing what the child is going to want . . . the more they can allow themselves to hold back and allow the student to do his own learning the more effective and better judged will be their interventions when they are really needed. There are two ways in which we can help the child to learn. One of them is by attempting to teach him; the other is by facilitating his attempts to teach himself. We need to give the child freedom to explore and to learn on his own . . . The child is self-stimulating and self-starting provided conditions are right for him.
>
> (Cashdan, 1976)

The teacher aims to stimulate, foster, support, and reinforce reading work carried out by the learner. The learner must actively search for information, relate this to things known, detect error even if he cannot solve the problem, use all his own resources, initiate his own word-solving of whatever kind, actively relate new discoveries to established knowledge and so on. It is important that the teacher does not narrowly characterize or label what the child is doing because this will reduce her sensitivity to unexpected links the child is able to make on his own.

The child must actively work on printed messages using all the sources of information and redundancy in the text that he is currently able to use, working on a sequence of learning judged to produce the quickest route to effective processing for that child at that stage of learning. *The teacher is more concerned to reinforce how the child worked to get the response than whether the child arrived at the precise correct response.* In this way the teacher is responding to the learner's construction of strategic control over reading and writing processes.

In oral language learning there is a well-known analogous body of interactions. Researchers have shown that mothers in conversation with their preschoolers rarely correct their incorrect grammar but respond to the meanings they are trying to express. In such an exchange it is the process of putting the ideas into words, the strategies by which language is generated, that are reinforced by the mother's response-in-reply, and the partially correct product in the form of the not-yet grammatical sentence is not as important as the approving of the developing generating system.

In the reading or writing situation the child can be praised for the quality of the reading work he did, whatever the correctness of the response. A prompt or question might be appropriate to then get to a correct response or it might be better to give the partially correct response no attention. The teacher observes signs of what might have led to the error response and of what might have triggered a self-correction. She records and collates instances in the record of the kinds of cues the young reader is using and what he ignores at errors, self-corrections and any word-solving behaviour. We have not been successful with young failing readers when we have not monitored the learning process closely.

Perhaps the fiercest theoretical debate around this issue of a literacy system which extends itself is not the novelty of the concept of strategies which allow the child to go beyond the information given and add to what he knows and to knowing that he knows. It is about who should control the formation of that strategic system. On the one hand some educators hold the firm belief that the teacher's programme can and must control the acquisition process in order to reduce learning failures. On the other hand some educators are so confident that 'the-child-can-do-it-alone' that they are highly critical of careful monitoring and special help. Both these positions need to produce explanations and solutions for the group of children who fail under programmes that implement what they advocate. A wide acceptance of a large category of learning-disabled children is no longer tolerable in the face of successful early interventions.

For educators who are disturbed by the increasing number of children who have been called learning disabled in the last decade, the possibility of teaching in ways that help children to develop their own literacy strategies is attractive. This calls for both the prescriptive teacher and the 'child-can-do-it-alone' teacher to have healthy doubts about the efficacy of their espoused programme for *every child*, to always question her own assumptions and check them thoughtfully against what her children are actually doing, and to hold a watchful brief for when the child's processing behaviour requires her to change her approach. Recent research has shown how well-adapted to children's learning needs are the responses of parents and non-teachers when they work in interaction with children sharing tasks for joint outcomes. Teachers can be equally supportive of the child's attempts if we see this as their major role in literacy learning.

Bruner (1974) saw the challenge to education as deciding how one managed to time the steps of pedagogy to match *unfolding* capacities, how one managed to *instruct* without making the learner dependent and how one managed to do both of these *while keeping alive zest* for further learning. It is not easy to rewrite that statement to take account of what we have been exploring. How does one manage to support the child's control of literacy activities from the beginning, to interact with an inner control one can only infer, and to progressively withdraw to allow room for the child to control the development of a self-extending network of strategies for literacy learning?

Resnick (1987) suggested the emphases and principles of such instruction. Reviewing important and recent evidence in *Education and Learning to Think* she wrote:

> Reorienting instruction in the three R's (the enabling disciplines) so that they incorporate more of the higher order processes seems a particularly promising approach to improving thinking skills. The three R's of the traditional basic school curriculum can become the environment for higher order education. Effective reading, writing and mathematics learning depend on elaboration, explication, and various kinds of meaning construction. Reorienting basic instruction in these curricula to focus on intentional, self-managed learning and strategies for meaning construction, rather than on routinized performances, will result in more effective basic skill instruction while providing a strong base for higher order skill development in other disciplines.

It is not clear whether Resnick is referring to the first steps in literacy learning but there are several developments in the teaching of literacy which are consistent with her view. The study of emerging literacy, changes in kindergarten programmes, the whole language movement, the 'real books' advocacy, and emphases on introducing children to a variety of texts and genres are developments which require various forms of meaning construction, and require teachers to engage in interactions with learners about texts.

My special plea would be that we recognize that *some children need extra resources and many more supportive interactions with teachers* to get them through the necessary transitions of reading acquisition to the stage where they can pick up most of the different kinds of information in print. As they read familiar texts or are challenged to engage in reading work on novel texts their literacy 'systems' which generate (a) correct responding and (b) effective problem-solving, provide them with feedback on the effectiveness of the strategies they used. Success encourages more risk-taking which, in turn, is likely to extend the range of strategies they try. Meanwhile more and more encounters with 'known' words gives them rapid and 'direct access' to a wider vocabulary of words that require little or no solving. Literacy activities can become self-managed, self-monitored, self-corrected and self-extending for most children, even those who initially find transitions into literacy hard and confusing.

Bibliography

Ahlberg, J. and A., *The Jolly Postman or Other People's Letters*, London: William Heinemann, 1986.

Anderson, P. (Ed.), *Linguistics In The Elementary School Classroom*, New York: The Macmillan Co., 1971.

Anderson, R. A., Osborn, J. and Tierney, R. J. (Eds.), *Learning to Read in American Schools*, Hillsdale, New Jersey: Erlbaum, 1984.

APIED, UNESCO Regional Office, Bangkok, *Textbooks and Reading Materials* Vols. I–III, Wellington: Department of Education, 1984.

Ashton-Warner, S., *Teacher*, London: Secker and Warburg, 1963.

Aslin, R. N. and Smith, L. B., Perceptual development. *Annual Review of Psychology*, 39, 1988: 435–73.

Au, K. and Kawakami, A., 'Vygotskian perspectives on discussion processes in small group reading lessons.' In P. Peterson, L. Wilkinson and M. Hallinan (Eds.), *The Social Context of Instruction: Group Organization and Group Processes*, New York: Academic Press, 1984.

Baghdan, M., *Our Daughter Learns To Read And Write*. Newark, Delaware: International Reading Association, 1984.

Bar-Adon, A. and Leopold, W. F., *Child Language: A Book of Readings*, Englewood Cliffs, New Jersey: Prentice-Hall, 1971.

Barnes, M., 'The blue forest.' In T. Clymer and R. L. Venezky, *Across the Fence*, Lexington, Massachusetts: Ginn & Co. 1982.

Beadle, M., *A Child's Mind*, New York: Doubleday & Co., 1970.

Begg, J. A., and Clay, Marie M., 'A note on teaching a preschooler to read: Some problems of evaluation.' *New Zealand Journal of Educational Studies*, 3, (2), 1968: 171–174.

Benton, A. L., *Right-Left Discrimination and Finger Localization*, New York: Paul Hoeber, 1959.

Berko, J., 'The child learning of English morphology,' *Word*, 14, 1958: 150–177.

Bertelson, P. 'The onset of literacy.' *Cognition*, 24, 1986: 283–284.

Bertelson, P. 'The onset of literacy: Liminal remarks.' In P. Bertelson (Ed.), *The onset of literacy: cognitive processes in reading acquisition*, Cambridge, Massachusetts: MIT Press, 1987.

Bettleheim, B., *Dialogues with Mothers*, New York: Free Press of Glencoe, 1962.

Biemiller, A., 'The development of the use of graphic and contextual information,' *Reading Research Quarterly*, 6, 1970: 75–96.

Birch, J. W. and Birch, J. R., *Preschool Education and School Admission Practices in New Zealand*, Pittsburgh: University Centre for International Studies, 1970.

Bissex, G., *Gyns At Work: A Child Learns to Write and Read*, Cambridge, Massachusetts: Harvard University Press, 1980.

Bloom, B. S., *Stability and Change in Human Characteristics*, New York: Wiley, 1964.

Bloom, L. and Lahey, M., *Language Development and Language Disorders*, New York: Wiley, 1978.

Board, P. E., 'Toward a Theory of Instructional Influence', Doctoral dissertation, Toronto: University of Toronto, 1982.

Brailsford, A., 'Early reading experiences: The literacy development of kindergarten children viewed from a cultural perspective.' Ph.D. dissertation, University of Alberta, 1984.

Brogan, M., 'I'll tell you about your painting,' *New Zealand Play Centre Journal*. 1981.

Brown, A., 'Metacognition: The development of selective attention strategies for learning from texts.' In M. L. Kamil (Ed.), *Directions in Reading: Research and Instruction*, Washington, D.C.: The National Reading Conference, 1981: 21–43.

Brown, A., 'Metacognitive development and reading.' In R. J. Spiro, B. C. Bruce and W. F. Brewer (Eds.), *Theoretical Issues in Reading Comprehension*, Hillsdale, New Jersey: Lawrence Erlbaum, 1980: 453–481

Bruce, D. J., 'The analysis of word sounds by young children.' *British Journal of Educational Psychology*, 34: 1964: 158–170.

Bruner, J. S., 'On perceptual readiness,' *Psychological Review*, 64, 1957: 123–152.

Bruner, J. S., Organization of early skilled action. *Child Development*, 44, 1973: 1–11.

Bruner, J. S., Organization of early skilled action. In M. P. M. Richard, *The Integration of a Child Into A Social World*, London: Cambridge University Press, 1974: 167–184

Bruner, J., *The Relevance of Education*, Middlesex: Penguin Education, 1974.

Bruner, J. S. 'Learning how to do things with words.' In J. Bruner and A. Garton (Eds), *Human Growth and Development*, Oxford: Oxford University Press, 1978.

Bruner, J. S., *Child's Talk: Learning to Use Language*, London: W. W. Norton & Co., 1983.

Bruner, J. S. and Garton, A., *Human Growth and Development*, Oxford: Clarendon Press, 1978.

Bruner, J. and Haste, H., *Making Sense: The Child's Construction of the World*, London: Methuen, 1987.

Bryant, P., *Perception and Understanding Young Children*, London: Methuen, 1974.

Bryant, P., 'Theories about the causes of cognitive development.' In P. L. C. van Geert (Ed.), *Theory Building In Developmental Psychology*, North-Holland: Elsevier Science Publishers, 1986.

Bryant, P. E., Bradley, L., MacLean, M., and Crossland, J. 'Nursery rhymes, phonological skills and reading.' *J. Child Language*, 16: 1989: 407–428.

Butler, D., *Babies Need Books*, London: The Bodley Head, 1980.

Butler, D. and Clay, M. M., *Reading Begins At Home*, Auckland: Heinemann Educational Books, 1979.

Cambourne, B., *The Whole Story*, Auckland: Ashton Scholastic, 1988.

Cashdan, A., 'Who teaches the child to read.' In J. Merritt, *New Horizons in Reading*, Newark, Delaware: International Reading Association, 1976: 80–85.

Cazden, C. B., 'Play with language and metalinguistic awareness: one dimension of language experience.' Organization Mondial pour l'Education Prescolaire, 1974: 6, 12–24.

Cazden, C. B., *Classroom Discourse: The Language of Teaching and Learning*, Portsmouth, New Hampshire: Heinemann Educational Books, 1988.

Chall, J. S., *Stages of Reading Development*, New York: McGraw-Hill, 1983.

Chapman, L. J., *Reading Development and Cohesion*, London: Heinemann Educational Books, 1983.

Charles, H., Glynn, T. and McNaughton, S., Childcare workers' use of 'talking up' and incidental teaching procedures under standard and self-management staff training packages, *Educational Psychology*, 4, 1984: 233–248.

Chomsky, C., 'Stages in language development and reading exposure,' *Harvard*

Educational Review, 22, 1972: 1–33.

Chomsky, C., How sister go into the grog, *Early years*, 1975: 36–39.

Chomsky, C., 'Invented spelling in the open classroom.' In W. von Raffles Engel (Ed.), *Word* (Special Issue entitled Child Language Today), 1976.

Chomsky, C., 'Approaching reading through invented spelling.' In L. B. Resnick and P. A. Weaver (Eds.), *Theory and Practice of Early Reading*, Vol. 2, Hillsdale, New Jersey: Erlbaum, 1979: 43–64.

Church, J. (Ed.), *Three Babies: Biographies of Cognitive Development*, New York: Random House, 1966.

Clark, M., *Young Fluent Readers*, London: Heinemann Educational Books, 1976.

Clarke, D. D. and Crossland, J., *Action Systems: An Introduction to the Analysis of Complex Behaviour*, London: Methuen, 1985.

Clay, M. M., 'Emergent Reading Behaviour.' Unpublished doctoral dissertation, University of Auckland Library, 1966.

Clay, M. M., 'The reading behaviour of five year old children: a research report,' *New Zealand Journal of Educational Studies*, 2, (1), 1967: 11–31.

Clay, M. M., 'A syntactic analysis of reading errors,' *Journal of Verbal Learning and Verbal Behaviour*, 7, 1968: 434–438.

Clay, M. M., 'Reading errors and self-correction behaviour,' *British Journal of Educational Psychology*, 39, 1969: 47–56.

Clay, M. M., 'An increasing effect of disorientation on the discrimination of print: a developmental study,' *Journal of Experimental Child Psychology*, 9, 1970: 297–306.

Clay, M. M., 'Language skills: a comparison of Maori, Samoan and Pakeha children aged 5 to 7 years. *New Zealand Journal of Educational Studies*, 1970: 153–162.

Clay, M. M., 'Orientation to the spatial characteristics of the open book,' *Visible Language*, 8, 1974: 275–282.

Clay, M. M., 'The development of morphological rules in children with differing language backgrounds,' *New Zealand Journal of Educational Studies*, 9, 2, (November) 1974: 113–121.

Clay, M. M., *What Did I Write?*, Auckland: Heinemann Educational Books, 1975.

Clay, M. M., 'Exploring with a pencil,' *Theory Into Practice*, 16, 5, (December) 1977: 334–341.

Clay, M. M., *Reading: The Patterning of Complex Behaviour*, Auckland: Heinemann Publishers, 1979 (2nd Edition).

Clay, M. M., *Observing Young Readers: Selected Papers*, Portsmouth, New Hampshire: Heinemann Educational Books, 1982.

Clay, M. M., *The Early Detection of Reading Difficulties: A Diagnostic Survey with Recovery Procedures*, Auckland: Heinemann, 1985 (3rd Edition).

Clay, M. M., 'Constructive processes: Talking, reading, writing, art and craft,' *The Reading Teacher*, (April) 1986: 764–770.

Clay, M. M., 'Implementing Reading Recovery: Systemic adaptations to an educational innovation,' *New Zealand Journal of Educational Studies*, 22, 1, 1987: 55–58.

Clay, M. M., *Writing Begins At Home*, Auckland: Heinemann Publishers, 1987.

Clay, M. M., 'Concepts about print: In English and other languages,' *The Reading Teacher*, 42, 4, 1989: 268–277.

Clay, M. M., 'Child development.' In J. Flood, J. Jensen, D. Lapp and J. R. Squire (Eds.), *Handbook of Research on Teaching the English Language Arts*, Newark, Delaware: IRA and NCTE.

Clay, M. M and Cazden, C. B., A Vygotskian interpretation of Reading Recovery. In L. C. Moll (Ed.), *Vygotsky and Education: Instructional Implications and Applications of Socio-Historical Psychology.* Cambridge: Cambridge University Press, (in press).

Clay, M. M., Gill, M., Glynn, T., McNaughton, T. and Salmon, K., *Record of Oral Language and Biks and Gutches,* Auckland: Heinemann Publishers, 1983.

Clay, M. M. and Imlach, R. H., 'Juncture, pitch and stress as reading behaviour variables,' *Journal of Verbal Behaviour and Verbal Learning,* 10, 1971: 133–139.

Clay, M. M. and Williams, B., 'The reading behaviour of Standard One Children,' *Education,* 1973: 13–17.

Cochran-Smith, M., *The Making of a Reader,* Norwood, New Jersey: Ablex Publishing Corporation, 1984.

Cole, M., John-Steiner, V., Scribner, S. and Souberman, E. (Eds), *Mind and Society,* Cambridge, Massachusetts: Harvard University Press, 1978.

Cowley, J., *Number One* (*Ready to Read* Series), Wellington: School Publications, 1982.

Cowley, J. & Melser, J., *Mrs. Wishy-Washy,* Auckland: Shortland Publications, 1980.

Dalgren, G. and Olsson, L. E., 'The child's conception of reading.' Paper presented to the American Education Research Association, San Francisco, California, April, 1986.

Daniels J. C. and Diack H., *The Standard Reading Tests,* London: Chatto and Windus, 1958.

Davies, M. R., 'Home Deprivation and intellectual development,' *Education,* 12, Wellington: Department of Education, (March) 1963.

Day, H. D. and Day, K., 'The reliability and validity of the Concepts About Print and Record of Oral Language,' Resources in Education, ED 179 932, Arlington, Virginia: ERIC Document Reproduction Service, 1980.

Deardon, R. F. D., *Theory And Practice in Education,* London: Routledge & Kegan Paul, 1984.

Department of Education, *Ready to Read,* Wellington: School Publications, 1963 (18 titles).

Department of Education, *Reading In The Junior Classes: with guidelines to the revised Ready to Read series,* Wellington: School Publications, 1985.

Diack, H., *Reading And The Psychology of Perception,* Nottingham: Peter Skinner, 1960.

Doake, D. B., 'Book experience and emergent reading behaviour in preschool children.' Doctoral Dissertation: University of Alberta, 1981.

Donaldson, M., *Children's Minds,* Glasgow: Fontana, 1978.

Downing, J., *The i.t.a. Symposium,* National Foundation For Educational Research For England and Wales, 1967.

Downing, J., 'Children's concept of language in learning to read,' *Educational Research,* 12, 1970: 106–112.

Downing, J. and Leong, C. K., *Psychology of Reading,* New York: Macmillan, 1982.

Downing, J. and Oliver, P., 'The child's conception of 'a word.'' *Reading Research Quarterly,* 9, 1974: 568–582.

Dunn, L. M., *The Peabody Picture Vocabulary Test,* Minnesota: American Guidance Service, 1965.

Dunn-Rankin, P., 'The similarity of lower-case letters of the English alphabet,' *Journal of Verbal Learning and Verbal Behaviour,* 7, 1968: 990–995.

Durkin, D., *Children Who Ready Early,* Teachers' College Press, New York, 1966.

Durkin, D., *Reading And The Kindergarten: An Annotated Bibliography*, Newark, Delaware: International Reading Association, 1969.

Durrell, D., 'First grade reading success study,' *Journal of Education*, 140, February, 1958.

Ehri, L. C. and Wilce, L. S., 'Do beginners learn to read function words better in sentences or in lists?' *Reading Research Quarterly*, XV, 4, 1980: 451–476.

Ehri, L. and Wilce, L., 'Movement into reading: Is the first stage of printed word learning visual or phonetic?' *Reading Research Quarterly*, 20, 1985: 163–179.

Elkind, D. and Weiss, J., 'Studies in perceptual development III: Perceptual exploration.' *Child Development*, 38, 1967: 553–561.

Elkonin, D. B., 'Development of speech.' In A. V. Zaporozhets and D. B. Elkonin (Eds.), *The Psychology of Preschool Children*, Cambridge, Massachusetts: M.I.T. Press, 1971.

Elkonin, D. B., 'U.S.S.R.' In J. Downing (Ed.), *Comparative Reading*, New York: Macmillan, 1973: 551–580.

Elley, W., 'What do children learn from being read to?' *SET* 1, Item 11, 1985.

Fellows, B. J., *The Discrimination Process and Development*, London: Pergamon Press, 1968.

Fernald, G. M., *Remedial Techniques In Basic School Subjects*, New York: McGraw-Hill, 1943.

Ferreiro, E. and Teberosky, A., *Literacy Before Schooling*, Portsmouth New Hampshire: Heinemann Educational Books, 1982.

Flavell, J. H., 'Cognitive monitoring.' In Dickson, *Children's Oral Communication Skills*, New York: Academic Press, 1982.

Flavell, J. H., 'On cognitive development,' *Child Development*, 53, 1982: 1–10.

Fodor, J. A., Bever, T. G. and Garrett, M. F., *The Psychology of Language*, New York: McGraw-Hill, 1974.

Fries, C. C., *Linguistics and Reading*. London: Holt, Rinehart and Winston, 1963.

Gardner, D. E. M. and Cass, Joan, *The Role Of The Teacher in The Infant And Nursery School*, London: Pergamon, 1965.

Gibson, C. M. and Richards, I. A. *First Steps In Reading*, New York: Pocket Books, 1957.

Gibson, E. J., 'Learning to Read,' *Science*, 148, 1965: 1066–1072.

Gibson, E. J. and Levin, H., *The Psychology of Reading*, Cambridge, Massachusetts: M.I.T., 1975.

Glynn, T. and McNaughton, S., 'The Mangere home and school remedial reading procedures: Continuing research on their effectiveness,' *New Zealand Journal of Psychology*, 14, 2, 1985: 66–77.

Goodacre, E., *Children and Learning to Read*, London: Routledge, 1971.

Goodacre, E., 'Hearing children read,' *Child Education*, June 1971.

Goodman, K. S., 'Analysis of oral reading miscues: applied psycholinguistics,' *Reading Research Quarterly*, 1, 1969: 9–30.

Goodman, K. S., 'Reading: a psycholinguistic guessing game.' In H. Singer and R. B. Ruddell (Eds.), *Theoretical Models and Processes of Reading*, Newark, Delaware: International Reading Association, 1970.

Goodman, K. S., 'A linguistic study of cues and miscues in reading.' In H. Singer and R. B. Ruddell (Eds.), *Theoretical Models and Processes of Reading*, Third Edition, Newark, Delaware: International Reading Association, 1985.

Goodman, K. S. 'Using children's reading miscues for new teaching strategies,' *The Reading Teacher*, 23, 1970: 455–459.

Goodman, Y., 'The development of initial literacy.' In H. Goelman, A. A. Oberg and Frank Smith (Eds.), *Awakening To Literacy*, Portsmouth, New Hampshire: *Heinemann Educational Books*, 1984.

Goodman, Y, 'A whole-language comprehension-centred view of reading development.' *Gnosis*, 7, (September) 1985: 2–8.

Goodman, Y. M. (Ed.), *How Children Construct Literacy: Piagetian Perspectives* , Newark, Delaware: International Reading Association, 1990.

Goodman, Y. and Altwerger, B., 'Reading: how does it begin?' In G. S. Pinnell (Ed.), *Discovering Language With Children*, National Council of Teachers of English, 1980.

Goswami, U., 'Children's use of analogy in learning to read: A developmental study,' *Journal of Experimental Child Psychology*, 42, 1986: 73–83.

Goswami, U., 'Orthographic analogies and reading development,' *Quarterly Journal of Experimental Psychology*, 40, 2, 1988: 239–268.

Gough, P., 'One second of reading,' *Visible Language*, 6, 4, 1972: 291–320.

Gough, P. B. and Hillinger, M. L., 'Learning to read: An unnatural act,' *Bulletin of the Orton Society*, 30, 1980: 179–196.

Grice, H. P., 'Logic and conversation.' In P. Cole and J. L. Morgon (Eds.), *Syntax and Semantics: Speech Acts*, 3, New York: Academic Press, 1975.

Guthrie, J. T., 'Reading comprehension and syntactic responses in good and poor readers,' *Journal of Educational Psychology*, 65, 1973: 294–299.

Haber, R. N., 'Visual Perception,' *Annual Review of Psychology*, 29, 1978: 31–59.

Haber, L. R. and Haber R. N., 'Perceptual processes in reading: An analysis-by-synthesis model.' In F. J. Pirozzolo and M. C. Wittrock, *Neuropsychological and Cognitive Processes In Reading*, New York: Academic Press, 1981.

Haber, L. R., Haber, R. N. and Furlin, K. R., 'Word length and word shape as sources of information in reading,' *Reading Research Quarterly*, 18, 2, 1983.

Harris, D., *Children's Drawings As Measures of Intellectual Maturity*, New York: Harcourt Brace, 1963.

Harris, M. and Coltheart, M., *Language Processing in Children and Adults: An Introduction*, London: Routledge & Kegan Paul, 1986.

Harris, T. L., 'Reading flexibility: a neglected aspect of reading instruction.' In J. Merritt (Ed.), *New Horizons in Reading*, Newark, Delaware: International Reading Association, 1976: 331–340.

Harste, J. C., Burke, C. L. and Woodward, V. A., *Children, their language and world: Initial encounters with print*, National Institute of Education, 1981.

Harste, J. C., Woodward, V. A., and Burke, C., *Language Stories and Literacy Lessons*, Portsmouth, New Hampshire: Heinemann Educational Books, 1984.

Hart, B., and Riseley, T., 'Incidental teaching of language in the preschool,' *Journal of Applied Behavior Analysis*, 8, 1975: 411–420.

Hart, N. W. M. and Walker, R. F., *Mount Gravatt Reading Series*, Sydney: Addison-Wesley, 1977.

Hart, N. W. M., Walker, R. F. and Gray, B., *The Language of Children: A Key To Literacy*, Sydney: Addison-Wesley, 1977.

Heath, S. B., 'What no bedtime story means: narrative skills at home and school,' *Language in Society*, 11, 1982: 49–76.

Hemming, J., personal communication, 1971.

Henderson, L., *Orthographies And Reading*, Hillsdale, New Jersey: Lawrence Erlbaum, 1984.

Holdaway, D., *The Foundations of Literacy*, Sydney: Ashton Scholastic, 1979.

Holt, J., *How Children Learn*, Pelican, London, 1970.

Horton, J., *On The Way To Reading*, Wellington: Department of Education, 1978.

Hutchins, P., *Titch*, London: Bodley Head.

Imperial Readers—First Primer, London: Thomas Nelson, 1890s.

Jansen, M., Jacobsen, B. and Jensen, P. E., *The Teaching of Reading Without Really Any Method*, Copenhagen: Munksgard (also Humanities Press, New Jersey), 1978.

Johns, J. L., 'First graders' Concepts About Print,' *Reading Research Quarterly*, 15, 4, 1980: 529–549.

Johnston P. H. and Winograd, P. M., Passive failure in reading. *Journal of Reading Behaviour*, 17, 4, 1985: 279–301.

Juel, C., Learning to Read and Write: A longitudinal study of 54 children from first through fourth grades, *Journal of Educational Psychology*, 80, 4, 1980: 437–447.

Juola, J., 'Development trends in visual search: determining visual units in reading.' In L. Resnick and P. Weaver, *Theory and Practice of Early Reading*, Hillsdale, New Jersey: Lawrence Erlbaum and Associates, 1979.

Karmiloff-Smith, A., *A Functional Approach To Child Language*, Cambridge: Cambridge University Press, 1979.

Klein, D. C. and Ross, A., 'Kindergarten entry: a study of role transition.' In Morris Krugman (Ed.), *Orthopsychiatry and the School*, New York: American Orthopsychiatric Association, 1958.

Kolers, P. A., 'Three stages of reading.' In H. Levin and J. P. Williams, *Basic Studies On Reading*, New York: Basic Books, 1970.

Landau, E. D., Epstein, S. E. and Stone, A. P., *Child Development Through Literature*, Englewood Cliffs, New Jersey: Prentice-Hall, 1972.

Lefevre, C. A., *Linguistics And The Teaching of Reading*, New York: McGraw-Hill Book Co., 1964.

Levin, E., 'Beginning reading—a personal affair,' *Elementary School Journal*, 67, 1966: 67–71.

Liberman, A. M., 'The speech code.' In G. A. Miller (Ed.), *Psychology and Communication*, Voice of America, Forum Series, 1974: 145–158.

Liberman, I. Y., Shankweller, D., Fischer, F. W. and Carter B., 'Explicit syllable and phoneme segmentation in the young child,' *Journal of Experimental Child Psychology*, 18, 1974: 201–212.

Lindfors, J. W., *Children's Language and Learning*, Englewood Cliffs, New Jersey: Prentice-Hall (2nd Edition), 1987.

Luria, A. R., 'The functional organisation of the brain,' *Scientific American*, March 1970: 66.

Lynn, R., *Attention, Arousal and The Orientation Reaction*, London: Pergamon 1966.

McLane, J. B. and McNamee, G. D., *Early Literacy*, Cambridge, Mass: Harvard University Press, 1990.

McConkie, G. W. and Raynor, K., 'Identifying the span of the effective stimulus in reading: Literature review and theories of reading.' In H. Singer and R. B. Ruddell (Eds.), *Theoretical Models and Processes of Reading*, Newark, Delaware: International Reading Association, 1976: 137–162.

McCullough, C., M., 'The language of basal readers.' In R. C. Staiger and O. Andresen (Eds.), *Reading: A Human Right and A Human Problem*, Newark, Delaware: International Reading Association, 1968: 67–72.

McDonald, G., 'Promotion, retention and acceleration,' *SET* 2, Item 3, Wellington: New Zealand Council For Educational Research, 1988.

McDonell, G. M. and Osburn, E. B., 'New thoughts about reading readiness,' *Language Arts*, 55, 1, 1978.

McKee, P., Brzeinski, J. E. and Harrison, M. L., 'The effectiveness of teaching reading in kindergarten,' Report of the Co-operative Research Project, Denver Public Schools, Colorado, 1966.

McKenzie, M., 'Shared Writing: Apprenticeship in writing,' *Language Matters*, 1–2, 1985: 1–5.

McKenzie, M., *Journeys Into Literacy*, Huddersfield: Schofield and Sims, 1986.

MacKinnon, A. R., *How Do Children Learn To Read?*, Toronto: Copp Clarke, 1959.

Maclean, M., Bryant, P. and Bradley, L., 'Rhymes, nursery rhymes and reading in early childhood,' *Merrill-Palmer Quarterly*, 33, 3, 1987: 255–282.

McNaughton, S. S., 'Instructor attention to oral reading errors: a functional analysis.' Unpublished Ph.D. Thesis, University of Auckland, 1978.

McNaughton, S. S., 'Learning in one-to-one reading instruction: outcomes of teacher attention to errors.' Paper presented to International Reading Association Conference, Dunedin, New Zealand, 1978.

McNaughton, S., 'Becoming an independent reader: Problem-solving during oral reading,' *New Zealand Journal of Educational Studies*, 16, 172–185, 1983.

McNaughton, S., *Being Skilled: The Socializations of Learning to Read*, London: Methuen, 1987.

McNaughton, S., Glynn, T. and Robinson, V., *Parents as Remedial Reading Tutors: Issues For Home and School*, Wellington: New Zealand Council for Educational Research, 1981.

McNaughton, S., Glynn, T. and Robinson, V. *Pause, Prompt and Praise: Effective Tutoring For Remedial Reading*, Birmingham: Positive Products, 1987.

McQueen, P. J., 'Motor Responses Associated with Beginning Reading.' Unpublished M.A. Thesis, University of Auckland Library, 1979.

Mahy, M., *A Crocodile In The Garden* (*Ready to Read* Series), Wellington: School Publications, 1983.

Malmquist, E., 'Sweden.' In J. Downing, *Comparative Reading*, New York: Macmillan, 1973: 466–487.

Marshall, J., 'Help for the hen.' In T. Clymer and R. L. Venezky, *Across the Fence*, Lexington, Massachusetts: Ginn and Company, 1982.

Masonheimer, P. E, Drum, P. A. and Ehri, L. C., 'Does environmental print identification lead children into word reading?' *Journal of Reading Behaviour*, 16, 4, 1984: 257–271.

Mattingly, I. G., 'The psycholinguistic basis for linguistic awareness.' In M. L. Kamil and A. J. Moe (Eds.), *Twenty-eighth Yearbook of the National Reading Conference*, Clemson, South Carolina: National Reading Conference, 1979: 274–278.

Mattingly, I. G., 'Reading, linguistic awareness and language acquisition.' In J. Downing and R. Valtin (Eds.), *Language awareness and learning to read*, New York: Springer–Verlag, 1984: 9–25.

Meade, A., 'Who talks to William? and Karla, and Susan, and Michael, and? Adult-child interaction, particularly in conversation, in early childhood centres,' *SET*, Wellington: New Zealand Council for Educational Research, 1982.

Meares, O., 'Some children talk about print,' Belmont Reading Clinic, 1972.

Meek, M., *Learning to Read*, London: Bodley Head, 1982.

Metropolitan Reading Readiness Test, Wellington: New Zealand Council For Educational Research, 1943.

Meyer, L. A., Greer, E. A. and Crummey, L., 'An analysis of decoding, comprehension and story text comprehensibility in four first-grade reading programs,' *Journal of Reading Behavior*, 14, 1, 1987: 69–98.

Miller, G. A., *Language and Speech*, San Francisco: S. F. and W. H. Freeman, 1981.

Moore, D. W., 'First and last, one and two, letter and word: Concept formation in Papua New Guinean community schools.' Paper presented at 4th National Conference on Mathematics, Lae, Papua New Guinea, 1981.

Moore, O. K., 'Orthographic symbols and the preschool child—a new approach.' In E. O. Torrance (Ed.), *New Educational Ideas: Third Minnesota Conference on Gifted Children*, Minnesota Center for Continuation Study, University of Minnesota: 1961: 91–101.

Morais, J., Cary, L., Alegria, J. and Bertelson, P., 'Does awareness of speech as a sequence of phonemes arise spontaneously?' *Cognition*, 7: 1979: 323–331.

Morrow, L. M., *Literacy Development In The Early Years: Helping Children Read and Write*, Englewood Cliffs, New Jersey: Prentice-Hall, 1989.

Morrow, L. M. and Smith, J. K., *Assessment for Instruction in Early Literacy*, Englewood Cliffs, N. J.: Prentice-Hall, 1990.

The Mount Gravatt Reading Series: A Developmental Language Reading Programme. (Level Two, No. 9, My Plant), Sydney: Addison–Wesley Publishers, 1977.

Murphy, L., *The Widening World of Childhood*, New York: Basic Books, 1962.

New Zealand Department of Education, The *Ready to Read* Series (I), Wellington: School Publications, 1963.

New Zealand Department of Education, The Revised *Ready To Read* Series (II), Wellington: School Publications, 1980.

New Zealand Educational Institute, *Reading Units For Junior School* (Rev. Ed.), Wellington: NZEI, 1978: 93.

Newman, B. M. and Newman, P. R., *Development Through Life*, Homewood, Illinois: The Dorsey Press, 1975.

Ng S., 'Error and Self-correction Behaviour in Speech and Writing.' Unpublished Ph.D. Thesis, University of Auckland Library, 1979.

Nicholson, T., 'Good Readers Don't Guess,' *SET*, 2, Wellington: New Zealand Council For Educational Research, 1986.

Nicholson, T., 'Taking the Guesswork Out of Teaching Reading,' *SET*, 2, Wellington: New Zealand Council For Educational Research, 1986.

Ninio, A. and Bruner, J., 'The achievement and antecedents of labelling,' *Journal of Child Language*, 5, 1, 1978: 1–15.

Nurss, J., 'Oral reading errors and reading comprehension,' *The Reading Teacher*, 22, 1969: 523.

Osborn, J., 'The purposes, uses and contents of workbooks and some guidelines for publishers.' In R. C. Anderson, J. Osborn, and R. J. Tierney (Eds.), *Learning to Read in American schools*, Hillsdale, New Jersey: Erlbaum, 1984.

Paley, V., *Wally's Stories*, Cambridge, Mass: Harvard University Press, 1981.

Palincsar, A. S. and Brown, A. L., 'Reciprocal teaching on comprehension-fostering and comprehension-monitoring activities,' *Cognition and Instruction*, 1 (2), 1984: 117–175.

Palincsar, A. S. and Brown, A. L., Interactive teaching to promote independent learning from text, *The Reading Teacher*, 39, 8, 1986: 771–778.

Pearson, P. D., 'Guided Reading: A Response To Isabel Beck.' In R. C. Anderson, J. Osborn and R. J. Tierney, *Learning To Read in American Schools: Basal Texts and Content Texts*, Hillsdale, New Jersey: Lawrence Erlbaum, 1984.

Peters, M. J., 'The influence of reading methods on spelling,' *British Journal of Educational Psychology*, 37, 1, 1967: 47–53.

Phillips, G., 'Story Reading to Preschool Children in their Home Environment: A Descriptive Analysis.' Unpublished Thesis, University of Auckland, 1986.

Phillips, G. and McNaughton, S., 'The practice of storybook reading to preschoolers in mainstream New Zealand families,' *Reading Research Quarterly*. (in press, 1990)

Pines, M., *Revolution in Learning*, New York: Harper and Row, 1967.

Price, H., 'Lo I am an ox!,' *Education*, 3, 1975.

Rasmussen, D. E. and Goldberg, L., *The Basic Reading Series*, Chicago: Science Research Associates, 1964.

Rayner, K., 'The role of eye movements in learning to read and reading disability,' *RASE* 6, 6, 1985: 53–60.

Read, C., 'Preschool children's knowledge of English phonology,' *Harvard Education Review*, 41, 1971: 1–34.

Read, C., *Children's Categorization of Speech Sounds in English*, Urbana, Illinois: National Council of Teachers of English, 1975.

Reid, J., 'Learning to think about reading,' *Educational Research*, 9, (1), 1966: 56–62.

Reid, J. F., 'Sentence structure in reading primers,' *Research in Education*, 3, May 1970: 23–37.

Reid, J. F., *Towards a Theory of Literacy in Reading and Related Skills*, London: Ward Lock, 1973.

Renwick, M., *To School At Five*, Wellington: New Zealand Council For Educational Research, 1984.

Renwick, M., Transition to school: The children's experience. *SET*, 2, 1987, Item 12: 1–6.

Resnick, L. B., *Education And Learning To Think*, Washington, D.C.: National Academy Press, 1987.

Richards, I. A., Review of 'Learning To Read: The Great Debate,' *Harvard Educational Review*, 38 (2), 1968: 357–364.

Ringrose, A., 'From sharing to independence: Writing in the Middle Infants,' *Language Matters*, 2 and 3, London: ILEA Centre for Language in Primary Education, 1987.

Robinson, S. M., 'Predicting Early Reading Progress.' Unpublished M.A. Thesis, University of Auckland, 1973.

Rodriguez, I., 'Administration of the Concepts About Print SAND Test to Kindergarten Children of Limited English Proficiency Utilizing Four Test Conditions.' Doctoral Dissertation, Texas Women's University, Denton, TX, 1963.

Russell, D. H. et al., 'The Ginn Basic Readers,' Boston: Ginn and Co., 1966.

Samuels, S. J., 'Effects of pictures on learning to read, comprehension and attitudes,' *Review of Educational Research*, 40, 1970: 397–407.

Schank, R. C. and Adelson, R. P., *Scripts, Plans, Goals and Understanding*, New York: John Wiley & Sons, 1977.

Schmidt, E., 'Hvad Ved Skolebegyndere Om Bogernes Sprog? Laese Rapport 6, Laesning,' Copenhagen, Denmark: The Danish Reading Association, 1982.

Seuss, Dr., *Green Eggs and Ham*, New York: Beginner Books, 1960.

Simpson, M. M., *Suggestions For Teaching Reading In Infant Classes*, Wellington: Department of Education, 1962. (Also published by Methuen, London, 1966.)

Singer, H. and Ruddell, R. B. (Eds.), *Theoretical Models and Processes of Reading*, Newark, Delaware: International Reading Association, 1976: 8–19.

Singer, H., Samuels, S. J. and Spiroff, J., 'The effect of pictures and contextual conditions on learning responses to printed words,' *Theoretical Models and Processes of Reading*, 2nd Edition, Newark, Delaware: International Reading Association, 1976.

Slane, J., An individual, audiovisual inservice course for teachers: The Early

Reading Inservice Course *PLET* vol. 16, No. 1. (February) 1979: 38–45.

Smith, F., *Psycholinguistics and Reading*, New York: Holt, Rinehart and Winston, 1973.

Smith, F., 'The role of prediction in reading,' *Elementary Education*, 52, 8, 1975: 305–311.

Smith, F., *Understanding Reading*, 2nd Edition, New York: Holt, Rinehart and Winston, 1978.

Smith, F., *Reading*, London: Cambridge University Press, 2nd Edition, 1985.

Solley, C. M. and Murphy, G., *Development of The Perceptual World*, New York: Basic Books, 1960.

Southgate Booth, V., Structuring reading materials for beginning reading.' In R. C. Staiger and O. Andresen (Eds.), *Reading: A Human Right and A Human Problem*, Newark, Delaware: International Reading Association, 1968.

Spache, G. E., *Toward Better Reading*. Champaign, Illinois: Garrard Publishing Co., 1963.

Spencer, M., *How Texts Teach What Readers Learn*, Victoria, British Columbia: Abel Press, 1987.

Spencer, M., 'Playing the Texts,' *Language Matters* 1, 1987: 1–5.

Stallman, A. C. and Pearson, P. D., Formal measures of early literacy. In L. M. Morrow and J. K. Smith (Eds) *Assessment for Instruction in Early Literacy*, Englewood Cliffs, N. J.: Prentice-Hall, 1990.

Stanovich, K.. Toward an interactive-compensatory model of individual differences in the development of reading fluency. *Reading Research Quarterly*, 16, 1, 1980: 32–71.

Stanovich, K. E., 'Matthew effects in reading: Some consequences of individual differences in the acquisition of literacy,' *Reading Research Quarterly*, XXI, 4, 1986: 360–406.

Stanovich, K. E., 'Perspectives on segmental analysis and alphabetic literacy,' *European Bulletin of Cognitive Psychology*, 7, 5, 1987: 514–519.

Strang, R., *The Diagnostic Teaching of Reading*, New York: McGraw-Hill, 1969.

Strickland, D. and Morrow, L. (Eds.), *Emerging Literacy: Young Children Learn To Read And Write*, Newark, Delaware: International Reading Association, 1989.

Strickland, R. G., *The Language Of Elementary School Children*, Indiana Bulletin of School of Education, Indiana University, 1962.

Taylor, D., *Family Literacy: Young Children Learning To Read And Write*, Portsmouth, New Hampshire: Heinemann Educational Books, 1983.

Taylor, D. and Strickland, D., *Family storybook reading*, Portsmouth, New Hampshire: Heinemann Educational Books, 1986.

Teale, W. H. and Sulzby, E. (Eds.), *Emergent Literacy: Writing and Reading*, Norwood, New Jersey: Ablex, 1986.

Temple, C. A., Nathan, R. G. and Burris, N. A., *The Beginnings of Writing*, Boston: Allyn and Bacon, 1982.

Templin, M., *Certain Language Skills in Children*, Minneapolis: University of Minnesota Press, 1957.

Tinker, M. A., 'Experimental studies on the legibility of print: an annotated bibliography,' *Reading Research Quarterly* 1, 1966: 67–118.

Tizard, B. and Hughes, M., *Young Children Learning*, London: Fontana 1984.

Tizard, B., Blatchford, P., Burke, J., Farquhar, C. and Plewis, I., *Young Children At School In The Inner City*, London: Lawrence Erlbaum, 1988.

Tompkins, G. E. and McGee, L. M., 'Visually-impaired and sighted children's emerging concepts about written language.' In D. Yaden (Ed.), *Metalinguistic*

Awareness: Findings, Problems and Classroom Applications, Portsmouth, New Hampshire: Heinemann Educational Books, 1984.

Tough, J., *The Development of Meaning*, London: George Allen and Unwin, 1977.

Tough, J., *A Place For Talk*, London: Ward Lock Educational, 1981.

Trelease, J., *The Read-Aloud Handbook*, Middlesex, England: Penguin, 1982.

Tumner, W. E., 'The role of language prediction skills in beginning reading.' In *New Zealand Journal of Educational Studies*, (in press).

Tumner, W. E., Nesdale, A. R. and Wright, A. D., 'Syntactic awareness and reading acquisition.' In *British Journal of Developmental Psychology*, 5, 1987: 25–34.

Venezky, R. L., 'Regularity in reading and spelling.' In H. Levin and J. P. Williams, *Basic Studies on Reading*, New York: Basic Books, 1970.

Vernon, M., 'The dyslexic syndrome and its basis.' In R. C. Staiger and O. Andresen (Eds.), *Reading: A Human Right and A Human Problem*, Newark, Delaware: International Reading Association, 1968.

Vygotsky, L. S., *Thought And Language*, Cambridge, Massachusetts: M.I.T. Press and Wiley, 1962.

Vygotsky, L. S., *Mind in Society*, Cambridge, Massachusetts: Harvard University Press, 1978.

Wade, T., 'Promotion Patterns in the Junior School.' Unpublished Dip. Ed. Thesis, University of Auckland Library, 1978.

Walkerdine, V. and Sinha, C., 'Developing linguistic strategies in young school children.' In G. Wells, *Learning Through Interaction*, Cambridge: Cambridge University Press, 1981.

Waterland, L., *Read With Me: An Apprenticeship Approach To Reading*, Lockwood, Gloucestershire: The Thimble Press, 1985.

Watson, B., 'An observation study of teaching beginning reading to new entrant children,' M. A. Thesis, University of Auckland Library, 1980.

Weber, R., 'The study of oral reading errors: a survey of the literature,' *Reading Research Quarterly* 4, 1968: 96–119.

Weber, R., 'A linguistic analysis of first grade reading errors,' *Reading Research Quarterly* 5, 1970: 427–451.

Wells, G., *The meaning makers: Children learning language and using language to learn*, Portsmouth, New Hampshire: Heinemann Educational Books, 1986.

Wertsch, J. V., *Vygotsky and the Social Formation of Mind*, Cambridge, Massachusetts: Harvard University Press, 1985.

White, D. N., *Books Before Five*, Portsmouth, New Hampshire: Heinemann Educational Books, 1984.

Wildman, D. M. and Kling, M., 'Semantic, syntactic and spatial anticipation in reading,' *Reading Research Quarterly*, 14, 2, 1979: 128–164.

Williams, B., 'The oral reading behaviour of Standard One Children.' Unpublished M.A. Thesis, University of Auckland Library, 1968.

Wood, D., *How Children Think and Learn*, Oxford: Basil Blackwell, 1988.

Zaporozhets, A. V. and Elkonin, D. B. (Eds.), *The Psychology of Preschool Children*, Cambridge, Massachusetts: MIT Press, 1971.

Zaporozhets, A. V., 'The Development of perception in the preschool child.' In P. H. Mussen (Ed.), 'European Research in Cognitive Development,' *Monographs Society Research Child Development*, 30, 1965: 82–101.

Zinchenko, V. P. and Lomov, B. F., 'The functions of hand and eye movements in the process of perception,' *Problems of Psychology*, 1 and 2, 1960.

Index